Praise for *Deliverology in Practic*
by Michael Barber, Nick Rodriguez, and E⌐

"Kentucky has seen significant increases in high school graduation rates and college- and career-readiness rates for graduates over the past 6 years. Our success in Kentucky is directly linked to our ability to implement strategies and keep all educators focused on success for ALL children. The Education Delivery Institute and deliverology provided the support and tools to enable our success."

Terry Holliday, Commissioner of Education,
Commonwealth of Kentucky

"Too often, the gap between policy ambition and implementation is wide. The protocols and practices advanced by deliverology have been instrumental in narrowing this gap in Massachusetts. As a result, state education policies are translating into practices that are benefiting students."

Mitchell D. Chester, Massachusetts Commissioner of
Elementary and Secondary Education

"In dealing with the challenges of getting more of our students to achieve their postsecondary goals, no program or approach is as comprehensive, focused, or as well-conceived as that offered by EDI. Deliverology works if you follow its processes and have people dedicated to its method of driving improvement."

Robert L. King, President of the Kentucky Council
on Postsecondary Education

"EDI's process of turning vision into action—and, most importantly, into results—has been just the catalyst we needed to meet our goal of delivering global-ready students. Their straightforward method and process bring reality to big dreams. No change agent should be without it."

Jason E. Glass, Superintendent,
Eagle County Schools, CO

"Deliverology gives district leaders the tools they need to drive, and monitor, real change for students at the school and classroom level. This essential book for system leaders builds on the approach set out in *Deliverology 101* and augments it with 5 years' worth of real life stories and experiences from public school systems across the United States."

Paul Kihn, Former Deputy Superintendent,
School District of Philadelphia, PA

"The best thing about the clear, practical methodologies the authors describe is that they really do help colleges and universities deliver on their goals for student success and completion. They provide a means for tracking progress toward long-term objectives—and getting back on track if there is some wandering along the way!"

Kevin P. Reilly, President Emeritus,
University of Wisconsin System

"EDI worked with my department to help us learn and apply a powerful set of deliverology tools for culture change in our state's unique context. We now have a focused set of goals and priority strategies which inform everything we do to improve education in Hawai'i, and routines that build shared team accountability for results that move the needle on our strategic goals. This has contributed significantly to the major improvements in student outcomes that we've seen in recent years."

Kathryn S. Matayoshi, Superintendent,
Hawai'i State Department of Education

"As a large urban school district that serves approximately 17,000 students, we have found the process of delivery to be empowering. It is the catalyst for action as we work to implement our district strategic plan, ensuring that we have the capacity to leverage specific elements of the plan in a multi-year time line. The consistent focus on student results and positive changes at the classroom level allow us to remain true to our vision of instructional excellence, for every student every day."

Kathleen A. Smith, Superintendent,
Brockton Public Schools

"'Poor implementation is like poison to a reform effort,' *Deliverology in Practice* reminds us. But poor implementation is the norm in education. *Deliverology in Practice* goes beyond platitudes and 'common sense' to set out a clear, step-by-step framework for large-scale implementation. It's a must-read for every policymaker seeking to spark improvement and every practitioner working to implement it."

Joanne Weiss, Former Chief of Staff,
U.S. Department of Education

"Never before have the stakes been higher for American higher education institutions. EDI provides a concise approach that system and campus teams can use to set goals, measure progress, and achieve outcomes. The tools they provide can help leaders make progress toward the goal, ground routine campus conversations around results, and ultimately achieve increased collaboration, streamlined processes, and improved student success."

John Morgan, Chancellor,
Tennessee Board of Regents

"At the Council of Chief State School Officers, we have worked closely with the Education Delivery Institute to improve our delivery against our goals. Today, we are better identifying our goals, measuring our progress, and delivering on results. We are still improving these processes every day, and now we are able to share these best practices with our member states."

Chris Minnich, Executive Director,
Council of Chief State School Officers

"Colleges are filled with smart people with great ideas and lots of data that never get integrated into decisions. This volume will change that. The delivery approach is amazingly both simple and effective, and this practical guide will walk anyone through to success."

Larry Abele, Provost Emeritus, Director of the Institute for
Academic Leadership, Florida State University

"*Deliverology 101* showed us what and why; *Deliverology in Practice* shows us how. This practical, case study–based guide from the excellent team at the Education Delivery Institute is an invaluable tool for education leaders and administrators wanting to drive efforts to improve student success and narrow achievement gaps—two of the most urgent challenges facing educational institutions today."

José Luis Cruz, Provost and Vice President for
Academic Affairs, California State University, Fullerton

"EDI has designed an effective process to connect external goals with internal operations."

Rick Melmer, Senior Advisor, CCSSO
and South Dakota Board of Regents

"This book is a field guide to effective education improvement efforts. If you are responsible for leading ambitious, complex change in public education, you will appreciate the wisdom of experience and the practical guidance contained in these pages."

Ross Wiener, Vice President and Executive Director of the
Education and Society Program, Aspen Institute

"At the heart of learning is the connection between teachers and students. In order to support what happens in the classroom, our school, district, and state leaders must be equipped to effectively implement bold, evidence-based policy reforms. *Deliverology in Practice* brings together a toolbox of protocols, rubrics, processes, and stories that education leaders at all levels can draw on as they work to raise outcomes and close achievement gaps."

Vicki Phillips, Director of Education,
College Ready, Bill & Melinda Gates Foundation

To Ezra, and to every child entrusted to our care

Deliverology in Practice

How Education Leaders Are Improving Student Outcomes

Michael Barber

Nick Rodriguez

Ellyn Artis

A Joint Publication

FOR INFORMATION:

Corwin
A SAGE Company
2455 Teller Road
Thousand Oaks, California 91320
(800) 233-9936
www.corwin.com

SAGE Publications Ltd.
1 Oliver's Yard
55 City Road
London EC1Y 1SP
United Kingdom

SAGE Publications India Pvt. Ltd.
B 1/I 1 Mohan Cooperative Industrial Area
Mathura Road, New Delhi 110 044
India

SAGE Publications Asia-Pacific Pte. Ltd.
3 Church Street
#10-04 Samsung Hub
Singapore 049483

Executive Editor: Arnis Burvikovs
Senior Associate Editor: Desirée A. Bartlett
Editorial Assistant: Andrew Olson
Production Editor: Melanie Birdsall
Copy Editor: Deanna Noga
Typesetter: C&M Digitals (P) Ltd.
Proofreader: Christine Dahlin
Cover Designer: Candice Harman
Marketing Manager: Amy Vader

Printed in the United States of America

ISBN 978-1-4522-5735-8

This book is printed on acid-free paper.

Certified Chain of Custody
SUSTAINABLE FORESTRY INITIATIVE
Promoting Sustainable Forestry
www.sfiprogram.org
SFI-01268
SFI label applies to text stock

15 16 17 18 19 10 9 8 7 6 5 4 3 2 1

Contents

Preface

When *Deliverology 101: A Field Guide For Educational Leaders* was published in 2011, many U.S. states were gearing up to implement the ambitious school reform agenda set out in Race to the Top, either as winners in that federal competition—such as Massachusetts or Tennessee—or as states that simply wanted to do the right thing—such as Kentucky or Louisiana. At the same time a number of large public university systems were determined to reduce their often shocking drop-out rates and narrow the gaps in graduation rates between students in general and Latino and African-American students.

Deliverology 101 was written to help leaders of those systems implement these ambitious agendas with greater urgency and greater rigor and therefore achieve more universal impact than might otherwise have been the case. The Education Delivery Institute, founded at around that time and using *Deliverology 101* as its curriculum, has worked with some of these states and system leaders over the intervening 5 years, to assist them in their endeavors.

In the light of that profound and varied experience, *Deliverology in Practice* updates and refines the content of *Deliverology 101*. Most important, it provides numerous, recent examples from around the United States of how to go about delivering and, at a granular level, what the challenges and opportunities are. It is therefore much more grounded in the daily reality of getting things done in U.S. education systems than its predecessor could ever have been.

In the preface to *Deliverology 101*, I made the bold claim that if the content of that book were followed through consistently, results would improve. Everything I have seen in the United States and elsewhere since then reinforces my view that that is the case. *Deliverology in Practice* provides further insight and evidence to support this view.

Nick Rodriguez and Ellyn Artis, my coauthors on *Deliverology in Practice*, have spent most of those last 5 years working tirelessly and with significant success alongside state colleagues to assist them in their delivery efforts. As I discovered while working on this book with them, they have, as a result of that experience, become deeply expert in what the President of the World Bank, Jim Yong Kim, calls the Science of Delivery. The depth of their knowledge and insight has pushed my thinking forward and helped me question and refine some aspects of my thinking. As a result, the collaboration with them on *Deliverology in Practice* has been a wonderful learning opportunity for me.

All three of us hope that *Deliverology in Practice* will be a worthwhile and enjoyable read, but most of all, we hope it will assist its readers accelerate and intensify the work they do to improve outcomes for students of whatever age.

Success in the 21st century, for individuals, countries, and indeed humanity as a whole, depends on more, better, and deeper learning for everyone at every stage of their lives. Bringing that about depends on many things—one of the most important of which is the capacity to deliver successful education reform at scale. We are confident that *Deliverology in Practice* will enable its readers to do that.

—Sir Michael Barber
Founder of the Education Delivery Institute

Acknowledgments

A book that purports to tell the story of a growing movement is necessarily indebted to the leaders and the members of that movement. A whole community of people contributed to making *Deliverology in Practice* possible.

First, we thank the practitioners who have worked with us over the last 5 years to create the stories that it tells. There are too many of them to name here, but you'll see them acknowledged again and again throughout these pages: teachers, professors, deans, principals, superintendents, nonprofit and philanthropic leaders, and other courageous public servants who have committed their lives to achieving meaningful results for the students they serve. Each of them is a source of inspiration for us and the work that we do to support them.

Second, we thank the team at EDI. Kathy Cox, our founding CEO, is the person most responsible for growing EDI into the organization it has become today; without her leadership, we wouldn't have any stories to tell. Richard Eyre, Ashleigh McFadden, Lauren Kurczewski, and Lisa Smith have been the best editorial support team we could have asked for; they not only pushed this book over the finish line, but are also responsible for the launch of its excellent digital companion, available at http://www.deliveryinstitute.org/resources.

And every other member of the EDI team, past and present, has contributed energy and effort to bringing this book to life, whether by doing the work it chronicles or by lending us ideas and experiences that proved crucial to the writing: Omoaluse Amenkhienan, Ashley Bittner, Omari Burnside, Catherine Cullen, Rebecca Davis, Alycia Deihs, Tom DeWire, Mike DiConti, Eliza Dilberti, Luli DiMauro, Jaye Espy, Louise Feroe, Regina Fuller, Jonathan Gagliardi, Sharon Gaskins, Corey Gordon, Alex Harris, Krissy Haynes, Jordan Jampol, Sara Kerr, Ethan Lin, Lisa Lin, Mykia Long, Jackie Maniglia, Rebecca Martin, Monica Martinez, Lexi Miltenberger, Chris Navia, Marc Raffel, Aasha Rajani, Duncan Robb, Emily Russel, Ellen Spolter, Sharron Steele, Lauren Strickland, Jennifer Swayne, and Colin Welch. We also thank our friends at Isos Partnership, who are former members of the Prime Minister's Delivery Unit, for their support in helping stand EDI up as an organization, particularly Simon Day, Richard Page-Jones, Simon Rea, and Leigh Sandals. Fenton Whelan, a deliverologist extraordinaire who has helped establish the approach around the world, also provided invaluable guidance.

Third, we thank Arnis Burvikovs and the editorial team at Corwin, for persevering through this project with us and believing in it even in those moments when we doubted ourselves.

Fourth, we thank our families and friends, whose support and forbearance made it possible to do the hard work of writing. A few personal notes are below.

—Nick, Ellyn, and Michael

Thank you to all my family and my friends for your constant support, love, laughter, pushes, and prayers. You have collectively helped shape me into the person I am—while still making me strive to be so much better. And thank you God—for your faithfulness through it all.

Thank you to my coauthors—I simply adore you both and am glad to call you my friends.

—Ellyn Artis

To Wensa: thank you for your kindness, your encouragement, and your patience through the years this took. Apart from Christ, you are the best thing that ever happened to me—and you will always be my only Muse.

And, above all, I thank God for giving me the strength to complete this work. To Him be all the glory.

—Nick Rodriguez

⊙ PUBLISHER'S ACKNOWLEDGMENTS

Corwin gratefully acknowledges the contributions of the following reviewers:

Lydia Adegbola
Assistant Principal
NYC Department of Education
Elmsford, NY

Matthew Deninger
Manager of Delivery Unit
Massachusetts Department of Elementary and Secondary Education
Malden, MA

Peter Dillon
Superintendent of Schools
Berkshire Hills Regional School District
Stockbridge, MA

Cathy Galland
Facilitator of Educational Operations for Secondary Schools
Springfield Public Schools
Springfield, MO

Lisa Graham
Interim Director, Special Education
Berkeley Unified School District
Berkeley, CA

About the Authors

Sir Michael Barber has been chief education advisor at Pearson since September 2011, and he is the founder of Delivery Associates.

In 2001, he founded the Prime Minister's Delivery Unit (PMDU) in No. 10 Downing Street, which he ran until 2005. In this role, he was responsible for ensuring delivery of the government's domestic policy priorities across health, education, crime reduction, criminal justice, transport, and immigration. The sustained focus on delivery from the heart of government, and the processes the PMDU developed, was a significant innovation in government and of interest to numerous other countries and global institutions such as the IMF and the World Bank. Tony Blair described the PMDU as "utterly invaluable."

From 2005 to 2011, he was a partner at McKinsey & Company, where he played a leading role in creating a public sector practice and founded the global education practice. In 2009, he founded the Education Delivery Institute in Washington, DC, a not-for-profit organization that works with leaders of American education systems to apply systematic delivery approaches to improving outcomes in schools and public higher education.

Since 2009, on behalf of the British government, he has visited Pakistan more than 30 times to oversee a radical and, so far, successful reform of the Punjab education system.

He is the author of numerous books and articles, such as *How to Run a Government* (2015) and *Instruction to Deliver* (2008), which tells the story of his time in Downing Street and was described by the *Financial Times* as "one of the best books about British government for many years." *Deliverology 101* is the textbook on how to deliver in government and was written as the curriculum for the Education Delivery Institute (EDI).

Nick Rodriguez is the leader of the Education Delivery Institute's (EDI) K–12 practice. In this role, he is responsible for growing and maintaining a network of K–12 education leaders who are transforming the way they work to serve students. In his work at EDI, he has originated or helped to lead some of EDI's longest-standing partnerships with education systems that are on the cutting edge of reform, including Massachusetts, Kentucky, and Hawai'i. These systems have successfully adopted the practices of *Deliverology* to achieve remarkable results for students in recent years.

A member of the organization's founding leadership team, Nick began his work at EDI as its program director, where he helped to develop and continuously refine EDI's tools for helping education leaders to adopt the delivery approach. Nick began his career in education over 15 years ago when he served as the student member of the California State Board of Education and as a youth advocate and trainer with the California Association of Student Councils. Prior to joining EDI, he was an engagement manager with McKinsey & Company's education practice, where he advised education leaders on policy and implementation at the district, state, and national levels in the United States and abroad. His previous books include *Deliverology 101*, a resource that helped launch the movement to improve implementation in American education.

 **Ellyn Artis** served as a founding partner for the Education Delivery Institute (EDI), where she now serves as the Director of Higher Education. She has a long history of working with postsecondary and K–12 leaders to implement strategies that increase the numbers of students who graduate from high school college- and career-ready and complete a postsecondary credential—all while narrowing equity gaps. She leads the higher education team in their efforts to engage with campus, system, state, and nonprofit leaders in planning and implementing student success and completion strategies. This includes leaders from the California State University System, the Kentucky Council on Postsecondary Education, the Tennessee Board of Regents, and the University of Missouri System, among others. Ellyn also supports campus leaders as they use Student Success ImpleMENTOR™ tools and resources (www.successimplementor.org) to scale strategies and deliver improved retention and completion rates for all students.

Prior to her time at EDI, Ellyn worked at the Education Trust, where she was responsible for supporting higher education systems that agreed to halve their college-going and college-completion equity gaps as part of the Access to Success Initiative. She also coached and advised an array of state and district leaders as part of the Strategic Consulting Group at the Annie E. Casey Foundation. She currently lives in the District of Columbia but is proud to hail from Flint, Michigan.

Introduction

The American Implementation Problem

This is a book about delivering results.

That word—results—is common language in education reform today. It's an "of course" in the conversation, a given when we think about helping students learn, preparing them for college during their K–12 years, and helping them succeed in postsecondary education and beyond.

What's more, we (mostly) agree both on the outcomes we want *and* on the broad shape of the reforms necessary to achieve them. The last several years have been a time of great ferment in education. Race to the Top has prioritized a few key initiatives in nearly every state: rigorous college and career-ready standards, tools to measure and support effective teaching, longitudinal data systems, and a focus on the lowest-performing schools. Postsecondary institutions and systems, galvanized by President Obama's goal to once again lead the world in postsecondary attainment by 2020, have embraced an ambitious agenda around both college access and completion, with a small handful of common reforms like academic mapping and early alert being tested, refined, and improved on campuses across the country. This consensus, however fragile, has undoubtedly been good for students; it has elevated them to the center of the conversation, and these last several years have seen encouraging signs of progress on a host of outcomes, from National Assessment of Educational Progress (NAEP) proficiency to high school graduation rates to college access and degrees conferred.

But we all know that it hasn't been enough—at least not thus far. We've seen improvements, but they've been slower than we'd like. Progress is uneven; some systems are making gains while others are stalled. And we have even further to go when it comes to closing the achievement gaps that separate students of color, English-language learners, students with disabilities, and the economically disadvantaged from their more privileged peers. We should be proud of what we've accomplished, but few of us are satisfied. Which leads us to a discouraging question: if we can't achieve a breakthrough now, during what seems like a rare moment for education reform, when can we? What's holding us back?

The culprit's name is a single word: *implementation*.

In the last several years, policy—the "what" of reform—has driven this work. In many states, the passage of a big bill (usually with a number indicating its high priority, like "Assembly Bill 1") heralded the most important changes, and the same story played out in the boards and commissions that write the regulations pursuant to these statutes. Meanwhile, implementation—the "how" of reform—has gotten far less attention.

Instead, we want to believe the comforting fiction that policy makes things happen all by itself—that once a law or a regulation directs a system to do something, it will be done. In short, everyone wants to deliver results, but we're fuzzy on the part where we define how we actually *deliver* those results.

There's something uniquely American about our implementation problem. As Ben Jensen, an expert on international education reform, put it, "America is one of several countries that separates policy from implementation. But in high-performing countries, the policy *is* the implementation plan!" Leaders in these other systems would laugh you out of the room if you proposed an abstract "policy" without a clear and serious blueprint for how it would be implemented. But we do it here all the time.

There are many reasons for this, the most prominent of which is in our Constitution: we separate the people who set policy from the people who implement it at every level of government. There are good reasons for this, but the unwelcome side effect is a major disconnect between the two. Policymakers craft laws with little consideration for how to provide the right conditions for implementation or how the mandates they're creating affect the practitioners who must carry them out.

This separation persists over time; the American system, with its nonexecutive legislatures and boards, allows policymakers to have long careers that never bring them anywhere near the messier challenges of actually getting the work done. Practitioners do their best to make sense of the policies they're given. They're talented leaders, usually highly credentialed in the "what" of reform; they're experts in topics ranging from instruction and pedagogy to financial aid to institutional research.

Unfortunately, there has not been a clear path to becoming an expert in implementation; certainly, nobody goes to school to study it. Many leaders have learned to do it on their own. But for the most part, when it comes to our overall approach to delivering results, we leave it to chance.

That's why we wrote this book.

⊙ DELIVERY, THEN AND NOW

Nearly 5 years ago, we published *Deliverology 101* to help education leaders take on the new implementation challenges they faced. Like many others at the time, we saw opportunity in the wave of reforms that was taking shape and recognized that strong implementation would be critical to success. The purpose of that first book was to introduce a generation of reform leaders to the **delivery approach**, which makes implementation into a discipline that can be taught, learned, and applied in any context.

The delivery approach is based on the experiences that Michael, one of this book's three coauthors, had in creating and leading the Prime Minister's Delivery Unit (PMDU) from 2001 to 2005. Tony Blair had set up the PMDU to help his government achieve 20 high-priority public service goals, ranging from improved educational outcomes to drops in street crime. Michael and his colleagues took on this challenge by focusing relentlessly on four disarmingly simple questions:

1. What are you trying to do?

2. How are you planning to do it?

3. At any given moment, how will you know whether you're on track to succeed?

4. If you're not on track, what are you going to do about it?

The questions define the approach: delivery is nothing more and nothing less than a set of tools, techniques, and systems for asking and answering these questions consistently and rigorously. During their time of service to Blair, Michael and his PMDU colleagues both invented these tools and proved their value: in those first 4 years, the government hit 80% of its targets and made significant progress on the other 20%.

Deliverology 101 was our attempt to codify this approach and translate it to the American education context. It's a practical field guide that gives reform leaders a step-by-step framework for undertaking a **delivery effort**: a concerted and purposeful application of the delivery approach to help an education system set and achieve ambitious goals for students. And as the book was published, we launched the Education Delivery Institute (EDI), a nonprofit that partners with education leaders to implement their reforms at scale using the tools of this approach. This partnership was designed to be two-way: from its earliest days, we set EDI up to receive as much as it gave, continuously learning about and updating the delivery approach by capturing the stories of practitioners who were applying it. The idea was to provide both the tools for implementation and a center of excellence that would continuously improve them.

In the years since, EDI has had the privilege of partnering with over 100 education systems and organizations to apply the delivery approach to their work. They include leaders at every level of the system: schools, colleges and universities, school districts, state systems of K–12 and higher education, and education philanthropies and nonprofits. We've struggled alongside our partners to navigate the complexities of implementing an incredibly ambitious reform agenda. We've celebrated their successes and shared in the inevitable failures as well.

So what have we learned?

When we wrote *Deliverology 101*, we saw the opportunity that lay ahead. But we also issued a warning: "the presence or absence of the capacity to deliver," we wrote, "will make the difference between a once-in-a-generation opportunity seized and a once-in-a-generation opportunity missed." Today that opportunity survives, but it's at risk. On the one hand, there are education systems and leaders that are delivering on their promises for students:

- The Kentucky Department of Education has steadily improved its high school graduation rate and nearly doubled the proportion, from 34% to 54%, of its students who graduate college and are career ready since it adopted the delivery approach in 2010.
- Since incorporating the tools of delivery into its implementation of Race to the Top in 2012, the Hawai'i Department of Education has seen gains of 7 and 11 points in reading and math proficiency in high school. At the same time, the University of Hawai'i System has already attained its goal of awarding 25% more degrees and certificates by 2015 while simultaneously narrowing their Native Hawaiian student graduation gap.
- The University of Missouri–St. Louis saw a dramatic improvement in a key indicator, achieving a record-high first-year retention rate of 78% in 2012.

These are just a few examples of what our partners have accomplished using simple but powerful tools for setting goals, planning the strategies to achieve them, and regularly monitoring performance. There are many more that are in earlier stages of implementation but have early signs of progress: movement in leading indicators, widespread buy-in for the reforms, and evidence of consistent implementation across their systems.

But for every success story, there are multiple others that turn out differently. Some leaders have lost the confidence of a field that's frustrated with reforms that seem scattershot, even incoherent, because they weren't properly planned. Others have gotten public pushback because they didn't get ahead of the narrative on reform or build the necessary stakeholder relationships to maintain the consensus for it. Still others simply don't have the evidence to be able to say whether any progress is being made at all, either because they didn't define their goals or the feedback loops to measure them; they're working hard, but with no clear sense of whether it's the right work.

Poor implementation is like poison to a reform effort. It demoralizes the front line. It excites the opposition. It frays the coalition supporting it, peeling off people who can use it as an excuse to defect while maintaining that they still support the reform in theory. Tim Daly (formerly of The New Teacher Project) has a name for this—the "implementation dodge"—but when implementation actually is poor, the critics have a point. Moreover, poor implementation deprives us of an important tool for innovating in policymaking. Good implementation gives rapid feedback on the effectiveness of a reform; in effect, it allows the "how" to check the sensibility of the "what." At every stage, from goal-setting to planning to monitoring, the questions of delivery force us to get a lot clearer about what we're actually doing. But if implementation isn't working, we never get to that point, and policy continues to be made in a vacuum.

So of all the lessons we've learned, the biggest one is this: now, more than ever, delivery is an essential discipline for every education leader. We used to think that the delivery approach was mostly for people at the state level, laboring in offices far from the front line, in need of help to see how their work impacted students. But as we started to experiment with it in other venues, we discovered that delivery resonated with leaders at every level—even school or campus leaders, who are nearly as close to the students as you can get. No matter where we went, everyone seemed to struggle with the same challenges.

This is why we have to think of delivery as a *discipline*: a skillset, just like instruction or research methods or classroom management, that should be a requirement for every education leader to possess. They still don't teach it in school. But what's needed in our field is a movement that takes implementation seriously, that insists that any reformer worth their salt be proficient with these tools. In this world, EDI wouldn't be the organization that teaches everyone how to do this; it would merely be a gathering place for practitioners who are learning faster about the science of getting things done than we could ever hope to do.

⊙ WHAT ARE WE TRYING TO DO?

In hopes of advancing toward that vision, we've written this book.

Deliverology in Practice improves on the original (we hope) in at least three ways. First, it updates the framework and tools to reflect the lessons we've learned from our work over the last 5 years. Our three coauthors are well suited to this task. One of us—Michael—is the inventor of the approach, who has since helped it spread around the world. The others—Nick and Ellyn—are two original leaders of EDI who have been involved with nearly every partnership the organization has built over the last 5 years. We've drawn on all our collective wisdom and experience to update what we know about the delivery approach.

As for the approach itself, the four questions of delivery remain absolute, and the 15 elements of delivery introduced in *Deliverology 101* have held up fairly well. Figure I.1 shows the current version.

The only real difference is in Part 3, Plan for Delivery. Here, we've added an element that specifically takes on the **delivery chain**, which has turned out to be one of the most important tools in the approach. Other than that, the elements are the same:

- **Develop a foundation for delivery:** Set clear goals for students, establish a **Delivery Unit** (like the PMDU) to help your system achieve them, and build the coalition that will back your reforms.
- **Understand the delivery challenge:** Analyze the data and evidence to get a sense of your current progress and the biggest barriers to achieving your goals.
- **Plan for delivery:** Develop a plan that will guide your day-to-day work by explicitly defining what you are implementing, how it will reach the field at scale, and how it will achieve the desired impact on your goals.
- **Drive delivery:** Monitor progress against your plan, make course corrections, and build and sustain momentum to achieve your goals.
- **Create an irreversible delivery culture:** Throughout your delivery effort, identify and address the change management challenges that inevitably come with any reform.

Figure I.1   The Delivery Framework

 **1 Develop a foundation for delivery**

A. Define your aspiration
B. Review the current state of delivery
C. Build the Delivery Unit
D. Establish a guiding coalition

 **2 Understand the delivery challenge**

A. Evaluate past and present performance
B. Understand root causes of performance

 **3 Plan for delivery**

A. Determine your reform strategy
B. Draw the delivery chain
C. Set targets and establish trajectories

 **4 Drive delivery**

A. Establish routines to drive and monitor performance
B. Solve problems early and rigorously
C. Sustain and continually build momentum

 5 Create an irreversible delivery culture

A. Build system capacity all the time
B. Communicate the delivery message
C. Unleash the "alchemy of relationships"

As with the previous book, each chapter is aligned with an element of the framework. It explains the core principles of that element and the tools, practices, and techniques that work best to apply it in any context. Some things turned out to be more important than others (like the delivery chain example above). Others have mattered less and were simplified or even eliminated. We've learned more about the details of these tools than could ever fit in one book, so throughout each chapter, we've embedded links to additional resources on our website, **www.deliveryinstitute.org/resources.** These include more detailed examples of the tools and exercises to help you use them. We hope that you find them helpful and give us feedback to improve them even further.

Second, this book is written for a broader audience than the first one. As we said, we started our work mostly with *state* systems of K–12 and higher education. In this book, by contrast, **system** means any education organization of any size, at any level. It could be a state system; it could be the federal government; it could be a school district; it could be a department or a division of a university, an individual school, or a nonprofit. Whatever corner of our field you are a part of, that's the system you're trying to change when you read this book.

Specifically, we have three audiences in mind for any given system and some advice for how each should read this book:

- A **system leader** is exactly what it sounds like: the person leading the education organization that's trying to improve its results. If you're a system leader, your role is analogous to the one Tony Blair played with the original PMDU: you're the one who sounds the call for improvement and decides to undertake a delivery effort. You give it the backing and the resources it needs, starting with the delivery leader (the second role on this list). It may not be necessary for you to learn about the details of every tool in this book. For that reason, we've included a system leader summary at the beginning of each chapter that gives you the highlights of what you need to know to play your role.

- A **delivery leader** is the person or team that the system leader designates to manage the delivery effort. If you're a delivery leader, you're responsible for helping the system leader set and achieve their goals, no matter what. You play a role analogous to the one Michael played in leading the PMDU—and depending on the size of your system, you may lead a Delivery Unit of your own (for more detail on the role that Delivery Units play, see Chapter 1C of this book). The tools in this book are particularly important for you to master; you'll often find yourself facilitating teams through them or building the capacity of others to use them.
- Finally, **system staff** includes anyone who works in the education organization that's trying to improve its results. You are the people who are actually responsible for doing the work of implementation; a delivery effort both holds you accountable for this work and supports you to do it. If your system undertakes a delivery effort, you can use the tools in this book to anticipate and respond to the changes it brings for you: in particular, being asked to set goals, plan for delivery, and report on progress to the system leader. But even if your system leader isn't doing delivery, you can still adopt the tools in this book in your sphere of influence. In that case, congratulations: you've just redefined the "system," and you're now the leader!

Each chapter will close with a short reflection on its key implications for each of these three role groups.

Finally and most important, this book improves on its predecessor by highlighting the experiences of those American education leaders who have undertaken the delivery approach over the last 5 years. There are stories of both success and failure here—both of which were incredible sources of learning both for us and for the leaders involved. For obvious reasons, we've anonymized the most challenging cases. But we want to emphasize that we have nothing but respect for all our partners, including the ones who have struggled. Their work is difficult—as yours no doubt is—and we might not have done any better in their shoes. When they run into barriers, it is as much our challenge and our problem as it is theirs. In the end, we point out failures not to pass judgment, but to give you the same experience of learning that failure has given us.

These stories are written in the first-person plural; they often describe the work that a given leader has done in the context of their partnership with EDI. As such, there are places where this book risks looking a bit like an advertisement for the services that EDI provides to education leaders. For this, we ask your forgiveness in advance. The stories we have to tell are the ones born of these partnerships, and in many cases, there was no way to tell them completely without noting the role we played. In any case, we wrote this book so that people like you can take these tools and use them without seeking help from EDI. We'd love to meet and work with you one day if you think it would help, but if not, this book and the associated online resources should provide a viable alternative.

One last note: by the time you read this book, many of the systems highlighted will have changed or moved on from the exact approaches described in these stories. The delivery approach is flexible and evolving; our partners innovate with and iterate the tools every day, including several instances when we updated our stories even as we were writing this book. But at some point, we had to stop and concede that a snapshot of a system's work—even if it's out of date—is still informative. In fact, in some cases, we deliberately took examples from specific points in time to highlight a particular lesson learned in that moment. Of course, there will be some systems that have abandoned the approach or failed in some way by the time you read their stories. It's a result we try to minimize (and so far the track record is good!), but one that is inevitable in the messy course of implementation.

Wherever they are now, we thank all our partners for making this book possible. We're grateful for the privilege of working with them, for the chance to learn from them, and the permission to share their stories with you. We know that you'll benefit from them as much as we have.

Our implementation problem may be uniquely American. But for the last 5 years, the work we've done has helped us craft a uniquely American solution. We hope that it provides you with a tangible resource for reform and that it motivates you to join this growing movement to deliver outstanding results for all students.

Part 1

Develop a Foundation for Delivery

 **Develop a foundation for delivery**  Understand the delivery challenge  Plan for delivery  Drive delivery

 Create an irreversible delivery culture

Every strong delivery effort has a few prerequisites that must be put in place before you begin: a clear idea of what your system should deliver, an understanding of where and how delivery must improve, a talented team who will run the delivery effort, and sufficient alignment among key players to get things done. Together, these elements are your foundation for delivery.

This part of the book will help you build these elements out in four chapters:

- Define your aspiration
- Review the current state of delivery
- Build the Delivery Unit
- Establish a guiding coalition

Your foundation for delivery will set the stage for everything that follows.

Chapter 1A

Define Your Aspiration

 **Develop a foundation for delivery**

 **Understand the delivery challenge**

 **Plan for delivery**

 **Drive delivery**

 Create an irreversible delivery culture

System Leader Summary

Your aspiration helps you answer the first question of delivery: "What are you trying to do?" It defines an outcome connected to your moral purpose, it defines how you'd like to see that outcome move, and it can be broken down into no more than a handful of **goals**—each with a **metric**, **target**, and **goal leader** who holds primary responsibility for achieving it. An aspiration is most useful when it is widely shared across your system—which is why aspiration-setting is as much an exercise in communication as it is in visionary thinking.

As **system leader,** you're the direction-setter in chief. You'll ultimately be the owner of the aspiration and the chief communicator of it. Even if you designate your delivery leader to facilitate the process outlined in this chapter, your input is vital at every step. Be clear about what you want to accomplish—and then overcommunicate it by a factor of 10.

◉ IS THIS REALLY NECESSARY?

When we first started to write *Deliverology 101*, this first chapter posed an immediate challenge. A question loomed in the back of our minds: is this chapter really necessary? Don't education leaders articulate their aspirations already?

In the last few years, we've learned that this chapter is not only necessary but critical to everything that follows. An aspiration is like delivery as a whole: our most common mistake is to assume that it is already there, that articulating it is a natural skill that leaders already possess. But without effort and discipline, most systems will not have a clear, well-defined, and widely shared aspiration. Without that, your work is rudderless.

That's why the first question of delivery is always "What are you trying to do?" What are you trying to achieve for your students? This consistent focus on the ultimate outcome is one of the hallmarks that sets the delivery approach apart from others. Without alignment around the aspiration, your delivery effort is hamstrung from the very beginning.

Nevertheless, this seemingly obvious question has tripped up more than one leadership team we've worked with. One K–12 system convened a working group to articulate a long-term vision for their system. They asked a variation on our first question: "What is the purpose of this system?" Surprisingly, the question generated some intense disagreement. Some contended that, because they were so far from the classroom, their purpose must be limited to serving and equipping schools so that they could serve their students.

Others argued the opposite: no matter how far away we are, they said, our purpose must be to improve student achievement. Otherwise, when our schools don't perform, we'll be tempted to wash our hands of the outcome, kind of like the teacher who says, "I taught it; the students just didn't learn it!"

It took several hours and a great deal of discussion, but the team finally agreed on the latter view: the system's purpose was to serve students and improve their achievement.

Why was this conversation so difficult? The farther a person gets from the front line, the more difficult it is to make the connection between the cubicle and the classroom. So it's not surprising that some people plead powerlessness to influence outcomes and feel little or no responsibility for student success.

The delivery approach prevents this from happening. If a focus on outcomes is good enough for those at the front lines of education, it's good enough for those who lead them. In fact, leaders bear a special moral burden: we must hold ourselves just as accountable for how students perform as the teachers and faculty who work with them every day. Otherwise, what are we trying to do?

◉ CORE PRINCIPLES

An aspiration is a system's answer to three questions:

1. What do we care about?
2. What are we going to do about it?
3. How do we measure success?

In practical terms, this means that an aspiration defines an outcome connected to a moral purpose, broadly defines how we would like to see that outcome move, and can be broken down into no more than a handful of goals with specific goal metrics and targets.

Target-setting doesn't necessarily happen at this stage. As long as you have a metric for each goal, you can set targets later on (for more on this, see Chapter 3B). On the other hand, sometimes the aspiration will be expressed as a series of targets from the start. It all depends on the environment where you operate and the number of external factors that influence your choices. For example, when the Louisiana Department of Education began their delivery effort in 2009, they expressed their aspiration as a continuum of student outcome targets that begins in preschool and culminates with postsecondary success, either in college or via an Industry Based Credential (see Figure 1A.1).

For many years now, the Kentucky Council on Postsecondary Education has expressed their aspiration in terms of 5 questions:

1. Are more Kentuckians ready for postsecondary education?

2. Is Kentucky postsecondary education affordable for its citizens?

3. Do more Kentuckians have certificates and degrees?

4. Are college graduates prepared for life and work in Kentucky?

5. Are Kentucky's people, communities, and economy benefiting?

Their assessment of progress always comes back to metrics and measures related to these five questions.

Notice something here that both Kentucky and Louisiana have in common: their aspirations lend themselves to clear measurement, but they also lend themselves to clear communication of the vision for students (more on this later).

Figure 1A.1   Louisiana's Aspiration in 2009

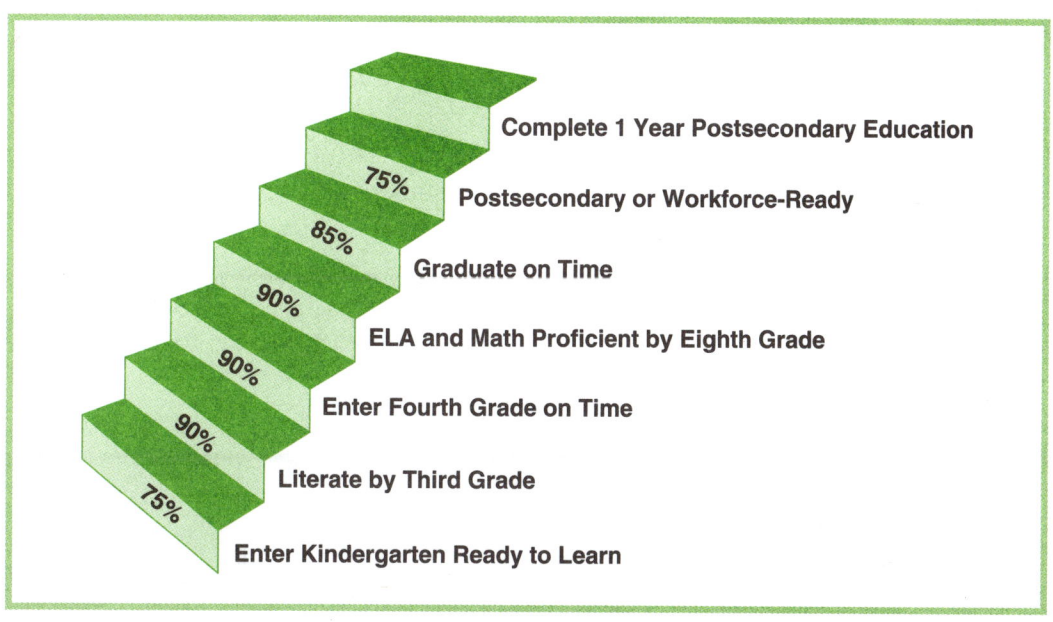

There is one more quality that makes a strong aspiration: it must consist of goals we can assign to specific people. In many systems, these people are known as **goal leaders**. In the original Prime Minister's Delivery Unit, the staff referred to them as the "single named officials" who would be responsible for the delivery of each priority: "This should be the person who spends most of his/her time on the priority and has sleepless nights, worrying about hitting the targets."[1]

This implies a big shift in the way we think about organizations and how they operate. People are not normally responsible for goals; they are responsible for programs, projects, initiatives, or other inputs. The result is that programs, projects, and initiatives get managed—but we have little confidence that the overarching outcomes will change. To appoint people as goal leaders is to declare that we value the results of our work more than work for its own sake.

Being a goal leader is difficult. It requires a person to exert influence over anyone and everyone who could have a significant impact on the goal they manage. This inevitably means influencing others without explicit authority to do so—either peer to peer or often with someone higher up on the organization chart. The best goal leaders are:

- Senior enough to be respected throughout a system (they are usually members of the leadership team);
- Flexible enough to wear two hats (managing their goal while continuing to manage a division of the office); and
- Willing and able to build the necessary relationships across divisions to break down siloes and exercise influence without authority.

The most common model for goal leadership is to find a qualified senior team member and assign to them the goal whose **center of gravity** is in the division that they manage. So, for example, in many K–12 systems that have goals to increase student proficiency, the goal leader is the person who heads the curriculum and instruction office. This reflects the fact that instructional reforms (especially in the era of Common Core Standards) are a major strategy for achieving this goal.

But the fit isn't perfect. Many of these same systems also have goals for college and career readiness—usually defined by high school success measures but closely related to proficiency at all grade levels. And educator effectiveness can be both a goal (increasing the number of effective teachers and leaders) and a strategy to achieve proficiency and college and career-readiness goals.

You can see the challenge: very few student outcome goals line up cleanly with the work of the functional divisions of an education system. Most goals will draw on the work of multiple offices, which is why goal leadership requires a special skill set.

With these principles in mind, what should we do to define a system's aspiration? There are three steps:

1. Identify existing aspirations and goals;

2. Prioritize and refine the aspiration; and

3. Communicate the aspiration.

Identify Existing Aspirations and Goals

No system starts from a blank slate, and most have articulated goals in some form or fashion. It's important to identify these goals to understand our starting point. What kinds of statements of purpose, goals, or objectives has your system defined already? Some sources to consult include:

- Strategic plans;
- Mission statements;
- Legislative mandates;
- Publicly known commitments made by the system leader or other leaders (e.g., a governor, a mayor); and
- Commitments made to the "next" level up (e.g., school commitments to districts, state system commitments to the federal government).

Prioritize and Refine the Aspiration

Once you have identified your existing goals, you must choose which ones will matter most. Which are the most important? How feasible is it to de-emphasize the unimportant ones? What will it take to narrow down the list? The challenge most systems face is not a lack of aspiration but an incoherent abundance of it; as we all know, a focus on "30 high-priority goals" means a focus on nothing at all.

You'll also need to consider the opposite: are there goals that are missing from the current list and will need to be added? Is there a grade span or content area that is not as well covered as it should be? Do the goals reflect the system's relative priority on access, success, and equity? And does each goal have at least one clear metric that you can use to measure success?

The last question to consider brings it all together: can we tell a coherent story about how the goals add up to an overall aspiration for students—regarding their life chances, economic opportunity, or other moral purpose? Sometimes you start with this statement and fill the goals in around it, but sometimes it arises from the collection of goals you have chosen.

Communicate the Aspiration

Depending on your circumstances, the process of communicating the aspiration may begin early. Some leaders will involve key stakeholders in the creation of the aspiration itself. When the California State University (CSU) system started its Graduation Initiative in October 2009, they began the work with a kickoff event with leaders from every campus; one intent of this event was to set and agree on goals for each campus that would add up to an ambitious but realistic system goal. This process generated early buy-in for the goals from the leaders who would be most critical to achieving them—and created champions to communicate those goals to other stakeholders.

> Please visit EDI's website at www.deliveryinstitute.org/1A for a guide to brainstorming your aspiration.

Identifying High-Priority Goals
in the Hawai'i Department of Education

When the Hawai'i Department of Education (HIDOE) began its delivery effort in early 2012, the State Board of Education was already in the midst of reevaluating its strategic plan. The plan contained several goals and objectives. In addition to that, HIDOE already had established goals in its Race to the Top plan and was about to establish additional goals for its Elementary and Secondary Education Act (ESEA) waiver application to the U.S. Department of Education (DOE).

With all these potential goals, it was important to establish priorities for the department. The Assistant Superintendent for Strategic Reform, Stephen Schatz, worked with several stakeholders at HIDOE and at the State Board of Education to produce a list of critical goal areas: third-grade proficiency, eighth-grade proficiency, college readiness (ACT benchmark), graduation, and college-going rate. However, several stakeholders pushed back, and the draft list got significantly longer.

As a solution, leaders at HIDOE identified their high-priority goals as "critical lagging indicators," and framed the remaining goals as leading indicators for these measures (see Figure 1A.2). The result was a set of priority goals that reflected the best input of the state's stakeholders but also allowed the team to narrow their focus to a vital few.

Figure 1A.2   HIDOE Goals, Targets, and Leading Indicators

Goals	Student Success	Staff Success	Successful Systems of Support
Metrics	• Reading and math proficiency (Grades 3–8, 10) • College and career readiness • Graduation rate • Postsecondary enrollment rate • Equity in Achievement • Attendance • Ninth-grade promotion	• Effective teaching	
Leading Indicators	• School safety • Cocurricular and extracurricular activities • Vocational training • Lifelong learning, character, and citizenship • Student connection to community • Parent satisfaction with school responsiveness • Percentage of accredited schools	• Educator hiring pool • Educator training • Employee turnover • Teacher ratings and improvement plans • Administrator ratings and improvement plans • Professional development alignment • Student perception of learning experience • Pilot career development/ladder participation • Leadership placement • Leadership skills training	• Academic review teams • School facilities • Reliable technology resources • Internet access • Technology support satisfaction • Financial operations • Internal program evaluations • Funding sources review • School administrative burden reduction • Parent communication • Understanding and support of DOE priorities • Stakeholder organization satisfaction • Parent and community engagement

Other leaders will prefer to articulate a vision of their own and then lead from the front, communicating and selling that vision to stakeholders at every level. Either approach can work, as long as it leads you to a well-defined, well-understood, and widely shared aspiration.

In any case, overcommunication is the key: find ways to make sure that your aspiration works its way into every public and private conversation that your system leader and team have and have them encourage others to do the same. For more information on how to do this, please see Chapter 5B: Communicate the Delivery Message.

This step can cause some anxiety. Many leaders worry that publicly naming some things as priorities will offend staff whose work is not included on the list. This is a large driver of the pressure to include everything on the list in the first place. You need to be aware of this challenge, but you can't shy away from it. Instead, think carefully about how to craft a message that elevates the priorities but honors the ongoing work that must continue. This will be a recurring theme with other things that we have to prioritize—in particular, the strategies we will discuss in Chapter 3A.

One Line in a Speech:
The President's Goal for Higher Education

In his first joint address before Congress in 2009, newly elected President Barack Obama set out an ambitious goal for the nation. The United States had fallen to 16th in the world according to its share of certificates and degrees awarded to young adults, placing it behind Korea, Canada, and Japan, among others. President Obama issued a challenge: that the United States should once again lead the world with the highest proportion of college graduates. This meant an increase of at least 8 million degree holders by the end of the next decade. The White House and the Department of Education then broke down this goal into specific targets for states and publicly shared those targets.

The president's goal has catalyzed the movement for increasing degree completion in the higher education community. Nearly two thirds of states have established public completion goals and are now working to achieve those goals. National college and university associations like the American Association of State Colleges and Universities (AASCU) and the Association of Public Land-grant Universities (APLU) created Project Degree Completion, an initiative committing hundreds of campus leaders to significant increases in undergraduate baccalaureate degrees by 2025.[2]

The effect has been reminiscent of President Kennedy's goal of landing a man on the moon by 1970. Both statements drew on the public's concern for the well-being of our nation to illustrate the necessity for change. Both created a sense of urgency to improve the nation to be able to compete internationally. And both have spurred action. We famously met Kennedy's goal, and we are striving mightily to meet Obama's.

◉ LESSONS FROM THE FIELD

Use Your Aspiration as a Leverage Point

Ronald Reagan once quipped that the closest thing to eternal life on this earth is a government program.[3] Whatever one's politics, those of us who have worked in public organizations will know that these words have at least some truth to them: when we manage programs without managing outcomes, the programs tend to take on a life of their own, regardless of whether they are actually useful.

A good aspiration can change this dynamic. When it is clearly defined, we've seen system leaders insist to their colleagues that *all* their work must justify its existence by demonstrating its contribution to student success. A shared aspiration gives these leaders the moral high ground to make the argument that some programs should be eliminated or changed. The questions you should ask will look something like this:

- Do we agree that this student outcome goal is the most critical thing we are trying to achieve?
- If that's true, then do we also agree that we should be directing our resources to strategies and projects that are likely to make the biggest impact on this goal?
- If that's true, then why would we continue program X, when the evidence suggests it has no impact at all?
- OR is it possible to change program X to give it a higher likelihood of contributing to this goal—or should we eliminate it?

Simple, logical questions such as these won't win the day all on their own—especially when the person answering is deeply and emotionally invested in the status quo. But they're more effective than you might think, especially when you ask them in public settings.

Don't Underestimate the Communication Challenge

Aspiration-setting is as much an exercise in stakeholder management as it is in logic or problem solving. Defining the right set of goals is important; getting the right people to agree to them is even more important, and much more difficult. We've seen many systems where an aspiration existed, but few people knew or understood it; the practical effect was that the aspiration had no real force. Conversations about the aspiration can be contentious, of course, but they force participants to surface the objections that they do have and to make them explicit so that leaders can deal with disagreement or people who are not on board. Overinvest in this area, and it will pay dividends for your delivery effort.

Don't Get Tied Up by Terminology

Finally, the specific words that we use here—goal, target, and so on—are less important in and of themselves than the establishment of a common language around a system's aspiration. This is important to keep in mind, because the performance improvement literature has spawned countless terms, many of which can have interchangeable and flexible definitions.

Performance Improvement Terms (A Partial List)

- Vision
- Goal
- Objective
- Target
- Milestone
- Desired Outcome
- Strategic Plan

- Project Plan
- Project Charter
- Strategy
- Project
- Initiative
- Action Step

For the purposes of this book, we've attempted to use a consistent nomenclature, starting with the definitions of words in this chapter. However, the words are less important than the concepts behind them. If a system finds, for example, that they are accustomed to using the word "objective" to describe what we call a "target" in this book, we almost never recommend that the system adopt a new term in their work with us. Instead, we work to communicate the definition of "objective" so that system staff all have the same mental model of what an objective is. Consistency and shared language are far more important than the use of specific labels.

For this reason, we often find ourselves working with higher education and K–12 systems who don't even use the word "delivery" to describe what they're doing. Again, the actual substance of what they are doing matters far more than what they call it.

⊙ KEY CONSIDERATIONS FOR SYSTEM LEADERS AND STAFF

If you're a **system leader**, you're the owner and most critical communicator of your aspiration. Your system—both the staff and the field—is looking to you to set the direction of the entire enterprise. You need to be clear about what you want to accomplish and overcommunicate it by a factor of 10.

If you're part of the **system staff**, you may or may not see an aspiration set by your system leader. But no matter what your circumstances, you can always bring clarity to your work by asking fundamental questions: "Why am I doing this? What am I attempting to accomplish?" If your system has a well-defined aspiration, these questions help you link your work to it. If they do not, then you should define an aspiration—preferably with specific goals— to guide the work in your sphere of influence. A grants manager for a dual credit enrollment program, for example, might set a goal for the impact of their work on college and career readiness and college enrollment for high school graduates in their program.

Finally, **delivery leaders** are responsible for making sure that the aspiration exists. You cannot organize your system for delivery, or do much of anything at all, if you don't have a clear sense of what your system is trying to accomplish. Do what is necessary to facilitate this conversation. On the one hand, it may mean pushing your system leader or even volunteering to lead the work of aspiration-setting yourself. On the other, it may mean trying to pull together and make sense of a patchwork of existing half-starts and well-intentioned efforts at strategic planning—and managing the stakeholders behind each of these to reach consensus on a common and coherent aspiration.

⊙ CONCLUSION

"What are you trying to do?" is a simple, powerful, and underestimated question. We drift easily; it is human nature to for us to let our work be driven by those things that are tangible, right in front of us, urgent, and/or interesting to us. We all need to do a better job of defining and keeping our eyes on the horizon.

Delivery efforts always begin by ensuring that this horizon is well defined, well understood, and agreed to by a critical mass of those responsible for the work. With an aspiration in place, your delivery effort can begin in earnest.

⊙ NOTES

1. Barber, M., Kihn, P., & Moffit, A. (2011). *Deliverology 101: A field guide for educational leaders.* Thousand Oaks, CA: Corwin.

2. Obama, B. H. (2009, February 24). Address to Joint Session of Congress. Retrieved from http://www.whitehouse.gov/the_press_office/Remarks-of-President-Barack-Obama-Address-to-Joint-Session-of-Congress/

3. Reagan, R. (1964, October). A time for choosing. Speech presented at the Republican National Convention in San Francisco, California.

Chapter 1B

Review the Current State of Delivery

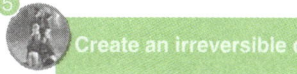

System Leader Summary

A **capacity review** is a rapid but thorough diagnostic of your system's current capacity to deliver results for its students. Using a combination of evidence from stakeholder interviews and your own self-review, a small team delivers an assessment of how well your system is currently implementing each of the 15 elements of delivery. This allows you to avoid reinventing the wheel, build on areas where your practices are already strong and shore up areas of challenge. This chapter provides a guide for how to conduct a capacity review, working either with an outside facilitator or with a team you appoint.

The capacity review requires an investment of time by you and your leadership team: about 2 to 4 hours over a 2-day period. But the benefits are worth it: you'll get a reasonably accurate snapshot of your current capacity to deliver, a sense of where you should spend your time as you begin your delivery effort, and buy-in from your leadership team about the value of the delivery approach and the next steps to take.

⊙ WHERE DO WE START?

The 15 elements of delivery are the basis for our big claim: do these things consistently and rigorously, and you will significantly improve results for your students.

This is easier said than done. Fifteen elements is a lot—more than you'll have time to focus on all at once. It made sense to start with your aspiration, but where do you go from there?

You might try to pursue each of the elements in order, but you'll run into two problems. First, delivery is not a linear process. Doing the elements "in order" may be the right choice for some, but not for all.

Second, many systems are already pursuing some of these elements on their own. Because many elements of delivery are intuitive, you'd be hard-pressed to find a system where *none* of them are present, at least nominally. Who wouldn't have a strategy? Or some kind of plan? Or an analysis of their data? Some of these things are so steeped in common sense that we'd be embarrassed to admit it if we weren't doing them.

And that's the problem. Tell a person that they should adopt the elements of delivery, and their (justifiable) reaction may be to feel insulted that you think they don't do these things. Moreover, they might ask, who are *you* to tell them how to improve? If you're a delivery leader, an outside party like EDI, or even a system leader, you don't truly *know* their work, do you?

At EDI, we recognized the potential of this problem early on, and our answer to it was a process called a capacity review.

A capacity review is a rapid but thorough diagnostic of a system's current capacity to deliver results for its students. You can conduct this diagnostic internally or with support from an external partner (most of EDI's engagements begin with a capacity review).

A capacity review delivers an assessment of how well a system is currently implementing each of the 15 elements of delivery. The core tool for doing this is EDI's **capacity review rubric**, a piece of which is shown here in Figure 1B.1 (for the full rubric, please see EDI's website, **www.deliveryinstitute.org/1B**).

For each of the 15 elements of delivery, the rubric lists key questions to consider, followed by written descriptors of what a "weak" or "strong" delivery will look like. These descriptors follow a four-point scale, which helps prevent a convergence to the middle and forces a real judgment about how strong or weak delivery is:

1. **Red:** Weak delivery, with either absence of the element or very poor execution of it

2. **Amber-Red:** Some aspects of the element exist, but there is still significant work to do

3. **Amber-Green:** The element is in place and in fairly good shape but could use additional improvement

4. **Green:** Strong delivery, with exemplary (but not perfect) execution of the element

Figure 1B.1 Sample Row From Capacity Review Rubric

Aspect of Delivery	Questions to Consider	Weak Delivery (R)	Strong Delivery (G)	Current State and Rationale
1A. Define Your Aspiration *Does the system have a clearly articulated and shared aspiration?*	• Has your system clearly articulated an aspiration? In other words, does your system have an answer to the question "What are we trying to do?" • Is the aspiration sufficiently ambitious and realistic (i.e., will achievement mean a substantial improvement in student outcome measures statewide)? • Is the aspiration shared by all relevant stakeholders? • Has the aspiration been translated into a manageable number of goals that are clearly defined and measurable?	• Aspiration is vague and lacks definition regarding students impacted, change to be accomplished, and time to impact • There are numerous, or even contradictory, aspirations that do not present a coherent picture of system goals • Aspiration lacks ambition; little progress is required to achieve it • Aspiration is not well communicated; relevant stakeholders unable to articulate it • The aspiration has not been translated into a manageable number of goals or those goals lack clear definition and metrics	• Aspiration is well defined regarding students impacted, change to be accomplished, and time to impact • System has single overarching aspiration aligned at all levels • Aspiration is ambitious—achievement will require significant, but possible, improvement • Stakeholders are clear about the aspiration and its definition and could articulate it if asked • A manageable number of clearly defined goals and quantifiable metrics have been identified	R Red AR Amber-Red AG Amber-Green G Green

23

A small team can gather the necessary feedback and range of perspectives to make judgments on this rubric with a few weeks of preparation time and 2 days on the ground at the system office. During this time, they review existing data and documents about the system's current work, conduct interviews and focus groups with key internal and external stakeholders, and through the system's leadership team facilitate a self-assessment of their work against the rubric. They combine this assessment with their own judgments from other evidence to produce a snapshot of the system's current capacity to deliver.

The team backs each judgment with evidence from the review and uses the whole picture to arrive at a series of focused recommendations for the system leader to build their delivery effort and achieve their aspirations for students.

This process helps address several challenges we identified above. First, it gives leaders an accessible entry point to applying the delivery methodology in their systems—where to start, as it were, in establishing a delivery effort.

Second, the capacity review explicitly acknowledges the system's current strengths and encourages leaders to build on them. The process places a heavy emphasis on identifying areas where the system is already doing delivery. Sometimes—nearly always, in fact—it will be called something else, of course. A delivery plan may be an "operational" or "strategic" plan. A routine

Figure 1B.2   Sample Heat Map of Capacity Review Judgments

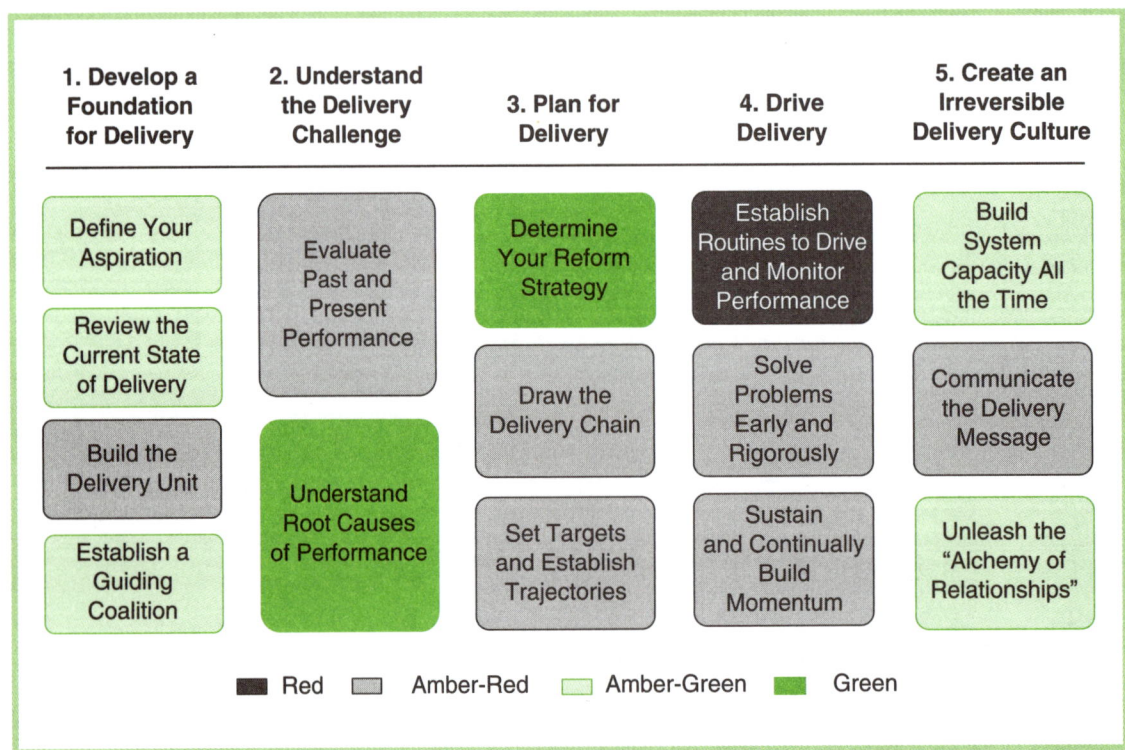

may be a "performance management system." But, as we've already noted, labels matter far less than the substance beneath them.

In this way, the capacity review takes a central challenge of the delivery methodology—that people think they're doing it already—and turns it into an advantage. "Here are the things you are doing well," it says, "and here are our recommendations for you to take that work to the next level." This not only honors the work that people have already done, but it also gives you an important foundation for the work you're about to undertake. You wouldn't want to build a delivery plan from scratch without acknowledging or even borrowing from an organization's strategic plan. You wouldn't want to undertake a goal-setting exercise while ignoring goals that a state board or board of regents has already set. And so you wouldn't want to begin—or even fully scope—a delivery effort without the vital information that a capacity review supplies.

Third, the capacity review process is both rapid and accurate. At EDI, we often laugh at our naïveté when we first proposed the process in *Deliverology 101*. There, we said that it could take up to a month on the ground to conduct. This was in line with the conventional wisdom about reviews and diagnostics, which could range from 6 weeks for a consulting firm to several months or even years for a research organization. These processes invariably ask for more time and effort than most system leaders can reasonably give, and they often return information too late to make a difference.

The capacity review takes an 80/20 approach to this problem—getting answers that are 80% right in 20% of the time. Over the years, our partners have been consistently impressed by how quickly our teams could come to know and understand their systems using these tools. This allows for a fast start to delivery that imposes a minimal time commitment for leaders (no more than 2 to 3 hours per senior leader, and no more than an hour for most other stakeholders).

Finally, and most important, the capacity review process gets everyone on the same page about what must be done. The combination of external perspectives—the review team—and internal views—the leadership team self-assessment—creates a dialogue about the current state of delivery that invests people in the delivery work. In a sense, the judgments and recommendations are less important than the conversations that lead to them—conversations in which leaders discover their own strengths and weaknesses and become motivated to do something about them. If you're an external reviewer or a Delivery Unit that plans to help with follow-up on the capacity review, the process will allow you to get to know the system and the system to get to know you, which will facilitate collaboration in the future. For these reasons, going through the capacity review process makes it significantly more likely that the recommendations will be implemented.

As we've learned these lessons, the capacity review has become a centerpiece of EDI's work with our partner systems. Done properly, this holistic, 360-degree process has a power all its own; it's a great way to align stakeholders to get moving on a range of issues, including delivery but that goes beyond it as well.

Figure 1B.3 Capacity Review Process

	Set Up the Review	Prepare for the Review	Conduct the Review	Determine Implications
Timing	60–90 minutes	2 days in a 3-week period	2 days on-site	Within 2 weeks after review
Major Outputs	• Dates set • Team in place • Relationships established	• Fact pack assembled • Interviews and focus groups scheduled and prepared	• Compiled evidence • Self-assessment results • Report with overall results and recommendations	• Decision on whether and how to move forward with delivery effort
Activities	• Meeting or phone conversation to explain process and gain agreement to undertake it • Designate team members	• Review documents pertinent to aspiration • Analyze performance data on aspiration • Schedule interviews and focus groups and prepare materials for them	• Conduct interviews and focus groups • Compile evidence and arrive at initial judgments • Conduct leadership team self-assessment • Assemble and present final report and recommendations	• Discuss and scope the shape of delivery effort and external support needed (if applicable) • Adjust staffing as appropriate to set up for delivery effort

⊙ CORE PRINCIPLES

Figure 1B.3 summarizes the capacity review process.

> Please visit EDI's website at www.deliveryinstitute.org/1B for a complete capacity review rubric that you can use as you conduct your capacity review.

We now briefly describe how EDI undertakes each of these steps, with some notes for leaders hoping to conduct capacity reviews on their own. As we go through the steps, it will be important to keep three principles in mind:

1. **Understanding, not evaluation:** The purpose of the review is to build a shared understanding of the current state of delivery in the system, not to evaluate performance in any way.

2. **An external perspective:** Whether with a partner like EDI or through some other means, it's important to ensure a strong outsider's view as part of the review process. Otherwise, your system will risk myopia about what strong delivery truly looks like.

3. **Transparency:** There must be open and honest dialogue between the system leader, system staff, Delivery Unit, the external partner, and any others who are intimately involved, with clear communication to all about the purpose of the process.

Set Up the Review

This may seem mundane for a first step, but it's important. Once a team has agreed to do a review, the first order of business is to identify a 2-day period that can accommodate a capacity review schedule. To facilitate this part of the discussion, we like to show the leadership team a "typical" capacity review schedule like the one in Figure 1B.4.

You can see here that the biggest challenge will be finding a 2-hour time block when the leadership team can be together—possibly twice in one day if the system leader wants them to return for the final report. The schedule also gives an overall sense of the other types of interviews that will need to be identified and set up.

Once you have a date, you can assign a few key roles and responsibilities:

- A **system coordinator** who arranges and schedules the capacity review activities;
- A **partner coordinator** (if there is an external partner); and
- A **review team** of about four people, with a balance of "outsider" and "insider" perspectives on the system.

Prepare for the Review

Once the dates have been set and the team has been named, the system coordinator and partner coordinator will work with their teams to prepare for a review.

Figure 1B.4   Sample Capacity Review Schedule: K–12

Day 1

Time	Team A Schedule	Team B Schedule
9:00–9:30	Introduction and kickoff with Commissioner and senior leadership team	
9:30–10:30	Interview State Board Chair	Interview Legislative Education Committee Chairs
10:30–11:30	Principal focus group	Superintendent focus group
11:30–12:30	Interview Commissioner	Mid-level manager focus group: student support, legislative affairs, communications, HR
12:30–1:30	Lunch and check-in about current findings	
1:30–2:30	Regional office staff focus group	Interview Deputy Commissioner
2:30–3:30	Business and philanthropic leader focus group	Teacher focus group
3:30–5:30	Break to record evidence	
5:30–9:30	Dinner; discuss evidence and arrive at initial judgments and recommendations	

Day 2

Time	Full Team Schedule
8:30–10:30	Self-assessment exercise with full senior leadership team
10:30–12:00	Break to synthesize evidence, produce final report and recommendations
12:00–1:30	Present final report and recommendations to Commissioner

There are three aspects of preparation that are important. The most urgent of these is arranging interviews and focus groups to fill the schedule. There are three categories of interviewees to consider, each of which includes some typical roles (these are written for the state system level, but can be easily adapted for campus, school, or district use). Use these in Figure 1B.5 as a starting point for your list.

As the interviews and focus groups are scheduled, the team can prepare protocols for conducting them. This is mostly about taking the questions in the rubric, finding the ones that are most relevant to the particular audience in question, and adapting them to speak directly to that audience.

You will also want to add a simple introductory script that sets the tone for the interview. For interviewees who do not know much about you and your work, use this time to give them context. Stress that the interview is nonevaluative and confidential (that is, no attributable information will be shared with system leadership). In most cases, especially interviewees in the field or in mid-level management positions, it will be important to emphasize that this is really an assessment of the system leadership's work, not of their own.

Figure 1B.5   Potential Interviewees for a Capacity Review

Role Type	K–12 Roles	Higher Education Roles

Internal leaders: part of the system and inside the system office	• System leader
	• Deputy
	• Chief Academic Officer
	• Chief Accountability Officer
	• Chief Financial Officer
	• Chief Operating Officer
	• Chief Talent Officer
	• Chief Innovation Officer
	• Chief Information Officer
	• Directors of key programmatic areas, including:
	
	   o Curriculum and instruction (or teaching and learning)
	   o Teacher and leader effectiveness
	   o School turnaround
	   o Title programs
	
	• Project or performance management director(s)
	• Data analysts
	• Mid-level managers in any of the above divisions
		• System leader
		• Vice-Provost/President of Academic Affairs
		• Vice-President of Student Affairs/ Associate Provost for Student Affairs Officers
		• Chief Financial Officer
		• Chief Operating Officer
		• Chief Information Officer
		• Director of Institutional Research
		• Directors of key programmatic areas, including:
		
		   o Initiatives on graduation and/or equity
		   o Financial aid
		
		• Project or performance management director(s)
		• Mid-level managers in any of the above divisions

The field: part of the system but outside the office	• Regional office leaders • District superintendents • Principals • Teachers	• Campus presidents • Campus provosts • Academic Senate leaders
External organizations: outside the system and outside the office	• Governor's office staff (especially the Governor's Education Policy Advisor) • Legislators (especially chairs of education committees) • Leaders of statewide advocacy groups invested in these issues • Local education philanthropies • Union leaders • Business community leaders • Representatives from workforce development	

To tailor your questions for your specific system, you'll need to understand as much as you can about that system's context. This is where the second element of preparation—a **fact pack**—becomes important, particularly for external partners. The time that you will have to interview and interact with system leaders and staff will be limited. To make the most of it, you'll need to know as much as possible prior to the interviews and use it to guide your interactions. A well-researched fact pack, provided to every member of the review team, will help them agree about the most important lines of inquiry to pursue.

The general outline of a fact pack consists of a few elements:

- **Overview of the system:** Its location, number of districts/schools/campuses, staff, students and demographic data, and other salient facts.
- **Governance and structure:** Basic information on how the system is governed, with biographies of key leaders.
- **History of reform and recent news in the system:** Usually a legislative and policy history that gives a sense of how we got to this point in recent years.
- **Information on current delivery activities:** Goals, mission and vision and values statements, major initiatives currently under way, plans that guide them, performance management routines or systems in place, and capacity-building or stakeholder engagement efforts being undertaken. There may be multiple goals, strategies, or other elements like these floating around a system. But that's all right; the point of the capacity review is to identify this and point it out.
- **An overview of student performance data:** Nothing too sophisticated here, just a few basic statistics on student performance as they relate to the goals you could find.

To assemble a fact pack, you need two things: access to student data and the opportunity to review key internal documents. For the first, you can often get what you need through public sources, but if not, you can ask for standard information from the system coordinator. For the second, ask the system leadership team to identify and provide any existing documents that speak most to the questions in the categories above. Are there vision and goal statements? Strategic plans? Documents they've used to communicate externally about their work? News articles summarizing recent history? The system team should not have to do any work to compose anything—this is purely an exercise of finding what already exists.

There's only one last consideration: communicating with those who will be interviewed or otherwise involved. Though you will, of course, introduce yourself and the work at hand in each interview, it always helps to have some introductory context from the people setting up these interactions. (We cannot tell you how many interviews we have begun with the question, "What do you know about why we're here?" only to hear the answer, "Nothing—I was just told to show up." Not the greatest foot to get off on!) This can take the form of a note from the system leader (facilitated by the system coordinator) or a one-pager to hand out to interviewees ahead of time.

Communicating like this will help you avoid misinterpretations of the work you are doing in the capacity review. This is important, particularly since the default response to an external "review" tends to be one of suspicion.

Conduct the Review

Now you're at the most critical and difficult step. Your 2 days of focus groups, interviews, and self-assessment exercises will be intense, but it's where everything comes together to produce your report and recommendations.

As we saw from the schedule above, the first day of the capacity review consists of interviews and focus groups using the protocols you've designed.

The protocols will be a helpful guide, but this part of the process is really about getting to know and understand the people you meet, their perspectives, and their suggestions. Often, the first question in many of our protocols—"what are the top three strengths and weaknesses of your system?"—takes up half the time. It's amazing what you can learn by listening carefully and asking the right follow-up questions.

Toward the end of the day, each team member will review the notes for the interviews and focus groups they recorded and synthesize the evidence. The central goal is to translate the qualitative evidence gathered throughout the day (and the preparation period) into evidence that allows the review team to make a judgment. What does the evidence collectively tell us about the system's current work with respect to each of the 15 elements of the delivery framework? You can find a tool for categorizing and sorting this evidence on EDI's website, **www.deliveryinstitute.org/1B**.

This sets the review team up for their main exercise on the evening of Day 1— debating the evidence and arriving at initial judgments against the rubric. The review team uses the evidence, the rubric, and their collective knowledge of what good planning and implementation look like to drive this discussion.

There is a simple protocol to follow here, which is very similar to what you will do the next day with the leadership team self-assessment:

- Ask everyone to examine the evidence for one category of the rubric and compare it to the corresponding descriptors. Ask each person to independently determine where they think the system is—Red, Amber-Red, Amber-Green, or Green—and ask them to think of the two to three pieces of evidence that they have to support that claim.
- After everyone is done reflecting on their own, ask them to "vote" their rating for that element in a way that is visible to everyone else.
- Discuss and record evidence of strengths and weaknesses from the group that voted.
- Push the team to get to consensus on a final rating.
- Repeat this process for the remaining rows of the rubric.

As you finish Day 1, you'll want to consider your judgments all together and do some internal calibration. You can assemble all the judgments in one place and look at the "heat map" that results, in a format similar to the one we shared at the beginning of this chapter (see Figure 1B.6).

This is an important opportunity to do a sense check of the ratings that you gave and to make sure that they square with your overall understanding of the themes that have emerged during the review. Some questions that you might ask about the heat map in Figure 1B.6, for example:

- Are targets and trajectories and delivery routines the two most important things for this system to focus on? The two Red ratings send the message that they are. If this isn't the case, the ratings aren't quite right.
- Are there really no Greens? Are all the Amber-Greens equally good, yet none are quite great yet? Do none stand above the rest as a core strength? Pushing for differentiation of results can be useful.

Figure 1B.6 Sample Heat Map of Capacity Review Judgments

1. Develop a Foundation for Delivery	2. Understand the Delivery Challenge	3. Plan for Delivery	4. Drive Delivery	5. Create an Irreversible Delivery Culture
Define Your Aspiration	Evaluate Past and Present Performance	Determine Your Reform Strategy	Establish Routines to Drive and Monitor Performance	Build System Capacity All the Time
Review the Current State of Delivery		Draw the Delivery Chain	Solve Problems Early and Rigorously	Communicate the Delivery Message
Build the Delivery Unit	Understand Root Causes of Performance	Set Targets and Establish Trajectories	Sustain and Continually Build Momentum	Unleash the "Alchemy of Relationships"
Establish a Guiding Coalition				

■ Red   ▢ Amber-Red   ▢ Amber-Green   ▇ Green

- There are a lot of Amber-Reds, and there is more red than green on this map, suggesting a system that has a lot of work to do. Does this seem right? How do these ratings compare with the ratings that we've seen in other systems? Internal differentiation of results is good, but it must be calibrated against the team's knowledge of what "green" looks like in other systems.

The team should also consider its initial recommendations. If these were the final judgments, what would be the overall themes that emerge? What specific next steps would you recommend to the system leader to get things moving as quickly as possible? You will want to sketch out your overall impressions to carry in and test the next day.

The next morning, one or more members of the review team will facilitate the leadership team self-assessment. The protocol for this is very similar to the one described above, with just a few differences. First, leadership team members will rely on their own knowledge of the system to make judgments on the rubric rather than on the evidence you have gathered. In fact, you will not want to share your initial judgments or evidence with them at this point but listen carefully to their "insider" perspective to see how it is similar to or different from yours.

Second, you'll need to take additional time up front to set the tone of the exercise, reminding participants that the discussion is a confidential opportunity for the leadership team to step back from their day-to-day work and reflect together on the system's capacity to deliver results for students. In particular, if the system leader is participating, you'll want them to role model the importance of transparency and vulnerability in talking about the system's strengths and challenges.

The end results will be similar in format to the ones that the review team produced the night before. They will give you additional evidence that you need to finalize your judgments and recommendations. But in truth, your objective here is more ambitious than that: the most important purpose of the leadership team self-assessment is to familiarize the team with the elements of delivery, to help them reflect and agree on their strengths and challenges with respect to these elements, and to emerge from the process committed to doing something with the results.

Over the years, we've found that there's something universally powerful about the self-assessment. The combination of objective criteria and skilled facilitation creates an open space where even the most Pollyanna-ish teams challenge themselves to be honest about their weaknesses—and, likewise, where the most cynical teams learn to find and celebrate their strengths. As a result, we've found that the review teams' judgments diverge very little from what the leadership teams discover on their own. In fact, they're usually harder on themselves. When the process is done well, it causes the team to buy in to the final results and recommendations.

After the self-assessment, there's a short window—usually 2 to 3 hours long—in which the review team combines their initial judgments with the evidence from the self-assessment, agrees on adjustments to the final ratings, and finalizes the recommendations to present to the system leader.

There's no single prescribed format for arriving at overall recommendations. They will depend on not only the ratings that you give but also the evidence under those ratings and the overall story told by that evidence. There are a few questions to consider:

- What are the themes that emerge—consistent findings that seem to cut across the rating categories? Is one issue a root cause of weakness in several areas? Conversely, is there a common source of strength identified by multiple stakeholders, such as a particular initiative or recent accomplishment?
- How do the various areas of strength and challenge relate to one another? Are some linked to others? Is there a sequence of cause and effect you can follow?
- What seems to be most urgent to get right first? If you were the system leader and could do only three things in the next 6 months, what would they be?

Depending on your answers to these questions, your recommendations will focus on different things. In some cases, it's a straightforward matter of addressing the areas of red in the heat map, and the recommendations are categorized almost entirely by delivery element (see Figure 1B.7).

For other systems, the focus will be more on cross-cutting challenges. In one K–12 system doing a capacity review for the second time, we divided the recommendations into three overall categories: actions for leadership, actions for the Delivery Unit, and actions for everyone else to take.

Figure 1B.7   Sample Recommendations: Higher Education System

Relationship With Campuses

- Establish clear rules of engagement for how system would like to work with campuses on implementation of strategic agenda
- As part of discussing and presenting the strategic agenda to campuses, identify 4 to 5 high-impact strategies or action steps, which all campus presidents can sign up to work with the system on

Goals and Target Setting

- Set clear system-level goal(s) that correlate(s) to strategic priorities
- Use the bottom-up approach to target setting, establish appropriate benchmarks and clear principles for negotiating targets with campuses

Building Delivery Capacity

- Decide how a delivery team could help implement the strategic agenda at the system and campus levels
- Determine the structure, skills, and resources needed
- Consider how campuses can be engaged in the delivery team

Delivery Planning

- As a next stage of developing the strategic agenda, produce detailed plans for the 4 to 5 high-impact strategies identified
- Determine approach to campus-level planning

Whatever form they take, your recommendations should be brief. As we've said all along, the capacity review is thorough, but it's also rapid; teams have to turn around their recommendations in the space of a few hours after gathering most of the evidence over the course of 2 days. This is a feature, not a bug: we've found that the sense of pace and urgency from this process allows the team to deliver on its promise of producing findings that are 80% right in 20% of the time. As a result, the recommendations are sharp, simple bullet points that are primed for executive-level action. With more time and resources, we'd be able to produce the 50-page reports that have become standard in most diagnostic activities. Unsurprisingly, however, no system leader we've worked with has ever asked for one.

The last step of the on-site process is to present your recommendations to the system leader. Many leaders ask for their leadership teams to be present at this time to hear the results and to discuss them. If you've done your job well, nothing in the report should be too surprising, particularly to the leadership team who participated in the self-assessment. The similarity of your findings with theirs will build long-term credibility for your work with them, and it will give you the runroom to deliver a tough message or two where necessary—a place where you disagree with their ratings, for example, or a specific piece of feedback delivered privately to the leader. Sometimes your disagreement will be positive, as you encourage the team to play up its strengths more than they are willing to do.

During this step, listen for the reactions and receptiveness of all the leaders assembled in the room. You should leave with a fairly good sense of their overall posture toward the findings and recommendations, which leads us to the last step of the review.

Determine Implications

With the on-site review completed, you have one question left to answer: what will the system do about the recommendations? And if they are working with an external partner, how (if at all) will that partner be involved in supporting this work?

In EDI's work with partner systems, the time right after a capacity review is an important on/off ramp. The capacity review has given us an intimate view of the system, its strengths, weaknesses, and, most important, its commitment to undertaking a delivery effort. At the same time, it has allowed the system leader and staff to take the measure of us as a potential partner, to experience what work with us would be like, and to evaluate whether we are a good fit for them. This is the point where we decide together what the scope of a partnership, if any, will look like.

Even if you're not working with an external partner, this is the time to decide whether you want to pursue a delivery effort. You've just engaged in a rigorous dialogue about the delivery framework and how well you are currently executing against it; there will be no better moment to circle everyone around this approach as the way to improve student outcomes—or to deliberately choose another direction.

There have been a few (rare) instances when one of our capacity reviews clearly indicated that further partnership was not a good idea. It wasn't that the ratings were red—our whole mission, after all, is to help leaders get from red to green. Rather, it was the disconnect between those ratings and the perceptions of the leadership team—and an unwillingness to even consider some of the more challenging feedback in the review. In situations like these, further work to undertake a delivery effort isn't in anyone's interest; the leadership team clearly wants to go in a different direction, so your resources are best spent elsewhere.

If the decision is a yes, then there are a few other questions to consider:

- Is your aspiration sufficiently strong and clear? As we saw in the last chapter, delivery efforts anchor on the aspiration. You'll save a lot of time by getting this piece right before putting the others into place.
- Who will be responsible for managing the delivery effort, and who will they rely on to do this work? We will cover this in more detail in the next chapter on Delivery Units, but the capacity review results can help you unearth talent that can be devoted to the effort.
- Based on the strengths and weaknesses identified in the report, what aspects of delivery should be your focus in the next few months? This will guide the learning that you do during that time, both from this book (which chapters to read first!) and other delivery-related resources.
- How will you operationalize any other specific recommendations in the capacity review report? Can the Delivery Unit (if there is one) take it on right away? How involved will the system leader or other leaders have to be?

The Difference a Capacity Review Makes

In early 2014, EDI conducted a capacity review with the Eagle County School District in Colorado. The final report included the following ratings (see Figure 1B.8).

Figure 1B.8   The capacity review summary for Eagle County shows both areas of strength and opportunities for growth.

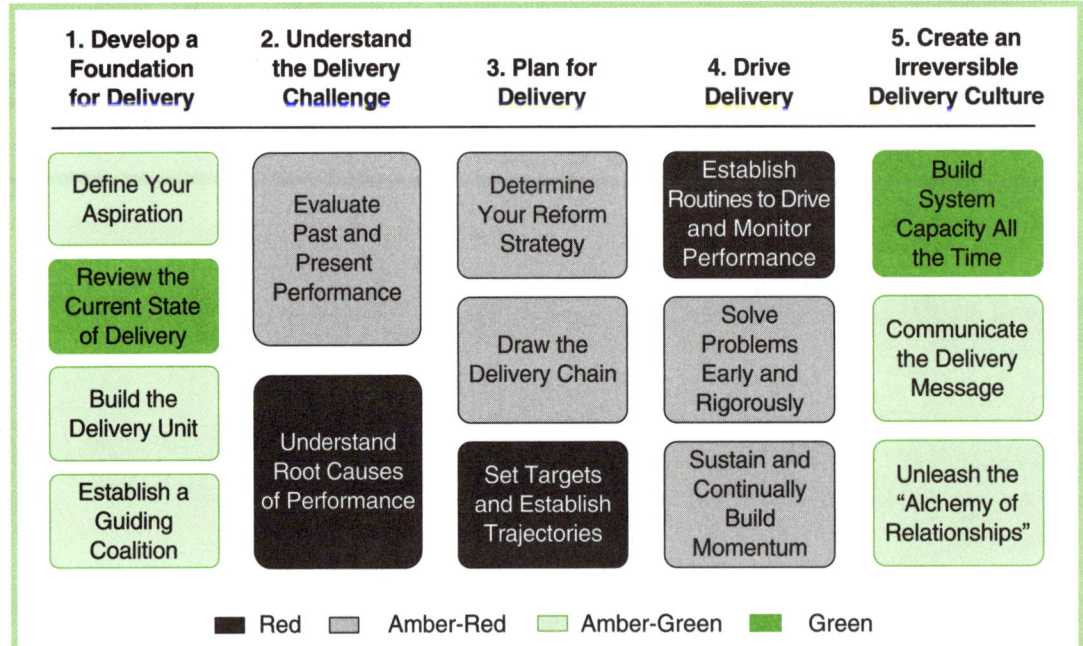

There was a clear foundation for delivery, due in large part to the work that the superintendent and his team had done over the past several months to get out into the community, meet with key stakeholders around the district, generate a clear vision for the district, and communicate that vision widely.

At the same time, the ratings showed that the details of implementing the vision were less clear. The EDI team focused its recommendations on addressing this challenge (see Figure 1B.9).

In the following months, EDI supported the Eagle County district team to set clear student outcome goals and create more detailed plans for each of the strategies outlined in their vision document.

As a result, the Board of Education and the superintendent adopted a shared Strategic Plan that fleshed out the superintendent's vision in August 2014. In September 2014, District Office staff began to implement routines for monitoring progress that include regular updates to the superintendent as well as regular updates to the Board.

This is a "textbook" use of a capacity review: the recommendations created a blueprint and impetus for action, which set the district on a course to launch its delivery effort within 6 months. In the words of Eagle County Superintendent Jason Glass: "The EDI Capacity Review brought an authentic and genuine view on how well positioned our organization was to move on our aspirations. Simultaneously supportive and honest, the process allowed us to clearly see those areas which needed a lot of attention, as well as areas where we could build on past work. The total experience was incredibly engaging and left us poised for the work ahead."

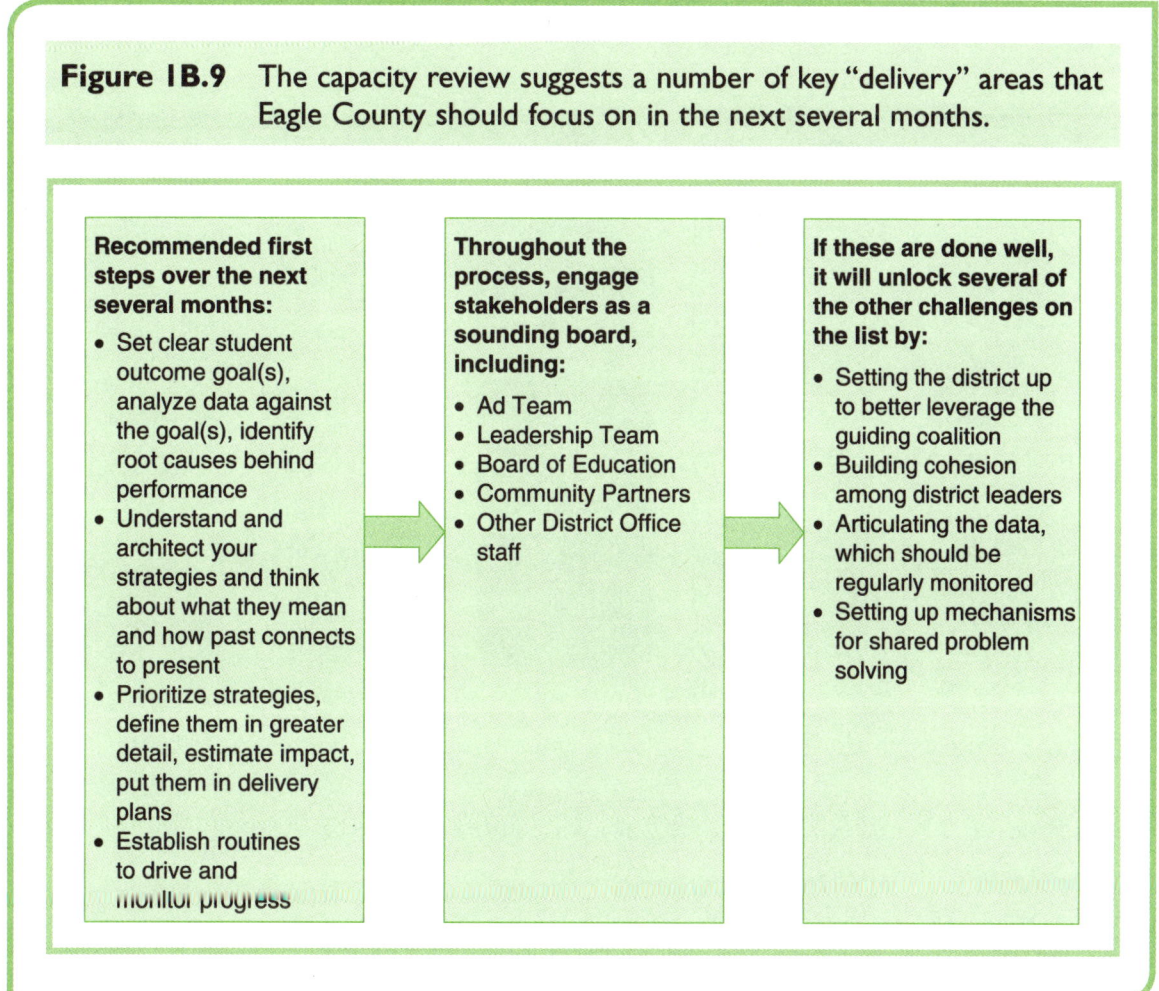

Figure 1B.9   The capacity review suggests a number of key "delivery" areas that Eagle County should focus on in the next several months.

Recommended first steps over the next several months:

- Set clear student outcome goal(s), analyze data against the goal(s), identify root causes behind performance
- Understand and architect your strategies and think about what they mean and how past connects to present
- Prioritize strategies, define them in greater detail, estimate impact, put them in delivery plans
- Establish routines to drive and monitor progress

Throughout the process, engage stakeholders as a sounding board, including:

- Ad Team
- Leadership Team
- Board of Education
- Community Partners
- Other District Office staff

If these are done well, it will unlock several of the other challenges on the list by:

- Setting the district up to better leverage the guiding coalition
- Building cohesion among district leaders
- Articulating the data, which should be regularly monitored
- Setting up mechanisms for shared problem solving

⊙ LESSONS FROM THE FIELD

There Are Common Patterns in Capacity Reviews

While every capacity review produces different results, there are some common patterns that emerge for systems undertaking delivery efforts for the first time. Figures 1.B.10 and 1.B.11 show "average" results for EDI's capacity reviews since it began this work in 2010.

A few patterns emerge, which can serve as starting hypotheses for you as you approach your first capacity review:

- There is often at least a foundation for delivery: Nearly always, the first part of delivery contains some bright spots. There is generally some kind of aspiration at the leadership level. However, the average aspiration rating (1A) is lower because many aspirations are not widely shared or understood in their systems. While some systems start with Delivery Units and others do not (1C), most are able and willing to be self-reflective about their practice, which is why they are doing the capacity review in the first place (1B).

Figure 1B.10 Average Capacity Review Results From Higher Education Systems

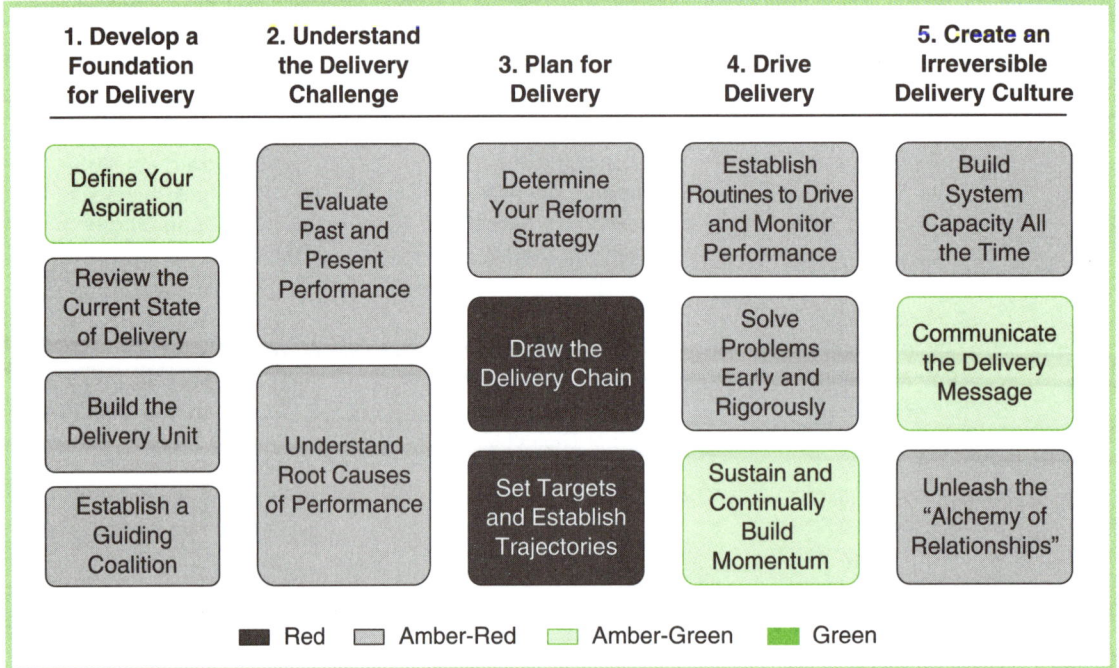

Figure 1B.11 Average Capacity Review Results From K–12 Systems

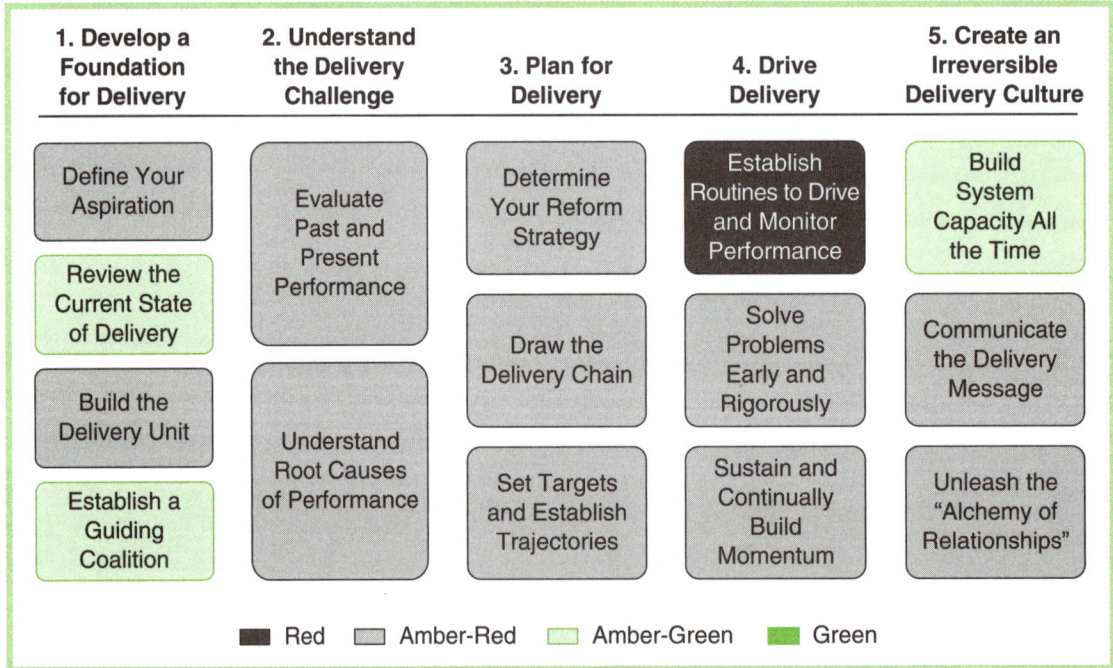

- Data is a mixed bag: The Amber-Red ratings across Part 2, Understand the Delivery Challenge, are rooted in a theme that is almost universal in our field, and which we explore further in Part 2: we have plenty of data, but we're not very skilled at using it to drive insights and decisions.
- Core "delivery" elements are the biggest challenge: as you might expect, those elements that are most unique to delivery—particularly delivery

plans (Part 3) and routines (4A)—have some of the lowest marks. Often this is because efforts to build these things do not yet exist.

- There are other bright spots: System leaders usually have a strong sense of the strategies they want to pursue (3A), even if they could be articulated and planned more clearly. Strong leadership teams tend to build a culture of problem solving (4B), though it could be more deliberate. And some system leaders do a good job of building capacity in their systems (5A) and engaging stakeholders (5B).
- Many systems start from a low point: As the amount of red makes clear, these are systems that could use significant help. This is not surprising: delivery is a relatively new discipline, and while many practice parts of it, few practice the whole. What makes these systems different is that they wanted to do something about it.

Empathy Is Critical to This Work

One of the biggest mistakes that many external partners make is to criticize the systems they work with, usually behind their backs. This is a challenge among consultants generally: the temptation to feel a sense of superiority as you rifle through the dirty laundry that your partner has aired for you, to marvel at how *those people* could have let things get *this bad*.

We are all susceptible to this mindset—but we can't stress enough how important it is to fight it. Not only is it unfair to your partner, but it's also wrong on its face. For the most part, consultants—even the best ones—add their greatest value not by being smarter or harder working than their partners, but simply by having some distance from the situation and some space to think differently about it. Many of *those people* could do your job, perhaps better than you!

The converse is also true: you might be hard-pressed to do your partner's job better than he or she does. As we stress again and again throughout this book, the challenges of delivery are not unique to certain types of "bad" systems or leaders. Rather, they are universal byproducts of both our human nature and the central irony of delivery: we think implementation is obvious, so we pay little attention to it, thus we're not very good at it. Some of the most talented leaders we know have overlooked some seemingly "easy" things because of this—and we would, too, if we were in their shoes.

For these reasons, *empathy* must be your guiding mindset: acknowledgment of how difficult this work is and that you are capable of making (even likely to make) the same mistakes as those who are doing it. That empathy must be combined with optimism that your outsider's perspective can genuinely help—but empathy must come first. This is why one of EDI's core values is *abiding respect for educators* in our partner systems.

This attitude is important for your capacity review, but as we will see, it is critical to every task you will undertake in your delivery effort.

The Capacity Review Can Be a Dipstick

A capacity review is not just a great way to kick off a delivery effort; you can also use it to check progress over time. As your delivery work grows and matures, system and delivery leaders will want to form a new review team every 12 to 18 months, if possible, to revisit these questions of delivery capacity and refocus their efforts.

A handful of systems have done this in partnership with EDI. For example, the Massachusetts Department of Elementary and Secondary Education (ESE) undertook an initial capacity review in July 2010. The initial results looked like Figure 1B.12.

This first review revealed several areas of focus for ESE. In particular, the department had no targets, trajectories, or delivery routines, even though it was just about to finalize an ambitious application for its Race to the Top (RTT) grant.

The review helped the team adjust its RTT application—and when ESE emerged as one of the winners, they worked through their Delivery Unit to create clear targets and trajectories for their goals, produce delivery plans to achieve them, and establish routines to keep the Commissioner apprised of performance against these plans.

Eighteen months after the initial review, ESE partnered with EDI to undertake a follow-up review using a nearly identical process. The results are shown in Figure 1B.13.

As a result of the delivery focus, ESE had formalized and communicated its aspiration, built a strong Delivery Unit and guiding coalition, and established many of the "standard" practices of delivery. However, the review also showed that other challenges, particularly around communications, had emerged in the meantime.

Figure 1B.12   Massachusetts Capacity Review: July 2010

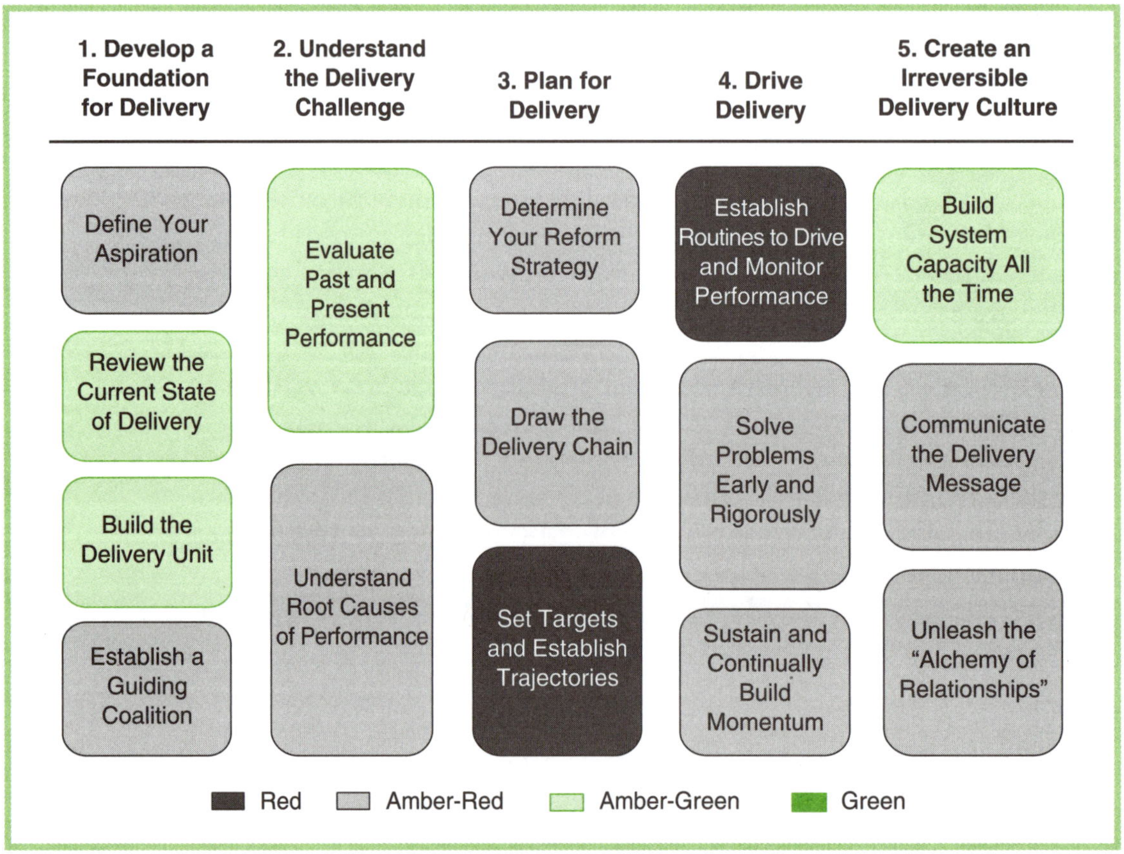

1. Develop a Foundation for Delivery	2. Understand the Delivery Challenge	3. Plan for Delivery	4. Drive Delivery	5. Create an Irreversible Delivery Culture
Define Your Aspiration	Evaluate Past and Present Performance	Determine Your Reform Strategy	Establish Routines to Drive and Monitor Performance	Build System Capacity All the Time
Review the Current State of Delivery		Draw the Delivery Chain	Solve Problems Early and Rigorously	Communicate the Delivery Message
Build the Delivery Unit	Understand Root Causes of Performance	Set Targets and Establish Trajectories	Sustain and Continually Build Momentum	Unleash the "Alchemy of Relationships"
Establish a Guiding Coalition				

■ Red   ■ Amber-Red   ▢ Amber-Green   ■ Green

Figure 1B.13   Massachusetts Capacity Review: January 2012

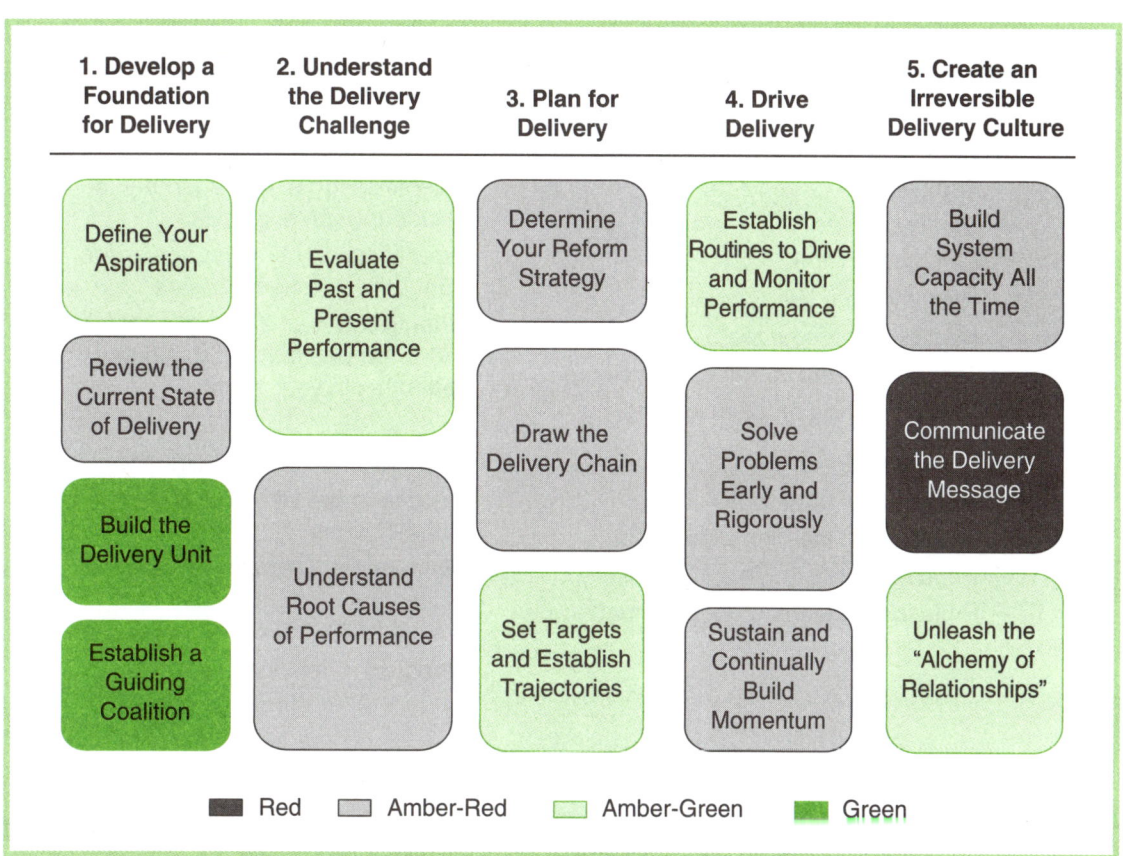

This second review influenced the focus of the agency in the months that followed and allowed the team to reaffirm their commitment to this work. Regularly reviewing capacity, even if it is with a shorter-form internal review, is a great practice for continuously renewing your delivery effort.

The Capacity Review Goes Beyond Delivery

The power of the capacity review process need not be restricted to the delivery framework; we've found that it can be used to assess a system against any well-constructed set of criteria.

We learned this lesson a few years ago, when the Council of Chief State School Officers (CCSSO) partnered with us to work with a network of K–12 systems on implementing the Common Core State Standards (CCSS). Part of our partnership included reviewing the capacity of these systems to implement the Common Core.

To do this, we worked with CCSSO to design a rubric (see Figure 1B.14) that was specifically tailored to Common Core implementation (for states: **http://www.deliveryinstitute.org/file/CCSS-rubric-state**; for districts: **http://www.deliveryinstitute.org/file/CCSS-rubric-district**).

Notice that there are some aspects of delivery included here, mostly under "systems alignment and systems change." But the remaining rows of the rubric have more to do with content specific to Common Core implementation.

Figure 1B.14   State Education Agency Common Core Implementation: Progress and Capacity Rubric

Rubric elements:

- Systems alignment and system change
  - Aspiration
  - Clarity of roles
  - Leadership
  - Plan and time line
  - Budget and resources
  - Technology and information systems
  - Monitoring and problem solving

- Educator supports
  - Instructional materials
  - Professional learning for teachers
  - Educator preparation and licensure
  - Professional learning for principals

- Student supports
  - Identification of and supports for students with disabilities
  - Identification of and supports for English-language learners
  - Identification of and supports for other groups that need additional attention in your state

- Communication and engagement
  - Engagement with education stakeholders
  - Engagement with the broader community
  - Building momentum through productive relationships

This combination of the "what" and the "how" is powerful. Tools like these allow system leaders to quickly understand the quality of implementation of an initiative that they know is critical to success.

Since then, there have been more developments like this. We have partnered with the Bill & Melinda Gates Foundation to create a rubric to assess a district's implementation of the research-based Measures of Effective Teaching (MET) principles **(http://www.deliveryinstitute.org/educational-topic/k12/teacher-and-leader-effectiveness-tle)**. We have partnered with the Access to Success (A2S) network to create a framework with criteria for successfully scaling up high-impact practices in higher education systems. And we have partnered with the U.S. Department of Education to create a rubric to gauge the sustainability of Race to the Top reforms (http://www2.ed.gov/about/inits/ed/implementation-support-unit/tech-assist/sustainability-rubric-full.pdf). Indeed, the joke at EDI is that we're "rubricologists": any time there is a hot topic in education reform, we're ready to make a rubric for it.

Why do we keep making rubrics? They're not a cure-all, but they fill an important gap in our knowledge. In K–12 and higher education, we wish we knew far more about implementation quality than we currently do—information that occupies the middle ground between rigorous student outcome results and mere anecdotes about progress (more on this in Part 2). A rubric fills this gap with a set of well-defined criteria that gets everyone on the same page about what "good" looks like. In fact, the very act of creating a rubric helps us all get clearer about what we are really trying to accomplish and how (the first two questions of delivery!). The capacity review allows people to use the rubric to translate their subjective perspectives into more objective, actionable evidence.

A rubric can't tell us everything that we need to know. But it's a surprisingly powerful tool for helping us know a lot more than we do now.

⊙ KEY CONSIDERATIONS FOR SYSTEM LEADERS AND STAFF

If you're a **system leader**, the capacity review is a gift: a process that can give you a reasonably accurate snapshot of your current capacity to deliver, and align your team around that snapshot, with a small investment of time. Whether you're working with an external partner or appointing your own internal review team, ask them to follow the process in this chapter. You can trust that process to help you decide what to do next.

If you're part of the **system staff**, you can use the capacity review to clarify what you're trying to do and how. Be transparent in the interviews and self-assessments; use the opportunity to air your concerns and crystallize them in a productive way. The capacity review process isn't a gotcha; it's a baseline from which your leaders can continuously improve this work. If you lead a particular division in your system, you can also apply the capacity review process to yourself, both to support your own work and to role model the value of the exercise to others.

Finally, **delivery leaders** have two important things to think about. First, consider whether you'd like to join the capacity review team. If it's internal, you should almost certainly join it and even lead it. But if you're working with an external partner, there may be an advantage in sitting back, letting the team do its work, and participating by contributing your perspective in interviews and the self-assessment. It all comes down to whether the system will benefit more from your learning how to conduct a process like this (which is similar to other delivery work you will be doing) or from guarding against any biases you may bring in the review.

Second, pay attention to the results of the review and their implications for how you build your team. The review will identify places where excellent delivery is already happening. Some leaders in these areas will make excellent candidates to join your delivery team; others will be natural leaders for goals and strategies as you undertake the delivery planning processes outlined in Part 3. Either way, use the review results to develop a perspective on who needs to play what roles in the months to come.

⊙ CONCLUSION

We began this chapter by wondering where you start your delivery effort. Hopefully we've made the answer clear: in a world of limited time and resources, we must do some up-front work to understand what we're already doing well, where we fall short, and how we can best bridge the gap. The capacity review is the most efficient way we've found to do this.

Beyond that, the capacity review symbolizes an important hallmark of what makes delivery different from other approaches for improving implementation: its flexibility. Unusually for a "methodology," delivery places a high value on adapting its tools to the surrounding context. Delivery has no ego; if our partners have found a better way to get something done, we celebrate their work and use it to revise our own tools.

The capacity review embodies this ethos by seeking first to understand before setting a course of action. It gives us the context we need to understand which tools are needed most urgently, which are not a good fit, and which need to be adjusted. We emerge from it with a clear idea of what to do next to establish this approach in a system, all without reinventing the wheel or offending the people who are already doing good work.

The capacity review is the gateway to the rest of your delivery effort, which begins now.

Chapter 1C

Build the Delivery Unit

 Develop a foundation for delivery

 Understand the delivery challenge

 Plan for delivery

 Drive delivery

 Create an irreversible delivery culture

System Leader Summary

Distractions abound when you lead a system—so much so that it can be difficult to focus on the discipline of delivery. For this reason, we recommend that you establish a **Delivery Unit**: a person or team responsible for driving the achievement of your aspiration, no matter what. Led by your delivery leader, the Delivery Unit is the one group in your system that you can count on to be immune to distractions, even when you yourself have to respond to them. This chapter describes the role of the Delivery Unit and how you should organize it and build its capacity.

Your Delivery Unit's relevance will depend on your support. Carve out a small but significant set of resources for the Unit, staff it with talented people, back them publicly, and give them a singular charge: to master the tools and practices in this book and embed them in your system's ongoing work. If you've found the right people, they will do the rest; in fact, as they build trust with you, they will learn to guide and manage you through the rest of this book.

⦿ WHY BUILD A DELIVERY UNIT?

In Homer's *Odyssey*, one of the many dangers that the hero, Odysseus, faced on his journey home were Sirens, a brood of dangerous creatures whose sweet song would lure sailors to veer off course and run aground on the rocky island they inhabited. Odysseus wanted to avoid this, but he still wanted to hear the sirens' song. So he instructed his crew to plug their ears with wax and to tie him, ears unplugged, to the mast of their ship. It worked: when the ship came in range, Odysseus heard and was enchanted by the Sirens' song—but much as he might try to convince his crew to untie him and direct the ship toward the island, they rowed on, wax in their ears, safely toward their destination.

A system leader who undertakes a delivery effort is rather like Odysseus. He or she wants to hear the sirens' call; in fact, a system leader must be willing to spend his or her own personal time and attention engaging with the inevitable distractions and crises that arise in the course of their work. But even as that happens, a system leader must have a crew that can be counted on to be immune to the sirens, rowing toward the system's aspiration and focusing on student results no matter what kinds of distractions arise. That crew is the Delivery Unit.

The idea of a Delivery Unit preceded the idea of delivery itself. It was for the purpose of running a new "Prime Minister's Delivery Unit" that Michael first went to serve at No. 10 Downing Street; it fell to that Unit, once established, to actually invent the practices and disciplines of delivery.

And invent they did: the various chapters of this book all derive from that original work and the work of the people who have replicated it elsewhere. That original Delivery Unit was a vanguard: taking the best of management practices from multiple sectors, they created something new and well suited to achieving results in education systems.

Today, over a decade later, it's worth asking the question: now that we know so much more about delivery, is a dedicated Unit still necessary? Aren't the commonsense principles of delivery supposed to be *everyone*'s job, and not just that of a separate Unit? In fact, doesn't that separateness create the risk of a "delivery silo" to add to those that already exist in education systems?

Though we know that delivery can take hold with or without one, we continue to believe that a dedicated Unit is the best investment a system can make to maximize the likelihood of delivering results. There are a few reasons for this:

- Though we know much more about delivery, it's a discipline that's constantly being renewed and reinvented. Delivery Units provide a focal point for continuing to reflect on and improve delivery tools and practices.
- Like most aspects of good management, delivery is also a neglected discipline. It's certainly true that delivery—the focus on results for students—*should be* everyone's job. But we have seen too many leaders make the naïve assumption that talented people, qualified people, and/or experienced people automatically know what it takes to drive results. The truth is that the disciplines of delivery are counterintuitive; they don't come naturally to even the highest performers. A Delivery Unit will build the capacity of every leader to adopt these disciplines.

- The crises of the moment will inevitably distract even the most focused system leaders and managers from the work of achieving results for students. Without a Delivery Unit, there will be no advocate for delivery, which will put the focus on outcomes at risk. Sometimes, the sirens' song is simply too powerful to resist.

A Delivery Unit provides consistency, a calm and steady presence whose role it is to continue to ask the four key questions of delivery:

1. What are you trying to do?

2. How are you planning to do it?

3. At any given moment, how will you know that you are on track to succeed?

4. If not, what are you going to do about it?

To these four questions, a Delivery Unit will add a fifth: How can we help? When It functions well, a Delivery Unit gives coherence to a system's delivery effort, supplying influence without authority to complement the system's formal line management structure.

> "Someone needs to manage to the aspiration. Otherwise, the aspiration is something that a board votes on every 12 months and gets neglected. Delivery ensures that someone is watching out for the outcomes we all want. And unless it's someone's job, it's no one's job."
>
> —Matt Deninger,
> Delivery Leader,
> Massachusetts Department
> of Elementary and
> Secondary Education

◉ CORE PRINCIPLES

The steps for building a Delivery Unit are fairly straightforward: you need to establish one, and then you need to build its capacity and culture.

Establish the Unit

A Delivery Unit is the person or team responsible for driving the achievement of system aspirations, no matter what. The theory of action is simple: if a system leader creates and backs a small, flexible, and highly capable team that can focus on results, then that team will help the leader exercise meaningful influence over the activities of that system to drive toward those results.

It sounds simple, but it's kind of revolutionary. You don't need to overhaul everything all at once. You don't need to reorganize your entire system as a first step. Start at the top, start focused, and start small, and you can have the impact you want on the larger whole. Bigger changes may come later, but your Delivery Unit will help you commit to those changes with confidence that they're the right ones to make.

A Delivery Unit plays five roles:

1. **Plans and planning:** Delivery Units ensure that a system has priority goals and that each goal has a plan for how it will be achieved. They work with a system's goal leaders to facilitate or drive this planning as necessary.

2. **Monitoring and reporting:** When plans are in place, Delivery Units set up the right routines to consistently monitor progress against each goal.

3. **Evaluation and follow-up:** Between these routines, Delivery Unit members work with goal leaders and their teams to arrive at a shared view of progress, to tease out the implications for the work, and to align system resources to keep things on track.

4. **Capacity-building:** Delivery requires a shift in mindsets and capabilities from the top to the bottom of a system. This shift begins within the Delivery Unit itself, but the Unit must take advantage of every opportunity to "teach" delivery to system staff—including formal training, everyday interactions, and job-embedded coaching.

5. **Communication and relationship management:** Because their job is to exercise influence without authority, Delivery Units must be experts at managing relationships throughout the system—with goal leaders, with other system staff, and with the system leader.

To play these roles, the ideal Delivery Unit will be a dedicated, independent team established according to three principles. First, the delivery leader who leads the Unit should report directly to the system leader. This person must have the trust of both the leader and the leadership team—in particular, the system leader must be ready to back up the delivery leader when things get difficult. This relationship can be set up through a variety of existing arrangements and organizational structures. Some Delivery Units live inside a larger but related function—such as data, research, evaluation, and/or planning. Others are Chief Academic Officers or sit in that office. And others are Delivery Unit leaders by another name—Chief Performance Officer, Chief Accountability Officer, and so on.

Second, the Delivery Unit should sit outside the line management hierarchy of the system, neither managing nor being managed by the goal leaders and teams they work with. This allows them to provide an objective perspective on the system's progress toward its aspirations.

Finally, the Unit should include some of the most talented and capable people in the system—problem solvers, relationship managers, data analysts, and expert coaches. They are not necessarily the most senior people in a system, but these Delivery Unit Consultants should know how to work with and earn the respect of people at all levels.

Once you've established a Unit, how should you organize their work? For most Delivery Units, relationships with goal leaders and their teams are the most critical ones to build. This is why Delivery Units usually organize their staffing so that each team member is an "account manager" for one or more goal leaders. In Figure 1C.1 is a typical structure for a K–12 system.

Ownership for the system's 10 goals was divided according to three student-centered content areas: Literacy; Science, Technology, Engineering, and Math (STEM); and College and Career Readiness (CCR). Responsibility for these goals rested with the chiefs for each of those content areas, who reported directly to the superintendent. Each content team was directly supported by a Delivery Unit Consultant, who worked closely with the team to prepare for stocktakes and monthly meetings, perform the necessary analyses, and solve

Figure 1C.1 Delivery Unit Relationships With Goal Leaders in a K–12 System

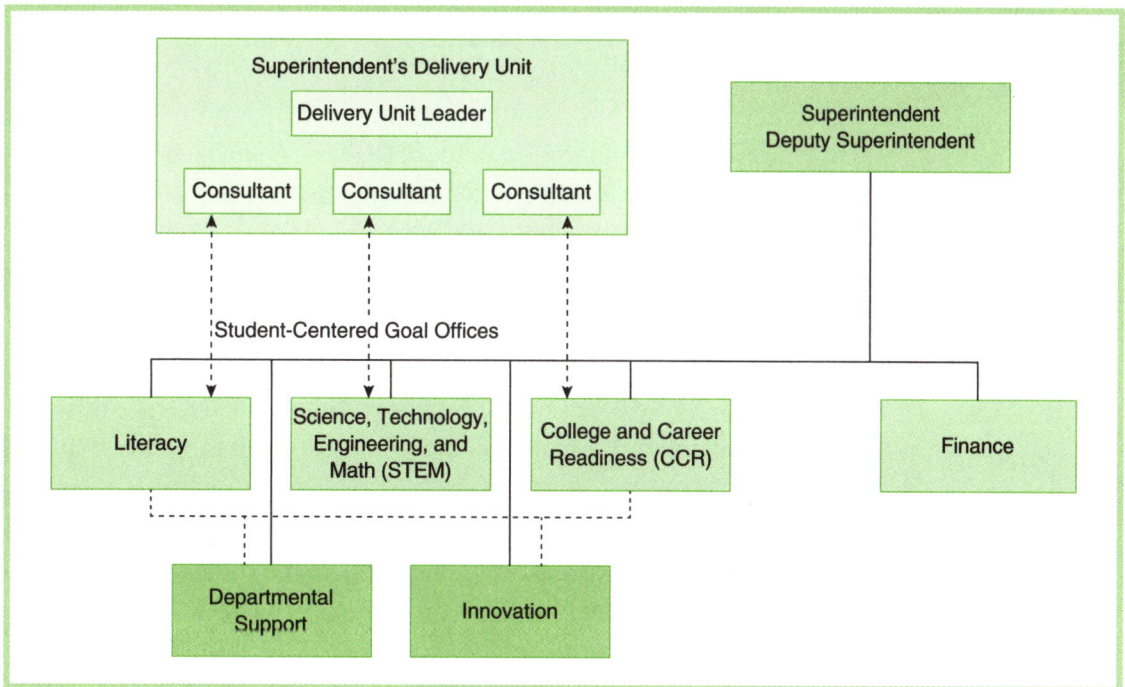

problems when goals were off-track. The benefit to this structure is that the Delivery Unit Consultants become very familiar with the content area they support and can form a strong relationship with the goal leaders to provide a good balance of challenge and support.

In some systems, the most important "goal leader" is actually a local leader. This is particularly true in higher education systems, where campus presidents and chancellors hold disproportionate sway. Recognizing this, the University of Missouri System's delivery leader assembled her Delivery Unit with leaders from each of its four campuses. This structure

Please visit EDI's website at www.deliveryinstitute.org/1C for more information on establishing a Delivery Unit.

The Experience of Goal Leadership

Being a goal leader means taking the journey of delivery alongside the Delivery Unit. It's a tough experience, but it can be a rewarding one. Dale Sims, Vice Chancellor for Business and Finance at the Tennessee Board of Regents and a goal leader for that system, explains:

"The process of goal setting and implementation of a specific plan to deliver on those goals has helped me to prioritize and assess the work related to my strategy. By virtue of the fact that through the system of routines, I am constantly reviewing progress on the pieces involved in implementing my strategy with team members as well as with the Chancellor, other board staff, and the Board, we can make almost real-time adjustments to the work. This has resulted in avoiding investment of time and resources in something that won't get us to our goal."

ensured a direct line of communication to the people who would feel the most responsibility for driving progress toward the system's goals.

Build the Unit's Capacity and Culture

Once you've carved out a space for your Unit, set it up, and recruited a few stars, you'll have the raw materials you need. Delivery is such a new discipline, however, that nearly every team member will inevitably be learning on the job. The key is to set the Unit up so that they can learn faster than anyone else.

This means that the Unit must embody a culture of delivery so thoroughly that its work is infectious. After the PMDU's first year of operation, Michael tried to sum up this emerging culture in five words:

1. **Ambition:** The Delivery Unit should constantly challenge performance and ask difficult questions, holding everyone—including themselves—to a high standard.

2. **Focus:** Delivery requires that we identify the things that are most likely to help us achieve our goals and prioritize them relentlessly. The Delivery Unit must lead this charge.

3. **Clarity:** The Delivery Unit should be able to cut through complex situations and get to the heart of every matter it addresses with a combination of rigorous problem solving, fact-based analysis, and effective communication.

4. **Urgency:** Most systems are biased toward inaction. The Delivery Unit must have the opposite bias, keeping awareness of the timetable for achieving results on the front of everyone's minds.

5. **Irreversibility:** Success is insufficient if it is ephemeral; the Delivery Unit must obsess with how they get the changes they make to *stick*.

Building this culture is partly about what you tell the team, but it's also about what the team does together to reinforce these values. Ultimately, you will build the team's culture by doing the work laid out in the rest of this book and by offering capacity-building supports along the way. For more tools and resources on capacity building, please see Chapter 5A.

Delivery Units in a Resource-Constrained Environment

Dedicated does *not* necessarily mean full-time. Several systems, particularly in higher education, have achieved promising results by drawing their delivery teams from the part-time contributions of existing staff. In these systems, the delivery team is a cross-functional group who takes advantage of the talent and credibility of people throughout the different units of the system office, as this example in Figure 1C.2 from the University of Wisconsin System shows.

Figure 1C.2 The University of Wisconsin system distributed delivery responsibilities among multiple offices.

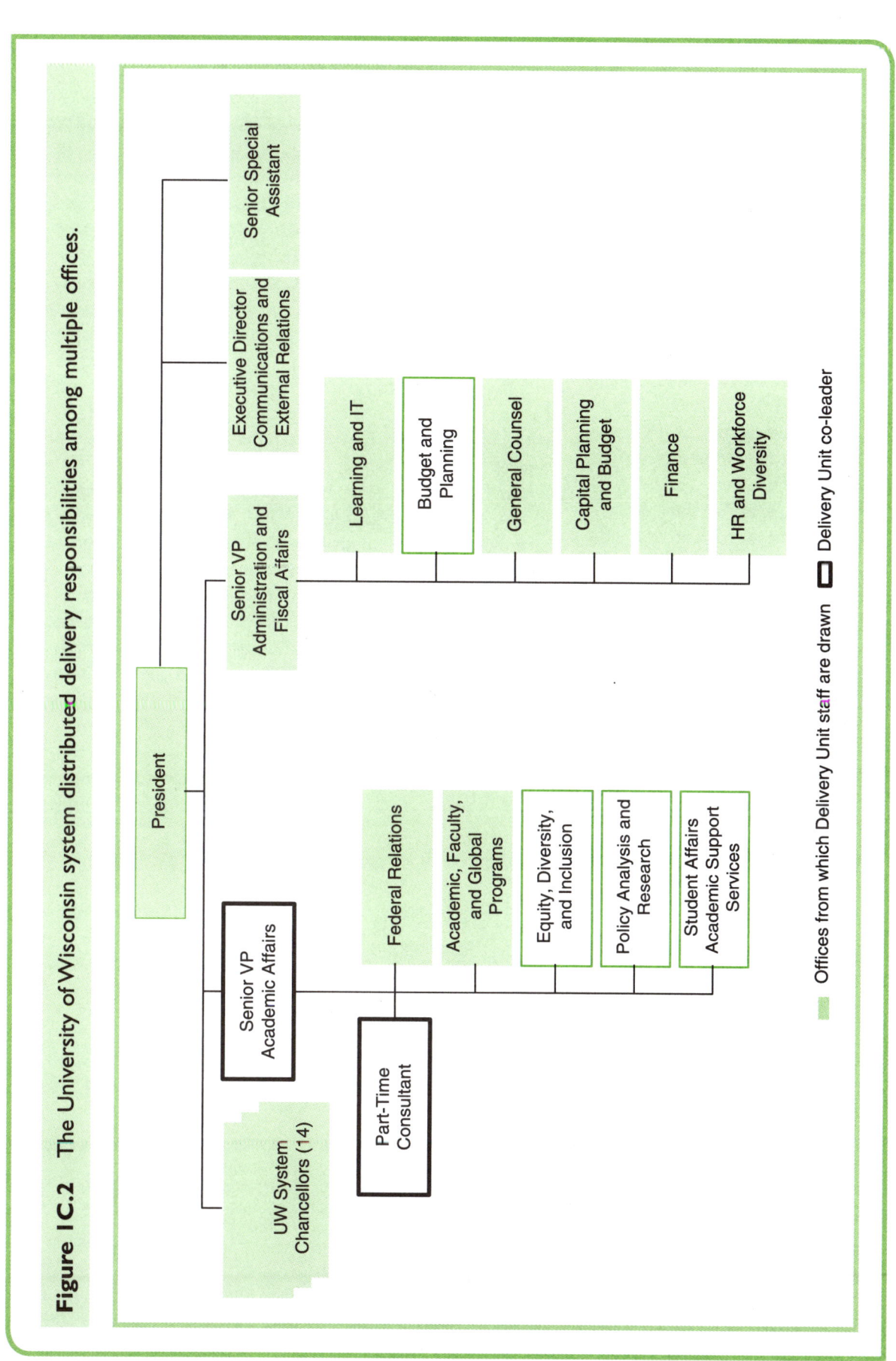

- Offices from which Delivery Unit staff are drawn ☐ Delivery Unit co-leader

The Massachusetts Delivery Unit

"Implementing delivery principles at ESE over the past few years has shifted the conversation to clarify not only what we are trying to accomplish but also how we are going to accomplish it, ensuring that we focus on improving student outcomes. At the heart of this approach has been the Delivery Unit: a dedicated team of three people that drives the department forward and constantly brings the conversation back to academic indicators and student outcomes."

—Mitchell Chester, Commissioner of Education, Massachusetts

In 2010, Commissioner Mitchell Chester established a Delivery Unit for the Massachusetts Department of Elementary and Secondary Education (ESE). He appointed Carrie Conaway, the head of the Office of Planning and Research, to head the Unit. Carrie was a strong choice for delivery leader for several reasons: her talent, her trusted relationship with the Commissioner, and her relationship with the senior staff. Her office was also outside the line management hierarchy for most of the people who were managing ESE's goals (see Figure 1C.3). Carrie did have a day job, however—leading the planning and research work—so she appointed a deputy and dedicated two analysts to work with that deputy to drive the delivery effort full time.

Each Delivery Unit member was assigned responsibility for a particular goal leader and team, for whom they provided support and challenge toward meeting the goal.

One year later, in a capacity review for ESE, the results showed that the Delivery Unit had made great progress in establishing the disciplines of delivery throughout the agency. Stakeholders throughout the agency, from mid-level leaders to the Commissioner, voiced their respect and praise for the Unit's work.

Figure 1C.3   Simplified Organization Chart for Massachusetts Delivery Unit and Goal Leaders

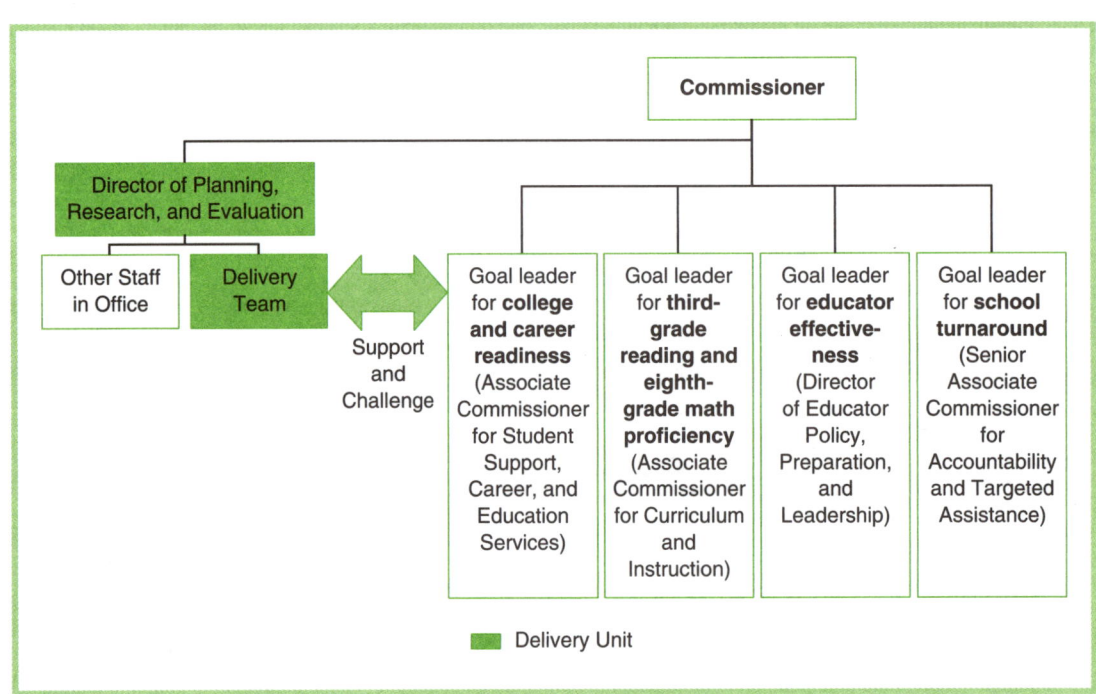

⊙ LESSONS FROM THE FIELD

Be Clear About Roles

The Delivery Unit is still a new concept. As such, the potential for misunderstanding is great, and you will need absolute clarity on the role that the Unit plays. A group of talented people is a magnet for every possible "special project" that your system's leader and staff can dream up: we have seen delivery leaders mistaken for "czars" that run particular high-profile initiatives, dismissed as "mere" project managers, and pulled into the very firefighting activities that they are supposed to avoid.

For this reason, remember and emphasize what a Delivery Unit does *not* do. Though the work is related, a Delivery Unit is not a project management office. Three things distinguish Delivery Consultants from project managers: (1) their focus on outcomes rather than inputs, (2) their role in synthesizing and interpreting rather than just aggregating information about performance, and (3) their sense of ownership of the delivery effort at a leadership level.

> "If you overplay your hand, you sound arrogant; if you make unreasonable demands, you weaken yourself for the next time; if you claim to speak for the Prime Minister on an issue but don't really, you risk ridicule; and if you are rude, aggressive or ill informed, you bring the Prime Minister himself into disrepute. Worse still, if you persistently do any or all of these things, in the rumor mill that is government the world over, the word soon gets back to the man himself. And if he loses confidence in you or your Unit, the game is up."
>
> —Sir Michael Barber[1]

A Delivery Unit is also not a goal leader. Goal leaders are ultimately accountable for achieving the system's aspirations and for managing a system's strategies to that end. They have direct ownership over the work: they are curriculum developers, conveners of faculty committees, managers of contracts with vendors, and so on.

By contrast, Delivery Units do not manage the day-to-day work; instead, they work with and through goal leaders and other system staff to ensure that things stay on track. They do this by striking the right balance between supporting the work (and the people who do it) and challenging it to be better. It is their distance from the day-to-day that gives them the perspective and objectivity necessary to do this.

To protect this role, Delivery Units must clearly delineate and overcommunicate it to others. This communication starts with the system leader and the Delivery Unit itself; over time, goal leaders must reinforce this message to their teams as well.

Don't Assume Credibility; Earn It

Many of the principles we've covered are designed to increase the Delivery Unit's credibility—in particular, a Unit that reports directly to the system leader and is not in the line management hierarchy will enjoy some independence and will be more likely to be taken seriously. However, this kind of "structural" credibility only lasts so long. As Michael used to tell his staff at the PMDU, the Prime Minister's name would help you get your foot in the door with goal leaders; after that, you were on your own. And it's easier than you think to mess things up.

A Delivery Unit can threaten others in a system. In addition to the fact that *any* change is disruptive, the very existence of a Delivery Unit can give the impression that others aren't capable of doing their work on their own.

Nothing could be further from the truth; in fact, the point of a Unit is to free everyone else to focus on the substantive work that they do best. Nonetheless, the potential for misunderstanding is real.

Ultimately, Delivery Units maintain their credibility and relevance by the quality of their relationships and their success at helping others buy in to this approach. The tools and processes in this book are necessary for the work to be effective, but they are not enough on their own. Early on in a delivery effort, Delivery Units must demonstrate that, while they will not always agree completely with the goal leaders that they work with, they will always be respectful and helpful. As one delivery leader once said to us, "I define success as people wanting to work with us because they know we are going to make them look good."

Delivery Units must therefore adopt a posture of humility toward the leaders they work with and strive to earn their trust. Invoking the system leader's name—or any kind of formal authority—should be a last resort.

◉ KEY CONSIDERATIONS FOR SYSTEM LEADERS AND STAFF

If you're a **system leader**, we encourage you to find the resources to build a Delivery Unit. The most important role you will play is in your endorsement of this Unit's work as your primary means for focusing your system on achieving your aspirations. This means guiding your leadership team to work with the Unit, publicly communicating about the importance of its work, and backing them up when they receive the inevitable pushback. It takes a certain degree of confidence and humility to allow a Delivery Unit to "manage" you in the way that they are supposed to; by showing that you trust them to do this, you will set an example for your leadership team and staff.

The tools and practices outlined in this book will help **system staff** focus your work on achieving results, whether or not there is a Delivery Unit helping you do this. Ultimately, your adoption of this different way of working will determine whether delivery is a passing fad or a catalyst for lasting change. As you read this book, consider how it can inform your individual work, regardless of whether there is a larger delivery effort under way. It may be possible, for example, to dedicate a portion of your team's time to focusing on delivery. If your system does have a Delivery Unit, consider how they can be an asset in helping you achieve results for students—and be willing to give them feedback about how they can best work with you.

Finally, **delivery leaders** must pay special attention to building a positive "brand" for the Delivery Unit as soon as possible. The system leader has placed his or her trust in you and has allocated precious resources to your Unit; your job is to demonstrate to everyone that your existence is worth the cost. For more on building the Delivery Unit brand, see Chapter 5C: Unleash the "Alchemy of Relationships."

⊙ CONCLUSION

Whatever it's called and however it's arranged, dedicated capacity to focus on delivery is a critical condition for success. The up-front investment, and the disruption caused by the early work, will be a source of tension. But this is a natural consequence of the shift that delivery brings; what feels like added work is in fact the addition of the *right* work, which must then be offset by a willingness to drop those things that aren't as important. Courage is required throughout a delivery effort, but the early stages, in which a Delivery Unit begins its work, are some of the most critical.

⊙ NOTE

1. Barber, M. (2008). *Instruction to deliver: Fighting to transform Britain's public services* (Rev. ed.). London, UK: Methuen.

Chapter 1D

Establish a Guiding Coalition

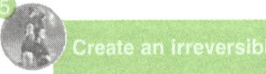

System Leader Summary

Public leadership isn't just an act of will; it depends on the support of other leaders around you. This is what John Kotter calls a **guiding coalition**: a critical mass of people, with the right types of formal and informal influence, who agree profoundly with you about the aspiration you're trying to achieve and the work you're doing to achieve it. By building and engaging a coalition *before* you need them, you have people you can rely on when things get difficult.

Most leaders are natural coalition-builders, and the lion's share of the work in coalition-building will fall to you as system leader. This chapter takes a process that is instinctual for many and breaks it down into manageable steps, both for your benefit and the benefit of your leadership team. The more you can bring them and your delivery leader into your efforts, the more likely your guiding coalition will be a deliberate, focused effort that maximizes the value of the relationships you build.

⊙ WHO CAN YOU COUNT ON?

Good implementation depends on strong leadership. We've seen that already in our discussions of aspiration-setting and capacity reviews: we need the system leader and the leadership team to share a collective commitment to the aspiration, and to improving delivery, in order to get anything done. What's true in this early work will be true throughout your effort.

This principle extends beyond the leadership of your system. To keep both implementation—and the policy that supports it—on track, you'll need a critical mass of powerful internal and external stakeholders to be aligned around your aspiration and the work you're doing to achieve it. This group is what John Kotter called a guiding coalition: a small team of 7 to 10 people, in key positions of influence, who agree profoundly with you about what must be done and how to do it.[1] They answer a fundamental question: *who can you count on* to support your work, no matter what?

Consider the recent history of education reform. When EDI was first founded in 2010, a common agenda was taking root in systems all across the country. In higher education, a new president's commitment to making the United States first in the world in degree attainment resulted in a flurry of state legislative activity aimed at college completion. In K–12, the Race to the Top (RTT) competition had an impact far beyond the initial grantees; nearly every state changed law or policy to adopt reforms aligned with the RTT agenda. In nearly all these cases, guiding coalitions made change possible: key state legislators, executive officials, policy advisors, system leaders and staff, advocacy groups, business leaders, and others worked together to build the necessary consensus.

Five years later, the landscape is different. Enthusiasm for the completion agenda has waned in some states. A range of critics are pushing back against the RTT reforms. In the face of this opposition, some systems have retreated and undone some of the changes they made at the outset of this movement. But others have stood their ground.

A big part of the difference between these systems was in the strength and durability of their guiding coalitions; those that maintained and invested in these relationships had much better results than those that did not. So again, *who can you count on?* When a legislator proposes a bill to undo the reform you're trying to implement, who can you count on to stop it? Do you have friends in the legislature who can whip votes against it? Credible advocates who will testify against it? A governor who will veto it?

A guiding coalition can take many forms, but getting the right people is crucial. A good guiding coalition isn't a leadership or management team; it's not even a steering committee. Rather, it's a group that brings together sources of power from a variety of contexts, giving you the right combination of clout to keep your work on track.

Guiding coalitions play at least four roles. First, they contribute expertise and guidance. Like Roosevelt's famous Kitchen Cabinet, they're a valuable sounding board for your work, and their opinions should shape the strategic decisions you make.

Second, guiding coalition members often contribute directly to the work—or at least remove obstacles to it. Think of the board member who shepherds a crucial proposal through to passage. Or the well-respected faculty member who leads her colleagues in a course redesign initiative. Or the human resources director who eliminates a bureaucratic barrier to hiring the people you need. Each of these people is marshaling a unique source of power to help drive delivery forward.

Third, guiding coalition members serve as champions for your work. Your challenge is not just to build credibility amongst influential leaders; to sustain your reforms, you'll need a durable base of support that extends all the way to front-line implementers and the public at large. This is what Michael Fullan calls the "ever-widening circles of leadership" (see Figure 1D.1).[2]

System leaders and the Delivery Unit can't hope to reach all these people on their own. The guiding coalition is your first circle of leadership, a force multiplier that helps you reach to the circles beyond.

Finally, guiding coalition members use their influence to support and defend your work at critical moments. More than anything else, your coalition is a set of relationships you invest in *before* you need them. Reforms that take years to build can be demolished in a heartbeat if leaders are caught unaware by opposition. When crisis strikes, you'll need to have your support lined up already or you'll be overwhelmed. If you ask for help only during tough times, there will be understandable cynicism about your motives. So at any given moment, you must be ready to answer the question: who can you count on?

⊙ CORE PRINCIPLES

The steps for building a guiding coalition are straightforward: identify the coalition, engage its members, and then rely on them to support your work. For the

Figure 1D.1   Widening Circles of Leadership

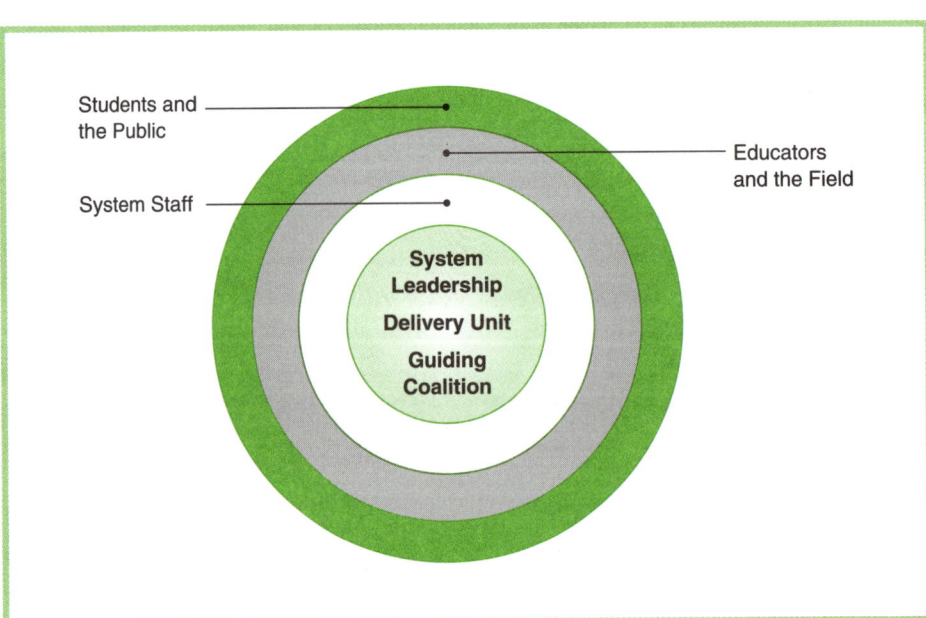

purposes of this section, we'll assume that you need one guiding coalition for your overall aspiration. Some systems may find that they need different (though probably overlapping) coalitions to support different parts of their agenda. This same approach applies to those cases but must be undertaken multiple times.

Identify the Coalition

You'll need a small group—7 to 10 people, as we noted above. Inevitably, you'll have many more options than that. For this reason, you need to narrow and prioritize the possibilities and come up with a short list.

The first step to a short list is to make a long one. Who are the 20 to 30 people with the highest potential to help you achieve your aspiration? Figure 1D.2 gives a list of likely groups of people to consider.

In considering who to put on this initial list, think about what they would bring to the coalition. Kotter identifies at least four types of power that you should consider:

1. **Position power:** Do they have formal authority that is essential to policy or implementation? This could mean that they manage a team or an organization whose support is vital, or that they have constitutional or statutory authority to make certain critical decisions.

Figure 1D.2   Potential Guiding Coalition Members

Level	K–12	Higher Education	Both
State	• Secretary of Education and staff • State Board of Education members and staff • State Education Agency leaders and staff • Regional leaders • Local superintendents • Principals • Union and professional association leaders • School board association leaders	• Higher education governing board members and staff • System office leaders and staff • Faculty Senate leaders and members • Campus presidents, chancellors, provosts, and department chairs	• Governor's office (particularly education policy advisors) • Legislature (particularly education committee chairs or their advisors) • P-20 Council members and staff • Advocacy organization leaders and staff
Local	• School board members • Key central office staff • Principals • Department heads and other teacher leaders • Teachers • Union leaders • Parents	• Provosts and vice provosts • Key campus staff • Department chairs • Faculty senate leaders • Faculty members	• Mayoral and/or county office executives and staff • City council members or equivalent • Leaders of local philanthropies • Leaders of community-based organizations

2. **Credibility:** Do they have informal authority that comes from respect or reputation—particularly with one of the broader circles that you need to influence? These aren't necessarily the people with the most impressive titles or jobs—but almost anyone you ask will know who they are. Perhaps it's a particular principal or campus provost who inspires respect and admiration amongst their peers. If they're with you, many others will be, too.

3. **Expertise:** Do they have power because they have deep knowledge of your work? An expert in education labor law might be the right person to help you navigate the legal implications of your teacher and leader effectiveness work, for example. Or a dean who has served at the campus for 30 years might know "how things work" at that institution—and therefore, how to change the way they work—better than anyone else.

4. **Leadership:** Do they have power because they are strong leaders? You will need your guiding coalition members to be competent people who you can trust to act on your behalf and to do so effectively.

Once you've made your list, eliminate the names of people who are staunchly opposed to your work, either because they disagree with your aspiration or your fundamental approach to achieving it. Time is too precious and the agenda is too important to invest in coalition members who are irreversibly hostile to your priorities. Prioritize leaders who you have a reasonable chance of bringing together around your aspiration, values, and strategy.

Once you've narrowed the list, select the 7 to 10 people you will focus on. To do this, it's helpful to answer three questions for each name:

- How powerful are they relative to the others? Rate on a 4-point scale: Low, medium, high, very high.
- What kind of power do they have? Position power, credibility, expertise, leadership? Some combination?
- What is the sphere of influence where they exercise that power?

Lay the answers to these questions out in a table like the one in Figure 1D.3.

Figure 1D.3 Worksheet for Identifying a Guiding Coalition

Person	Power	Type of Power	Sphere of Influence
Superintendent's chief of staff	High	• Position • Leadership	• Central office • Superintendent
School board president	Very high	• Position	• School board
Teacher in district who was named state teacher of the year	Medium	• Credibility	• Teachers
District science director	Medium	• Expertise	• Science educators and experts

At this point, you have the information you need to discuss and debate the merits of including each person with your leadership team. Is the group sufficiently powerful to give you what you need? Is there sufficient diversity, both of the types of power being exercised and where these people are influential? (One leader we worked with included military leaders in his coalition to support the Common Core Standards—it was a conservative community, and the military knew that better standards meant better recruits.) Does the group cover the constituencies you need to cover to be successful? And do they have the potential to work well together?

There's no single rule for who you choose, but laying out all the information will help you consider the options together and assemble a coalition that makes the most sense for your context.

> Please visit EDI's website at www.deliveryinstitute.org/1D for an exercise on identifying and prioritizing members of your guiding coalition.

Engage the Coalition

Your guiding coalition will only be as helpful as the strength of the relationships that you have with its members. As we've already said, you need to invest in these relationships before you need them.

This is the point where some leaders may balk. After all, many of these potential guiding coalition members are busy people. Even if we need to build a relationship now, we may be hesitant to ask for too much, fearful that the goodwill of others is a finite and exhaustible resource.

Paradoxically, the opposite is true: asking for help is the best way to get a person to help you in the future. Ask for advice; it's much more difficult for a person to oppose an idea if they've advised the person promoting it. Ask for action; the work they do for you now will actually beget the work they are willing to do for you later. And ask them to ask others for help; the effect will multiply. To use Ben Franklin's words, "If you want to make a friend, let someone do you a favor."

There are a range of options for asking for help. You can hold individual meetings with your guiding coalition members. If you need the members of your coalition to engage in more collective action, gathering them as a group to ask for help may be the best course of action.

At this point, you're crossing into the territory of more "formal" groups. The Arizona Ready Education Council is one example of a group like this. Founded in 2005 as the Governor's P-20 Council, the Arizona Ready Education Council was renamed in 2011 by Governor Jan Brewer to advise on and champion the implementation of *Arizona Ready*, her P-20 reform plan for the state. During Governor Brewer's tenure, the Council included a wide range of influential stakeholders: the president of the board of regents, the state superintendent, local superintendents and college presidents, leaders of philanthropic organizations, and business community leaders. It was chaired by Dr. Craig Barrett, the

> "Many people spend their whole lives resisting having others do favors for them. In doing so, they forfeit not only the gift directly offered, but something far more important: the power that comes from receiving. Never forget the basic accounting principle at work here: an account receivable is an asset. Those who have helped you in the past are more likely to help you again."
>
> —Chris Matthews[3]

former CEO of Intel Corp. and an activist in education policy both in Arizona and in the country as a whole. In this and its previous incarnations, the Arizona Ready Council provided a kind of built-in guiding coalition for the state's reforms for nearly a decade.

If you need your guiding coalition to coordinate its activities like this, you'll face the challenge of bringing a group of leaders with strong perspectives to consensus. You'll need to engage in expert facilitation to get the most out of these interactions—looking for common ground, confronting opposing beliefs, and building trust continuously.

When Coalitions Build Themselves:
The Role of External Groups

Sometimes an external organization can do much more than act as a member of your coalition; they can assist you in building and maintaining it. Over the last several years, several state K–12 systems have seen the birth of external organizations that have allowed leaders to "outsource" some of their coalition-building:

- The oldest and best known of these is Kentucky's Prichard Committee for Academic Excellence, a nonprofit organization that has guided Kentucky's P-20 reform efforts for over 30 years.
- The Massachusetts Business Alliance for Education (MBAE) was formed to be the eyes, ears, and voice of the business community in that state for shaping the policies and practices of public school reform. Most recently, in 2014, they released "The New Opportunity to Lead," a comprehensive blueprint for the future of education reform in the state.
- Founded in 2009, the Tennessee State Collaborative on Reforming Education (Tennessee SCORE) was instrumental in building a coalition for K–12 education reform that has endured through two governors and twice as many Education Commissioners. SCORE engages in advocacy, publishes reports on the state of education in Tennessee, and holds regular Institutes to bring together thought leaders in the education conversation in the state.
- The Colorado Education Initiative (CEI, originally the Colorado Legacy Foundation) goes beyond advocacy to partner directly with state and district leaders to support innovation and implementation. CEI raises and targets resources to incubate innovative ideas, arm educators with effective tools, identify proof points, and move promising practices into more schools.

If you have an organization like this in your community, consider how you might partner with them to build and maintain a coalition. If you don't, consider how you might start one.

Rely on the Coalition

This may go without saying, but it's all there is left to do: asking for help, early and often, is the most important activity you can undertake to maintain your coalition's cohesion and sense of purpose. Sometimes this coalition-building will be proactive. EDI recently worked with the Council of Chief State School Officers (CCSSO) to support a handful of states as they set up College and Career Readiness Commissions on implementation of new academic standards. The states gather the Commission members several times a year to ensure they are informed about the state-level work and to discuss potential support that members can provide—writing an op-ed supporting the standards, for example, or meeting with a key stakeholder who needs to be persuaded to support the work.

Sometimes your work with a guiding coalition will involve asking for support on a specific difficult decision—the closure of a program, a staff shakeup at a struggling school, the publication of new data on campus performance. These situations are half proactive and half reactive: on the one hand, you know that you are about to make a decision that will trigger some opposition, and you want to prevent it, but on the other hand, you will need to be prepared to meet and react to that opposition if it does arise. When you encounter them, you should alert your guiding coalition members, ask them to lay the groundwork for the news, and prepare them to back you up.

Finally, sometimes you'll need to call on your guiding coalition to defend against an unexpected threat to your agenda. These are the moments when you learn who your true friends are. But why learn then when you can know ahead of time? Remember that building a guiding coalition is about always having a sure answer to the question we asked at the beginning of this chapter: who can you count on?

⊙ LESSONS FROM THE FIELD

Formality Is Overrated

We've noted that guiding coalitions can take many forms: they can be a loose network of individual relationships that the system leader has, or they can be formally appointed bodies like the Arizona Ready Education Council. We don't think one is necessarily better than the other, but we have noticed a tendency among leaders to gravitate toward formal structures. There's a risk with this approach: we can become complacent, believing that the structure of a guiding coalition substitutes for the thing itself.

An example of this is the committee structure that has become a common vehicle for overseeing the development of teacher and leader evaluation systems at the state and local levels. Many of the laws authorizing these evaluation systems mandated the convening of committees of stakeholders—system leaders, representatives of principals, representatives of teachers, and so on—to oversee their design and implementation. The idea is sound: create a structure for a guiding coalition that can lead (and therefore back) a difficult and challenging reform.

But as you might have predicted, results vary. Some of these committees have successfully overseen the implementation of their new systems. Others have become the graveyards of progress: deadlocked, stalled, or just plain incoherent. Having a structure in place doesn't create alignment by itself. Given a choice between a structure—even one that comes with resources—and the determination to do the hard work of coalition-building detailed in this chapter, the smart leader will choose the latter every time.

Members of a "council" or "committee" may also get confused about their purpose. There is something about formal structure that makes us all think that we should have formal authority. Even the Arizona Ready Education Council, profiled earlier in this chapter, struggled with this identity problem: Are we a decision-making body? Should we vote to approve things? Or are we just here to advise the governor and to work on behalf of her agenda? Being designated as a "council" muddies the water around these questions.

At best, a formal structure will add symbolic value and some organizational heft to your guiding coalition. At worst, such a structure will be *no more than* a symbol, a fig leaf that some leaders use to give the impression of engagement without actually doing anything. Be careful not to let this happen.

Build Your Coalition in Reverse

The approach we've laid out in this chapter takes the players on the field as a given and assumes that you have to work with them. But another possibility is for you to exercise influence over *who gets selected* for some of the more powerful positions. Perhaps you can't work well with the head of a particular community organization. But when they move on to a new role, can you have some influence over who replaces them? Even as you recruit powerful people into your coalition, keep your eye on the powerful *positions*. When they turn over, push to fill them with people who support your aspiration and are eager to do something about it.

Take a Moment to Be Deliberate

Most system leaders have a natural instinct for coalition-building; identifying and engaging the key players will come easily to them. However, our experience is that many leaders are not as strategic as they could be about who they spend their time with and why. Moreover, a disadvantage of being naturally talented at something is that you're not as explicit with others about how it works. As a result, many leaders inadvertently keep coalition-building to themselves and don't enlist the aid of their leadership teams or Delivery Units.

You may not need to spend too much time in this chapter, but we would encourage you to take a moment to step back and consider your current efforts using the exercises we offer here. They're fairly simple and intuitive, but they will help you clarify and affirm your current course of action—or discover a gap in your work that you need to correct. They will also bring others into the conversation and help them support you in your coalition-building efforts.

⊙ KEY CONSIDERATIONS FOR SYSTEM LEADERS AND STAFF

If you're a **system leader**, a lot of this work will fall to you. Embrace your role as the coalition-builder, but ask for and take advice from your team about who needs to be in your coalition and what you need from them. Your team is a valuable sounding board for helping you maximize your efforts in this area.

If you're part of the **system staff**, remember that power in a guiding coalition takes many forms. Beyond the obvious leaders in your system's coalition, are there others that your system leader has overlooked? You might have unique knowledge of the formal and informal power centers, both within your system office and in the field. Use this knowledge to identify other critical guiding coalition members to include.

If you're a **delivery leader**, it'll be your job to facilitate and support your system leader in the work of coalition-building. Push them to be explicit with you about what they're trying to do and whose support they will need to do it. Use your knowledge of the emerging delivery effort to give your input on who the coalition should include, how you should engage them, and what you should ask for.

You may also find yourself having to build your own internal guiding coalition, as Michael did when he led the PMDU. Think of the 7 to 10 key people inside your system—and possibly adjacent to it—whose support will be necessary to help you maintain the delivery approach in your system. Remember that, like any other reform, delivery is subject to the same risks and threats of opposition or resistance. Who can you count on to protect that work?

⊙ CONCLUSION

One or two people, even in powerful positions, will always struggle to achieve dramatic change. But 7 to 10 people in key positions, who agree about what they want to do and how they want to do it, can change the world. Indeed, as the famous quote from Margaret Mead goes, the world has never been changed by anything else.

Your guiding coalition is the last building block of your foundation for delivery. Until this point, you've defined your aspiration, gotten clear about where you're starting from, and set up a team to drive the work. A guiding coalition brings it all together, aligning the right people behind the aspiration and ensuring that you will have sufficient runway to focus on achieving it in the months and years to come. Cherish this gift, and—more important—count on it.

◉ NOTES

1. Kotter, J. (2012). *Leading change.* Boston, MA: Harvard Business Review Press.

2. Hargreaves, A., & Lieberman, A. (2010). *Second international handbook of educational change.* New York, NY: Springer.

3. Matthews, C. (1999). *Hardball: How politics is played, told by one who knows the game.* New York, NY: Simon & Schuster.

Part 2

Understand the Delivery Challenge

 **Develop a foundation for delivery**

 **Understand the delivery challenge**

 **Plan for delivery**

 **Drive delivery**

 **Create an irreversible delivery culture**

Once you know what you're trying to do, how will you know what to do about it? Before making plans, it's important to go to your aspiration and ask: what will it take to achieve it? And what factors are standing in our way?

This is what it means to understand the **delivery challenge**: the nature and size of the barriers to the delivery of your aspiration, an assessment of what your system is currently doing to overcome them, and a view on how that work could be improved. The next two chapters lay out a diagnostic process that will help you:

- Evaluate past and present performance
- Understand root causes of performance

Unfortunately, this is the step that our partner systems are most likely to skip. Those who have used these tools, however, have reaped the benefits: more consensus around the "problem" they're trying to solve, a better fact base for planning (Part 3), and a reference point for monitoring progress (Part 4). Understanding the delivery challenge sets you up well for the core work of delivery. As you read these chapters, consider how you can apply them in your context—as quickly as you can, but as thoroughly as you need to.

Chapter 2A

Evaluate Past and Present Performance

 **Develop a foundation for delivery**  **Understand the delivery challenge**  **Plan for delivery**  **Drive delivery**

 Create an irreversible delivery culture

System Leader Summary

Once you know your goals for students, you can analyze the data to see how far you are from achieving them and to understand the major barriers you face. Systems do this by looking for **performance patterns**: themes or trends in the data that are consistent and recurring across different types of analyses.

We have more and more data in the field of education, but it seems to be telling us less and less. Data alone won't solve our problems; instead, we must use **hypotheses** to bring our own intuitions and beliefs to data analysis, continuing in a cycle of inquiry that brings us closer and closer to understanding what's going on. The tools in this chapter will help you set up this cycle.

As system leader, you will be a key consumer of this data. Insist that the leaders around you bring you not just analysis, but insight. Give your Delivery Unit the resources that they need to lead this charge, but make it clear that it's everyone's job to analyze, interpret, and understand the data underlying their work.

⊙ THE PARADOX OF DATA

The idea of a needs analysis is familiar to most of us; to know where to go, we have to start by understanding where we are. At the same time, most education systems have access to an unprecedented amount of data. The last decade has brought a great deal of focus and attention to this topic in our field, so much so that being "data-driven" is almost a requirement to be taken seriously at all.

For all this, we've found that good needs analyses rarely happen in education systems. In fact, much of the conversation in our field is one of frustration that the data don't seem to do what we need it to do. This is the paradox of data: we're getting more and more of it, but it seems to tell us less and less.

There are a number of reasons for this. First, and most ironically, the very abundance of data in our field may lull us into a false sense of security. Enthralled with the idea of "Big Data," we think that if we just collect enough of it, the numbers will tell us what we need to know. Moreover, we have an unrealistic notion of what the data can tell us; we think that the numbers can give us a precise answer to every question we have. In the grip of this idea, we pursue perfect data sets while overlooking what imperfect information can tell us.

All this speaks to a worrying trend in the way that we view data: we behave as if it can substitute for real thinking about what's going on. But that can't be true. As Nate Silver, the data journalist behind fivethirtyeight.com, puts it: "The numbers have no way of speaking for themselves. We speak for them. We imbue them with meaning." And when we shirk this responsibility, the numbers do very little to help us. We must do the hard work of drawing insight from the information we've collected. Or, in Silver's words, "Before we demand more of our data, we need to demand more of ourselves."[1]

How can we do this? With so much data and so many choices about how to analyze and interpret it, you could spend forever running the numbers. In the face of this, it can be tempting to throw up your hands and just go with your gut. But there's a middle ground: we can best understand current performance by working through hypotheses. This provides us with a rigorous way of thinking about the data both before and after we analyze it.

In fact, the best data analysis occurs in an iterative cycle of forming hypotheses, gathering the right data to test them, and using the results to confirm, reject, or reshape those hypotheses for further analysis (see Figure 2A.1). This allows us a way to use our beliefs to inform and guide our work.

This approach isn't just a good idea that is practical for system leaders; it's also the way statistical analysis is meant to be done, going all the way back to the work of Thomas Bayes, a pioneer in this field. Silver summarizes it well: "[The Bayesian approach] encourages us to hold a large number of hypotheses in our head at once, to think about them probabilistically, and to update them frequently when we come across new information that might be more or less consistent with them."[2]

Whether we're working with formal statistics or rougher information, this is the approach we need if we're to develop an understanding of current performance to inform the work of our delivery effort.

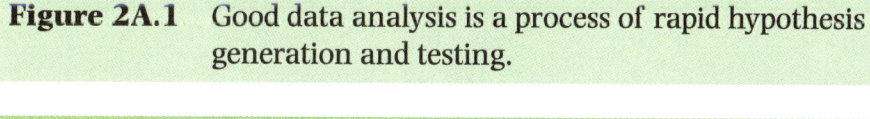

Figure 2A.1 Good data analysis is a process of rapid hypothesis generation and testing.

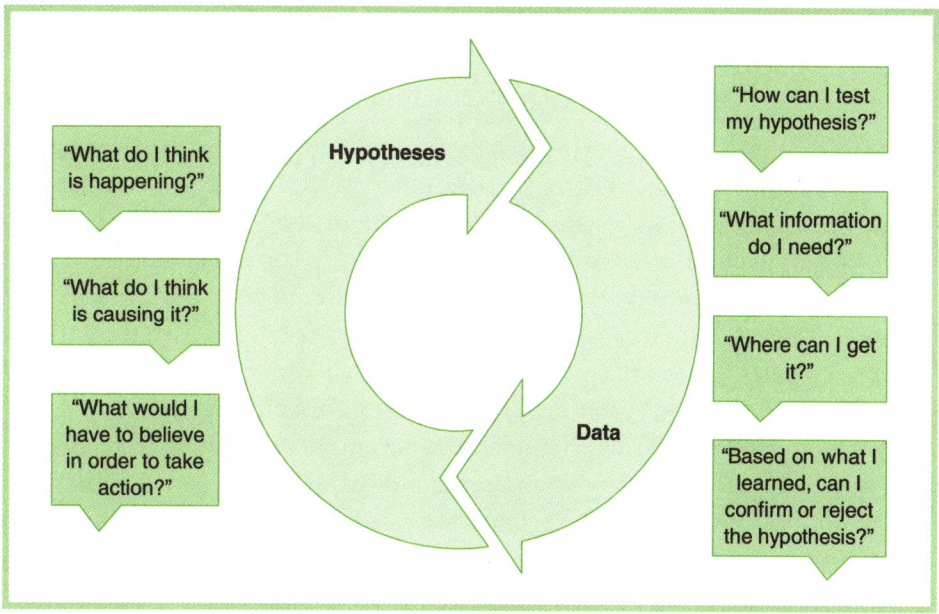

◉ CORE PRINCIPLES

The objective of this chapter is to help you identify performance patterns: themes or trends in your system's performance that are consistent and recurring across different types of analyses. These patterns summarize the current state of performance in your system and help inform the work you'll undertake.

There are four steps to do this:

1. Choose your data

2. Develop hypotheses

3. Analyze data to test hypotheses

4. Identify patterns of performance

As you go through them, it will become clear that this process is not meant to be confined only to your needs analysis. We return to it again and again, any time you need to look at evidence to understand current progress. In particular, you'll see its echo in Part 4, where we explore what it looks like to analyze performance after implementation has begun.

Choose Your Data

To analyze performance, you'll need to decide what data to start with. A hypothesis could be helpful here, but at the beginning, a more fundamental question should guide you: what data can tell us how we are performing against the system aspiration?

There are three types of measures to consider as you answer this question. First, **goal metrics** are used to measure the achievement of the goals that you defined in your aspiration (Chapter 1A). In most cases, they should measure actual student outcomes. In K–12, for example, if your aspiration is to help every student leave school college and career ready, the associated goal metric might be the college- and career-ready graduation rate. In higher education, goal metrics tend to be completion or graduation rates.

Of course, if you only rely on goal metrics, you may not get the information you need in time to make a difference to the outcome. As one of our partners likes to say, "Data analysis is too often an autopsy—it looks backward rather than forward." That's why you need **progress metrics** to help you understand or predict your future performance on the goal metrics. Progress metrics satisfy at least one of two criteria: (1) they are mathematical components of the goal metric or (2) when reported, they are correlated in some way to the future performance of the goal metric, "leading" you toward an estimate of that future performance.

For example, retention in higher education meets both these tests. For the first, retention from the first year to the second year must happen if a student is to graduate within 6 years. The graduation rate is at least partially determined by retention rates. For the second, we can also determine the likelihood of graduation based on patterns in first-year retention. In both cases, progress measures give us a way of making judgments on the likelihood of achieving our goals based on interim progress. Figure 2A.2 gives a list of the best leading indicators for student success in higher education, as determined by The Education Trust in its work with the Access to Success (A2S) initiative.[3]

Figure 2A.2   Leading Indicators of Postsecondary Success

Leading Indicators

Remediation:
- Begin coursework in first term
- Complete needed remediation

Gateway Courses:
- Complete college-level math/English in the first year or two
- Complete a college success course

Credit Accumulation and Related Behaviors:
- High rate of course completion (80%)
- Complete 20 to 30 credits in first year
- Earn summer credits
- Enroll full time
- Enroll continuously, without stop-outs
- On-time registration for courses
- Maintain adequate academic performance

Definition

Measurable academic patterns students follow that **predict the likelihood they will reach milestones and ultimately earn a degree**

Sometimes, progress metrics include **process metrics**— indicators that tell us whether the work we're doing to impact the goals is happening (and whether it's happening well). These are an important part of the picture, and we cover them in more detail in Chapter 3B.

> Please visit EDI's website at www.deliveryinstitute.org/2A for an exercise on identifying goal, progress, and perverse metrics.

Finally, **perverse metrics** may be necessary to guard against unintended consequences. Whenever you focus on one particular goal, the risk is that other desirable things will be crowded out. For example, a system focusing on its turnaround schools would want to continue to monitor performance in its other schools—especially those just above the threshold. Systems that have achievement gap goals must be especially careful of this. We all aspire to see equity gaps closed, but we don't want them to close because the performance of the higher-performing student groups has decreased.

Identifying perverse metrics ahead of time can become part of a powerful messaging strategy for your delivery effort. Naysayers may critique your goals by invoking the potential unintended consequences; your response, as Michael's was in the original Delivery Unit, should be to agree to check. This takes the excuse off the table and allows you to move forward.

As you identify these metrics, prioritize the ones that are clearly linked to your aspiration, easier to collect, and actionable for your team. This last one is particularly important; to borrow a phrase from Dan and Chip Heath, there's nothing more demoralizing than an analysis that is "true but useless."[4] Choose the metrics that will have the clearest implications for the work you're trying to do.

Once you've selected your data, the next step is to form your initial hypotheses about what you think it will say.

Develop Hypotheses

A hypothesis is a *tentative* statement about the relationship between two variables that is verified or rejected through further investigation. A hypothesis focuses your analysis and prevents "blind research," in which data are gathered that you find to be irrelevant after the fact.

There are five criteria that make a hypothesis robust:

1. Is it **testable**? Can you prove or disprove it with available data and a reasonable amount of effort?

2. Is it **plausible**? Does it broadly comport with existing evidence and theory? This is just a sense check—you do not necessarily want to rule out more far-fetched hypotheses, but the bar to prove them will be higher.

3. Is it **debatable**? If it can't be wrong, it's simply a statement of fact and unlikely to help.

4. Will it lead to **insight**? If you shared your hypothesis with the system leader, would it sound naïve or obvious?

5. Is it **actionable**? If you test it, will the result point directly to an action or actions the system might take?

Most important, a good hypothesis answers a question you care deeply about. In our case, the questions are about performance patterns. On which aspects of our aspiration are we performing well—and how well? On which aspects are we performing poorly—and how poorly?

To know what kinds of hypotheses to generate, we'll need to consider the analyses that we would use to test them. Edward Tufte writes that the heart of all quantitative reasoning is a single question: "Compared to what?"[5] A data "analysis" is merely a *comparison* of two or more different aspects of your data. Is proficiency similar to or different from, what it was a year ago? Are some campuses performing better than others? How are their underrepresented minority students doing compared with others? This is also known as **benchmarking**: comparing data in a way that helps you get a sense of what performance is versus what it should be.

The dilemma of the data analyst is to choose which comparisons to make. There are three ways to benchmark performance data:

1. Against history (the past);

2. Against peers (similar systems); and

3. Against yourself (variations within your system).

Moreover, for each benchmarking method, you also face a choice about how you would like to break down the data: by geography (districts/schools/campuses), by performance (proficient vs. advanced, percentiles of performance), or by student characteristic (race, socioeconomic status, and so on), among others. These methods, and various ways to combine them, are summarized in Figure 2A.3.

Figure 2A.3   Benchmarking Analysis Cheat Sheet With Sample Questions

Benchmarking Method	Ways to Break Down Data			
	By Whole System	By Geography	By Performance Band	By Student Characteristic
Against History	What is the trend in system performance?	What has been the trend in performance of districts?	How fast has the top quartile grown in the last 3 years?	How fast have our underrepresented minorities grown in the last 3 years?
Against Peers	How does my system compare to similar ones?	How do my urban districts compare to other urban districts with similar characteristics?	How does my top quartile of students compare to the top quartile in other countries?	How are my special education students doing compared to the national average?
Against Yourself	N/A	How does performance vary across our campuses?	How does my top quartile of students compare to the bottom quartile?	What is the achievement gap between Pell Grant recipients and nonrecipients?

As you can see, the number of analyses you could run to compare your data is practically infinite. Your hypothesis guides your choice of analysis by stating clearly what you believe the performance pattern could be.

We can now refine our definition of a performance pattern: it's a theme or trend in your system's performance on a particular metric that is *consistent and recurring* across different types of analyses like these. What do you expect will be true, no matter how you slice the data? For example, the chart in Figure 2A.4 shows four analyses of the trend in fourth-grade math proficiency across the state of Ohio. For each one, the solid line represents the achievement of economically disadvantaged students and the dashed line represents their peers. Each individual chart shows the data only for a specific student group.

There are at least two clear patterns visible across these four analyses. On the one hand, everyone's achievement is rising over time. On the other hand, the gap between disadvantaged students and their peers is stubbornly persistent—and in some cases, it has gotten larger over time.

This type of analysis can include progress metrics and leading indicators. The chart in Figure 2A.5 shows reading growth during the school year for students at three campuses of a charter school. It's broken out by campus and

Figure 2A.4   Example: Performance Patterns in Ohio

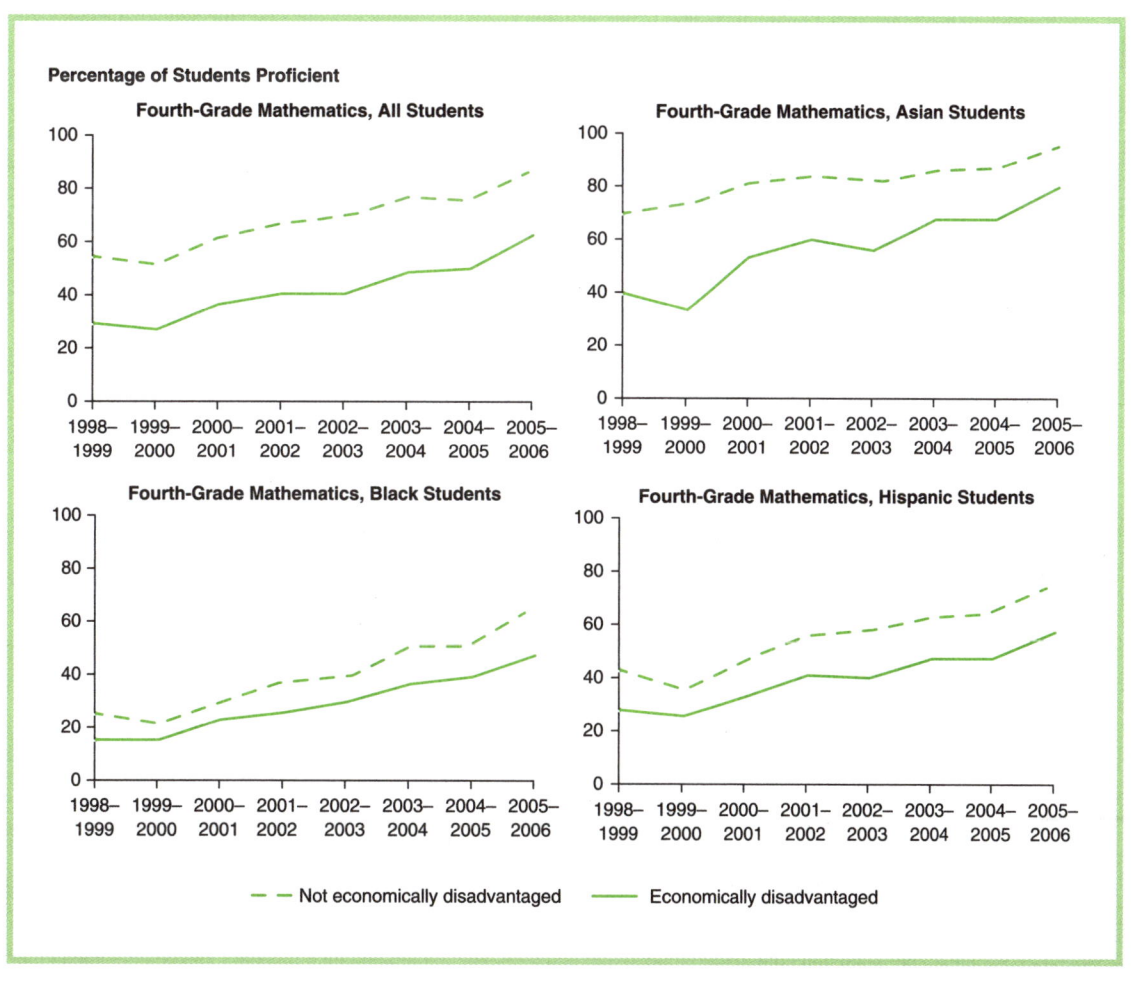

Figure 2A.5   Performance Patterns at the School Level

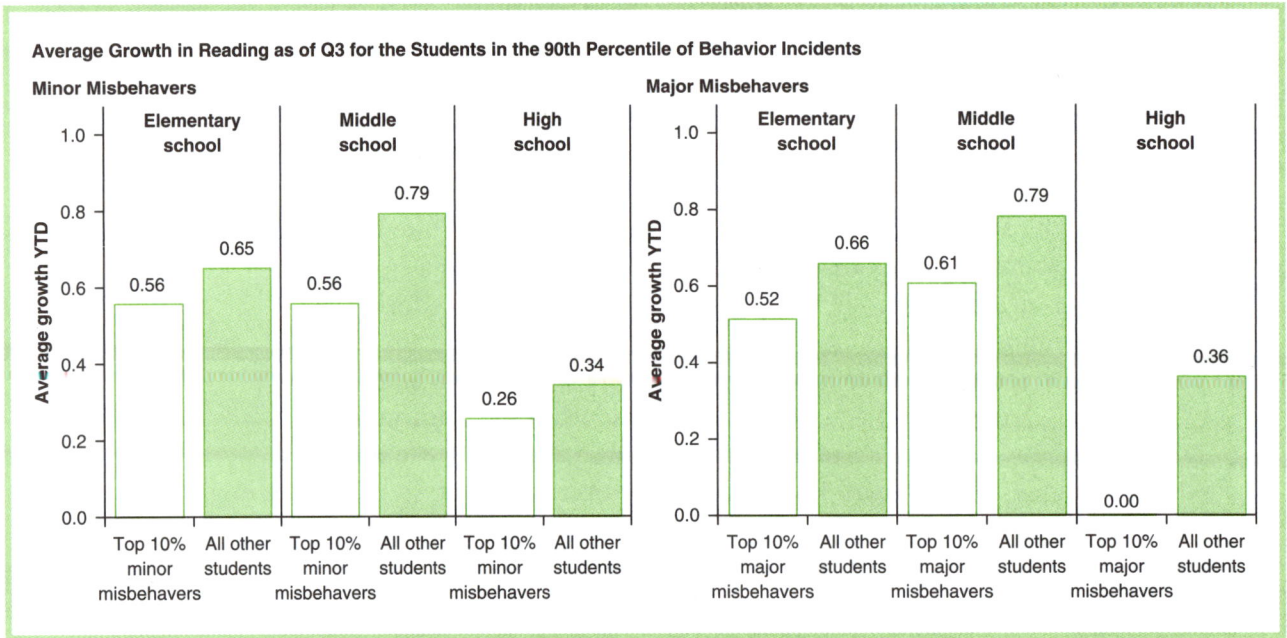

by student behavior status—comparing the top 10% of misbehavers in each school with their peers.

Again, the pattern is clear: the white bars are always lower than the dark green ones. Misbehavior seems to correlate to lower academic growth, on every campus, for both major and minor misbehavior.

These are examples of performance patterns because they're true across multiple cuts of the data. A good hypothesis will reverse engineer this process and try to guess what the patterns are *before* doing the analysis. So, for our Ohio example, you might hypothesize that achievement gaps are staying constant even as proficiency goes up. You would then ask yourself, "What kind of benchmarking should I do to test that hypothesis? And what data would I need in order to do it?" The result might be the four charts above, or something like them. And that's the point: a good hypothesis should lend itself to specific and focused analyses for you to do, saving you the time of digging through all the data systematically.

How should you come up with your first hypothesis? This is where Nate Silver's wisdom is important: make the best guess you can, and don't shy away from bringing your initial beliefs to the table. You should rely on the shared hunches, expertise, insights, and experience of your team members, content colleagues, and colleagues in data or institutional research offices. Between you and others you work with, you have a lot of collective wisdom that should serve as a good starting point.

More important, you should prepare for the possibility that your hypothesis is wrong. In fact, that's what separates a hypothesis from a mere bias or belief: a hypothesis flushes that belief into the open, makes it testable, and then uses the evidence to prove or disprove it. You needn't worry about whether your first hypothesis is right; if you're committed to analyzing the data and revising your beliefs accordingly when you get the results back, you'll eventually find your way to an accurate understanding of the facts.

Analyze Data to Test Hypotheses

With one or more hypotheses in hand, you have what you need to prioritize the data to collect and the analyses to perform. One concrete way to go from hypothesis to analysis is to construct a simple work plan:

- The starting point is the issue and hypothesis, which you already know.
- From there, you define a specific analysis for each hypothesis that you've identified and translate that into a specific "end product" that you'll need to produce. (As management consultants like to say, it helps draw the data analysis charts that you want before you've even gathered the data for them.)
- For clarity's sake, it then helps to put a stake in the ground: what would the data have to say for you to confirm the hypothesis?
- Finally, list your sources: where you will get the data, who will do the analysis, and by when.

The template in Figure 2A.7 on the following page gives an example of a work plan from an analysis we did with California University of Pennsylvania.

The university had recently started a program, called Support for Success (S4S), to help improve retention rates among academically at-risk students. University leaders wanted to know whether it was effective, so they worked with us to form and test a hypothesis: that students who attended the program were more likely to be retained.

At first, there didn't seem to be a noteworthy correlation between S4S course attendance and retention once other factors were taken into account. But, as it turned out, there was a correlation among students with mid-range high school GPAs (see Figure 2A.6).

Figure 2A.6 Retention rates were 10 percentage points higher amongst students with above average attendance at S4S.

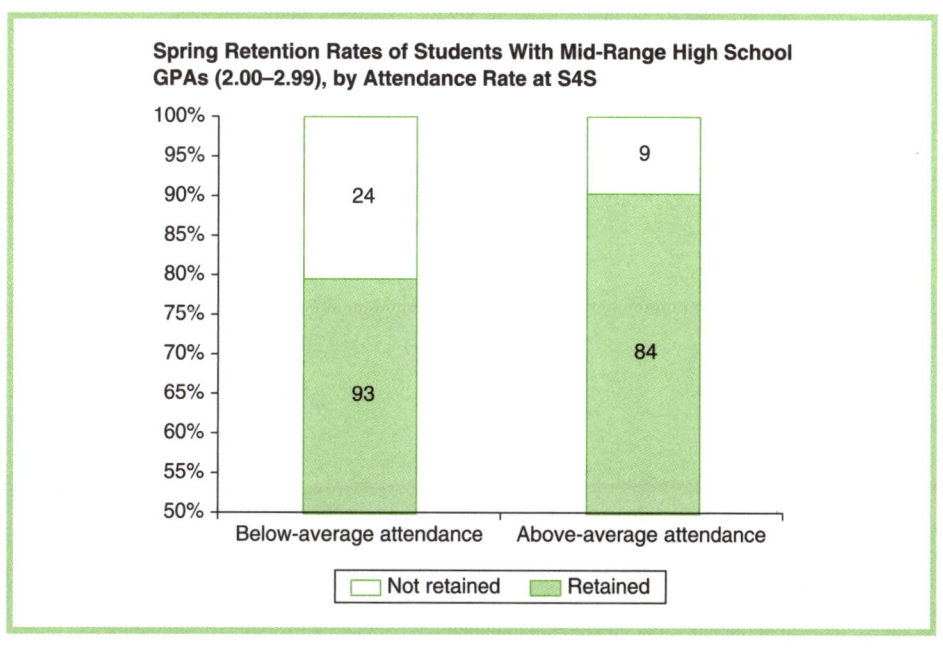

Spring Retention Rates of Students With Mid-Range High School GPAs (2.00–2.99), by Attendance Rate at S4S

Figure 2A.7 Work Plan Template With Example: Retention Rates for California University of Pennsylvania

	Issue	Hypothesis	Analysis	End Product	Hypothesis Is True If . . .	Sources
Definition	What is the key unresolved question?	What do you think the answer might be?	What work must you do to prove or disprove the hypothesis and resolve the issue?	What will the output of the analysis be?	Where will your data and evidence come from?	Who will do the analysis, and by when?
Example	Was the Support for Success (S4S) program effective in improving student retention rates?	Students who attend the S4S program more frequently are more likely to be retained.	Analyze retention rates of students and compare to their attendance rates at S4S.	A stacked barchart showing the number of students retained and not retained with percentage highlighted, for both the above-average and below-average attenders of S4S.	Retention rate is higher for the students who had above-average attendance at S4S.	Institutional Research Department

Using these data, university leadership could be confident in a decision to increase S4S program funding. The hypothesis had to be modified slightly along the way, but it turned out to be true.

If you complete a rigorous work plan, going and doing the analyses should be relatively easy. The challenge here is to actually complete the work plan—in particular, to use your hypotheses to conceptualize what the analyses should be. This can feel daunting to many of us, because knowing what data analysis to do is often a matter of pattern recognition: we have a hypothesis to test, we've seen or done an analysis before that fits the situation, and we remember and recall it. Those of us who are new to this have no such library to draw on.

Two things are worth remembering. First, you can get a lot of mileage out of simple charts and graphs. Some people make the mistake of believing that more and different and more complicated visualizations are always better; these people often sacrifice clarity, coherence, or overall story line in their attempt to follow this rule. The real test of whether you should conduct an analysis is different: does it help you prove or disprove the hypothesis? If it does, but you find yourself returning to the same boring bar chart time after time, this is fine—in fact, it is better in some ways, since your audience will get used to seeing data presented in this way and will be able to read and interpret it more quickly.

Second, for this reason, it's helpful to keep a playlist of your "greatest hits" in data visualization handy as a way of triggering ideas for analyses. Sometimes we need our memories jogged for pattern recognition to kick in.

Solutions in Search of a Problem: EDI's "Greatest Hits" Playlist

Over the years, EDI has supported state, district, campus, and school leaders in analyzing and interpreting their data. What follows is a sampling of some of our own "greatest hits"—analyses that we still return to now to inspire our future work.

Benchmarking Against Yourself, by Student Characteristic

In our work with one school district, we used a stacked bar chart to analyze the distribution of behavioral incidences caused by various students (see Figure 2A.8). The dark gray, light green, and dark green bars represent students at and above the 90th percentile in terms of number of misbehavior incidents. The right side shows the percentage of students that fall into these categories, while the left side shows the percentage of behavioral incidents they cause.

The message is clear: a small share of the students is causing a majority of the incidents in the elementary and middle schools. Stacked bar charts are useful for mapping this kind of disproportionality.

(Continued)

(Continued)

Figure 2A.8   Stacked Bar Chart Comparison: Behavioral Incidents and Top Misbehavers

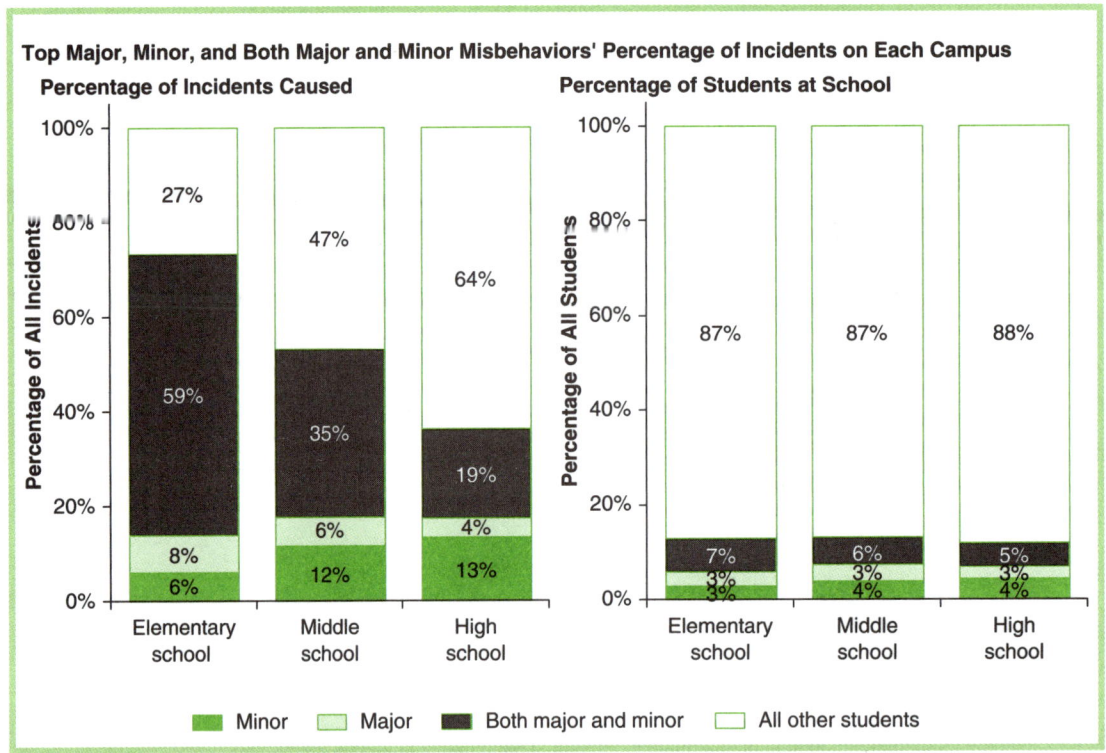

Top Major, Minor, and Both Major and Minor Misbehaviors' Percentage of Incidents on Each Campus

Benchmarking Against Peers, by Geography

Scatterplots are a great way to discover whether two variables of interest are correlated. In Figure 2A.9, each dot represents a state that participates in the National Assessment of Educational Progress (NAEP). The question we wanted to answer here was: does a concentration of low-income students in a state lead to better or worse outcomes for low-income students? The states are plotted on two variables: the percentage of their students that are economically disadvantaged (X-axis) and the average scale score of their low-income students (Y-axis).

There does seem to be a correlation: the more low-income students a state has, the worse its low-income students perform. The trend is represented by the diagonal line going through the middle of the chart. But at the same time, the chart is an opportunity to find exceptions to the rule—bright spots that light the way for others. Anyone above the trend line, for example, is performing better with their low-income students than the correlation would suggest they should; some states, like Massachusetts and Texas, are performing significantly better.

Benchmarking Against Yourself, by Geography

Maps are another visualization tool. At their most basic, you can use two colors to differentiate between high and low performers, as with this analysis of performance in Georgia (see Figure 2A.10). The gray districts represent trouble spots that might merit additional focus.

Figure 2A.9   Scatterplot Example: NAEP Results for Low-Income Students

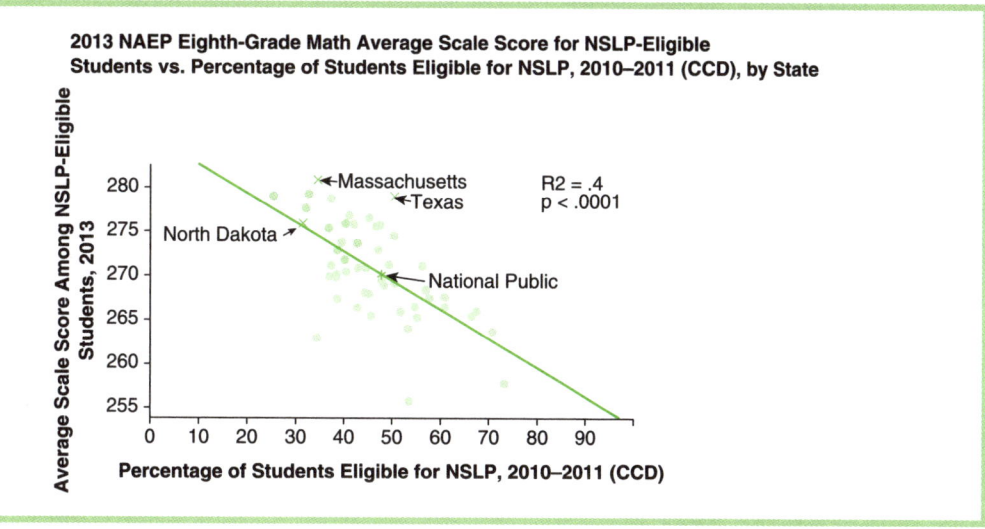

2013 NAEP Eighth-Grade Math Average Scale Score for NSLP-Eligible Students vs. Percentage of Students Eligible for NSLP, 2010–2011 (CCD), by State

Figure 2A.10   Map Example: Science Proficiency in Georgia

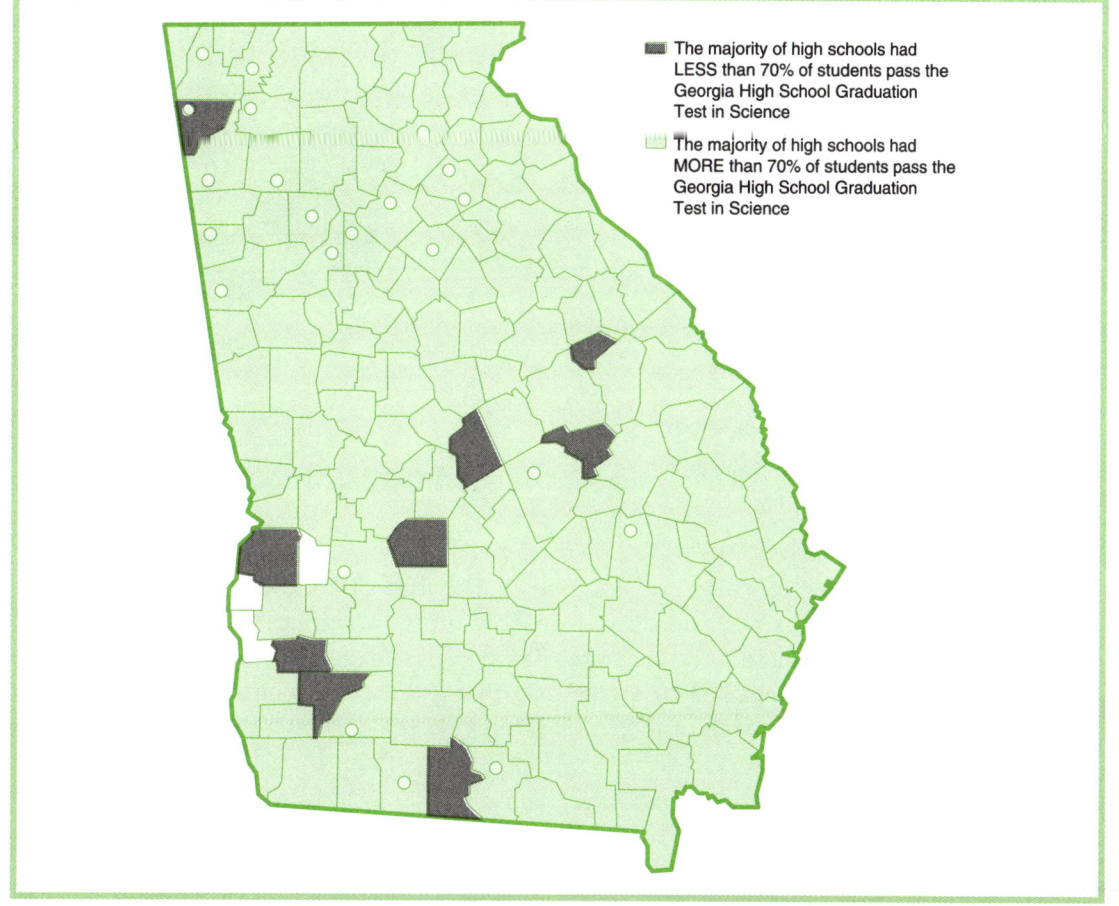

Source: Georgia State Superintendent of Schools, Kathy Cox

(Continued)

(Continued)

Map analyses can be more complex as well. The analysis of Hawai'i's system (see Figure 2A.11) covers two variables related to college and career readiness: the graduation rate in each district, and the percentage of graduates who enroll in college. The resulting 2 x 2 matrix captures four "types" of districts: those with high graduation and enrollment rates are doing well, while those with low levels of both are doing poorly. It is the intermediate cases that are interesting: the light gray districts have high graduation rates but low college enrollment rates, implying that there may be an opportunity there. The light green ones have low graduation rates but high college enrollment rates, leading to a worry that they may be providing "all for some" rather than "some for all."

Figure 2A.11   Map Example: College and Career Readiness in Hawai'i

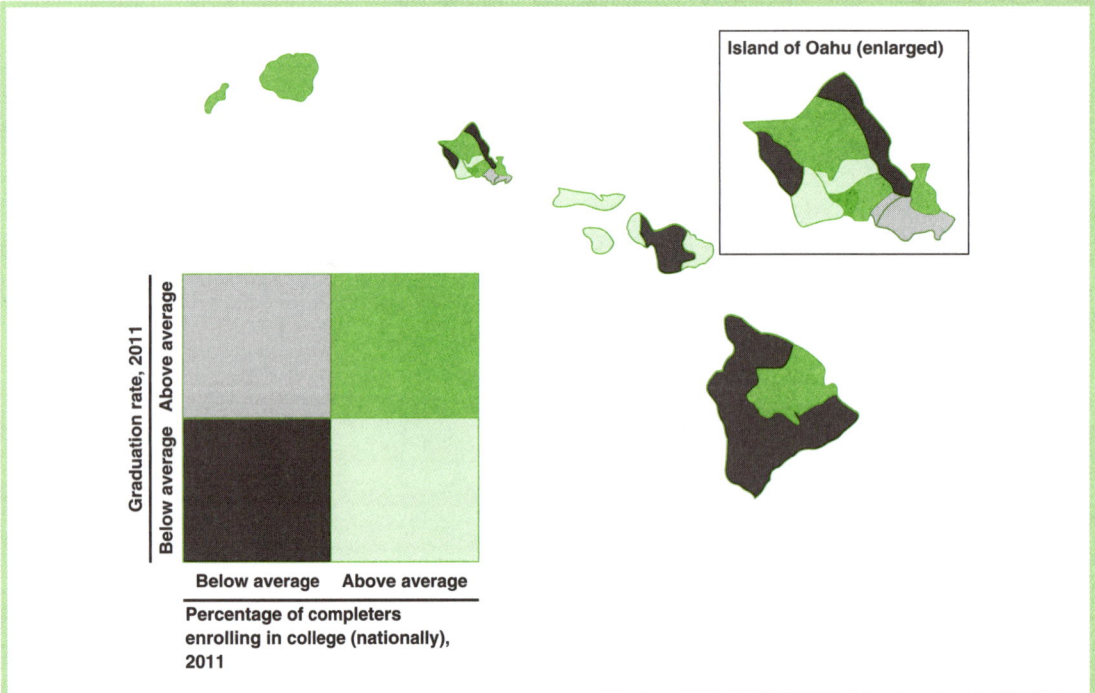

Maps can also be used to gauge process metrics. The map of Kentucky districts in Figure 2A.12 districts color codes each one based on how many milestones they have met on a check list for the implementation of the state's Teacher and Leader Effectiveness system. The "regular" map is also accompanied by a tree map that gives a sense of the relative student population of the districts in each of the color categories.

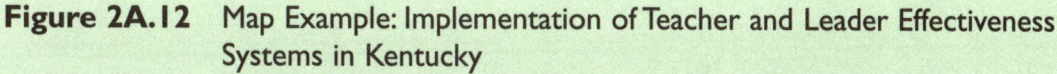

Figure 2A.12   Map Example: Implementation of Teacher and Leader Effectiveness Systems in Kentucky

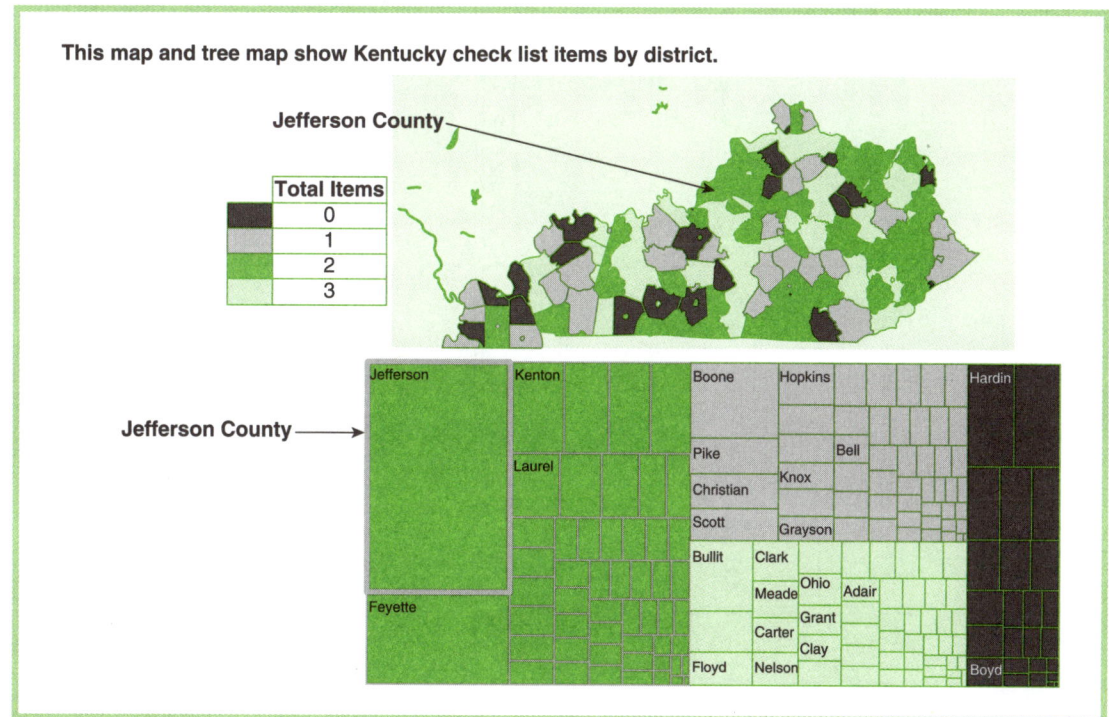

This map and tree map show Kentucky check list items by district.

Benchmarking Against History and Against Yourself, by Student Characteristic and Subject

Finally, in our partnership with the state of Massachusetts, we analyzed the achievement gaps in their NAEP scores using a series of trend charts (see Figure 2A.13).

This is an example of what Edward Tufte calls *small multiples*: multiple analyses, stacked side by side and on top of one another, with one or more variables changing for each analysis. Recall Tufte's assertion that the heart of quantitative reasoning is a single question: "Compared to what?" Small multiples "answer directly by visually enforcing comparisons of changes, of the differences among objects, of the scope of alternatives. For a wide range of problems in data presentation, small multiples are the best design solution."[6]

(Continued)

Figure 2A.13 Small Multiples: NAEP Scores in Massachusetts

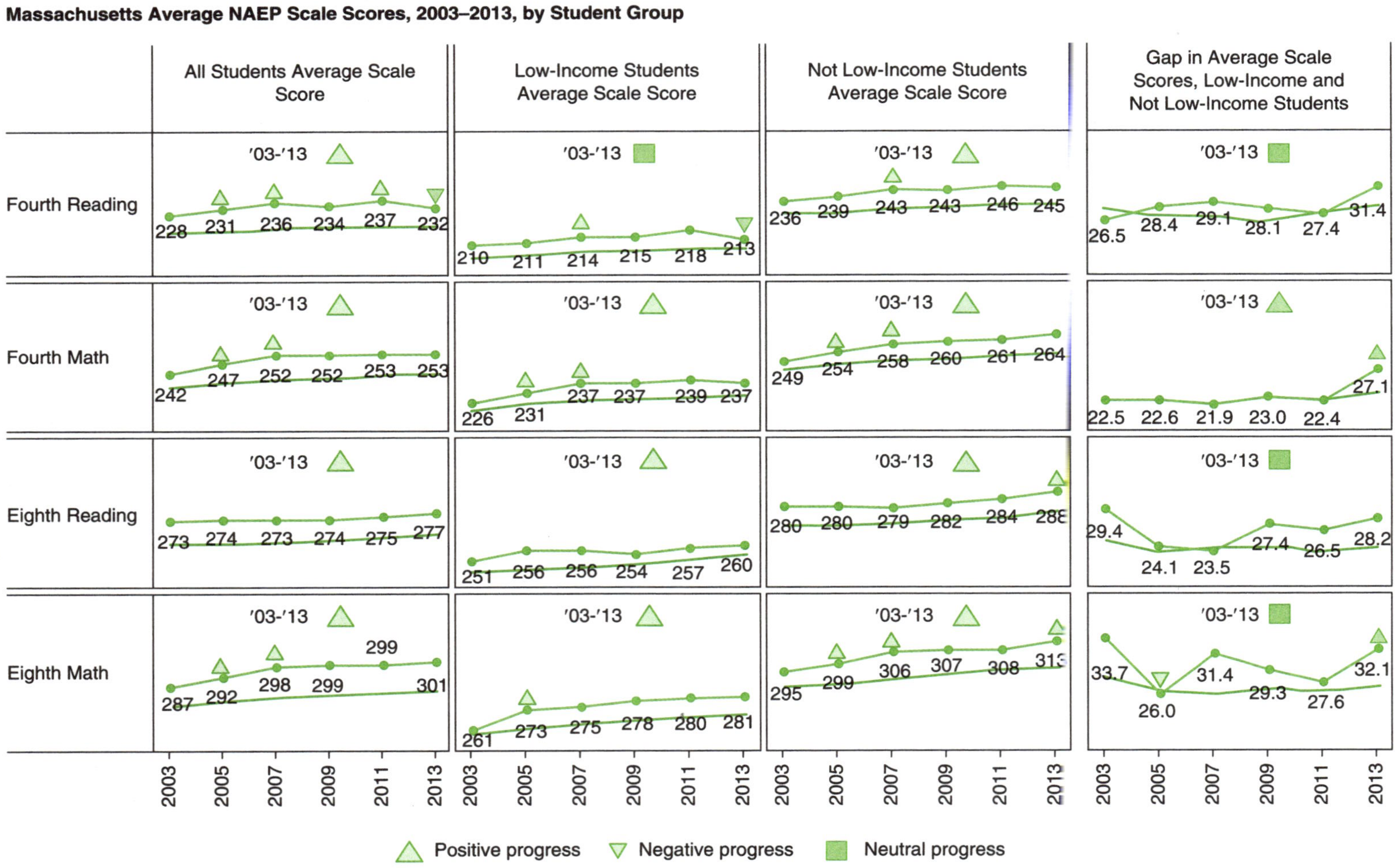

Massachusetts Average NAEP Scale Scores, 2003–2013, by Student Group

△ Positive progress ▽ Negative progress ■ Neutral progress

Each analysis will lend you some additional insight about performance patterns. At the same time, each will almost invariably lead you to imagine another that you could do. This is a normal part of the cycle of inquiry between hypotheses and data, and you can mediate it by asking the following questions of each analysis (see Figure 2A.14).

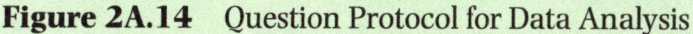

Figure 2A.14   Question Protocol for Data Analysis

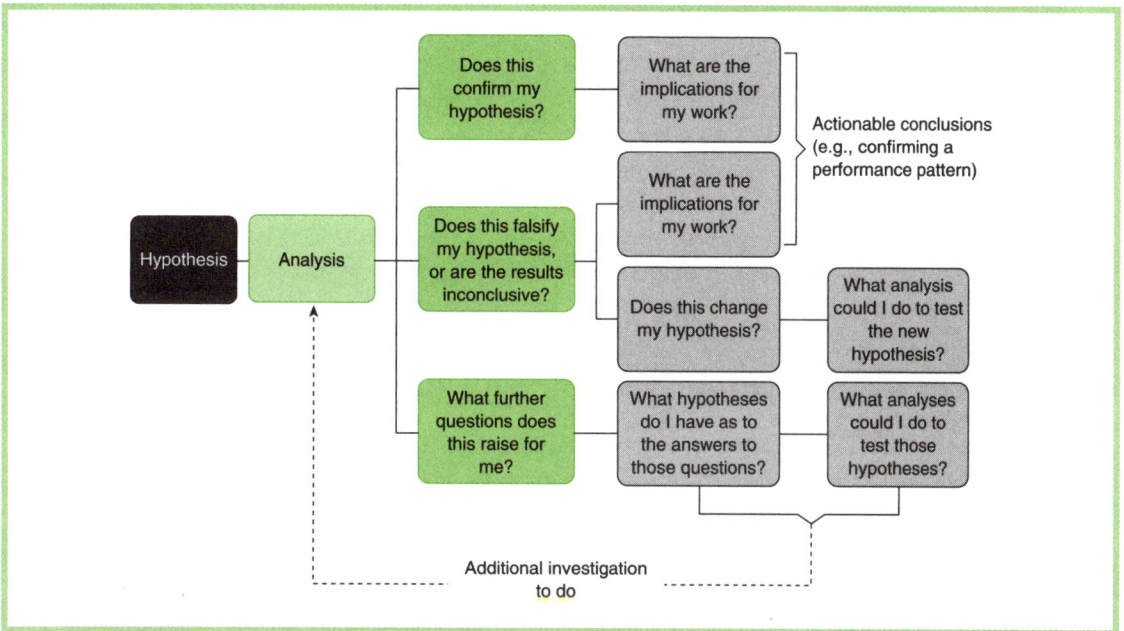

These questions lead every analysis to consider one or both of two things:

1. Actionable conclusions—what we learned from the analysis that will inform our work.

2. Further investigations to conduct, either because we could not prove our hypothesis (and we need to test a modified one) or because the analysis raised some additional questions for us.

And so the cycle continues, until you reach a set of actionable conclusions that you're satisfied with. When this occurs is a matter of judgment; you should go deep enough to build a relatively robust set of conclusions, but you also need to know when to stop. Keep asking the question: does the potential additional value from this next analysis exceed the cost to me of doing it?

Notice something here: while we've laid out these steps to encourage you to start with a hypothesis and then go to analysis, that doesn't necessarily have to be the order you pursue. You can start with an analysis—any analysis—and by applying the question protocol above, you can draw conclusions and form hypotheses about the next set of analyses to perform. The cycle of inquiry is a cycle, after all, which means that your entry point can be anywhere.

One last note: some data analyses will inevitably be more complex than others, or they will involve more raw data. The more this is the case, the less clear the

Exploring the Data Together

In the early stages of our partnership, the Hawai'i Department of Education (HIDOE) worked with us to design exercises and tools for their Complex Area Superintendents (CASs—the leaders of local districts) to explore their data and look for performance patterns.

One popular tool was created using Google Motion Charts, which allow the user to select up to four variables to compare (the X-axis, the Y-axis, and the color and size of the bubbles) and observe how they change over time.

We gave the CASs these charts, with the ability to manipulate them to include a number of variables collected over the last several years: results from the Hawai'i State Assessment (HSA) in reading and math, school size, and student demographic information. Figure 2A.15 gives an example of what these charts looked like.

The exercise for CASs was drawn straight from the question protocol given above: as you explore the data, identify performance patterns and implications for your work, and identify additional questions you have and ways to answer them through further analysis.

Both the exercise and the tool helped reinforce a shift, already under way in the department, toward a more transparent display and discussion of data about performance across the state. The data were not new or exotic; what made this experience different was the way we framed the information and encouraged systematic inquiry around it.

Notice that we didn't ask these CASs to start with a hypothesis. Instead, they started with a large amount of data that invited exploration. From there, we asked them to draw conclusions and develop sharper hypotheses to inform the next round of analyses. The cycle of inquiry can begin anywhere.

Figure 2A.15 Bubble Charts for Hawai'i Districts: Tenth-Grade Reading by School

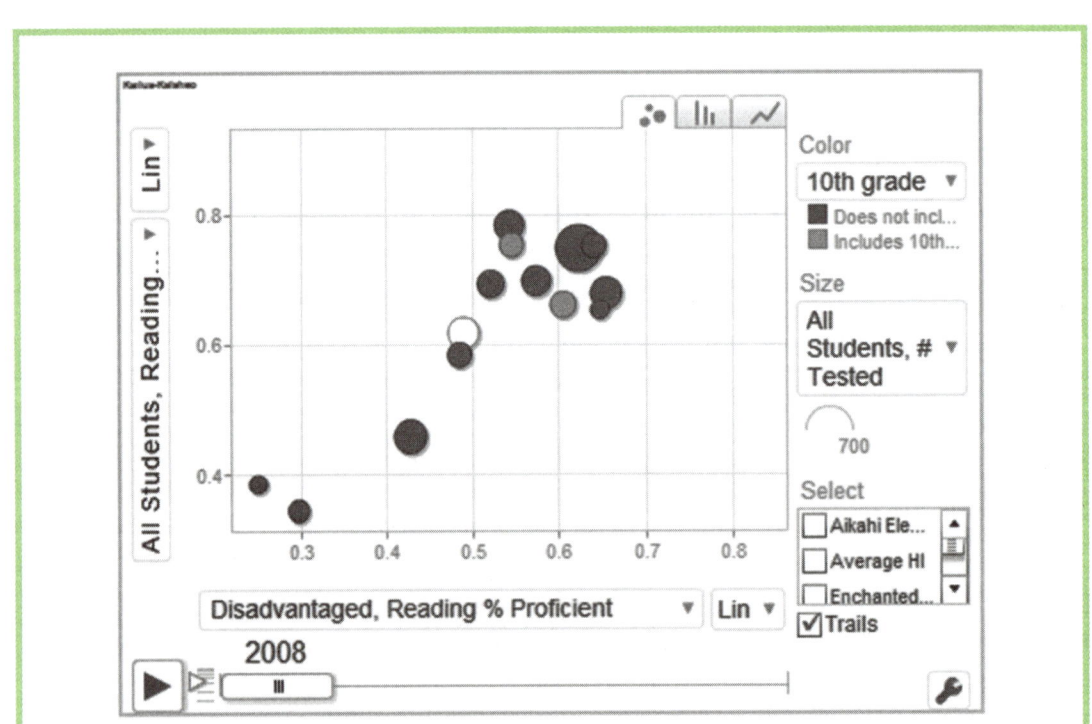

message from the data will be. Analyses like these are useful in the early stages, when you're exploring the data for patterns or helping others do so. Over time, as you solidify your conclusions, the cycle of inquiry should move you from analyses that invite exploration to those that tell a clear story—the last step in the process.

Identify Patterns of Performance

At this point, you've mined the data and captured the most important performance patterns. This last step is to move from hypothesis to conclusion: what story does the data tell? And how will you communicate it to others?

We've all seen this done badly. (In fact, if we're telling the truth, most of us have done this badly ourselves at some point.) We've neglected the presentation because we spent too much time on the analysis. Or we've understood the takeaway so clearly that we didn't take the time to start at the beginning and walk people through the logic that got us there. Or, wanting to be seen as data-driven, we've shared analyses that weren't truly related to the work we were doing. Or we've made our charts so unwieldy (or even ugly!) that the audience wasn't willing to take the time to engage with them.

The insights you gain are only useful if they're accessible to others. However, others won't have the time to dig through and understand that data (as you've just done). In presenting the results of your analysis, you must give them a shortcut that brings them to where you are. That shortcut is the story you tell.

As you go through the cycle of inquiry, the building blocks of this story will emerge. Insights will surface and will harden into conclusions as you confirm them with further analysis. You'll want to arrange these insights into a coherent story line, each point of which is backed up by a specific analysis.

To take an example: in 2006, Michael and Nick were part of producing a report by Achieve and McKinsey & Company[7] on building a world-class education system for the state of Ohio. Part of that report was a diagnostic of current system performance—a summary of the key performance patterns. The report captured the main story line with three charts (see Figures 2A.16, 2A.17, and 2A.18).

In each case, the chart supports the overall headline, which is one bullet point of the story line. And each headline builds on the one before it. Most important, however, the charts are *selective* about what data they display; they do not give the audience every possible cut and angle.

Some would argue that this gets dangerously close to "cherry-picking" the data: selecting only those data elements that tell the story that you want to tell, while ignoring other evidence. This is certainly a risk, but what we're advocating here is something that we call *authentic cherry-picking*: picking out data analyses that are illustrative of broader patterns that you've already uncovered. The four slides were backed up by literally hundreds of analyses our team had done; we saved the audience this work by synthesizing and selecting the right data to illustrate what we had learned as efficiently as possible.

Over the years, we've found that poor data presentations happen most often because people aren't comfortable doing this kind of selective storytelling. Fearful of accusations of cherry-picking and bias, they try to bring the audience in to discover the patterns themselves and inundate them with

Figure 2A.16   In the last several years, most aggregate indicators in Ohio have been moving in a positive direction.

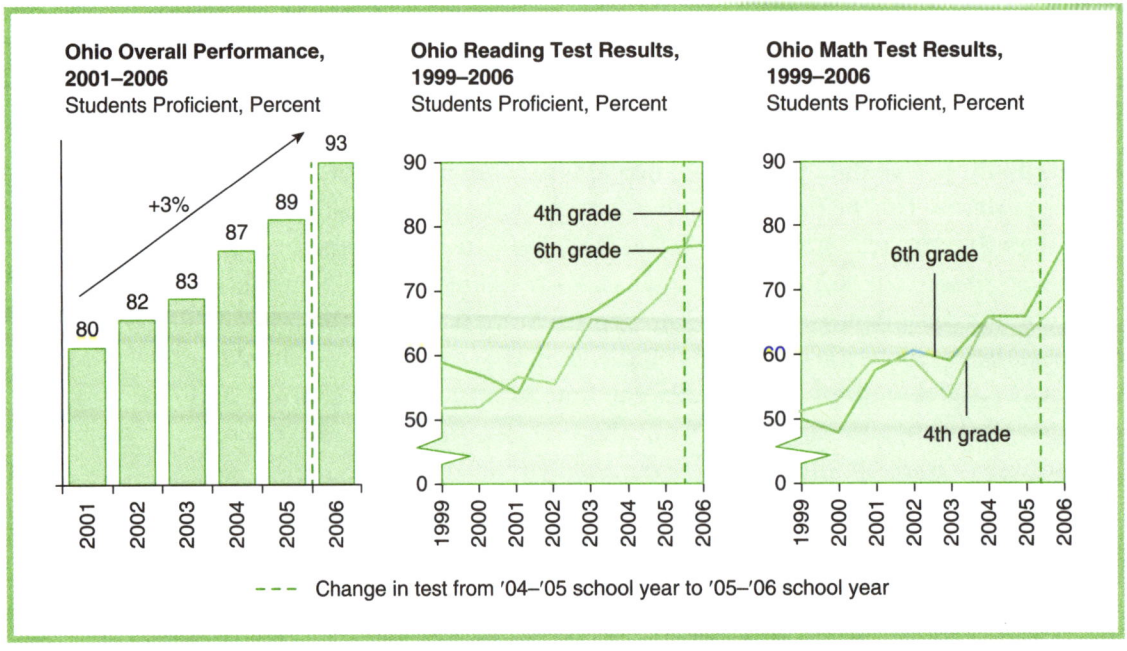

Source: Ohio Department of Education—Interactive Local Report Card

Figure 2A.17   In fact, major subgroups have outpaced the statewide average in achievement gains.

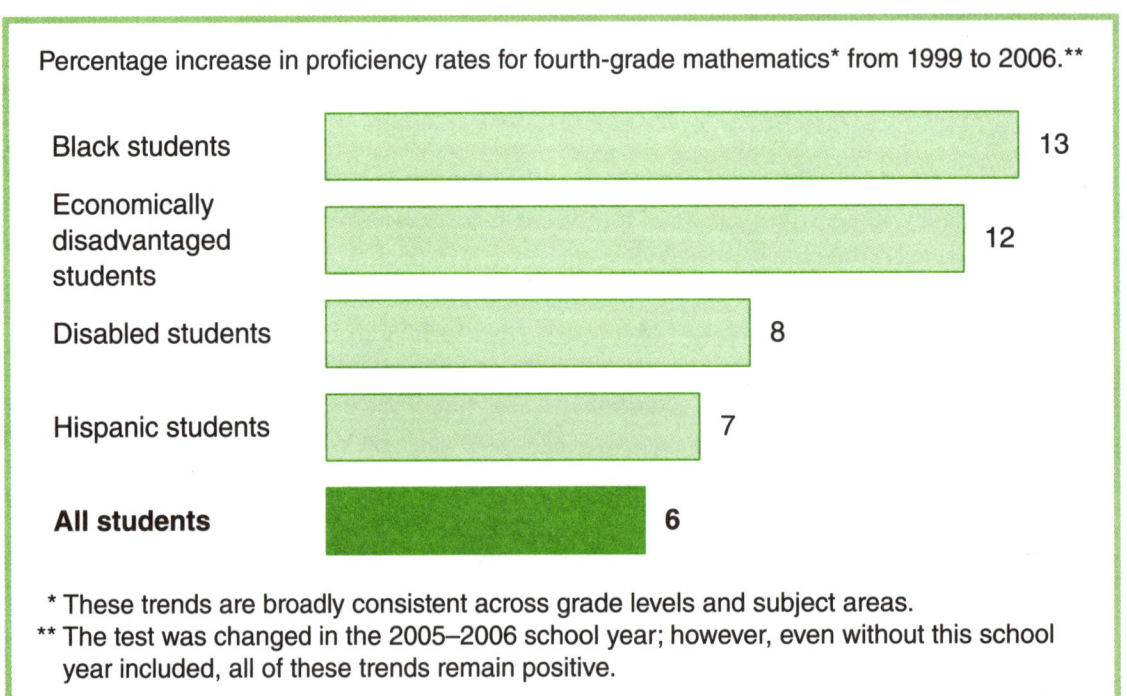

Source: Ohio Department of Education—Interactive Local Report Card

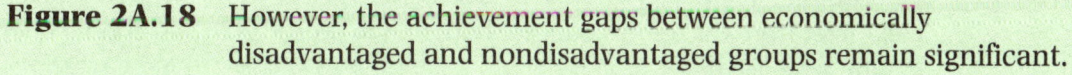

Figure 2A.18   However, the achievement gaps between economically disadvantaged and nondisadvantaged groups remain significant.

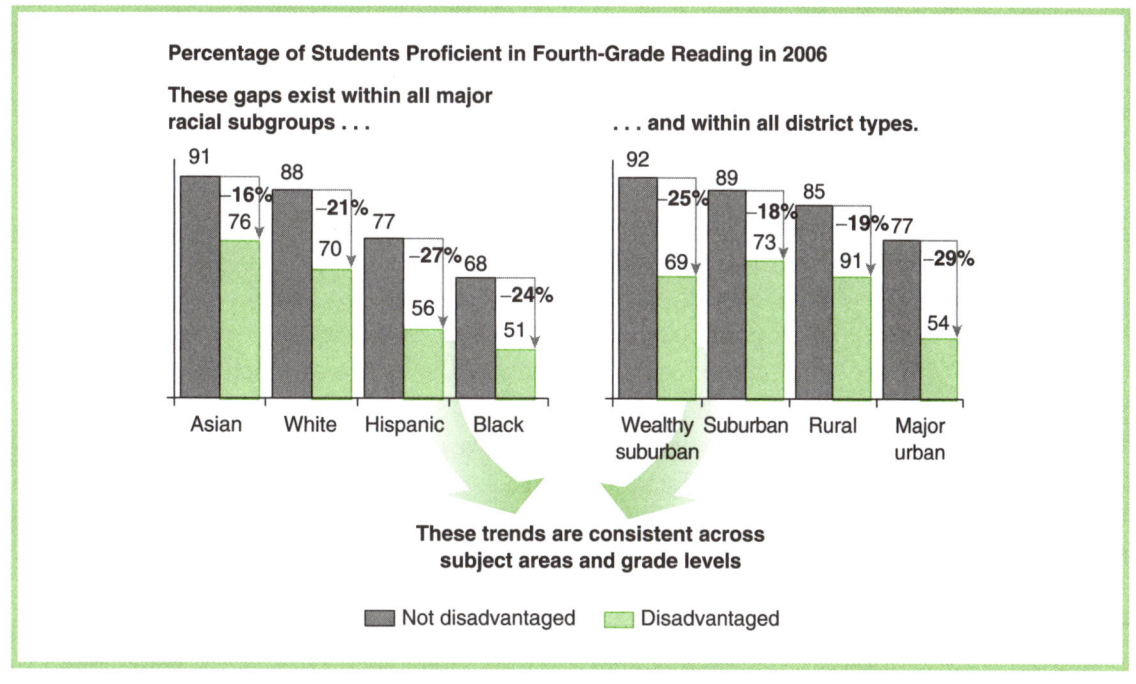

Source: Achieve, Inc.

rawer forms of the data. As we said before, analyses that invite exploration are helpful in the early stages. But at the end of the process, when it's time to draw conclusions, inviting more exploration will lead to endless discussion, frustration, and a lack of action.

Remember Nate Silver's words: The numbers can't speak for themselves. Your audience is looking for a set of actionable conclusions, which you can only give by making some calls about what the data say and shaping your story accordingly. For more on the process of storyboarding, please see Chapter 5B and the section on the Minto Pyramid Principle.

Inevitably, though, even your best data presentations will lead to further questions, which may start the cycle of inquiry over again. Do this as many times as it makes sense for you, until all the key decision makers have a shared and robust understanding of your system's performance.

⦿ LESSONS FROM THE FIELD

Don't Let the Perfect Be the Enemy of the Good

As we noted at the beginning of this chapter, a common mistake we make is to believe that data can do more for us than it actually can—that a more perfect data set can substitute for the judgment and thinking we have to do to understand what it means. In fact, the opposite is true: good thinking can compensate for a lack or poor quality of data, by helping us be clear about what we can and can't infer from the information we have and to prioritize the additional information we'd like to get.

This is especially important to remember in our field. Despite the abundance of data in education, we have a habit of constantly lamenting that we don't have more. As a result, we've been to far too many "data meetings" in which the entire conversation was thwarted by a discussion of what we "should" be looking at instead of what we had right in front of us. Hold yourself to too high a standard for what constitutes good data, and you'll become a helpless hostage to that standard. As Michael Fullan reminds us, "Statistics are a wonderful servant but an appalling master."[8]

How, then, should we think about the quality of our data? We should start by remembering that the bar for "validity" should be far lower when we're putting the information to use internally. If the data is available, we should try to make use of it, warts and all. We need to use the cycle of inquiry to make the most out of the data we do have *before* we consider making a (usually unrealistic) wish list of other data to collect. Again, we often get this backward: we wish for more data and believe that meaningful analysis will be impossible until we get it. This gives new meaning to the oft-used phrase "analysis paralysis": not an overabundance of analysis, but an unwillingness to begin for fear that the results might not be sufficiently rigorous.

Changing this will require a culture shift in most systems. Not only will you have to get over your own fear of using the data in this way, but you'll also have to help others do the same. Lead your teams through the cycle of inquiry confidently, reminding them that it improves both the data and the analysis with every turn.

Be Flexible in the Face of New Information

At the same time, you don't want to commit the opposite error: becoming so enamored with your hypothesis that you care little whether the data to test it exists or whether the analysis proves it true or false. We're all subject to what psychologists call the confirmation bias: the tendency to look only for data or information that supports our preexisting beliefs. If we're not careful, this bias will poison our hypotheses, our means of testing them, or both.

To guard against bias, we can do two things. First, we can construct our hypotheses so that they are clearly falsifiable. And second, we can be ready to change our beliefs in the face of information that disproves our hypotheses. If we are to reap the benefits in efficiency of being hypothesis-driven, we must also confront the inherent risks.

Build Capacity

One corollary of our misplaced standard of data quality is a near-universally disqualifying standard for analytical talent. This plays out in both higher education systems, where much of the analysis lives in the institutional research division, and in K–12 systems, where "data analyst" is often a separate job title and/or division. Good data analysts, the story goes, are proficient in statistical methods and software packages and often have graduate level experience in the social sciences. Training, such as it is, is accordingly geared to this very rarefied segment of the population.

The impact of this is to make data literacy a seemingly inaccessible skill, with no middle ground between zero and full rigor. We've striven to change this, working with K–12 and higher education systems to deliver workshops and trainings based on the material in this chapter. Our message is simple: data literacy and data analysis are essential skills *for everybody*, and the "middle ground" is where the vast majority of useful and actionable data analysis occurs.

Delivery Units will have to remember this in particular. You don't want to get stuck making one person in your Unit do all the analysis and become "the data person." Likewise, you don't want your Unit to play that role vis-à-vis the rest of your system. As you master the tools in this chapter, it's imperative that you teach them to others.

◉ KEY CONSIDERATIONS FOR SYSTEM LEADERS AND STAFF

If you're a **system leader**, you feel the paradox of data more acutely than anyone else: you have access to a wealth of information, but you don't have time to do all the analysis. When your staff and team want to discuss data with you, insist on two things:

1. They must be clear about the purpose of each data meeting: are they trying to convey a specific story or to explore the data with you? As the system leader, you should push your team to bring you more stories. Otherwise, you'll be frustrated that you don't have time to do the analysis that they really should be doing.

2. They must understand that it's everyone's job to analyze and interpret data. You can role model this by engaging with the data yourself, but you should also expect every colleague to bring a data-literate perspective to the conversation.

If you're a **delivery leader**, your job is to role model the use of the tools in this chapter and to build the capacity of others to do the same. At the same time, be careful not to become the person with a reputation for asking for too much unnecessary data. Always be prepared to back up your requests with a clear rationale grounded in a relevant hypothesis that you want to test.

Finally, if you're a part of the **system staff**, consider how you can bring this level of analytical rigor to your sphere of influence. What would it take to apply these tools in your day-to-day work? How can you help build a culture of data literacy and use among your colleagues? Demonstrating these skills will be immensely helpful to your team and to system leadership, and they will cause you to stand out amongst your peers.

⊙ CONCLUSION

The paradox of data can be resolved, but it requires a reframing and a reimagining of how we interact with information. Rather than being passive observers, we must actively engage our data to understand what it tells us. Throughout the process, we must be consistently transparent about our beliefs, how we test them, and how the evidence helps us update them. If we apply this discipline consistently, beliefs will eventually harden into facts that are strong enough to act on.

The result of all this will be the needs analysis we spoke of at the beginning of this chapter: a well-supported set of conclusions that gives you a clear and comprehensive picture of how well your system is performing against its aspiration. With that in place, you are ready to take the process a step further and dig into the root causes of performance.

⊙ NOTES

1. Silver, N. (2012). *The signal and the noise: Why most predictions fail—but some don't.* New York, NY: Penguin.

2. Ibid.

3. Offenstein, J., Moore, C., & Shulock, N. (2010). *Advancing by degrees: A framework for increasing college completion.* Washington, DC: Institute for Higher Education Leadership & Policy and The Education Trust. Retrieved from http://www.edtrust.org/dc/publication/advancing-by-degrees

4. Heath, C., & Heath, D. (2010). *Switch: How to change things when change is hard.* New York, NY: Broadway.

5. Tufte, E. (1995). *Envisioning information* (5th ed.). Cheshire, CT: Graphics Press.

6. Ibid.

7. Achieve, Inc. (n.d.). *Creating a world-class education system in Ohio.* Retrieved from http://www.achieve.org/files/World_Class_Edu_Ohio_FINAL.pdf

8. Fullan, M. (2002). The change. *Educational Leadership, 59*(8), 16–21.

Chapter 2B

Understand Root Causes of Performance

 **1** Develop a foundation for delivery

 **2** Understand the delivery challenge

 **3** Plan for delivery

 **4** Drive delivery

 5 Create an irreversible delivery culture

System Leader Summary

The hard data won't always tell you what you need to know to take action. The patterns of performance you uncover through data analysis will always beg the same question: Why? So once you've identified the most important performance patterns, you'll want to search for their root causes. The process is very similar to the last chapter: using "Why" as your guide, form hypotheses and investigate them. The difference here is that you're working with "softer" data: qualitative evidence, artifacts from the front line, and field work you conduct to fill gaps in your information. The answers you find will help you determine what strategies are best suited to help you overcome your barriers to performance.

The same lessons from the last chapter apply here: as system leader, you're the key consumer of this information, and you should always push your delivery leader and your team to understand the root causes of performance. In particular, this means encouraging them to be comfortable with seeking and using information from unconventional sources rather than letting "perfect" analysis be the enemy of actionable information.

◉ THE SOFT UNDERBELLY OF HARD DATA

You now know something about the state of performance in your system. You understand your areas of strength, and you know where your most persistent challenges are. What you don't know yet is why these performance patterns persist. Why are graduation rates so low? Why is enrollment declining amongst Pell students? Why are achievement gaps widening in reading? Your goal metrics can establish these patterns, and your progress metrics can show you the proximate causes (e.g., low retention drives low graduation rates). What they can't do is tell you about the root causes.

This reveals a limitation in your performance patterns: they're based primarily on hard (quantitative) information. And, as management expert Henry Mintzberg puts it, hard information has a "soft underbelly".[1]

- Hard information can tell you a lot about a few things, but nothing about other things that matter: the reactions of faculty to the implementation of a particular strategy, for example, or the quality of a particular training you gave.
- Hard information is often too aggregated for effective use in decision making. Privacy rules prevent all but a few local leaders from examining data at the student level; the resulting aggregation forces us to throw out a lot of information.
- Much hard information arrives too late to be of use. We are painfully aware of this fact in our field, where some of the most important data only become available once or twice a year.
- Most important, a surprising amount of hard information is unreliable. The numbers and statistical tables give the veneer of accuracy, but the collection and cleaning process is subject to the same biases and mistakes as that of any other information.

All this is reason to pay more attention to "softer" information—observations, qualitative evidence, and the like—to understand what's really going on. Soft information is also subject to plenty of bias, of course. But it provides guidance that aids action. To paraphrase Mintzberg: what educator, faced with a choice between today's rumor that a student was thinking of dropping out and tomorrow's fact that he had done so, would hesitate to act on the first piece of information?

The performance patterns we've identified with hard data help us pinpoint the problem, but without an understanding of the root causes, we'll have little insight into the solution. This is the critical step we must take to bridge the gap between data analysis and action.

We take this step by extending the hypothesis-driven approach we explored in the last chapter to the next level of information underneath our performance patterns. The principles behind this approach will be the same, but several of the tools will be different.

Above all, the most important tool is the question "Why?" It will drive most of the hypotheses you test at this stage of the process, and it will help you uncover the actionable information that you'll need for delivery planning.

⊙ CORE PRINCIPLES

There are three steps to doing effective root cause analysis. As you will see, they're similar to the steps from the last chapter:

1. Form hypotheses about root causes

2. Investigate root causes by testing hypotheses

3. Tell the story

The same cycle of inquiry governs these steps. As with your work on discovering performance patterns, you can take the steps out of order, but we encourage you to begin with a hypothesis.

Form Hypotheses About Root Causes

Remember the definition: a hypothesis is a tentative statement about the relationship between two variables that answers a question we care deeply about. At this stage, that question is about the root causes of the performance patterns we discovered in the last chapter. Why are we seeing these particular trends? And what does that suggest about how we can improve them?

These hypotheses will be different from the ones in the last chapter; they will go beyond comparisons of hard data and into the territory of causality, which is more difficult to pin down. You also don't have the same universal question that you had last time (How well are we achieving our aspiration?). Instead, you have a particular performance pattern—or a collection of them—and the task of understanding it better. Let's take a specific example: suppose you're a K–12 system leader who's discovered that, while achievement gaps in reading proficiency for most groups have been narrowing over the last 5 years, one achievement gap has persisted at the same level: the one between students with disabilities (SWDs) and their peers. Why does this gap remain? And what can we do about it?

It helps to develop a structure that will help you think through all the possible root causes efficiently. In Chapter 4B, we explore the idea (borrowed from our training with the problem solvers at McKinsey and Company) of a **hypothesis tree**—a tool for structuring hypotheses about a wide variety of problems that could arise during implementation. Using this approach, we can construct a typical checklist of hypotheses to explore as you dig into a particular performance pattern (see Figure 2B.1).

The two main branches of this tree are the two basic causes of any pattern of poor performance: external circumstances make good performance difficult, and our response to these circumstances is inadequate. Often both are true at the same time.

First, in the category of external circumstances, there are three types of hypotheses to consider:

1. **Performance expectations:** Are they particularly challenging? Have they gotten more so? For example, has your system eliminated or restricted some accommodations for SWDs, effectively raising the bar for them?

Figure 2B.1   Typical Hypotheses About Root Causes to Test

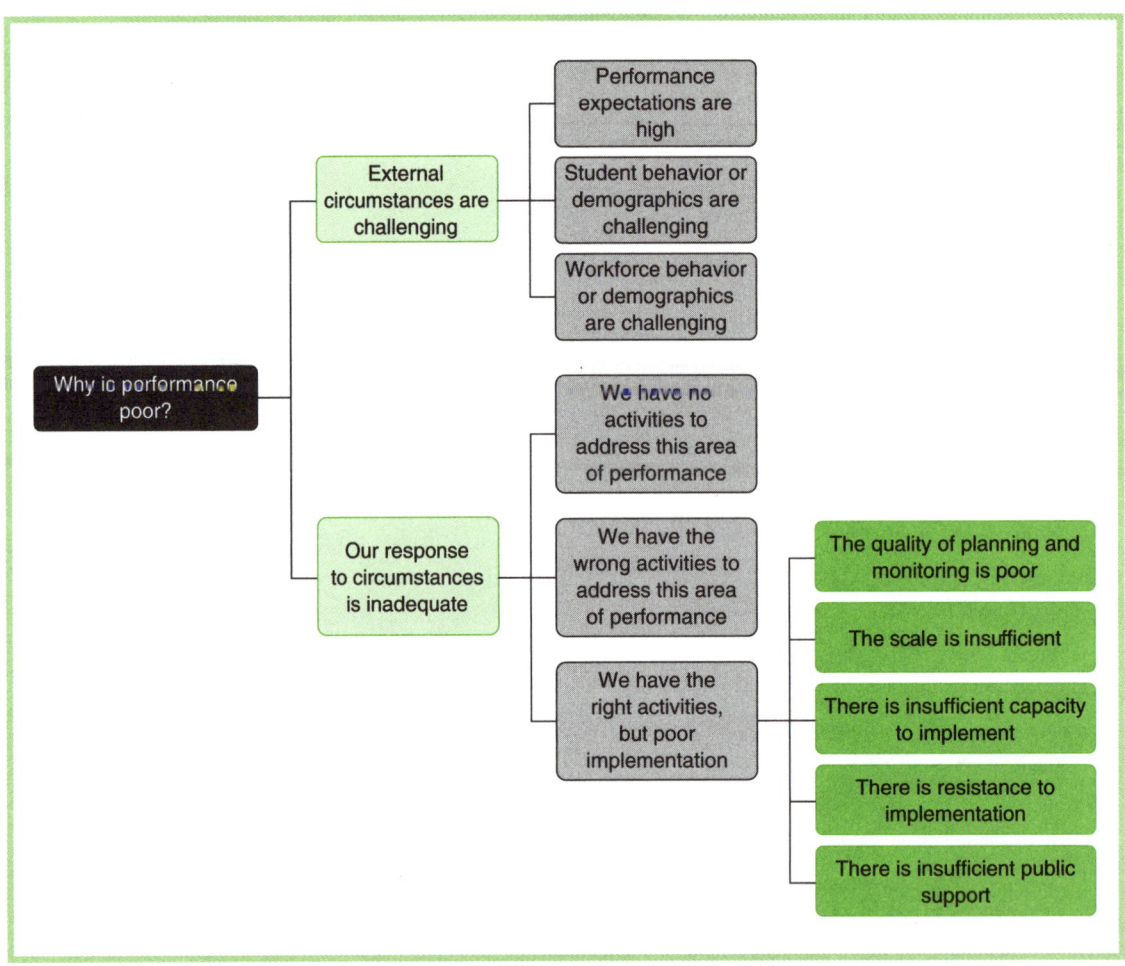

2. **Student behavior or demographics:** Is the proportion of SWDs in your system changing? Is the composition of disabilities *within* the SWD group changing? Is the rate (or accuracy) of identification changing?

3. **Workforce behavior or demographics:** Has any aspect of your system that serves SWDs changed? Have the skills, motivations, or assignments of the teachers who are closest to SWDs changed over time? What about resources for them? Policies to support them?

A caveat here: *external* does not necessarily mean "out of your control." The point of this category is not to help you develop an excuse for inaction or for ignoring the performance pattern; it's to give you context for what your response should be, and why it's currently falling short.

Your response is the subject of the second category of hypotheses, and it's where you're likely to find the most actionable information. We define your response to these circumstances in terms of one or more **activities**—ongoing programs, projects, or other substantive work—that your system is undertaking to improve performance in a particular area. For SWDs, for example, the programs under the Individuals with Disabilities in Education Act (IDEA) are examples of activities relevant to this area of performance.

There are three reasons why your activities may be inadequate:

1. You have no activities that address this particular area of performance: This is not common, but for some performance patterns, there may be no programs or projects in place to try to improve results.

2. Your activities are the wrong ones: This is possible but difficult to prove. Is the approach you're currently taking to serve SWDs wrong? Does research or experience or both suggest this?

3. You have the right activities but poor implementation: This is the most common challenge, and the area where you should spend the most time. There are five ways in which implementation could go wrong:

   - **Poor quality of planning and monitoring:** The activities may be poorly planned, the plan may not actually be driving the work, and/or leadership might be unclear. Those who do lead may have trouble monitoring progress.
   - **Insufficient scale:** This one seems basic but is the source of the problem more often than we'd like to admit. Many activities, particularly at the state level, are planned at a scale that is woefully insufficient, in the hope that the benefits will somehow be replicated on their own.
   - **Insufficient capacity to implement:** Those who are responsible for carrying out the activities—be they educators, administrators, or others within the system—may lack the skill to implement effectively.
   - **Resistance to implementation:** Likewise, these same people may simply not want to implement these activities.
   - **Lack of public support:** Finally, others who have influence on implementation—key stakeholders or the public at large—may not support the implementation of these activities.

As you form hypotheses, consider this checklist and consider what types of hypotheses you want to test (you can certainly test more than one at a time, but you should also prioritize so that the amount of work doesn't become overwhelming). Then write them out as specifically as you can. For example: "IDEA is the main program through which we serve SWDs, and our quality of monitoring is poor; we tend to monitor for compliance with the law rather than for practices that are likely to improve outcomes."

You will have noticed something by now: many of these hypotheses assume that you know what activities you currently have in place to address the performance pattern in question. For some of you, this will be fairly straightforward, especially if you already have a strategy for improvement, but for others, these questions will force you to identify and name your current approach to improving performance for the first time. We cover what it takes to fully develop or refine a strategy to improve performance in the next part of this book; for now, however, it's enough to conduct a quick review of your current activities.

Start by making a list. What are all the programs, projects, initiatives, and other ongoing work that are targeted toward improving the pattern of performance you're exploring? You may find it useful to identify colleagues who work in this area and develop the list jointly with them. Because different people bring different meanings and names to different activities, you'll need to check for overlaps and make sure that you emerge with a list that is finite, clear, comprehensive, and agreed by those involved. One tool for helping you do this is an **activity profile**: a list of questions that help you describe and characterize an activity so others will understand what it is.

Figure 2B.2 gives the basic questions to use, as well as an example drawn from our SWD scenario.

Notice that the questions and the answers to them are relatively clinical, almost boring. They aren't meant to help you design a breakthrough strategy; instead, they're meant to get everyone on the same page about what we mean when we use a common, easy-to-misinterpret label (like IEP for "individualized education plan") to describe an activity.

From that shared starting point, you can evaluate each activity to ask whether it may be contributing to the performance pattern in some way. Go through the checklist: is the activity well designed to make a positive impact on the performance pattern? Is it being implemented well? If not, why not?

One last note as you complete this step: it is worth remembering that you can and should go through a similar process for *positive* patterns of performance as well. Whether they're "bright spots" that buck a negative trend or genuine good news, we have as much to learn about what went right as about what went wrong. You can use similar questions to the ones listed above, just in reverse, to find out what your system's strengths are and how to build on them.

> Please visit EDI's website at www.deliveryinstitute.org/2B for an exercise on how to create an activity profile.

Investigate Root Causes by Testing Hypotheses

The process for testing hypotheses is similar to the last chapter: use the work plan tool to outline the specific analysis you'll have to do for each hypothesis. However, there's one challenge: most of our hypotheses about root causes will be about the quality of implementation of our current work, and quantitative data on implementation are often difficult to find.

This is where it will be important to supplement hard data with softer, more qualitative information. Specifically, there are four types of data and evidence that you can look at, defined broadly by their form—quantitative or qualitative—and their availability—readily available or created by you (see Figure 2B.3).

In the upper left-hand corner is the data we usually think of: "statistics," or quantitative data, that is collected by your system or by some other institution and available for analysis. These data usually include your goal metrics and many progress metrics. But, as we have shown, they are often insufficient for determining root causes and analyzing activities.

Figure 2B.2 Activity Profile Questions and Example

	Question and Guidance	Example: Individualized Education Plans (IEPs)
Description	• Describe the activity in one sentence.	• We require that all schools provide an individualized plan to guide the education of each SWD.
Goal(s)	• What student outcome goal or goals is the activity meant to impact? (Make sure that it includes the goal identified in the performance pattern you are investigating; otherwise, you can probably eliminate this activity.)	• Reading proficiency for SWDs • Math proficiency for SWDs • Graduation rates for SWDs
Rationale	• Why and how do we believe that the activity will have a positive impact on the goal(s)?	• By customizing education to the needs of a student with a disability, we can accelerate that student's learning and improve performance.
Success	• If the activity is occurring successfully, what will that look like? (Do NOT express in terms of the student outcome goal[s], since you already did that; instead, express in terms of what educators and/or students are doing that lead to that outcome.)	• Members of each student's IEP team know what that student needs and work in a coordinated fashion to deliver the right combination of services. • Students receive educational services appropriate to their current developmental level.

Figure 2B.3   Types of Data and Evidence

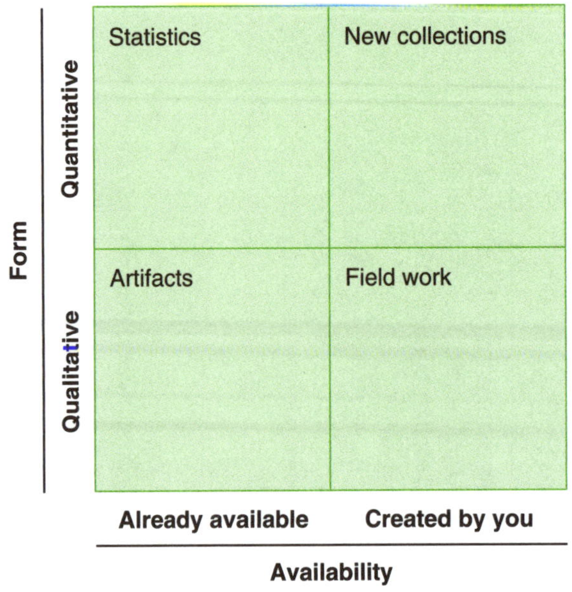

The second type of data is still quantitative, but it consists of data that you create. We call this "new collections," after the term that our system partners tend to use to refer to it. You might, for example, try to collect additional data on the implementation of programs targeted at SWDs to test hypotheses about the efficacy of these activities.

New collections can be difficult to justify because they represent a burden that systems put onto districts, campuses, schools, and the people in them to collect data. Systems already require the field to collect and report a great deal of data, so it can be difficult to ask for more. In some rare instances, a new collection is justified. But there are at least two options to try before you reach that point. First, you can try to place more of the burden of collection on yourself. We see examples of this in the feedback loops work that we describe in Part 3, in which the K–12 system offices for both New York and a state did most of the legwork to administer a survey of educator practice in the implementation of major reforms. Second, you can piggyback your work on existing data collections. This works particularly well with instruments such as surveys. Though you'll have less control over the timing, it's far less disruptive to insert a question or two into an existing survey than to create a new one.

The third type of data is "artifacts"—qualitative evidence that already exists and would be easy to collect. This category is useful when you're trying to understand how an activity is being implemented. Are principals giving accurate and thoughtful feedback to their teachers according to the new educator evaluation framework? An easy way to check would be to audit a random sample of written feedback reports that principals have uploaded. Is the course redesign initiative from the system affecting the way gateway courses are organized and taught? It might be useful to check the syllabi posted online as a starting point. Artifacts are an underestimated resource; they're right there in plain sight, and a little time spent with them can yield a great deal of insight about what's happening on the ground.

The final type of data deserves a bit more discussion: "field work," or qualitative evidence that you collect yourself. The original PMDU placed a great deal of emphasis on getting feedback from the field. This kind of work has a long history in well-managed organizations; most famously, the Toyota Production System, a method of continuous improvement that has been copied by businesses around the world, is built in part on the principle of "Genchi Genbutsu," which means "Go and See." Both the PMDU and Toyota understood one key fact: delivery doesn't happen in your office. It doesn't even happen in the data and reports that are passed between your office and the field. It happens in the field and on the front line. So if you don't know what is happening there, you're blind—no matter how much other data you have.

What does field work look like? There are four practices:

1. **Interviews:** These are one-on-one conversations with key individuals who are likely to give an important perspective on the current state of implementation.

2. **Focus groups:** A close cousin of interviews, focus groups include multiple people, usually grouped because they play the same or similar roles, to give a sample of perspectives on one or more issues.

3. **Experiencing the work:** You can put yourself in the shoes of someone on the front line by participating in one of the activities under discussion. For example, you might experience an advising website by logging in as a student, trying to select your courses, and seeing if the website offers the right information at the right time. This practice is not always possible, but it is highly recommended; it puts you at the heart of "going and seeing" what is really happening.

4. **Site visits:** A site visit is a more comprehensive variety of field work—a planned visit to a campus, district, school, or other site where the work is happening. A site visit not only incorporates every other practice described here, but also offers other opportunities, particularly for observing the work as it happens.

These practices will be familiar to you from Chapter 1B: a capacity review, after all, is just a very specific kind of field work built around a 2-day site visit. But they can be used for other purposes as well. In 2014, our partners in the South Dakota Department of Education were working with us to investigate whether it was possible to improve the alignment of the agency's resources—including funding streams, full-time employees (FTEs), and how people spent their time—with their goals for students (their hypothesis was that there was room for improvement!). Our team worked with them to design an "activity audit," which included an analysis of position descriptions for the entire department, an online survey of the entire staff, and interviews and focus groups with a cross-section of personnel.

"EDI coordinated a thoughtful school review with a team of both local and national practitioners to help us answer the question of whether we were organized to deliver on our mission. The framing of the review was just right and allowed the team to focus on the essential parts of our mission and look at multiple layers of the organization to reflect on alignment to our most valued goal—student achievement."

—Richard Pohlman,
Acting Head of School,
E. L. Haynes

The audit uncovered some important recommendations—in particular, it found that there was a great deal of potential for improving alignment of federal programs to agency goals.

In the same year, EDI helped facilitate a comprehensive school review for E. L. Haynes Public Charter School in Washington, DC. There were several questions that school leadership wanted to investigate, but in particular, they wanted to know how well the current academic program served students and how school culture helped or hindered that program. In partnership with a team of instructional experts, we conducted a 2-day site visit that involved intensive observation of classroom instruction, as well as recess, lunch, and passing periods. Before the school review, the team thought that the plan should focus mostly on questions related to building a stronger school culture. However, the evidence suggested something different: the reviewers found that the school's academic program needed greater attention in order to fulfill its mission. As a result, our subsequent work together led to a five-year strategic plan that aims to tackle how E. L. Haynes can best strengthen its academic program.

In both these instances, some carefully designed field work, drawing from a range of sources of "soft" evidence, helped our teams test out vital hypotheses about the root causes of performance that could not have been tested with any amount of hard data.

All four of these sources of data and evidence—statistics, new collections, artifacts, and field work—will help you fill out your work plan of analyses to test each of your highest priority hypotheses. Remember that this does not have to be a scientific process. In most cases, when you're looking for actionable information, something is usually better than nothing. Remember, too, that simpler is often better, both regarding the feasibility of your work and your ability to communicate the results.

These additional tools for gathering data—and creating it for yourself—will allow you to think more expansively about how to test your hypotheses. To go back to our SWD example, you might find yourself planning an analysis like the one in Figure 2B.4.

The analysis here consists mostly of gathering artifacts (IEPs) and field work (interviews with district special education coordinators). The information you get won't be perfect; IEPs don't tell you nearly enough about the quality of implementation, and the opinions of your interviewees will be subjective. But by combining and triangulating these sources, you'll be able to find out whether your hypothesis—about inadequate state support and compliance monitoring—is directionally true. What you learn will be good enough for action—which is the whole point. To borrow Lemony Snicket's words, "Even though there are no ways of knowing for sure, there are ways of knowing for pretty sure."

Analyses like these will yield rich information that will help you continue the cycle of inquiry, using data to sharpen and test your hypotheses further. As in the previous chapter, you'll eventually converge on a set of

Figure 2B.4 Work Plan Template With Example: Students With Disabilities

	Issue	Hypothesis	Analysis	End Product	Hypothesis Is True if . . .	Sources
Definition	What is the key unresolved question?	What do you think the answer might be?	What work must you do to prove or disprove the hypothesis and resolve the issue?	What will the output of the analysis be?	Where will your data and evidence come from?	Who will do the analysis, and by when?
Example	Why has our achievement gap for students with disabilities not narrowed, even as other gaps have shrunk over the last several years?	IDEA is the main program through which we serve SWDs, and our quality of monitoring is poor; we tend to monitor for compliance with the law rather than for practices that are likely to improve outcomes. As a result, district implementation varies widely and we have no system for addressing this variation.	• Interview a sample of district special education coordinators to find out whether they believe this is true. • Audit a sample of IEPs from these districts to check for similarities and differences in quality; compare to record of our own activities supporting districts.	Qualitative synthesis of findings from review that answers the questions: • What do districts feel held accountable for in implementing IDEA? • How does this affect the quality of their work?	• Coordinators consistently tell us that they are held accountable for compliance and not much else. • IEP quality bears little relationship to the amount or type of support and attention we give to a district.	• District special education coordinators • IEPs from districts • Records of our support activities with districts

conclusions about root causes. The last step is to bring them into your over-all story about performance.

Tell the Story

You've now done a level of analysis that goes deeper than the performance patterns you identified in the last chapter. As with the performance patterns, you'll want to communicate this information to others so they can use it to take action. The process here is very similar: look at your findings, select the ones that most efficiently illustrate the broader trend, and arrange them into a clear and coherent story line. In many cases, you'll want to insert these findings into the story of performance patterns that you've already developed.

You can use a short list of questions to test the quality of your story:

- Are the main points of the story clear?

  - Have we identified the key points that we want the audience to walk away with? If you read the headlines of each visual in the order they are presented, would the result be a coherent paragraph?
  - Have we identified the minimal amount of information that they will need to understand and believe these key takeaways? Have we avoided any analyses, data, or information that are extraneous (even if they are fascinating)?
  - For each point, have we used the data to lead to a clear conclusion or discussion questions about which actions to take?

- Is it readable, cohesive, and even beautiful?

  - Are the messages clear and does the prose synthesize the most important information efficiently?
  - Does each visual lay out the information in a way that aids under-standing?
  - Have we minimized the number of *types* of visuals that we use? How much time will we have to spend *explaining* to the audience what they are seeing rather than just letting them see it?

⊙ LESSONS FROM THE FIELD

Focus on Quality of Implementation

When we introduced the hypothesis tree of potential root causes, we focused on the second branch, about quality of implementation. Part of the reason for this, as we said, is that external factors can easily turn into excuses. But what if our activities simply aren't the right ones? Surely this is important; as several part-ners have asked us, isn't delivery—the *how* of implementation—a fool's errand if the actual content of the work—the *what*—is fundamentally flawed? Isn't that just a recipe for doing the wrong thing a lot better?

Yes and no. Of course, no amount of quality implementation could ever improve performance if the underlying activity is proven to be irrelevant to the goal, or even harmful to it. But *proven* is a strong word, and one that does not come easily in our field. Most activities targeted at a particular goal, whether deliberately or not, occupy a large middle ground between "proven to work" and "proven to hurt": they pass the plausibility sniff test (they *could* work), but research is inconclusive, or it's never been done.

For most of these activities, an old management saw applies: having the "right" activity matters far less than whether it's executed well. Because of the variation in quality of implementation, labels matter very little. It's almost meaningless, for example, when a school system tells you that they're doing Response to Intervention (RtI), or when a university says that they're engaging in course redesign—these labels are so ubiquitous that they've almost become meaningless buzzwords. Unless you know *how* they're being implemented, you know little about whether they will be successful. We think the reason so much research is inconclusive is because it doesn't usually capture that information.

As a result, we may be able to rule out some activities because research has definitively proven that there is *no* way to implement them well. But for the vast majority of activities, you're better off starting by asking whether implementation is going as intended (this implies that there *is* an intent, which is the first question you should ask!). Once you've done this, most of your job will be the hard work of improving implementation through better planning and monitoring (the subject of the next several chapters). And for some activities, you'll find that even when they're being implemented as intended, the resulting impact on performance isn't strong. Here you will have succeeded where research didn't: you'll be able to cross those activities off the list with confidence, knowing that they aren't the right ones to pursue.

Approach the Task With Humility

As we've seen, analyzing root causes inevitably brings you to closely examine your current activities. This is an important step to take, for two reasons. First, as you move into planning, you'll need to recognize that you're not starting from a blank slate. The current ongoing work will serve as an important foundation for your efforts. Second, this process is a useful way to get others to discover—alongside you—whether or not their current efforts are adequate. Just as the capacity review process invites introspection about how well your system is set up to deliver results, root cause analysis can be set up to help system leaders and staff examine their current assumptions about their work and agree, together, on what shifts they'll need to make to reach the goals.

However, there's an inherent risk in the process, as there was with the capacity review: that you will offend the owners of the current work by not taking it seriously enough. We've known too many Delivery Unit leaders (and made the mistake ourselves) who have too quickly assumed that the current work was not fit for purpose. Over the years, we've learned about the importance of understanding, acknowledging, and honoring the work that system leaders and staff have already done to try to improve performance. Your job is to use the tools and questions in this chapter to lead them through a process of collaborative, humble, and authentic inquiry into this work—one that is open to the possibility that some parts of it are going very well and that others are not.

This isn't just a matter of optics. In almost every case we've encountered, what may look like less-than-optimal behavior from outside is perfectly rational behavior from inside; a great deal of current work in most systems, effective or not, is the result of talented and caring individuals working hard to do the right things for students. As an outsider, you occupy a privileged position: your distance helps you ask questions that can help everyone break through to new insights about current performance. Approach this task with humility, and you're more likely to get a good reception.

⊙ KEY CONSIDERATIONS FOR SYSTEM LEADERS AND STAFF

If you're the **system leader**, you should push your team to use this process as an opportunity to examine your current work and improve it even further. For example, the "activity audit" in South Dakota was largely driven by the system head and her deputy, which lent special credence to the effort.

If you're a **delivery leader**, you have a particular responsibility for facilitating this process with humility and care, as per the above advice. Your job is to assume the best of intentions as you dig into the current work. In the words of negotiation experts Roger Fisher and William Ury, you always have the power of positive interpretation. Make it your goal to give everyone a graceful way to celebrate their successes and to admit, with no threat of shame, where their work may have fallen short.

Finally, **system staff**, especially those who have been in the system for a while, may find it uncomfortable to examine current work to see how effective it is. It's far too easy to conflate the efficacy of your work with your own personal efficacy. In reality, they're related but separate things. You may be good at your job, but choices made at the system level may prevent you from having an impact on the goal. This process is an opportunity to surface these kinds of issues and to fix them—or to realize, together, that a new direction is needed.

⊙ CONCLUSION

We began this chapter with a call to move beyond hard data and to ask "why" in the pursuit of the root causes of performance. The realization that hard data are often just as flawed as the softer stuff should have a liberating effect, opening us up to a range of creative sources of evidence that will help us make better and faster decisions. By using the cycle of inquiry from the last chapter to analyze this information, you'll be able to complete your understanding of the delivery challenge: how you're doing against your aspiration, what you're doing to reach it right now, and how well (or not) those efforts are working.

As we said at the outset, this part of the book is the step that our partners most often skip, probably because it's difficult to slow down and examine the data when you're operating with such a sense of urgency. As a result, many leaders are more comfortable going straight from aspiration to strategy. But the groundwork you lay here is for the longer term. Just as you benefited from getting everyone on the same page about your aspiration, you'll benefit from building consensus on the nature of the barriers that stand in the way of achieving it. Understanding the challenge will save you a great deal of trouble down the road, and it will set you up to take the next step: developing a focused plan to break down those barriers and significantly improve performance.

◉ NOTE

1. Mintzberg, H., Ahlstrand, B., & Lampel, J. (1998). *Strategy safari: A guided tour through the wilds of strategic management.* New York, NY: Free Press. Retrieved from https://planejamentoestrategico2s2011.files.wordpress.com/2012/08/s01_mintzberg_et_al_safari_ingles.pdf

Part 3

Plan for Delivery

 Develop a foundation for delivery

 Understand the delivery challenge

 Plan for delivery

 Drive delivery

 Create an irreversible delivery culture

---

System Leader Summary

Your aspiration answered the first question of delivery: What are you trying to do? This part of the book answers the second: How are you planning to do it? Specifically, what's your **delivery plan** for achieving the goals you've set out, and how does it account for the challenges you uncovered in Part 2 of this book?

This introduction to Part 3 explores how you should organize your planning effort (what we call an **architecture**), the core content that a delivery plan should contain, and a few ideas for the process of planning. Your delivery leader will be responsible for facilitating this process. You'll be the person who pushes the relevant goal leaders to take it seriously—mostly by reviewing the plans yourself and signaling your intent to use them as the main driver of your system's day-to-day work.

◉ THE TROUBLE WITH PLANNING

In the previous two parts of this book, we've covered the precursors to planning: well-articulated aspirations, a clear sense of current performance against those aspirations, and an understanding of the implications for your efforts to improve performance. We now have the information we need to develop high-impact, evidence-based delivery plans for achieving our aspirations.

The problem that delivery planning solves is not idleness; work would get done (and does get done) even in the absence of planning. In fact, that's often a problem: leaders think that planning is a luxury they can't afford, mostly because they have a fairly good idea in their own heads of what they ought to be doing, and they're too busy doing it to take time to plan.

We don't want to second-guess these leaders; they may know the right thing to do, and the work may be brilliant. But as long as the "plan" remains in their heads, they'll have limited leverage to ensure that the whole system implements it. This is why leaders often worry that they have no choice but to micromanage the work, or keep it in the hands of a small circle of trusted (and overworked) advisors. The process is self-reinforcing: limited leverage causes leaders to feel more pressure on their own capacity, which inclines them to take even less time for planning.

That's why we often emphasize delivery planning not as a tool for achieving blinding new insights about the work, but for getting everyone on the same page about insights they already have. The same rule that applied to the guiding coalition applies here: when the right people agree profoundly about what they're supposed to do, great things are possible. A good plan strikes a balance between centralized and distributed leadership: it pushes everyone in the system to focus on the leaders' aspiration and gives everyone the same mental image about the work necessary to achieve it, while also empowering people to bring all their talent and creativity to bear in finding innovative ways to carry out that work in their own contexts.

In this sense, a strong delivery plan amplifies the reach and effectiveness of a leader's vision in a way that nothing else can. Moreover, the planning process gives leaders a chance to reality-test the assumptions in their heads with each other and to make adjustments to improve the work before it starts. For all these reasons, planning is a fundamental pillar of the delivery approach.

But there's a problem: planning has a terrible reputation in our field. In our work with partners, we always ask about people's impressions of planning as a discipline; reliably, fewer than half ever report having a positive experience. The announcement of a planning process is often met with eyerolls—or worse. The need to plan is intuitive to us, but we resist it because many of us have never seen it done well, and we don't believe that this time will be any different.

What makes good planning so challenging? Author Neil Gaiman hints at why in his short story *The Map-Maker*. The fable is told of an emperor who ruled a vast domain and became obsessed with creating ever-larger maps of it, until finally the only map left to make was a life-sized replica of the land itself. For obvious reasons, he failed. "The more accurate the map," Gaiman writes, "the more it resembles the territory. The most accurate map would *be* [emphasis added] the territory, and thus would be perfectly accurate and perfectly useless."[1]

Planning works the same way. Make your plan too small and vague, and like a crudely drawn map, it won't do much to guide your work. Most of us have made plans like these when the planning felt like a compliance exercise; we checked the boxes and moved on.

Make your plan too large and detailed, though, and you'll find yourself in the map-maker's position, working endlessly toward a "life-sized" description of your work that is perfectly accurate and perfectly useless. Many of us have experienced these kinds of drawn-out planning processes, where the final product arrived way too late to make a difference in what anyone did. In cases like these, planning becomes a substitute for action; you would have been better off spending your time *doing* the work rather than refining the plan. Hence Michael Fullan's apt warning on the subject: "Beware of fat plans."[2]

Few of us have experienced planning in its best form: detailed enough to be meaningful, but light and flexible enough to drive and adapt to an organization's ongoing work. Getting this balance right can be difficult. But it's an ideal worth pursuing—because without a plan, the only way to deliver on your aspirations will be by accident or luck.

This introduction and the next three chapters contain the lessons we've learned about how to strike that balance. Because the individual components of delivery planning are really a unified whole, this part of the book is organized differently from the others. This introduction is longer than most because it provides an overview of what a delivery plan is, what makes it different from other types of planning, and how to organize your system to develop delivery plans. The three chapters that follow dig into the substance of delivery planning by detailing each of the core components that a delivery plan should contain.

⊙ CORE PRINCIPLES

In our work with partners over the last several years, we've articulated and refined a handful of principles and tools that will help you establish a relevant and practical planning process. There are three questions to answer at the outset:

1. How should we organize delivery planning?

2. What should a delivery plan contain?

3. How should delivery plans be written?

We will take on each of these questions in turn.

How Should We Organize Delivery Planning?

Delivery plans need to focus on the most important things, and they also need to fit coherently with any other planning that systems do—including project plans and/or organizational plans—as well as the planning undertaken by local campuses, schools, and districts. There can be an issue here with nomenclature. Sometimes, organizations have delivery plans without calling them delivery plans—they go by one of the other labels we have used above, like "strategic plan." We have to reiterate here that names matter less than the concepts they represent. At a minimum, every system needs four elements in place to organize planning:

1. A series of clear **goals** connected to their aspiration;

2. For each goal, a single **goal leader** who is responsible and empowered for developing and owning a delivery plan;

3. For each delivery plan, a series of **strategies** (or projects) for achieving the relevant goal (we'll learn more about how to define these in the next chapter); and

4. For each strategy or project, a single **strategy/project leader** who is responsible for its implementation. Strategy/project leaders also form a team to support each goal leader in the development of their delivery plans.

The relationship between these elements creates an architecture for delivery planning, as outlined in Figure 3.1.

Nearly any system that examines this list will find elements that they already have. The key is to identify these elements, see how they fit in with the greater whole, and build on them so that all the system's planning and resources are aligned with and directed toward their aspirations. This will look different in different contexts. Some systems will already organize their work into a series of strategies or projects, but have no goals. Others will have all the elements but don't make the connection between them explicit. Still others will have these elements on paper, but don't assign appropriate goal leaders and strategy leaders to own and drive the work.

The important thing to understand is that planning does not happen in a vacuum. It takes place in the context of other existing efforts to better define the work of a system. Anyone wishing to improve planning has to take this context into account and build on it where they can. A good architecture brings the old and new together, allowing you to coherently organize and describe the work.

Figure 3.1   Sample Delivery Planning Architecture

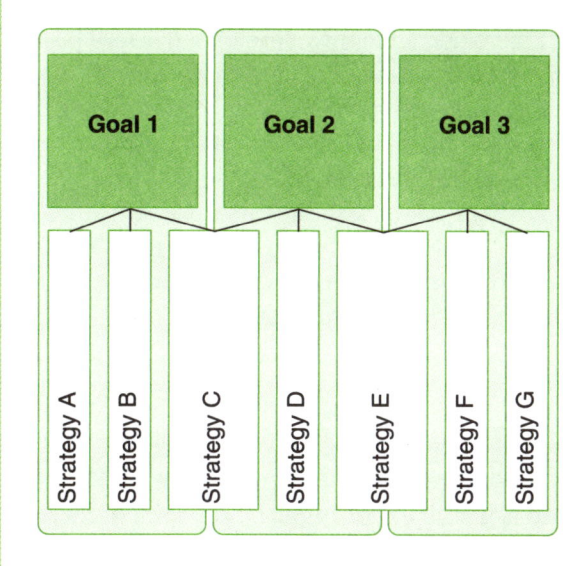

A single **goal leader** for each goal, responsible for developing the delivery plan

A single **strategy leader** for each strategy, responsible for supporting the development of the delivery plan and its implementation

□ Delivery Plans

Building on Existing Work: Strategic Planning and Delivery Planning in Kentucky

When we began our work with the Kentucky Department of Education (KDE), the department had just finished going through a lengthy and exhaustive strategic planning process. The result was a document that listed almost 30 projects being undertaken by the department.

The last thing that we wanted to do with our friends at KDE was to tell them to start over. Not only would it have been demoralizing, but it would also have thrown out a great deal of work that the team had invested in trying to articulate its main activities. Instead, our team worked with Commissioner Terry Holliday and his leadership team to prioritize KDE's most critical student outcome goals and put them at the center of the system's architecture for delivery planning. The plan already included an aspiration with a broad list of goals: increasing the number of college- and career-ready high school graduates, improving reading and math proficiency, and so on. Each of these goals was broken down further into metrics and targets. For example, the college- and career-readiness goal had two components:

1. Double the percentage of students who are college and career ready from 34% to 67% by 2015
2. Increase the average freshman graduation rate from 76% to 90% by 2015

(Continued)

(Continued)

Each goal was assigned a goal leader and the delivery planning process began. When each goal leader assembled a team to develop a delivery plan, one of their first tasks was to define the strategies (and their leaders) that they believed were most likely to help them achieve the goal in question. Each team used the projects in the strategic plan as the starting point for identifying these strategies. Occasionally, the team identified gaps and filled them by adding new strategies where necessary. But the architecture that ultimately emerged was a series of plans that were aligned with KDE's strategic plan and went further, prioritizing the most critical initiatives and aligning them to the agency's goals for student success.

With a clear architecture in place, you can then decide how to organize your delivery plans around it. Every plan has an **area of focus**—a topic that gives you a sense of what the plan is trying to accomplish. The area of focus for a project plan, for example, is the project, and its purpose is to complete that project to whatever definition of success the planner has come up with. Other plans focus on organizational units. A university system's office of academic affairs, for example, or a state education agency's department of assessment and accountability—these units might come up with plans to guide their work over the course of a fixed period of time.

However, plans like these are essentially focusing on inputs. What sets a *delivery* plan apart is the fact that its area of focus is an outcome of some kind. A delivery plan's definition of success must be aligned with the aspiration for students that we defined in Part 1 of this book. For this reason, we suggest organizing your delivery plans by goal: roughly one delivery plan for each goal that your system has articulated, with each plan "owned" by the relevant goal leader. For example, Massachusetts and Kentucky's K–12 systems both began their delivery efforts by adopting a handful of student outcome goals (about a half dozen for each), each of which consists of a handful of strategies to achieve it. In both of these systems, the goal was the area of focus: each goal had a delivery plan with a single owner—the goal leader. South Dakota's K–12 system made a similar choice, organizing their delivery effort around four goals and four plans (see Figure 3.2).

There are some exceptions to this rule. For the team at Eagle County Schools, there are more goals than there are strategies, and the linkages between them are complex (see Figure 3.3).

For this reason, Eagle County chose to make its strategies into the areas of focus. Accordingly, each strategy has a leader who is the focus for the delivery plan, and the team reviews the goals as a whole when the data come in. As we noted above, organizing in this way carries the risk of focusing too much on inputs rather than outcomes. You can manage this risk in two ways: (1) by ensuring that the plans for each strategy make explicit reference to the most relevant outcome data (e.g., teacher effectiveness data for the educator effectiveness system), and (2) by ensuring that the delivery

Figure 3.2   Sample Delivery Planning Architecture: Four Goals

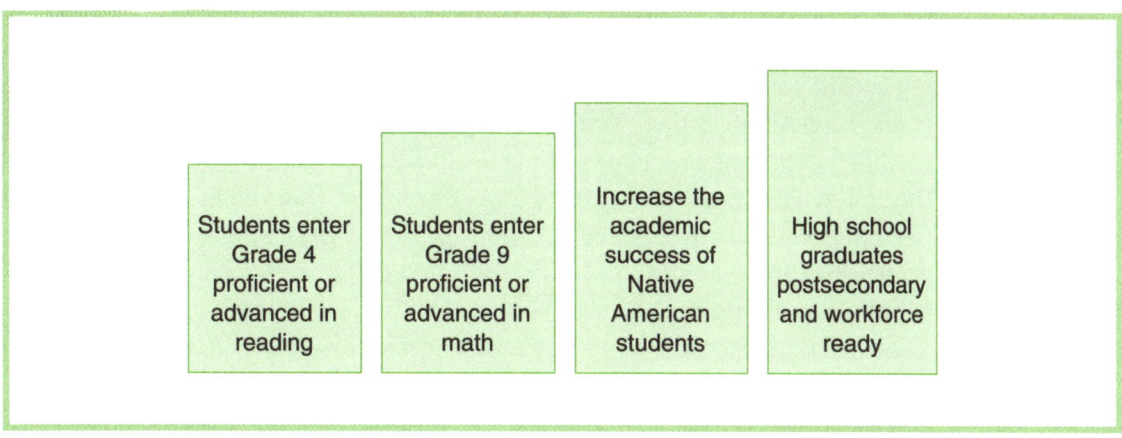

Source: South Dakota Department of Education. (n.d.). *College, career, and life ready: Preparing South Dakota students for success.* Retrieved from http://doe.sd.gov/outcomes/index.aspx

Figure 3.3   Delivery Planning Architecture for Eagle County Schools

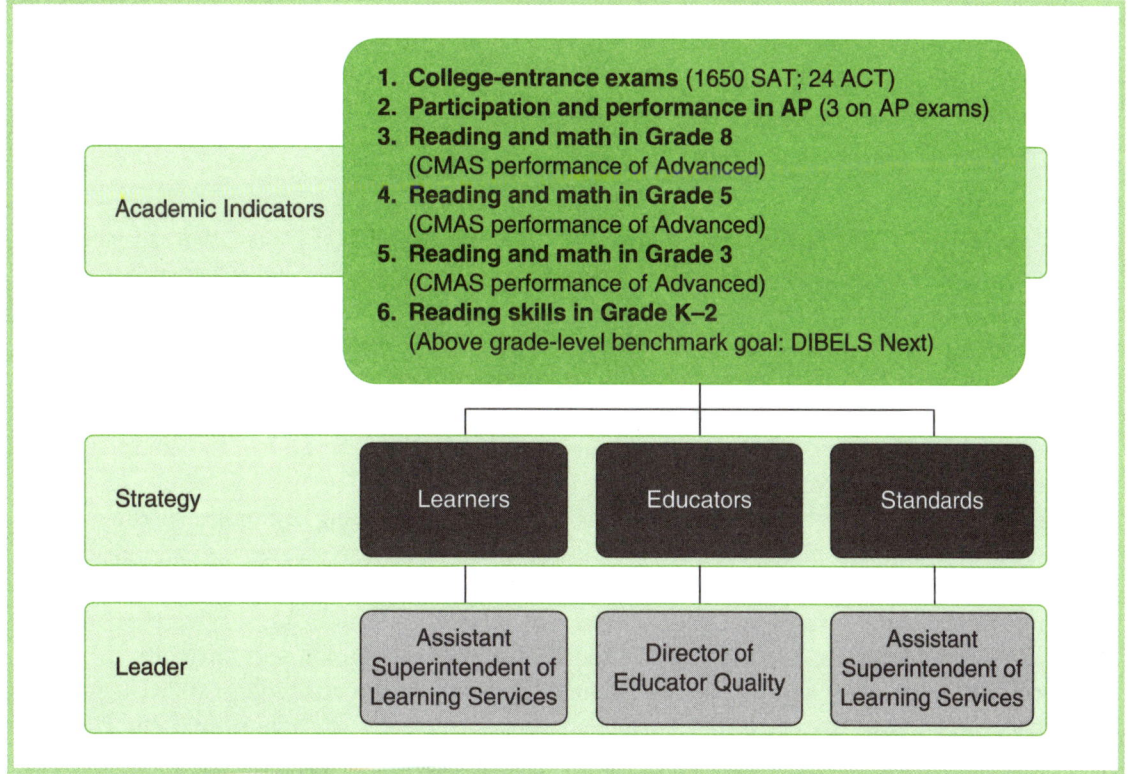

routines to monitor progress emphasize these data as well (for more on this, please see Part 4).

As these examples show, developing an architecture and organizing delivery planning around it can be a challenge because there's almost never a one-to-one correspondence between goals and strategies. Inevitably, some strategies support multiple goals; new college- and career-ready standards, for example, are likely to influence both proficiency rates *and* graduation rates, among other things. You'll need to work through this messiness. In some cases, this means doing what Eagle County did; in others, it means making a call (however imperfect) about which strategies best align with which goals. In general, assign strategies to goals using the same principle that we used for assigning goal leaders to goals in Chapter 1A: align each strategy to the goal where its *center of gravity* is and recognize that the fit won't be perfect (for college- and career-ready standards, the center of gravity is probably proficiency, for example). In some cases, you can have the same strategy contribute to multiple goals as well.

A system should also make the connection between its system-level goals and/or strategies and their counterparts at the local level. If you're a district superintendent, do you expect that each school will be held accountable for contributing to your district goals? If so, how is that reflected in your relationship with them? Similarly, when you have a state-level strategy, will its implementation require the buy-in of a significant number of your campuses, districts, and/or schools? And if so, how will you ensure that this strategy is somehow reflected in their local planning? As you design and organize delivery planning, keeping this connection in mind is very important.

Aligned Planning in Hawai'i

Like most systems, the Hawai'i Department of Education (HIDOE) has several layers: a district central office with a board of education, local "complex areas" (clusters of 2–4 high schools and their feeder schools), the schools themselves, and classrooms. When our partnership with them began, each level had its own planning process: the State Board of Education was working on a strategic plan, the district office had committed to a series of projects to manage under its Race to the Top (RTT) grant, complex areas had plans, schools had to complete Academic Plans every year, and teachers and principals had to plan for each teacher's professional development.

One of the HIDOE team's first steps was to take the planning architecture they had developed—six delivery plans organized around six big statewide strategies—and align all these other planning processes with it. The result looked something like Figure 3.4.

The core principle here is that there are a few state-determined "nonnegotiables" (the six strategies) and that at each successive local level, there is choice and flexibility to add to them. The state drew on its various guiding documents (the strategic plan, RTT goals, etc.) to come up with the statewide goals and the six strategies for achieving them. Those goals then cascade all the way through to the classroom level. They, along with the strategies, are "prepopulated" in the planning documents that complex areas and schools complete; these leaders must show how they will carry out the state strategies and contribute to the state goals.

That being said, each complex area and school must have flexibility to articulate goals and strategies that are important to them; the planning documents also allow for this so that planning is aligned at every level but flexible to local needs.

Figure 3.4 Aligned Planning for Results

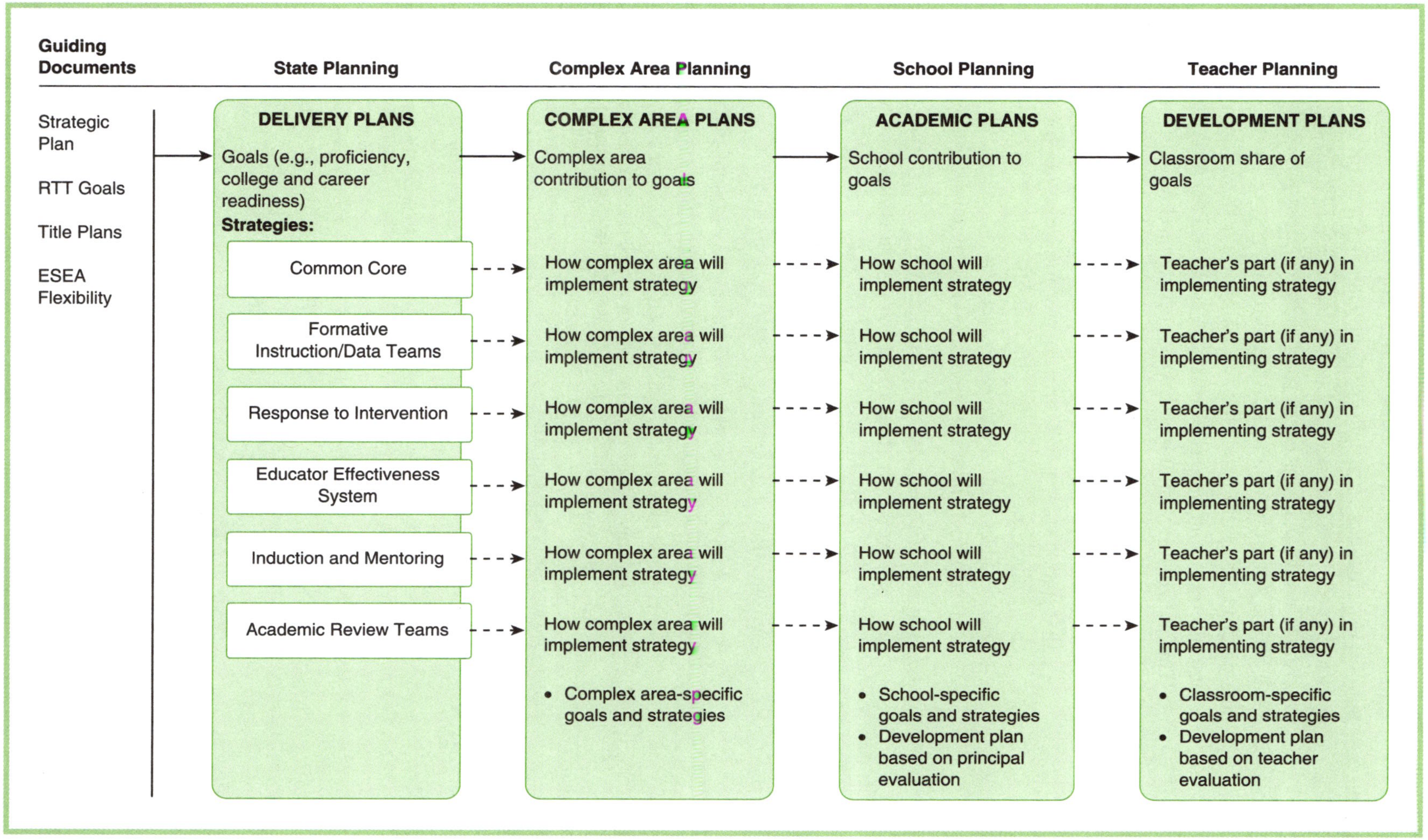

Guiding Documents	State Planning	Complex Area Planning	School Planning	Teacher Planning
Strategic Plan RTT Goals Title Plans ESEA Flexibility	**DELIVERY PLANS** Goals (e.g., proficiency, college and career readiness) **Strategies:** Common Core Formative Instruction/Data Teams Response to Intervention Educator Effectiveness System Induction and Mentoring Academic Review Teams	**COMPLEX AREA PLANS** Complex area contribution to goals How complex area will implement strategy How complex area will implement strategy How complex area will implement strategy How complex area will implement strategy How complex area will implement strategy How complex area will implement strategy • Complex area-specific goals and strategies	**ACADEMIC PLANS** School contribution to goals How school will implement strategy How school will implement strategy How school will implement strategy How school will implement strategy How school will implement strategy How school will implement strategy • School-specific goals and strategies • Development plan based on principal evaluation	**DEVELOPMENT PLANS** Classroom share of goals Teacher's part (if any) in implementing strategy Teacher's part (if any) in implementing strategy Teacher's part (if any) in implementing strategy Teacher's part (if any) in implementing strategy Teacher's part (if any) in implementing strategy Teacher's part (if any) in implementing strategy • Classroom-specific goals and strategies • Development plan based on teacher evaluation

What Should a Delivery Plan Contain?

A delivery plan doesn't follow one particular template or format. Rather, a handful of principles set a delivery plan apart: a focus on student outcomes, a connection of the strategies to those outcomes, and built-in reality checks on progress. The best plans give everyone a shared mental model of the work to be done, which empowers leaders throughout the system to implement with confidence. And, crucially, good plans contain within them the seeds of their own self-monitoring, which we cover in more detail in Part 4 of this book.

The ideal delivery plan has three components that reinforce these ideas:

1. **Reform strategies:** What can we do that will have the greatest impact on the goal? What is our theory of action—how and why do we believe that our strategies will have impact at all? Besides the reform strategies themselves, this component includes the clear assignment of leadership (goal leaders and strategy/project leads), measurable milestones for each strategy, and well-articulated resource requirements.

2. **Delivery chains:** How will each strategy reach the field at scale? And how will we know that this is happening? This component includes a description of the delivery chain for each strategy, the design of feedback loops for understanding the day-to-day quality of implementation, a definition of priority stakeholders and how to engage them, and the identification of risks and ways to manage them.

3. **Targets and trajectories:** What do we estimate will be the impact of each strategy on the goal over time? Is the resulting trajectory—and the target at its end—sufficiently ambitious? Is it realistic? What is our evidence for this? Targets and trajectories are the linchpin of a delivery plan, connecting tangible strategies with difficult-to-achieve aspirations.

These components are summarized in Figure 3.5.

Figure 3.5   Components of a Delivery Plan

This is the point—deciding what goes into a plan—where the risk of "overplanning" is strongest. You'll always be tempted to add more detail to this relatively short list. Remember, though, that if you really use it, the plan will change constantly. So there are diminishing returns to the amount of detail you add; indeed, the more detailed your plan, the more reluctant you'll be to revise it in the future, and the less likely you'll be to actually use it to drive your work. Keep your planning lean by sticking to the components listed here.

Each of these components is covered in detail in the three chapters that follow. For now, it suffices to say that they serve as criteria for assessing the quality of a plan. For this reason, we've combined them into a simple rubric, which is shown in Figure 3.6 and available in full on EDI's website, **www .deliveryinstitute.org/3.**

Goal leaders and their teams can use this rubric in several ways. First, they can use it to guide the writing of a plan—or the creation of a template that has the right prompts in it.

Second, they can use it to pressure test an existing plan—both internally and with external pairs of eyes. A self-assessment of an existing plan against this rubric is one of the most powerful exercises we've done with partners over the last several years; at EDI, we use the same exercise to evaluate our own internal delivery plan regularly. An external review using these same criteria can add an objective perspective to the exercise. EDI provides this kind of review to many of our partner systems, returning a series of traffic-light judgments and recommendations based on the criteria in the rubric. Figure 3.7 gives an example of feedback provided to the University of Wisconsin system on their delivery plan using an earlier version of the rubric.

Finally, the rubric can be used more formally to "approve" a plan, depending on the context and relationship between the planners and the Delivery Unit. We've most often seen this approach used in the context of approving local-level plans.

How Should Delivery Plans Be Written?

Once you've organized your delivery planning, identified leaders, and agreed on the substance of what you want to produce, there's only one question left: how will you get it done? To use an oft-derided phrase, what's your "plan for planning"?

This is another of those seemingly trivial questions that turns out to be quite important. People in education systems don't resist planning only because of their prior bad experiences; they're also busy trying to handle all the unplanned work that dominates in the absence of real planning. For this reason, you need a simple but deliberate plan for planning—one that quickly demonstrates the leadership's commitment to making this happen, the value of the planning process itself, and a respect for the busy schedules of the goal leaders and strategy leaders who will need to do the work. There's no perfect way to do this. As long as you have an idea of what to do and have made someone responsible, you can be fairly general in your guidance here.

Figure 3.6 Rubric for Assessing Delivery Plan: A strong plan will . . . .

	Criteria	Key Questions	Weak Plan ● (Red)	Strong Plan ● (Green)
Strategies	Articulate its aspiration	Have we defined a vision for what we want this plan to achieve in terms of outcomes? What will success look like? How will things be different?	• Aspiration is not well defined or is ambiguous • Desired outcomes are not specified	• Plan specifies an ambitious, easy-to-understand aspiration with a clear moral imperative • Plan defines the aspiration in terms of specific and measurable outcomes • Aspiration is linked to overall system commitments and goals
	Identify the relevant strategies	Have we defined a coordinated and coherent set of strategies that will collectively help us to achieve the aspiration? How and why do we believe that these strategies will work?	• No strategies are defined or strategies are vaguely defined	• Plan has defined a clear set of strategies that are based on benchmarking of best practices inside and outside the system • Strategies are defined and sequenced to work together to achieve the aspiration • Each strategy has a theory of action for how it will have an impact on the aspiration
	Assign leadership, management, and accountability	Have we defined a single person who is responsible for the plan as a whole and for each of the strategies? How will these people interact with other leaders and with the delivery team?	• Overall plan has no owner or multiple owners • Each strategy has no owner or multiple owners • Other roles not defined	• Overall plan has a single owner from the senior leadership team who is responsible for ensuring that the plan achieves the aspiration • Each strategy has a single accountable owner • Role of Delivery Unit in supporting leaders is well defined
	Describe the resources and support required	Have we identified the personnel, financial, technological, and other resources that are required for each strategy's success?	• Resources are not mentioned or are vague/unrealistic	• Plan gives a clear picture of how the strategies can be achieved with federal, state, and local resources available—or it specifies how the needed resources can be obtained

120

Category	Step	Question	Below Standard	At Standard
Delivery Chains	Identify the relevant delivery chain(s)	Do we know how each strategy will reach the field at scale? Have we specified who needs to do what, what capacity or motivation they will need, and who will engage them and how?	• Roles not well defined, or roles give an inaccurate/incomplete picture of realities on the ground	• Each strategy specifies clear roles at every level, from state to classroom, with clear analysis of how the necessary capacity and motivation will be developed at scale
	Create feedback loops for managing performance	Have we specified how we will know that each strategy is working? What indicators or subindicators will we use? Do we know how we will collect and monitor this information?	• No indicators given other than the main measure of success • Implementation time line is vague or nonexistent	• Each strategy has a defined set of indicators of success that is based on the delivery chain, including: - Specific and time-bound implementation milestones - Leading indicators of implementation quality • Plan includes mechanisms to monitor this information
	Anticipate and prepare for risks	Have we identified the major risks and weaknesses in the delivery chain that might throw the work off course? Do we know how we will manage them?	• No risks identified, or risk assessment is unrealistic, with no attempt at real solutions for management	• The plan details risks and constraints along the delivery chain, including weak relationships, chokepoints, funding shortfalls, and other major issues • There is a potential solution for managing each risk
	Prepare to manage stakeholders	Have we identified relevant stakeholders and how we will engage with and manage them effectively?	• No stakeholders listed, or listed without details on how they will be managed	• Relevant stakeholders identified • Each one analyzed to assess role, current perspective, and desired perspective • Approach detailed for communicating with and managing each stakeholder
Targets and Trajectories	Set a trajectory for implementation	Have we defined a clear measure of success—what it means to achieve the aspiration? What is our end target for this measure? Our intermediate targets? Why do we believe that our strategies will allow us to hit these targets?	• Measure of success not well defined • No linkage drawn between strategies and impact on the measure of success • No intermediate targets	• Plan defines a clear measure of success for the aspiration and a time-bound end target • Trajectory of intermediate targets comes from a series of evidence-based estimates of the impact that each strategy will have on the measure of success • Target and trajectory are validated by relevant benchmarks to ensure that they are ambitious and realistic

Figure 3.7 University of Wisconsin Initial System Delivery Plan Feedback

Criteria	G	AG	AR	R	Commentary
Articulate Its Aspiration	X				• Plan includes both access and success goals for all students as well as addresses equity gaps • Indicates the importance of the plan by tying into the overall goal/need with human/workforce needs for the state
Identify the Relevant Activities	X				• Detailed explanations on the various activities needed to accomplish goals • Includes robust and believable set of actions that campuses and/or the system has or will implement toward goal achievement
Identify the Relevant Delivery Chains			X		• Plan explains the working relationship between the system and the campuses • Could be improved with a discussion of the overall system delivery chain
Assign Leadership, Management, and Accountability			X		• Plan does not currently articulate who is responsible for the projects identified in the plan
Set a Trajectory for Implementation		X			• Trajectory has been defined but does not indicate how each activity impacts the trajectory (e.g., which are high-impact vs. low-impact time line)
Detail Performance Management	X				• Sets long-term and short-term reporting procedures • Identifies the metrics to be used to monitor performance
Incorporate Benchmarking				X	• Plan does not indicate if benchmarking was used in setting goals
Describe Resources and Delivery Unit Support		X			• Clearly lays out the role of the Delivery Unit • Details funding structures but does not present the staff required to carry out plan
Prepare to Manage Stakeholders and Users		X			• Plan clearly lays out all of the stakeholders (internal and external) and articulates how the overall goal relates to them • Needs to identify the communication strategy(ies) for each stakeholder group
Anticipate and Prepare for Risks	X				• Nicely identifies risks and appropriate mitigation strategies • Could be improved further by linking to relevant activities

■ Green   ▢ Amber-Green   ▨ Amber-Red   ■ Red

Approving District Success Plans in Delaware

Shortly after winning their grant in the first round of RTT, leaders at the Delaware Department of Education (DDOE) decided to revamp the state's "LEA [local education agency] Success Planning Tool" to serve as both the LEA Scope of Work for RTT (as required by the federal government) and the main delivery plan for each of its 19 LEAs. They designated the entire first year of the grant period as a time for LEAs to develop these plans.

To facilitate this process, Delaware created an LEA Support Program through which local superintendents and their teams met with state leaders once a month to work on their plans and receive guidance about state expectations. DDOE leaders also adapted the delivery planning rubric for use with LEAs and released guidance to their leaders that included the rubric itself, a planning template, and a sample plan.

In the first half of the year, monthly meetings focused on walking through the elements of the rubric and template, with interactive exercises to help leaders jumpstart the planning process with their teams. Then, in the second half, LEAs submitted the first drafts of their plans. DDOE assembled a team of leaders, including external reviewers from EDI, to review each plan and assign it a consensus rating on each element of the rubric. Education Secretary Lillian Lowery delivered the resulting ratings and feedback to each LEA leader in a series of review calls. In many cases, the plans required substantial revision to meet the criteria in the rubric. DDOE would not release subsequent years of RTT funding until state and LEA leaders had come to a consensus that the LEA's plan mapped out a plausible route to achieving their share of the state's goals for student outcomes.

> "The whole process was incredibly time-consuming, but we felt that the most important work we could do was empower the state's districts to fundamentally change student outcomes. Through a mix of support and challenge, we helped them develop plans that seemed both impactful and feasible, and perhaps most importantly, plans that had the buy-in of all major district stakeholders. As we supported districts and held them accountable for implementation in the years to come, it was extremely helpful that they had that foundation of ownership and community buy-in for their plans."
>
> —Rebecca Taber, Chief Performance Officer and Delivery Leader, Delaware Department of Education

The planning process struck a good balance, avoiding the extremes of a compliance-oriented "checklist" on the one hand and indifference to planning content on the other. The message from DDOE's leaders to their LEAs was this: This is not a question of whether you'll be funded, but of when and how. Through these ongoing feedback conversations, we will work together toward agreement on a plan that maximizes your likelihood of delivering on your goals for student success.

In our work with partners, there are a few planning models we have experienced that have worked. The first, which is closest to the model of the original PMDU, is to provide an up-front introduction to planning, review the rubric and some sample planning products, and give the relevant goal leaders a fixed time period (say, 4–6 weeks) to come up with draft plans. The Delivery Unit and system leader would then review the plan and give feedback for improvement, similar to the Delaware approach above.

There are many advantages to this approach. It avoids both the fact and appearance of micromanagement. It empowers goal leaders and gives them the

Please visit EDI's website at www.deliveryinstitute.org/3 for some examples of sample delivery plans to share in the K–12 and higher education contexts.

flexibility they need to produce plans that they really own. At the same time, it requires some patience. The first drafts of plans that come back will likely fall far short of the mark. Individual strategy leaders may struggle to produce their portions of the plan. Goal leaders who are new at this might not know how to organize their teams to produce what is needed. A system that chooses this path will have to be willing to (1) provide targeted support to individual goal or strategy leaders who need help on an as-needed basis and (2) use the feedback process to ask for significant revisions, not giving approval until the plan meets certain criteria.

A second approach is more hands-on: have the Delivery Unit facilitate a series of working sessions with goal teams, for the purpose of both giving them guidance on planning and stepping them through the actual work (see Figure 3.8 for a sample schedule of working sessions). Sometimes, the Delivery Unit will "pilot" this process with a team that is strong and likely to succeed, as a way of encouraging other teams and giving them a role model for the work. The K–12 systems in both Massachusetts and Kentucky have adopted versions of this approach, even going so far as to script out the specific types of workshops that they hold with each goal team.

Figure 3.8   Sample Schedule for the Creation of a Delivery Plan

Topic	Date	Time
Expectations Meeting	Wednesday, January 6th	1 hour
Delivery Workshop	Tuesday, January 12th	2 hours
Prioritize Strategies/ Intro to Trajectories	Wednesday, January 20th	4 hours
Delivery Plans	Wednesday, March 8th	2 hours
Trajectory Working Sessions	Tuesday, February 28th Wednesday, March 1st Wednesday, March 8th Thursday, March 9th	Teams to sign up for 2-hour blocks
Trajectory Review	Wednesday, March 22nd	4 hours
Delivery Chains	Wednesday, April 13th	3 hours
Draft Delivery Plan Due	Wednesday, April 20th	COB
Provide Feedback on Delivery Plan	Wednesday, April 27th	COB
Stocktake Prep	TBD	TBD
Final Delivery Plan Due to Commissioner	Wednesday, May 16th	COB
Stocktake	Week of May 22nd	TBD

The advantages of this approach are that they help provide the necessary support all along the way. They may also result in plans being produced more quickly. The tradeoff is that goal and strategy leaders might feel less of a sense of ownership of their plans. Less flexibility will mean that some take the exercise less seriously, as something to be complied with rather than a tool for unleashing their potential.

Finally, in some extreme cases, the Delivery Unit might take a heavy hand in working directly with a goal leader and their team to write a plan. A system should only take this step if they're dealing with a low-capacity team who can't be replaced; in particular, the approach may be beneficial if other teams are in need of an example that will help them write their plans independently.

Planning Templates: Yes or No?

A perennial debate in delivery circles is around whether a Delivery Unit should provide a template for a delivery plan to goal leaders. The original PMDU deliberately did not do this, fearing that it would make planning into a micromanaged, compliance-driven exercise.

This is generally our starting point as well, which is why a planning template is conspicuously absent from the tools in this book and on our website. However, many of our partner systems have asked for them, and in many cases, we've obliged. Sometimes, this is because the template is for local leaders outside the system office to do planning: if the system is unable to provide direct support to each of these leaders, the template provides some additional guidance on what to do. At other times, we do it at the request of goal leaders who are overburdened and want one less thing to worry about as they do their plans.

When we do provide a template, we always make sure to accompany it with a version of the rubric and point to it as the real standard of quality. We also try to provide an example of a high-quality plan, preferably from another system or context, to give leaders ideas about what the expectations are. Whatever you choose to do, the principle is what is important: encourage people to think for themselves and to put together plans that will really make a difference in their work rather than simply filling out a form.

In general, goal leaders and their teams must have clear responsibility for writing these plans, while the Delivery Unit's role must be to provide challenge and support. To account for the different scenarios above, the posture that a Delivery Unit takes toward delivery planning should be one that follows the progression of "I do, we do, you do." The eventual desire is for goal and strategy leaders to produce their own plans ("You do"). To the extent that the Delivery Unit needs to role model this work up front ("I do") or do it alongside these teams ("We do"), it should be for the purpose of moving toward that ultimate objective.

⊙ CONCLUSION

The need to plan is intuitive. Yet, in our experience with our partners (and ourselves), we're always inventing new excuses not to do it. This is because getting to a plan that really drives the work—detailed enough but not too "fat"—is really difficult.

This introduction has set out some overall principles that will lay the groundwork for a successful planning effort. In the three chapters that follow, we dig into the core elements of content in a strong delivery plan.

⊙ NOTES

1. Gaiman, N. (2010). *Fragile things: Short fictions and wonders*. New York, NY: HarperCollins.

2. Fullan, M. (2011). "The skinny." Retrieved from http://www.michaelfullan.ca/images/handouts/11_TheSkinny_A4.pdf

Chapter 3A

Determine Your Reform Strategy

 Develop a foundation for delivery

 Understand the delivery challenge

 Plan for delivery

 Drive delivery

 Create an irreversible delivery culture

System Leader Summary

A **strategy** is a deliberate and coordinated set of activities that is designed to help you achieve one or more of your student outcome goals. Together, the strategies you prioritize and implement constitute your overall **reform strategy**.

Your reform strategy is the "what" of your work. For this reason, you're the main person setting direction in this area; in fact, you probably already know the potential strategies that are most important to you. This chapter gives your delivery leader a guide for taking your ideas, prioritizing them, fleshing them out, and getting your team on the same page about what they really mean. As you and your team walk through this process, keep refocusing the conversation on one key question: how will the strategies we're contemplating help us achieve our goals? Be ready to refine your initial ideas—and the details of implementation—so that your reform strategy maximizes its impact on students.

⦿ HOW ARE YOU PLANNING TO DO IT?

The word *strategy* is a freighted term. It is the label for subfields in many disciplines, ranging from business to politics to military campaigns. Much has been studied and written about how to develop and choose your strategy in all these fields, and education is no exception. The last several years have born witness to important debates in higher education and K–12 reform, and both research and experience have identified core topics that are at the heart of the debate today—topics like improving the first-year college experience, implementing college- and career-ready standards, and changing the ways we support and develop educators over the course of their careers.

As we like to say at EDI, these things constitute the "what" of reform. If delivery focuses on the "how," where does a chapter on strategy fit in to this book? We don't hope to improve directly on the strategic thinking that experts across the country already practice. The aim of this chapter is more modest: to ensure that discussions of strategy are rooted in aspirations for student outcomes.

The challenge of strategy is not having one. Most of us are doing *something*. The question is: does it bear any discernible relationship to the result we are trying to achieve? A famous Sidney Harris cartoon from *The New Yorker* illustrates this well.[1]

Source: Cartoon Poster Print by Sidney Harris at the Condé Nast Collection. (n.d.), http://www.condenaststore .com/-sp/I-think-you-should-be-more-explicit-here-in-step-two-Cartoon-Prints_i8562937_.htm

We're a lot like the scientists, but we're less explicit about it: left to our own devices, we too easily fall in love with whatever we're currently doing, to the point where we forget to consider that the results (or lack thereof) may warrant a different course of action. If we drew it, the blackboard describing our strategies might look like this:

- Step 1: Do the things we're already doing, the way we've always done them.
- Step 2: Then a miracle occurs . . .
- Step 3: Students will learn!

Our key challenge is to ensure that every choice of strategy justifies itself, first and foremost, regarding its impact on our goals. If an aspiration is your answer to the first delivery question—"What are you trying to do?"—then a strategy is your most direct answer to the second—"How are you planning to do it?" The delivery approach may not dictate every aspect of your strategy, but it should be skeptical of strategies that can't articulate this linkage between inputs and outcomes.

⊙ CORE PRINCIPLES

A strategy is a deliberate and coordinated set of activities that is designed to help you achieve one or more of your student outcome goals. Together, the strategies you prioritize and implement constitute your overall reform strategy.

A strategy impacts your goal by bringing about some kind of *change* in the way that your system does business. This is an important point: sometimes leaders we work with confuse strategies with existing activities in their systems. "Classroom teaching" and "student advising" are not strategies, for example— but initiatives intended to change the way teachers teach or advisors advise would be.

This isn't to say that ongoing activities don't help students learn; of course they do (and to prove this, imagine what would happen to student learning if classroom teaching or student advising *stopped*). But because they already exist, there's little reason to believe that continuing them and doing nothing else will cause results to *improve further*.

Strategies do have an important relationship to these ongoing activities, however, because more often than not, strategies work through them. Specifically, a strategy can be designed to:

- **Add** a new activity (e.g., establishing a P-20 student longitudinal data system);
- **Improve** an existing activity (e.g., scaling up a successful freshman academy program); or
- **Remove** an existing activity (e.g., eliminating multiple planning requirements for school districts and/or campuses).

In Chapter 2B, we took an inventory of all the current activities you're doing that could potentially impact performance against our goals. Our evaluation of these activities is the starting point for deciding what you need to add, improve, or remove.

One last point about strategies: they always have a beginning and an end. Specifically, a strategy begins when planning and implementation begin—when one or more people are assigned to lead the effort and to achieve the promised result. A strategy ends when the change it brings about is a part of "business as usual"—that is to say, it's fully incorporated into the system's ongoing and sustainable activities, without extraordinary funding or personnel assigned to it. To give a prominent example from K–12, Common Core implementation is not a never-ending strategy; it ends when preparation, training, and support systems all reflect the expectations of the new standards as a matter of course rather than as a result of some special effort. This may take a long while, but it's still a finite amount of time.

Defining this endpoint is important, because it's the equivalent of setting a deadline for the success of your strategy. We've worked with leaders in the past who have insisted that a strategy they are undertaking is "perpetual." This blurs the line between a strategy and an ongoing activity, and it removes the discipline to accomplish certain things by a certain date. The endpoint is a major part of defining what success looks like (a topic we take up in the next part of this chapter). No strategy should be without one.

As noted in the introduction to this part of the book, a delivery plan can be anchored on a goal—including several strategies aimed at achieving it—or it can be anchored on one strategy and its impact on one or more goals. Either way, it's no understatement to say that a strategy is the fundamental building block of a delivery plan.

A Research-Based Strategy: the University of Hawai'i's "15 to Finish" Campaign

As part of its college completion agenda, leaders at the University of Hawai'i system decided to undertake a strategy aimed at improving first-year retention and ultimately graduation rates. Research indicated that one of the key determining factors in first-year retention was whether or not the student took at least 15 credits per semester. At the same time, they found that only one third of incoming students enrolled with 15 credits, and interviews with students and parents revealed that they thought 12 credits was the "normal" amount—even though 15 are required to graduate on time.

Thus, the University System began a campaign aimed to increase the number of students taking 15 credits per semester; aptly, they called this campaign "15 to Finish." The University System created radio and TV advertisements, placed ads in student newspapers, and created YouTube videos to spread the message to students and parents. They also worked with advisors to ensure there was a focus on 15 credits during orientation, during advising sessions, and in degree maps.

In its first year of implementation, the University of Hawai'i witnessed dramatic results: the percentage of incoming freshmen at the University's four-year campuses taking 15 or more credits rose from 36.4% to 52.8% in 2014. The percentage of freshmen in the community colleges taking 15 or more credits almost doubled from 7.5% to 11.4% in the same period.[2]

Now that you know what a strategy is, how do you develop one? There are three steps:

1. Define potential strategies;

2. Prioritize and refine strategies; and

3. Build out strategies.

Define Potential Strategies

When we first started doing this work with systems, we tried to keep this step simple by having leaders brainstorm ideas for strategies and then go straight to prioritization. In some cases—where most or all the strategies were already well understood by the group—this worked well enough. But in many groups, we encountered the same challenge: people didn't have a shared understanding of what each idea for a strategy really *meant*. This generated a great deal of frustration, because people talked past each other in discussions about prioritization.

This challenge reflects a broader truth that we've encountered before: the mere label of a strategy, like "teacher evaluation" or "credit recovery," doesn't give us enough information to evaluate and prioritize it. In many cases, having a robust conversation about priorities requires that we ask a few more questions about each strategy to define it better.

There's a fine line to walk here. On the one hand, you don't want to prioritize strategies without knowing what they really mean. But on the other hand, you don't want to create a full-blown plan for every potential strategy, only to discard half or more of them after prioritization. With this in mind, we developed a tool called the **strategy profile**. Like the activity profile that we introduced in Chapter 2B, it's a short list of essential questions that help you characterize a strategy for the purposes of delivery planning (see Figure 3A.1).

Answering these questions will actually last us through this and the next two chapters. The first six are relatively quick to answer, and they provide just enough information about each strategy to allow us to compare, contrast, and prioritize among them. We suggest that anyone proposing an idea for a strategy must be able to articulate answers to these questions before their idea can be seriously considered.

Figure 3A.1   The Strategy Profile

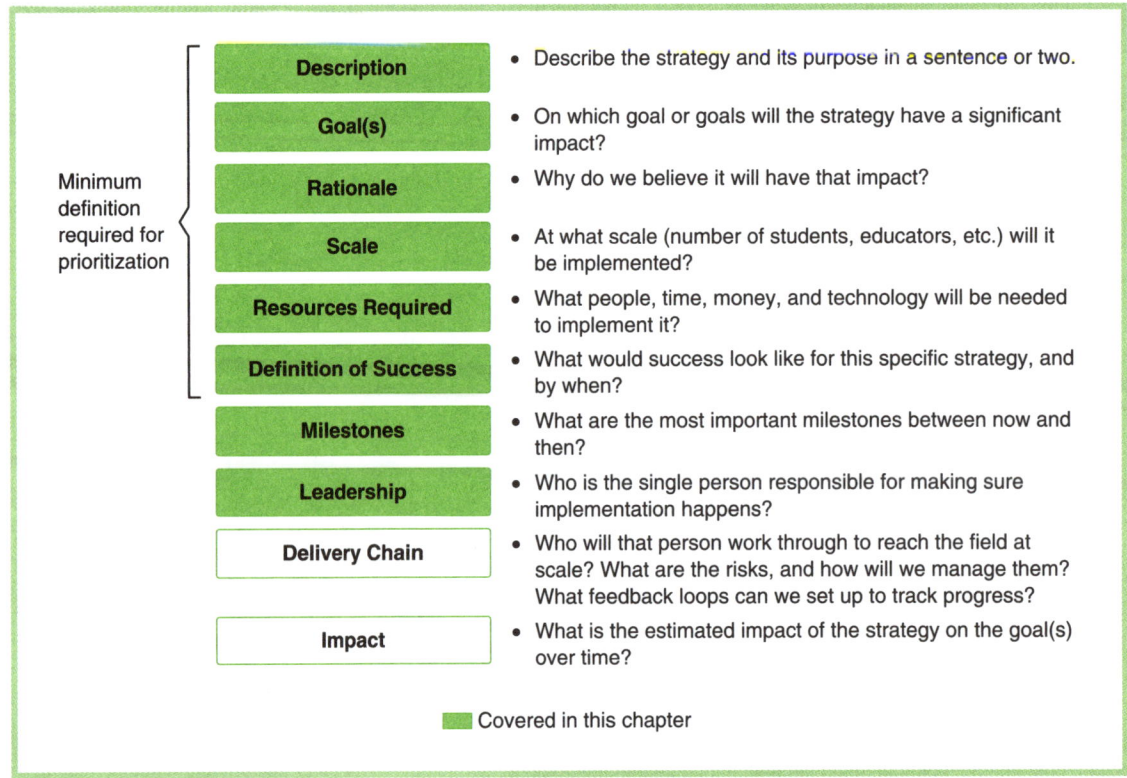

Description	• Describe the strategy and its purpose in a sentence or two.
Goal(s)	• On which goal or goals will the strategy have a significant impact?
Rationale	• Why do we believe it will have that impact?
Scale	• At what scale (number of students, educators, etc.) will it be implemented?
Resources Required	• What people, time, money, and technology will be needed to implement it?
Definition of Success	• What would success look like for this specific strategy, and by when?
Milestones	• What are the most important milestones between now and then?
Leadership	• Who is the single person responsible for making sure implementation happens?
Delivery Chain	• Who will that person work through to reach the field at scale? What are the risks, and how will we manage them? What feedback loops can we set up to track progress?
Impact	• What is the estimated impact of the strategy on the goal(s) over time?

Minimum definition required for prioritization — Description through Definition of Success

■ Covered in this chapter

1. **Description:** Can we describe the strategy and its purpose in a sentence or two? This can be more difficult than it seems, but it forces proponents of an idea to summarize it clearly. For example: one of the Delaware Department of Education's first Race to the Top projects was a data coach program, which provided data coaches to local schools to improve professional collaboration and use of data.

2. **Goal(s):** Which goal or goals will the strategy have a significant impact on? Again, it's important that you be able to define at least one. If there are too many goals related to this strategy, prioritize them with one more question: which goal or goals are *most directly* impacted by this strategy? For example, data coaches will ultimately impact student proficiency and graduation rates, but their most proximate impact will be on educator effectiveness.

3. **Rationale:** Why do we believe that the strategy will have that kind of impact on the goal(s)? However self-evident this may seem, it's important to spell out in clear terms. Is it a proven or promising practice inside your system or outside it? If not, can you tell a plausible story about why it is likely to work anyway? In the case of Delaware's data coaches, this was a relatively new idea, but the story was plausible: providing coaches will increase educator skill in using data to make instructional decisions, which will improve educator effectiveness.

4. **Scale:** At what scale will the strategy be implemented? Will it target your entire system, or just a part? For those targeted, what fraction will

actually be impacted? It's helpful to measure scale by number of students, where possible—for example, to say that a strategy to increase reading proficiency is intended for a state's 10 largest school districts, which contain 40% of the total students. This is the real sniff test for the seriousness of a strategy, which is why the question sometimes makes us uncomfortable. In Delaware's case, the data coaches were to be universally deployed across all school districts.

5. **Resources required:** What people, time, money, and technology will be necessary to implement the strategy? Keep scale in mind here.

6. **Definition of success:** With all this in mind, what would success look like for this specific strategy, and by when? This is the "endpoint" we referenced earlier. How will you know that the strategy worked as intended? You could do this by tracking the movement of the goal or goals defined above, but these are often difficult to attribute to one specific strategy (for more on this, see Chapter 3C on targets and trajectories). Therefore, it's helpful to focus on one or two measures of success that are specific to the strategy itself. These measures may have some overlap with the leading/interim indicators you defined in Chapter 2A. Or they may be drawn from your implementation milestones or delivery chain (more on that later in this and the next chapter). In our Delaware example, you might know you're successful when teachers across the state are consistently using data the way the coaches taught them to (without requiring additional support from those coaches).

We believe these questions strike a good balance between too much detail and too little, but how you approach this issue will depend on your context. Some groups of leaders will understand their strategies well enough to discuss prioritization with minimal extra effort; other groups may require even more detail than the questions provide. The point is to make sure that everyone has a shared understanding of all the potential strategies on the table, what they really entail, and their connection to your student outcome goals.

> Please visit EDI's website at www.deliveryinstitute.org/3A for an exercise and template for developing and defining new strategies.

Prioritize and Refine Strategies

We almost never have the capacity to take on and implement every good idea we have. Once you've clearly defined your potential strategies, you will need to prioritize the ones where you'll focus your attention. There are two criteria to consider:

1. **Impact:** What's the potential for the strategy to make a positive contribution to achieving one or more of your goals? From the strategy profile, the answer to this question will be based on the goals themselves, the rationale for how the strategy will impact them, and the scale. You should consider the performance patterns and root causes you uncovered in Chapters 2A and 2B; how well does the strategy explicitly address the biggest challenges? The better it does, the bigger impact it's likely to have.

2. **Difficulty:** Given your system's current capacity, how challenging will it be to implement this strategy and achieve the potential impact? From the strategy profile, the answer to this question will depend on your resource requirements—both human and financial—including the likelihood that the strategy will get the support from stakeholders that you need.

You can plot your strategies on a simple matrix to get a sense of where they fall with respect to these criteria (see Figure 3A.2).

The point of this exercise is not to concentrate only on high-impact, low-difficulty strategies. In fact, most of the partners we work with have trouble identifying very many of these. One definition of a "no-brainer," after all, is that someone has already thought of it—and in many systems, most of the easy things have already been done.

In fact, other than the low-impact and high-difficulty strategies (the ones to avoid), there are legitimate reasons to adopt items in any quadrant of this matrix. Low-impact, low-difficulty strategies may be important quick wins to generate momentum, while high-impact, high-difficulty strategies may be challenging but necessary "big ideas" to move your system forward. Use the matrix to select a balanced and coherent set of strategies that are collectively likely to deliver on your goal (or goals) for students.

Figure 3A.3 gives an example of one such matrix from the Colorado State University System with respect to its goal for improving graduation rates.

As you narrow down your list of potential strategies, you'll want to shift your focus to seeing how those strategies fit together and form a coherent whole.

First, consider the sequencing and interdependencies among the strategies. Do the ones you've selected fit together into a time line that makes sense? Where

Figure 3A.2   Prioritization Matrix

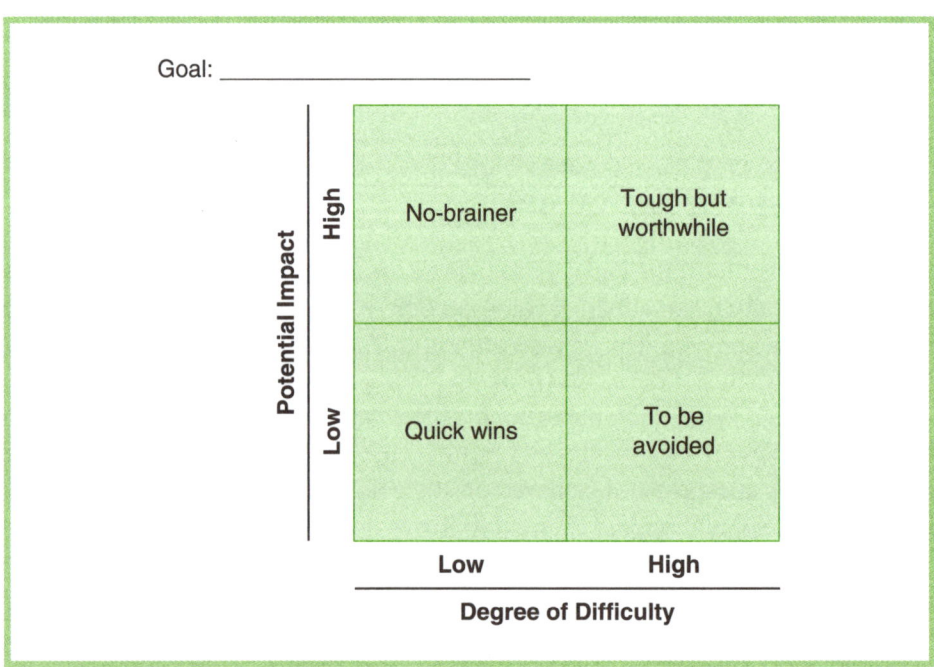

Figure 3A.3   Possible Initiatives by Estimated Difficulty and Impact

	Low	Moderate	High
High	• 30 first-year credits, including math/comp requirements	• Academic support coordinators	• Active and experiential learning • Reconfigure math series • Increase success in high-risk courses • Simplify structure of curriculum requirements • Promote understanding of • Science of Learning
Moderate	• Benchmark courses and capacity • Early graded feedback in 100-level courses	• Attendance in 100-level courses • Expand learning communities model → • Connect risk factors to support structures • Develop "early-start" model • Regular update of four-year plans	• Increase faculty mentoring • Faculty involvement in 100/200 courses → • Departmental engagement in curriculum redesign
Low	• Change of major implications • Analysis • Graduation orientation	• Three-year path to graduation • Intentional use of workstudy (numbers) → • Expand bridge strategies (scale) →	• Evaluate policy on major GPA

(Vertical axis: Estimated Impact — High, Moderate, Low)
(Horizontal axis: Estimated Difficulty — Low, Moderate, High)

are the dependencies, and does your time line account for this? Are there any missing pieces? Unnecessary pieces? Can you frontload "quick wins" to build momentum for more difficult things later?

Second, consider the **theory of action** behind your selection of strategies. A theory of action is a theme or set of themes that serve as overall guiderails for the set of strategies that you adopt. There's no standard way to express a theory of action—it varies by context—but there are common elements:

- **If-then statements:** These are the statements that establish the direct connection between the work you are choosing to do and the goals you seek. They help you establish the content of your strategies. At a micro level, there is an if-then statement in each strategy you have defined thus far: your rationale. At the macro level, you need to decide if there are any broad themes you would like to use to decide which strategies to adopt. For example, one strand of prevailing wisdom in higher education is that students don't make it to graduation because they have too many choices and too many paths they can take to failure. The theory of action follows: we must choose strategies that focus on narrowing the number of choices students have.

- **Governing principles:** If-then statements form the *what* of your theory of action; governing principles furnish the *how*. How do we believe our system is most effective at creating impact? What assumptions do we hold that tell us what *kind* of work we should and should not do? For example, most of our higher education partners at the system level believe they are most effective when they work alongside campus leaders to change faculty and staff behavior. Therefore, they have an implicit theory of action that they will prioritize strategies that rely heavily on engaging campus leaders. (An alternative theory of action would be to say, "We can't get traction with campus leaders, so we will focus only on things that are within our authority as a system office.") Our friends at the Massachusetts Department of Elementary and Secondary Education (ESE) rely, in part, on the idea of comparative advantage: even if we undertake this strategy, and what we produce is good, are we confident that it will be better than what's already being done out there, so much so that educators will gravitate toward it? ESE only adopts strategies where they're likely to be better at doing the work than anyone else.

The theory of action will be more important in some systems than in others. Some systems like to have one in place before they ever consider strategies; others like to build one and use it to evaluate the strategies they already have; others like to simply choose the strategies that have the most potential impact and be done with it. If you have or need to develop a theory of action, it becomes an important criterion for prioritizing which strategies are ideal for your system to adopt. Or, in some cases, it leads you to change something about how you intend those strategies to work.

Creating a Theory of Action With the Council of Chief State School Officers

In 2013, EDI supported the Council of Chief State School Officers (CCSSO) through a strategic planning process to guide their work through 2017. One of the first discussions that we had was fundamental: what will the architecture of the plan be? What are the overall goals, how do they relate to one another, and how do the strategies relate to those goals?

After much discussion and deliberation, CCSSO captured its overall architecture in the graphic in Figure 3A.4.

"Our theory of action enables CCSSO staff to readily see their contribution to CCSSO's goals and aspiration. Assigning goal and strategy leads to the work, then being able to refer to the relationship between the goals and the aspiration, has made accountability much crisper in our organization."

—Melissa Johnston,
Deputy Executive Director and
Delivery Leader, CCSSO

The Council adopted an overarching student outcome aspiration, represented by the top stair on the right hand side. To reach that aspiration, the Council identified five goals to work on. Four of them, in the middle of the diagram, are about influencing state policy and practice to implement key reforms, while the other one, on the left, is about improving the Council's organizational effectiveness to do this work.

This architecture of goals forms a theory of action for CCSSO: if we build an effective organization that provides strong services to states, then states will engage in high-quality implementation of critical reforms—and if they do that, then more students will graduate from high school prepared for college and the workplace.

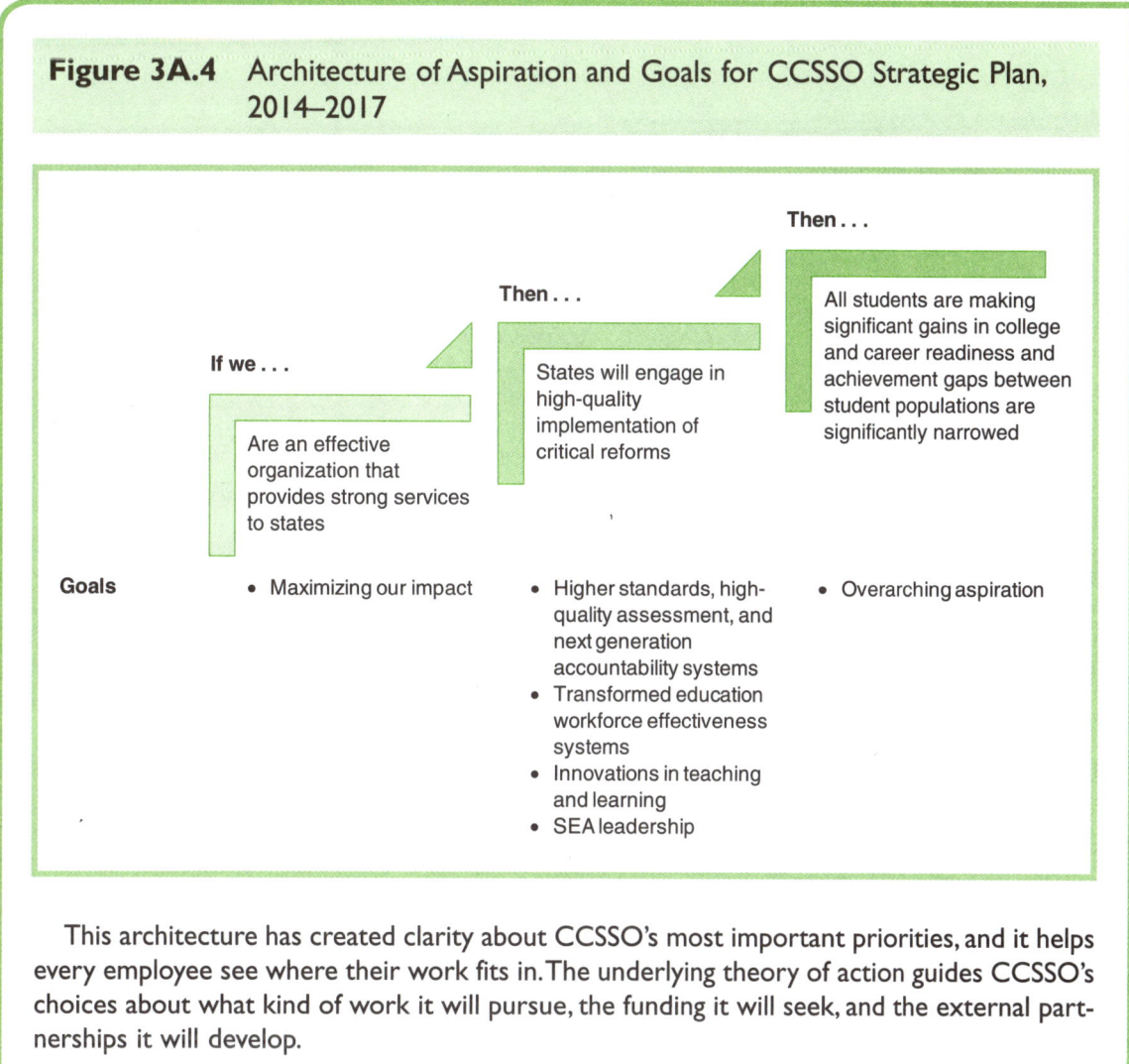

Figure 3A.4 Architecture of Aspiration and Goals for CCSSO Strategic Plan, 2014–2017

Then . . .

All students are making significant gains in college and career readiness and achievement gaps between student populations are significantly narrowed

Then . . .

States will engage in high-quality implementation of critical reforms

If we . . .

Are an effective organization that provides strong services to states

Goals

- Maximizing our impact

- Higher standards, high-quality assessment, and next generation accountability systems
- Transformed education workforce effectiveness systems
- Innovations in teaching and learning
- SEA leadership

- Overarching aspiration

This architecture has created clarity about CCSSO's most important priorities, and it helps every employee see where their work fits in. The underlying theory of action guides CCSSO's choices about what kind of work it will pursue, the funding it will seek, and the external partnerships it will develop.

Build Out Strategies

Once you've selected your high-priority strategies, you can invest the time and energy to flesh them out using the remaining questions in the strategy profile (see Figure 3A.5).

First, you should consider the key **milestones** for each strategy. If your definition of success is the endpoint, your milestones are your markers on the road to get there. What are the most important things that need to happen between now and the end date you've defined for the strategy?

> Please visit EDI's website at www.deliveryinstitute.org/3A for an exercise on prioritizing your strategies.

The definition of a milestone can be slippery; it's not quite an outcome, so what separates it from a task or an action step? Our guiding principle is that a milestone should be an *accomplishment* that demonstrates that the strategy is on track—the launch of a program, rollout to additional schools or campuses, training of key personnel, and other big events during the time line.

This is why we recommend that you choose five or fewer milestones for each strategy—not because five is a magic number, but because it forces you to focus

Figure 3A.5   The Strategy Profile

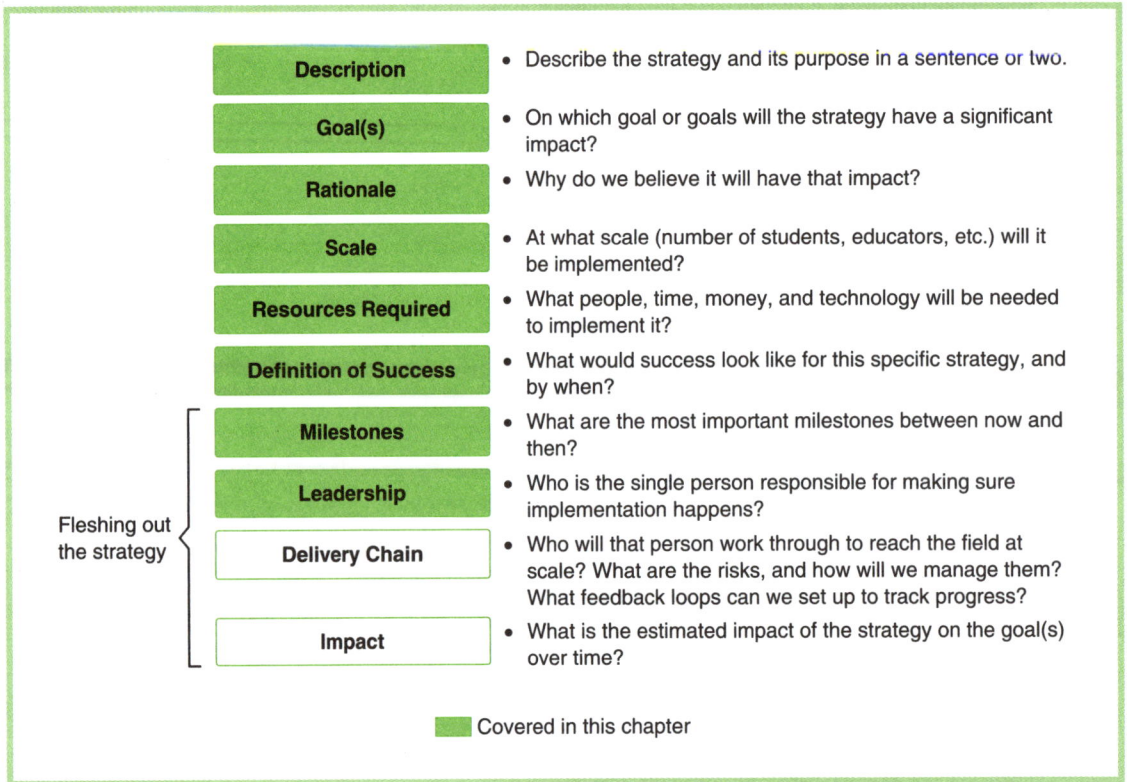

on the most important ones. Too many more than that, and you risk falling into the map-maker's dilemma, plotting out every step in a way that micromanages the work and limits your ability to adapt to changing circumstances.

We wouldn't be surprised if your five milestones are weighted toward moments that occur earlier in the time line. We can see the near future more clearly, and we need more specific guidance about what to do in that time frame. As we look further into the future, the view becomes more blurry—but that's all right, because you've also defined a clear end point. In their landmark management book *Switch*, Dan and Chip Heath talk about the power of combining this kind of long-term thinking—a "destination postcard" for the future—with short-term guidance on how to get started:

> You have to back up your destination postcard with a [short-term] behavioral script . . . What you don't need to do is anticipate every turn in the road between today and the destination. It's not that plotting the whole journey is undesirable; it's that it's impossible . . . When you're at the beginning, don't obsess about the middle, because the middle is going to look different once you get there. Just look for a strong beginning and a strong ending and get moving.[3]

Second, you should consider the strategy's **leadership**. Just as each goal should have a single responsible leader, so too should each strategy. Who will have sleepless nights worrying about making sure that the strategy is implemented successfully? As with goal leaders, the position or title of the person assigned matters far less than their individual capacity and determination to own the strategy and see it through. And as with a goal leader, the strategy leader is almost never the person doing all the work; rather, they are responsible for coordinating everyone else to get it done.

The last two questions in the strategy profile—**delivery chains** and **impact**—complete the process of fully fleshing out and defining a strategy. We cover each of them in more detail in Chapters 3B and 3C.

There are many different questions you could answer to characterize a strategy, but we've come to believe that these are the most important. In a world of limited capacity, they may be the only questions you have time to answer. But we don't think it's possible to get people on the same page about what they're actually doing with anything less than this.

⊙ LESSONS FROM THE FIELD

Work With What You Inherit

We have yet to work in a system where the list of potential strategies started as a blank slate; most systems have a number of strategic efforts already under way. In these cases, it makes sense to start with an inventory of existing strategies and add any new potential strategies you think may be missing. Then you can subject both the old and the new to the steps in this chapter. At times, leaders we work with have found that some of their longest-standing strategies were some of their most poorly defined. In other cases, they have found that some of their strategies did not stand up to the scrutiny of the most important question: the connection between the strategy and the system's goals. The strategy profile can be used both to generate new strategies and to evaluate existing ones.

At the same time, many education leaders find themselves with less freedom of action to choose their strategies than they might like. It might be because they already made decisions in the past or because they've inherited commitments from previous leaders, like the agenda of a governor or a legislature or commitments made to the U.S. Department of Education. Again, the situation may be different but the solution is the same: strategies are not finally defined by their labels, but by the way in which you design and implement them to achieve your goals. Your challenge is to take the strategies you've inherited and to use the tools in this chapter to ensure that each one will make a significant contribution to your goals for student achievement.

When Some Things Are Priorities, Others Aren't

Prioritization implies both high-priority and low-priority items. We've given some guidance on how to move forward with the former, but what do you do with the latter? It depends on what kind of low priority you are dealing with.

The easiest case is a low-priority potential strategy. Once you've identified it as a low priority, all you need to do is choose not to adopt it. The more difficult items are things you're already doing that need to be deprioritized in some way. This is much harder than it sounds. One leader we worked with in the Massachusetts Department of Elementary and Secondary Education started off his delivery planning by pledging to use "selective neglect" to draw resources away from low-priority items. After a few months of struggling to do this, the effort had become so frustrating that he renamed it "the myth of selective neglect."

Part of the challenge is that we don't know what we're allowed to discontinue. Every bureaucracy is required to do some things as a matter of law or policy—and it can be difficult to disentangle real mandates from mere traditions. One K–12 leadership team mobilized their people to solve this problem; they asked each person to make a list of all the things they do, and then they asked them to answer two questions for each item on the list:

1. Does it contribute to our student outcome goals (and if so, how)?

2. If it's a required activity, can you cite the statute or policy that requires it?

If an item didn't have a positive, substantive answer to either question, the team could consider discarding it with confidence.

Sometimes, knowing what to deprioritize is the most difficult part. But even when we have this knowledge, a powerful psychology of pride and self-consistency, one that equates "stopping something" with "failing," causes us to balk at a reduction in our own workloads. Across an organization, strategies develop constituencies among those who implement them—people who believe, rightly or wrongly, that their identities are bound up with the current work.

There are no easy answers to this problem, but one important thing to remember is that you aren't limited to just two options—"continue" and "stop." It's also possible to devote *fewer resources* to something without ending it entirely, to *delay* its implementation, or to *delegate* it to others in your organization who have more slack capacity. Any of these options requires a deliberate conversation by leaders and their teams—because without a collective decision and a clear message from the top, few individuals will feel empowered to deprioritize anything.

One last category to keep in mind is that of the ongoing activities we mentioned earlier. Almost nobody in a system gets to spend 100% of their time on "strategic" work. Even the most senior leaders have ongoing efforts to maintain, like certain public data reports or facilities management or transportation operations. Where does this work fit in, leaders ask us, if we can't connect it to one of the organization's big goals for students?

The short answer is that it doesn't necessarily fit in. If the elimination of an ongoing activity would have no negative impact on your student outcomes, you really should consider eliminating it (unless it's required by law). However, many activities are connected to student outcomes, just in a more indirect way. Again, the same test applies: if we eliminated transportation programs for students, would it worsen their results? How about food service on campus? These things aren't strategies that will show up in a delivery plan, but they're necessary to success nonetheless. If the strategies are the pillars of reform, these ongoing activities are the foundation. In recognition of this, one of our partners, the Hawai'i Department of Education, extended both delivery planning and routines to their operational divisions: facilities, fiscal services, IT, and human resources. This validates the work of these divisions and pushes them to connect it to the broader academic goals the department has set.

This approach carries some risks—most notably, the risk that you'll dilute the focus on your highest-priority strategies. Alternatively, you can acknowledge these activities in a space that's separate from your delivery planning. Because they're ongoing activities, you're not using them to bring about a change in outcomes; rather, you should focus on maintaining a certain level of service so that your other strategies can work. It may make sense to choose a series of indicators of the quality of each of these activities (e.g., meals served, number of facilities that pass inspection) and to set service level targets for each of these to monitor performance. Setting up and monitoring these kinds of targets is beyond the scope of this book, but many of the principles here—from data analysis to planning to monitoring—can be applied in this area if necessary.

◉ KEY CONSIDERATIONS FOR SYSTEM LEADERS AND STAFF

If you're a **system leader** or **system staff**, then you're in the driver's seat here. You will inevitably implement *some* kind of strategy, and your team can help you develop and lead it. But the hard work will be in leading that team through the above discussions and consistently refocusing the conversation on that key question: how will the strategies we're contemplating help us achieve our goals for students? No other question is more important for choosing your course of action.

At the same time, **delivery leaders** don't have an entirely passive role. Your job is to consistently ask the questions in this chapter and to apply them to the major strategies and operations of your system until you have confidence that they will make an impact on your goals for students. If the work under way already has a strong connection to the goals, then your primary task is to use the delivery planning process to ensure that this work is sufficiently captured on paper. If the connection is weak, then you may need to work with system leaders and staff to facilitate the conversations laid out in this chapter, using the exercises and prompts to help them articulate high-impact strategies that will make a difference for students. In this as in many other areas, your role is to let leaders lead but provide a backstop to ensure that they're set up to deliver on their aspirations.

◉ CONCLUSION

As we said at the beginning of this chapter, delivery tends to focus on the "how" of implementation rather than the "what" of strategy. But, as we have shown, we can't ignore this topic, because the choice and design of a strategy can make or break the success of implementation. While the delivery approach will not provide every tool for choosing a course of action—we aren't researchers, policy experts, or advocates—it will insist on holding these choices to the same simple standard that's at the heart of the methodology: the impact on students.

Your strategies are the building block of your delivery plans. In the next chapter, we flesh them out even further using a critical tool: the delivery chain.

⊙ NOTES

1. Harris, S. (n.d.). "I think you should be more explicit here in step two." [Cartoon Poster Print at the Condé Nast Collection]. Retrieved from http://www.condenaststore.com/-sp/I-think-you-should-be-more-explicit-here-in-step-two-Cartoon-Prints_18562937_.htm

2. Hawai'i Graduation Initiative. (n.d.). *15 to finish*. Retrieved from http://www.hawaii.edu/hawaiigradinitiative/15-to-finish/

3. Heath, C., & Heath, D. (2010). *Switch: How to change things when change is hard* (p. 93). New York, NY: Broadway Books.

Chapter 3B

Draw the Delivery Chain

 Create an irreversible delivery culture

System Leader Summary

The **delivery chain** is the set of actors (people or organizations), and the relationships between them, through which a given strategy in your delivery plan will be implemented. The tools in this chapter will help you answer the question at the heart of the delivery chain: starting with your strategic intent and ending with changes in practice at the front line, how—and through whom—does your strategy actually happen?

Drawing the delivery chain is critical to delivery planning: it lays out your assumptions about how each strategy will impact the field at scale, it helps you probe those assumptions for risks and weaknesses, and it allows you to test them regularly through the development of feedback loops about implementation. A strategy isn't really fully defined until you're able to specify its delivery chain; without one, it will be hard to know whether implementation is happening as planned. Impress this on your team and insist that they prioritize this work as part of their planning.

⊙ THE PROBLEM OF SCALE

Of all the tools we've used in our work with education leaders, few have been embraced as universally as the delivery chain. Even those who may not be sold on the entire delivery approach tend to believe in the importance of drawing the chain. One reason for this is that the chain is a ubiquitous and versatile tool in the discipline of delivery, having multiple uses ranging from planning to diagnosing and solving problems with implementation. If you're a leader struggling to deliver results for students, the delivery chain is more likely to be an immediate remedy for what ails you than many of the other practices in this book.

In the end, however, the delivery chain has proven so powerful because it gets to the heart of a challenge that most of us have experienced: the problem of scale.

In the previous chapter, you spent some time selecting the strategies you believe will make a significant impact on your student outcome goals. As you implement these strategies, your core challenge will not be getting them to work: invariably, in a large-enough system, a well-designed strategy will work *somewhere*. The bar is higher than that: your burden is to ensure that your strategy works *everywhere*.

Consider the size of the system you help lead. As of this writing, the University of Wisconsin System, a mid-sized higher education system, made up of 13 research and comprehensive campuses, 13 freshman-sophomore campuses, and a statewide UW-Extension with over 6,000 faculty.[1] The Kentucky Department of Education, a mid-sized K–12 system, has 174 school districts, 1,233 schools, and over 40,000 teachers. By contrast, the senior leaders, goal leaders and teams, and Delivery Units in these systems rarely add up to more than two dozen people. Every time you articulate a strategy and put it in a delivery plan, you are making the rather audacious claim that your small team in the system office can lead a change in behavior of hundreds or thousands of people throughout your state. In Michael Fullan's words, "For organizational or systemic change, you actually have to motivate hordes of people to do something"—and do it well.[2] This is the problem of scale.

In education, it has been fashionable to point to a different challenge: the problem of local control. Leaders at the state level see a field with university presidents or chancellors who have their own sources of influence and district superintendents who are hired by locally elected school boards. At the same time, district and campus leaders have a similar complaint: they have far less leverage over their principals, deans, or department chairs than they'd like to have.

While a dearth of formal authority is a hindrance, we don't believe it's the ultimate problem. To see this, consider the opposite: would absolute authority solve the problem? It might help, but it wouldn't be enough. As the English king Charles I, an "absolute" monarch who was beheaded by his own people, lamented shortly before his death, "There's more to doing than bidding it be done."[3]

And that's the rub: formal authority will *never* bring about transformational change on its own. The problem of scale asserts itself here: in a large-enough system, the "hordes" of people you need to motivate will find informal ways to undermine or circumvent your authority if they're so inclined. An old

Chinese proverb summarizes a point of view that's always available to the front line, no matter how powerful you are: "The mountains are high, and the Emperor is far away."

For this reason, it's influence *without* authority—persuading, equipping, training, and communicating—that makes the difference between a strategic reform at scale and a few random acts of improvement. An education leader's lack of formal authority merely paints this problem in sharper relief than usual.

The delivery chain is powerful because it addresses the problem of scale head-on. It provides a framework for laying out and describing who will need to do what in order to implement a strategy system-wide, for identifying the skills and motivation that each person will need to play their role, and for exercising every lever of influence available to you to make sure that this happens. In short, there must be some kind of delivery chain if there is to be delivery. If you can't specify it, nothing will happen.

⊙ CORE PRINCIPLES

The delivery chain helps you define your strategy more clearly, uncover potential risks, and create feedback loops that will make monitoring easier. We go through each of these steps below.

Define the Delivery Chain

A delivery chain answers one question: starting with the intentions of leaders at the system level and ending with the front-line behaviors and practices that you seek to change, how—and through whom—will a strategy actually get implemented? The delivery chain is the through-line that allows your strategy to reach the field at the necessary scale.

To do this, a delivery chain defines four things for any given strategy:

- The **levels** of your system: what are the layers between you and your students? These form the overall framework for your delivery chain. Some typical examples are given in Figure 3B.1.
- The **actors**—people or organizations—who have a role in implementing the strategy at each of these levels, and the number of each (e.g., 12 department chairs, 50 principals).
- The **role** that each actor plays in implementing the strategy, and what this implies about their **relationship** to other actors. Who will do what? How will that impact others? In doing this, it's important to specify the **beginning** and the **end** of the chain: who leads and initiates at the system level, and where will the ultimate change be felt at the front line? The end of the chain almost always centers on what students will experience differently.
- The **most direct line** of influence between the beginning and the end of the chain. This is a judgment call, but most delivery chains start with a certain amount of complexity. What is the most important set of **links** between you and the change you wish to see at the front line?

Figure 3B.1   Typical Levels of Implementation in Education Systems

K–12 Systems	Higher Education Systems
• State agency • Other state organizations (policy-makers, third-party organizations, etc.) • Region (names vary by state) • District/local education agency (including charter school authorizers or management organizations) • School • Classroom • Public (e.g., parents)	• System • Other state (policy-makers, third-party organizations, etc.) • Campus • School/college • Department • Public

There are several approaches to actually drawing the chain. Sometimes, we'll ask teams to brainstorm all the actors on cards and post them to a wall that has the levels drawn on it. Then we'll discuss how they relate to one another, rearranging the cards accordingly until we emerge with a clear picture. At other times, we find it helpful to begin with the end in mind, starting at the end of the chain with a clear picture of the "definition of success" the team created for the strategy as a whole: what will students experience differently if we're successful with this strategy? Then we work backwards from there: *who* will give the students that experience and how? What will *they* need in order to do that, and who will give it to them? And so on until you've reached the beginning of the chain.

A few examples will illustrate how this works. The first is given in Figure 3B.2.

Figure 3B.2   Delivery Chain for Aligning Teacher Certification With Common Core

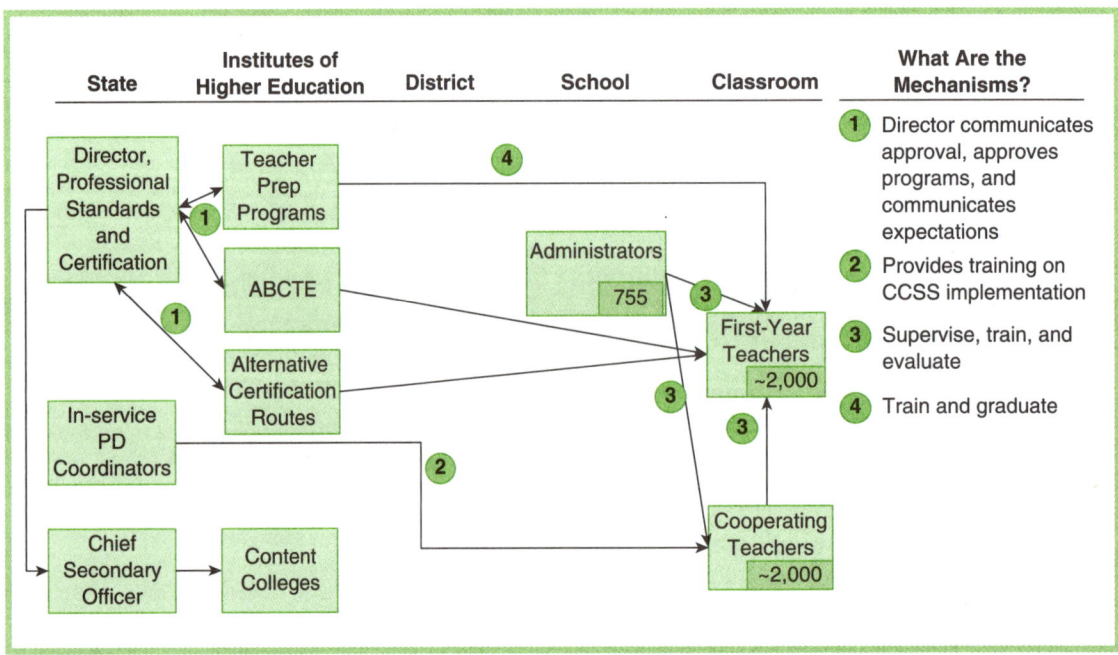

This is one of several delivery chains that a team developed for Common Core State Standards (CCSS) implementation; in this case, the focus is on aligning preservice teacher training and first-year in-service professional development and evaluation with the expectations of the new standards. All the above elements are illustrated here: the levels of the system include the state, district, school, classroom, and institutes of higher education that train teachers; a small group of actors on the left side of the diagram must exercise influence over a combined 4,000 first-year teachers and cooperating teachers that aid in their supervision; and the numbered circles illustrate the links in the chain.

The picture is fairly straightforward: the state's director of professional standards and certification uses her power of program approval to influence the content of teacher preparation programs and alternative certification programs that graduate first-year teachers. The director also works with in-service PD coordinators at the state department of education to equip and train cooperating teachers to reinforce this content in their supervision, evaluation, observation, and mentoring of first-year teachers.

The second example, in Figure 3B.3, comes from the University of Hawai'i System and its "15 to Finish" campaign, which we profiled in the previous chapter.

This delivery chain is a bit different, since it relies on multiple channels to reinforce the same desired behavior in students: enrolling in 15 or more credits per semester. But the same elements are visible: the actors involved in white boxes, the roles they play in green boxes, and a clear articulation of the many levers used to influence students. To take a few examples: the most direct "traditional" route is through the system Provost, who works with Vice Chancellors of Academic Affairs on the system's four campuses to promote "15 to Finish" through the advisors and faculty that interact most frequently with students. This work is reinforced in many other aspects of student life: through the Student Affairs office, which offers student incentives; through campus chancellors, who receive incentives to promote on-campus employment (which makes it easier for students to take 15 credits), and through the system's many student web portals in the bottom right portion of the chain, which encourage students to enroll in 15 credits even as they are making those decisions online.

> Please visit EDI's website at www.deliveryinstitute.org/3B for an exercise on drawing the delivery chain.

Partners often ask us whether they should draw the "ideal" delivery chain or the delivery chain as it currently exists. The answer, we've found, is that the distinction matters less than you think. In general, you should draw the delivery chain as you hope for it to work, keeping in mind the constraints and realities that you face in your system. The result will usually be something that does not look "ideal" but which may require some incremental changes to put into place. This can be the baseline for the conversations that follow about how to reach the field at scale.

Delivery chains have several uses in delivery planning, but first and foremost, they help you develop and pressure-test your highest-priority strategies. In the previous chapter, we noted that labels tell us little about what a strategy actually means. We introduced the strategy profile as a way of solving this problem (see Figure 3B.4).

Figure 3B.3 Hawai'i Graduation Initiative: "15 to Finish" Delivery Chain

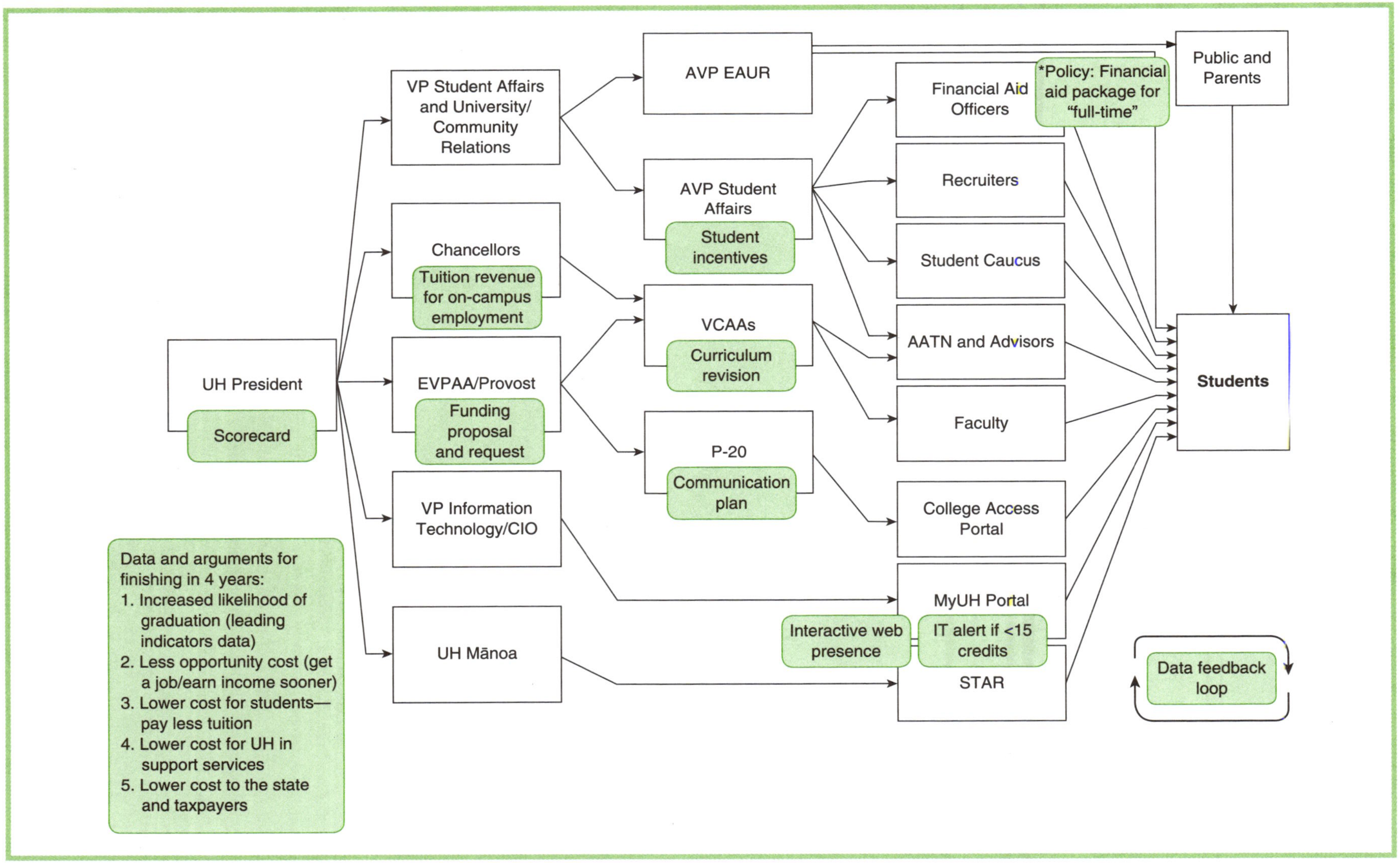

Data and arguments for finishing in 4 years:
1. Increased likelihood of graduation (leading indicators data)
2. Less opportunity cost (get a job/earn income sooner)
3. Lower cost for students—pay less tuition
4. Lower cost for UH in support services
5. Lower cost to the state and taxpayers

Figure 3B.4 The Strategy Profile

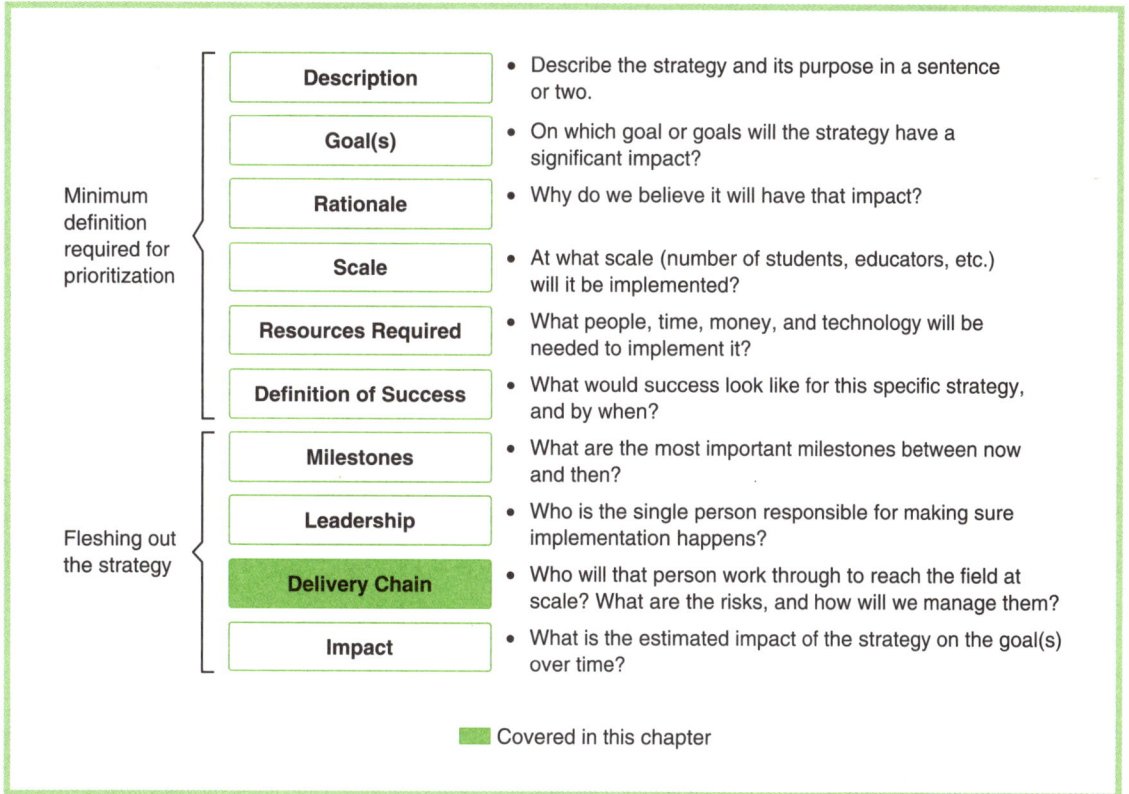

The first few questions are designed to give just enough information to allow you to prioritize your strategies. But once you've narrowed your focus, drawing the delivery chain is a critical step in laying out how each prioritized strategy will actually work in practice.

Consider the two previous examples. The labels "Aligning Teacher Certification with CCSS" and "15 to Finish" tell us something, but not much, about what these strategies actually mean. Answering the questions from the previous chapter—about each strategy's goals, rationale, definition of success, scale, and resources required—would give us a good start. But real delivery planning requires that we go further. How will a given strategy actually be implemented on the scale that we envision?

The delivery chain helps us answer this question. From looking at these two examples, we know that the team plans to issue guidance that teacher preparation programs are to use to bring their programs into alignment with CCSS. We know that the same team will develop aligned guidance for in-service PD coordinators. We know that we're relying on these two entities to reach educators in the field through training and supervision. By contrast, we know that the "15 to Finish" campaign is much more diffuse, relying on multiple actors throughout the system to reinforce the same message and behaviors. These are not extraneous details; they get to the heart of how a strategy is intended to work. Drawing the delivery chain isn't an exercise in addition to planning; it *is* the planning itself.

Identify Risks and Weaknesses

Once you've used the delivery chain to flesh out a strategy, you can use it to pressure-test and strengthen that strategy. In essence, a delivery chain is a series of assumptions about how implementation will work. These assumptions can and should be tested. The examples above raise several questions: Will the state's PD coordinators be able to reach 2,000 cooperating teachers? How will they do this? Is the "power of program approval" a strong-enough lever to ensure that teacher preparation programs change what they do? In Hawai'i, what will motivate faculty and advisors to play the roles we need them to play vis-à-vis their students? How will we ensure that the many actors involved don't work at cross-purposes from one another?

All these are examples of **risks and potential weaknesses** in the two strategies. By laying bare the assumptions of implementation, the delivery chain provides a map you can use to pinpoint where those assumptions are most likely to break down. Specifically, it's helpful to consider five things:

- **Individual links:** What is the quality of each critical relationship between the actors in the delivery chain? Which are the strongest links, and which are the weakest ones? This includes a consideration of both formal authority and informal influence.
- **Capacity:** How confident are we that each key actor has the necessary skill and will to play the role we envision? Are we doing enough to build that capacity?
- **Complexity:** How many actors are involved in the delivery chain? How easy or difficult is it to coordinate those actors to get something done? Is the chain unnecessarily complex?
- **Funding flows:** What are the major sources of funding and resources? Who controls those flows, and in which direction(s) do they go? Are they aligned with the flows of influence envisioned in the delivery chain?
- **Choke points:** Are there particular actors that you disproportionately depend on to get something done? What is the risk that they will be overburdened or not up to the task?

Identifying these kinds of risks is an important part of any planning exercise, but don't fall into the trap of just "admiring the problem." The whole point of identifying risks and weaknesses is to identify solutions to them. This may mean changing your emphasis to shore up certain relationships along the delivery chain, reconfiguring incentives or resources, or even redesigning parts of the delivery chain itself. Either way, any discussion of risks must include a discussion of how you will address them.

Develop Feedback Loops

Analyzing the risks and potential weaknesses in the delivery chain is a way of testing the assumptions of implementation in theory. **Feedback loops** allow you to test those assumptions in practice by regularly checking to see if the delivery chain is playing out as you thought it would. A feedback loop is a body of evidence that you commit to collecting to know whether your strategy is on track to deliver its promised results or if challenges exist that require more attention. Your starting point for thinking about this is the definition of success you created for each strategy in the last chapter: what evidence would help you measure that success? Feedback loops also allow you to measure the intermediate steps toward that definition of success (the progress metrics and process metrics we introduced in Chapter 2A)—and as such, they're particularly useful for helping you make mid-course corrections during implementation.

A delivery chain is the natural starting point for developing feedback loops because, as with risks and weaknesses, it provides a map from which you can "read" particular areas where you'll want to know more about the quality of implementation. You may choose to develop feedback loops in those areas where the links are weakest and the risks are greatest (in fact, shining a light on the problem using data may be the best risk mitigation tactic you have). Or you might choose to focus on measuring your definition of success, which is usually closer to the end of the chain and involves changes in front-line behavior.

Going back to the teacher certification strategy in our example, you can see how this plays out in Figure 3B.5.

The team has identified the most critical feedback loops they'd like to monitor to ensure that implementation is happening as intended. These range from hard quantitative data (the placement rates of newly certified teachers) to artifacts (aligned curriculum and lesson plans from preparation programs) to feedback from the key actors involved, which could be taken through surveys or spot interviews and visits. The delivery chain for "15 to Finish" provides a similar map for potential feedback loops: things like reports on student perceptions from

Figure 3B.5   Delivery Chain for Aligning Teacher Certification With CCSS

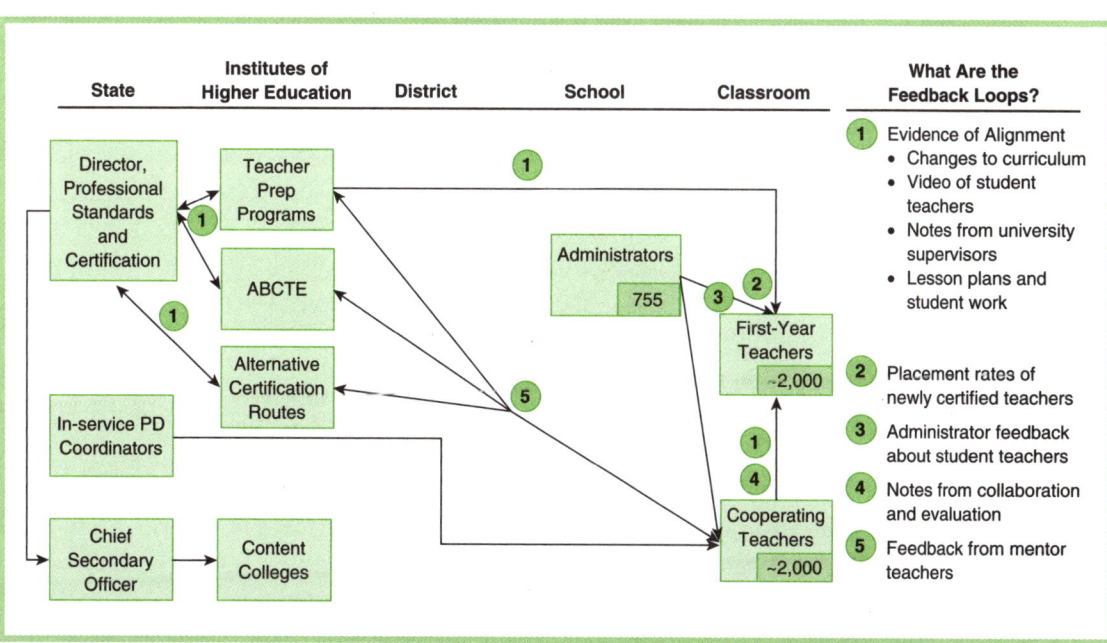

key players (like advisors and faculty), number of page views of "15 to Finish" material on student web portals, and, of course, actual student enrollment data. The delivery chain provides a rich source of vital and actionable information leaders can use to improve the implementation of their strategies.

How do you prioritize which feedback loops to develop? Start by looking at the delivery chain and prioritizing actors to focus on. Which ones are the most critical and/or the most challenging? What does the delivery chain imply about their role and our expectations for them? Then, for each role group, consider what questions you'd want to answer about how implementation is playing out for them. There are six categories to consider for each group:[4]

- **Inputs:** What did they experience? For example, did training take place as planned? Did the cooperating teachers receive the messages we intended for them to receive?
- **Reaction:** Did they like it? For example, how well were trainings and/or other communications received?
- **Learning:** Do they know the role they're expected to play as laid out in the delivery chain? For example, do Hawai'i's advisors now understand how they must advise students differently? Do cooperating teachers understand how their supervision and observation of first-year teachers must change to align with CCSS?
- **Support:** Are they being set up for success to play their role? Do their support and evaluation systems reinforce the expectations we have for them? For example, if we're asking cooperating teachers to supervise first-year teachers differently, have *their* supervisors—the principals in the buildings—been equipped to reinforce this?
- **Fidelity of implementation:** Are they actually changing their practices and playing their role in alignment with our expectations? For example, are we seeing faculty advise students to enroll in 15 or more credits per semester?
- **Outcomes:** Are students learning as a result? Is there evidence that the strategy is making its promised contribution to one or more student outcome goals?

These six types of feedback loops form a spectrum. On one end is evidence that, by itself, is just a series of "process" measures—but it has the advantage of being easier to gather and measure. On the other end is evidence that's much closer to real results for students—but it has the disadvantage of being more infrequently available and sometimes difficult to obtain. We often limit ourselves to these two extremes when we think about evidence of implementation; considering the full spectrum will give you access to a more balanced picture.

These six types of feedback loops will allow you to identify not just where implementation breaks down along the delivery chain but where it breaks down between inputs and outcomes. If we're off track, was it because we didn't do what we said we were going to do? Was it that we did the work, yet it failed to change the behavior of key players? Or did everything happen exactly as we thought it would but without the change in outcomes we expected? The answers to these questions will have important implications for your work: you could decide to amend a strategy or to scrap it altogether depending on where implementation breaks down.

Once you know what questions you want to answer, you'll want to identify the specific sources of evidence to answer each of them. As noted above, this evidence can be quantitative or qualitative, "rigorous" or more impressionistic. In Chapter 2B (page 100), we introduced a simple framework for thinking expansively about the evidence available to you: statistics, artifacts, new collections, and field work. Your feedback loops can draw from any of these categories. For those who want quantitative information, we've had particular success putting together surveys of people in role groups across the delivery chain. The qualitative sources of information—the interviews, the focus groups, the analysis of existing artifacts—will prove useful as a way of spot checking facts on the ground that are important but difficult to measure (such as changes in front-line learning, practice, and fidelity of implementation).

Not every strategy needs a full set of feedback loops. With your limited resources, you may want to do this exercise only for the most critical strategies—or you might find that you can monitor the implementation of several strategies through common sources of evidence.

By embedding feedback loops into the strategies in your delivery plan, you're strengthening those strategies in two ways. First, the availability of the information, and your ability to use it, is itself a form of leverage and influence you'll have over the field. There may be parts of the delivery chain where you have little authority over what a particular group does. But if you can make information available to that group that gives them insight into their own effectiveness (or lack thereof), you'll exercise a persuasive influence with them that can be meaningful. Second, the information from the feedback loops will help you make mid-course corrections and solve problems as they arise—a subject we cover in more detail in Part 4 of this book.

Feedback Loops in Two States

In 2012, leaders at the New York State Education Department (NYSED) decided to make an intensive push to develop feedback loops for their three most important reform strategies, including the Common Core State Standards (CCSS). They started with the delivery chain for CCSS (see Figure 3B.6).

Using this delivery chain, the team developed the questions they wanted to answer about implementation. They divided these questions according to the six categories given above, as well as by the major affected role groups. The team translated the research questions into an item bank of survey questions for educators and administered the surveys in early 2013.

New York's survey results are confidential, but other states have since used this item bank to conduct similar surveys on the quality of implementation of CCSS. Another state conducted a similar comprehensive survey in 2014 and has shared the results more widely.

Figure 3B.7 captures information on an important question: how often are district leaders observing educator practice for alignment with CCSS expectations? The results here indicate a great deal of inconsistency from district to district.

(Continued)

(Continued)

Figure 3B.6   Common Core State Standards Implementation in New York

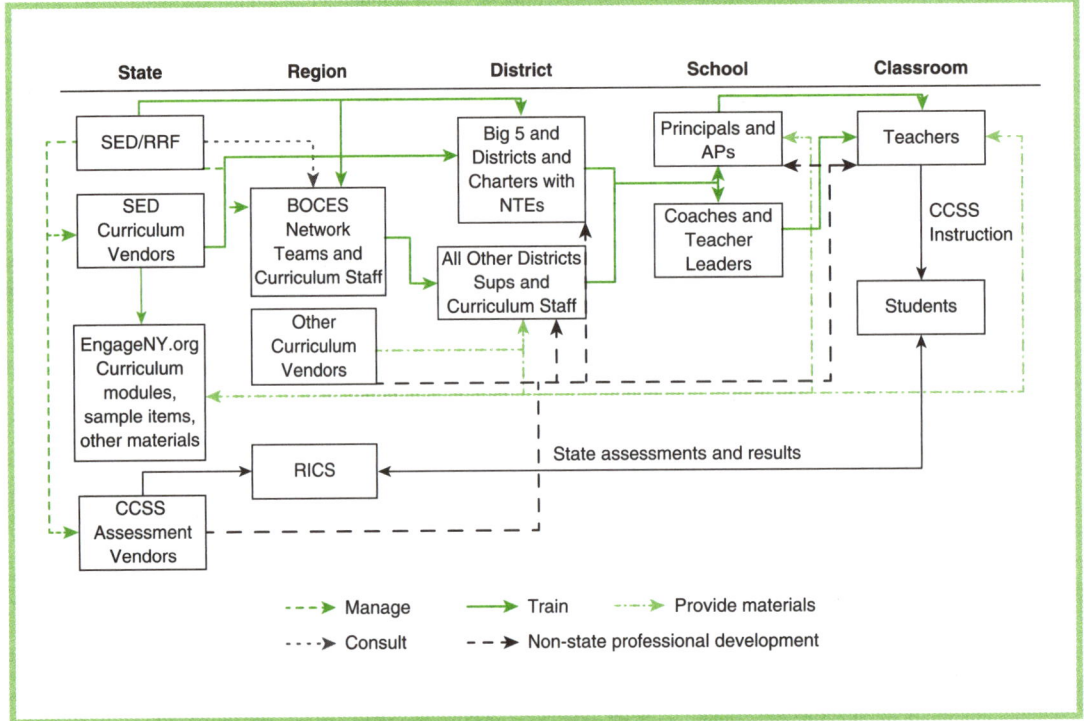

Figure 3B.7   Frequency of Observation of Teacher and Principal Practice for District Leaders

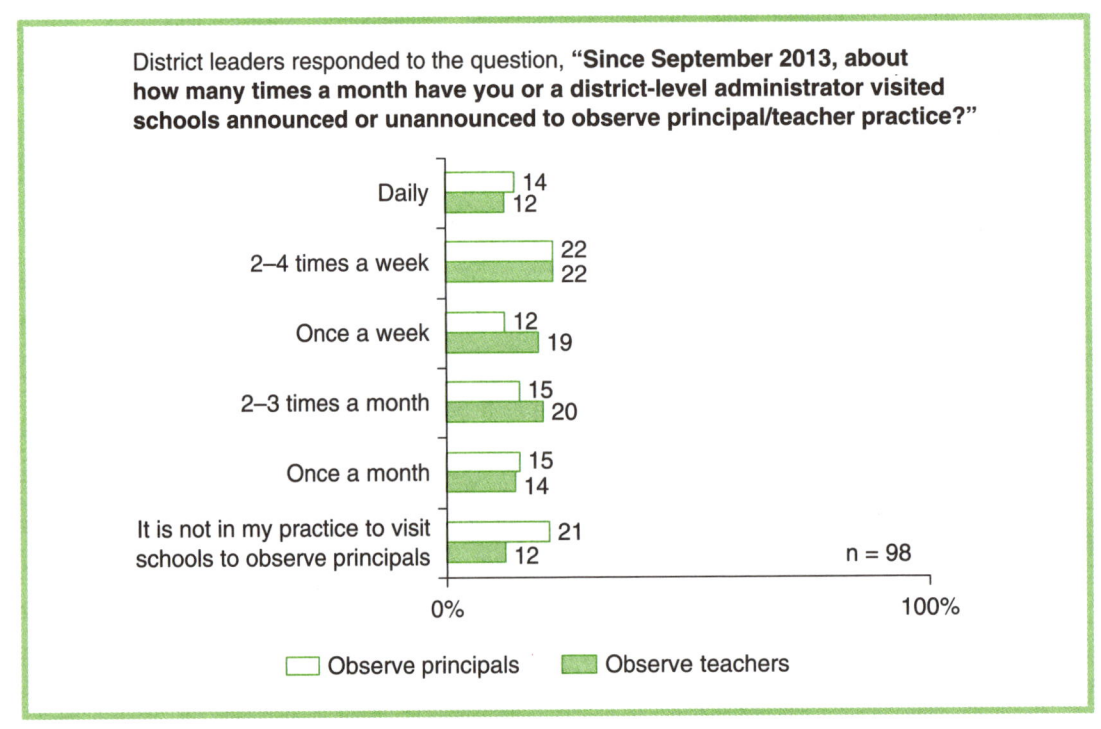

Most importantly, the survey results also helped leaders understand current classroom practice. Figure 3B.8 shows ELA teacher response to a question about what their students do on a day-to-day basis and divides the responses by their relative alignment to the Common Core. As you can see, aligned practices dominate, which is good news, but there may still be too much personal experience in writing assignments for students.

In this state, district-level results were provided to local superintendents as a source of evidence during a self-assessment against a Common Core Implementation Rubric developed by EDI and CCSSO. The exercise was designed to help the state and districts target their efforts to continue to improve implementation of the standards in classrooms.

These surveys have helped several leaders get a real and actionable grasp on how the delivery chains for their large reform initiatives are playing out in practice. The survey questions and underlying research questions can be found at EDI's website, **www.deliveryinstitute.org/3B.**

Figure 3B.8   Frequency of Student Classroom Practices, by Alignment to Common Core

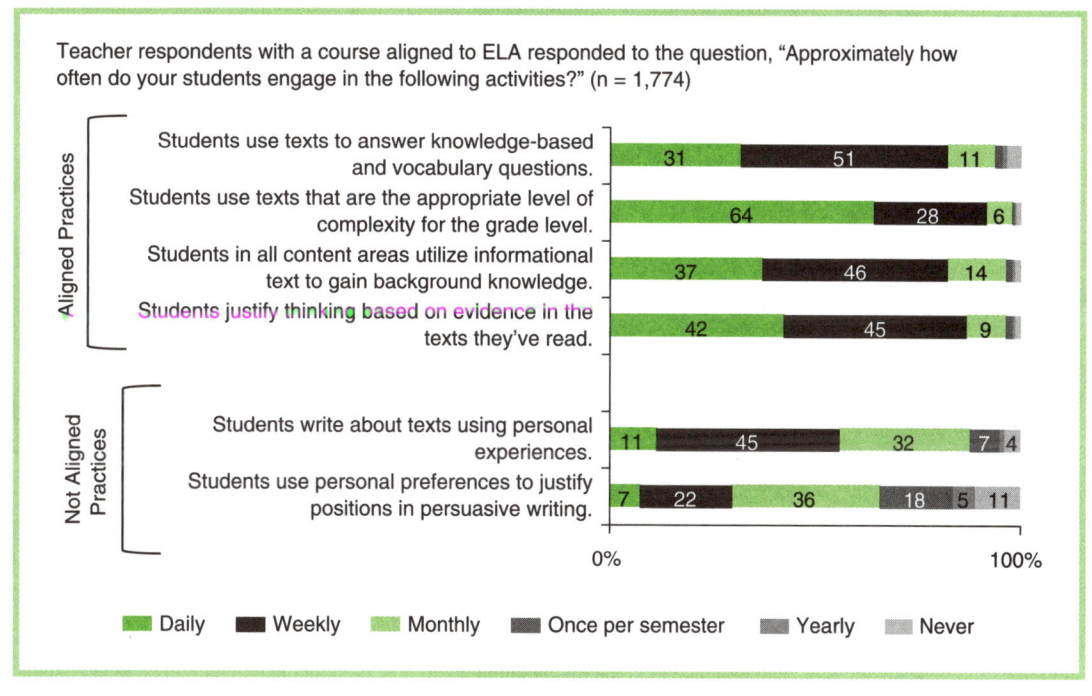

Teacher respondents with a course aligned to ELA responded to the question, "Approximately how often do your students engage in the following activities?" (n = 1,774)

LESSONS FROM THE FIELD

Work Through the Complexity

Despite its general popularity, we have occasionally encountered pushback when we've asked education leaders to draw the delivery chain. The most common objection is that it's a difficult exercise: education systems are complex and diverse entities, and the complicated realities on the ground tend to resist the simplicity of a diagram on a piece of paper. Most systems have multiple variations on the delivery chain, depending on who they are reaching out to: in K–12, the chain looks different for charter schools versus traditional schools, large versus small districts, or even different geographical areas, while in higher education, every campus arguably has significant variations in how (and through whom) things get done, not to mention the difference between 4-year and 2-year institutions. In light of this, some have wondered whether drawing the delivery chain distracts us from the more important work of planning our strategies.

In these conversations, we always return to a point we made earlier: drawing the delivery chain *is* planning your strategy. You really can't separate the two; a strategy without a plan to reach the field at scale is too vague to have a systemic impact. This isn't to downplay the challenge of complexity. But complexity is no reason to give up; rather, it's a sign that there's more work to do. It may be possible to simplify some elements of your delivery chain. If not, the delivery chain at least allows you to deal with that complexity in a comprehensive and rigorous way, accounting for the various paths that implementation can take.

One example of this comes from our partners at the Massachusetts Department of Elementary and Secondary Education (ESE). One of their strategies for improving third-grade literacy was to disseminate improved instructional materials to districts and schools. The Delivery Unit worked with the goal team to construct a delivery chain for this strategy. Figure 3B.9 shows the first draft.

The picture looks convoluted and messy—not unlike the reality it reflects. With some help from the Delivery Unit, the team was able to rationalize the chain and identify the two to three core pathways through which instructional materials would reach classrooms (see Figure 3B.10).

The most dramatic difference here is not that the underlying complexity has been eliminated, but that it has been described more clearly: not only are there multiple pathways to students (through preschool teachers, head start teachers, and PK–3 teachers), but the pathway to PK–3 teachers can run through any number of different roles at the district and school levels, depending on the type of district and type of school. This image allows us to grasp a complete and nonoverlapping list of potential pathways to students, which makes the chain a more useful tool for ensuring that implementation happens.

Use the Chain to Clarify Roles

As we noted above, it's highly unlikely that every delivery chain for every strategy will be unique. Delivery chains for a single system share too many of the same key players—faculty, deans, principals, and teachers, to name a few. For this reason, we've found that it makes sense for teams to look for points of interconnection where multiple strategies might be able to share the same delivery chain. A good example of this is training or communication: if each initiative runs its own training program, or its own communications strategy, each using a different vehicle and all demanding the time of the same people, it can be a recipe for frustration and a loss of credibility. On the other hand, if we pool our efforts to train or communicate across key strategies, we can improve the coherence of our work.

It sometimes helps to look at the delivery chain from a different angle: how will key players at the front line experience these strategies as they are implemented? We discovered the power of this question when we partnered with the Aspen Institute to host a conference for K–12 delivery leaders on teacher and leader effectiveness systems. One of the exercises we developed asked participants to think about this work from the perspective of principals and other school leaders—arguably the most important front-line implementers of the new systems.

We posed five questions for teams to answer about this role group:

- What **responsibilities** do they have in implementation?
- What **capacity** will they need to carry out this responsibility effectively?
- **How** will that capacity be built?
- What is the **LEA's role** in building this capacity?
- What is the **SEA's role** in building this capacity?

The resulting thinking was essentially a close look at one crucial link in the delivery chain—one that provided important insights and implications for how to design that chain (Figure 3B.11).

The exercise unlocked so much new thinking for one state team that they decided to do the same exercise for all their other major strategies—again, with a focus on principals. They compared the results across strategies and altered their overall delivery system to rationalize the state system's interactions with school leaders.

This idea of a **delivery system** is the next logical evolution of the delivery chain. It's useful to develop delivery chains to implement individual strategies, but the exercise often exposes a larger need to rationalize our overall systems of interacting with the front line. As you develop delivery chains, you may find that it makes sense to embark on broader work to develop your overall delivery system for reaching the field at scale. Think of it as building a robust pipeline through which you can deliver multiple strategies at once.

Other Uses of the Delivery Chain

We mentioned at the start of this chapter that the delivery chain is a ubiquitous tool—one that shows up and plays a role in many aspects of the discipline of delivery. As we've shown in this chapter, its most important use is as a tool for planning. But there are several other important areas where the delivery chain can come into play:

- **To pressure-test existing strategies:** As we noted in the previous chapter, most leaders start from a position of inheriting strategies and needing to know what to do with them. Just as the tools in the previous chapter can be applied to evaluate and improve existing strategies, the delivery chain can be used to do the same; simply take the same exercises and apply them to the existing strategy. Your work will either help you diagnose the major implementation challenges in the strategy and address or deprioritize it all togther.

- **To diagnose and solve problems:** We cover this in more detail in Part 4 of this book, but the delivery chain is a useful starting point for problem solving

Figure 3B.9 The Delivery Chain: Before . . .

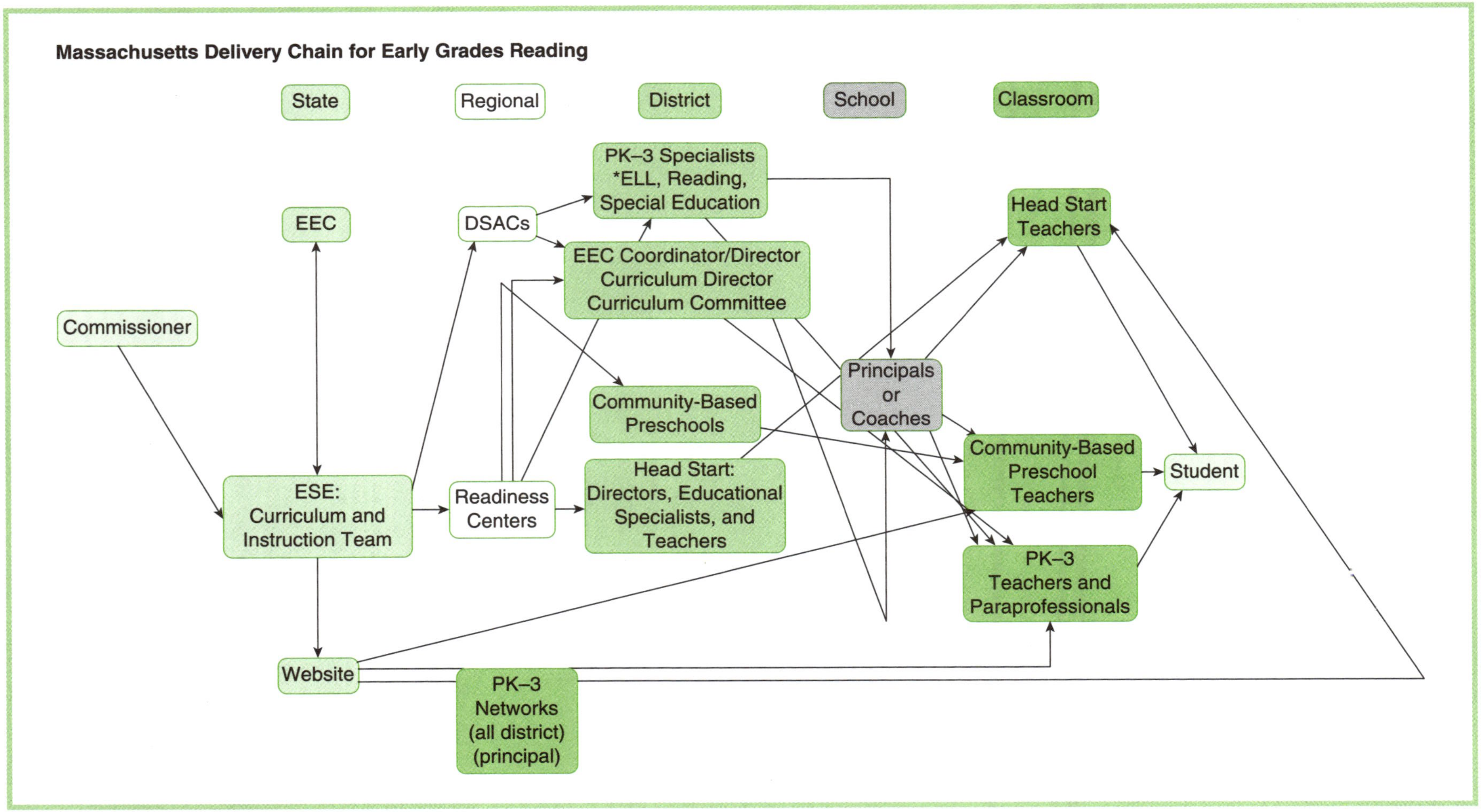

Massachusetts Delivery Chain for Early Grades Reading

Figure 3B.10 ... and After

Massachusetts Delivery Chain for Early Grades Reading

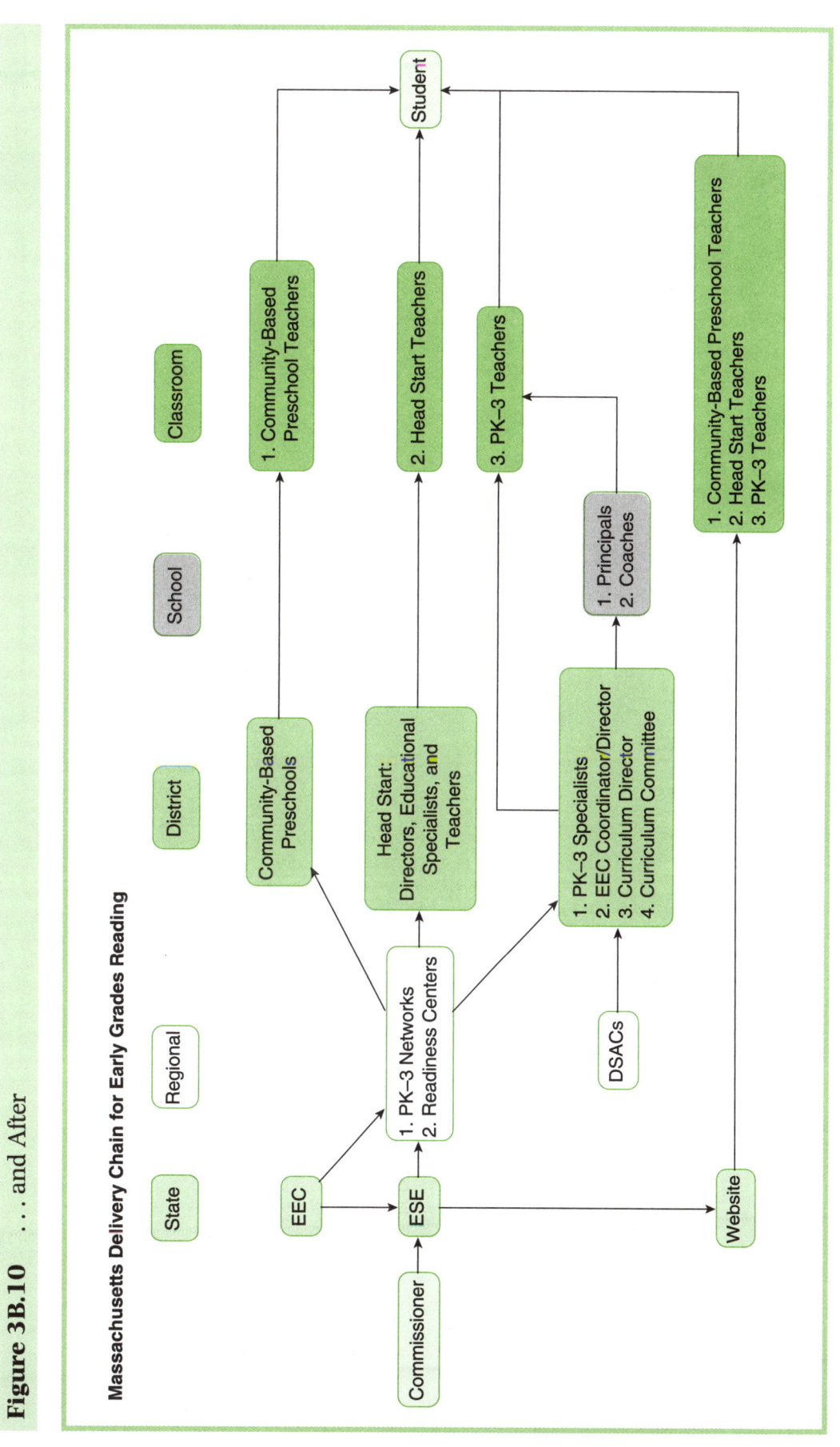

Figure 3B.11 Exercise 1: Identify Capacity Requirements

Job Position	Responsibility	Capacity Needed	How It Will Be Built	LEA Role	SEA Role
Principals	Training school staff (teachers and other evaluators) on their role in the system	Knows and supports local and state system	In-person, hybrid online training	Ongoing training with follow-up	LEAs and state/association to support districts
	Ensure alignment with district and state goals	Communication/interpersonal skills and strategy	Needs assessment; staff feedback	Empower principals to prioritize	Subsidizing vendors—training
		Knows current staff needs and capacity	Empower teachers to take on additional responsibilities	Labor management: getting feasible contracts	Collect/disseminate best practices—how?
	Do a lot of evaluations and observations	Time management skills and strategy/plan	Moving around resources to have additional administrators	Reforming HR systems	Collect/share examples of effective teaching
	Make sense of eval outcomes	Delegating evaluation and other responsibilities		Bringing principals together; working in groups, problem-solve, share best practices	Career ladders
	Identify PD needs effectively	Knowledge of best practices	Knowledge of technology systems in place	Works that into principal eval and coaching	Show them where money goes, relative to others, and give flexibility
	Working with teams and individuals	Data literacy	Ability to ID effective practices		
		Knows teacher performance standards and content skills			
			Evaluator training; ongoing calibration		

160

when a strategy seems to be off track. Just as you can "read" potential risks, weaknesses, and feedback loops off of the delivery chain for a strategy, you can also systematically work through a chain to consider all the possible places where implementation may break down.

- **To identify "bright spots":** A delivery chain is never just one chain; it's hundreds or thousands or even millions of individual chains, each reaching a different student. While the variability between them is a part of the problem of scale, it's also an opportunity that can be turned to your advantage. In any given system, the delivery chain is working well *somewhere*. Can you find the places where it's working? Can you learn lessons from the people in crucial roles who are making it work? Whether to solve a problem or just for general improvement, the delivery chain is a useful place to look for promising practices.

⊙ KEY CONSIDERATIONS FOR SYSTEM LEADERS AND STAFF

The delivery chain keeps us honest about whether our strategies are having an impact where it really matters: at the front line. If we don't use it as a central organizing principle of our planning, we run the risk of having strategies that seem to make sense in the abstract but bear no relationship to what students are actually experiencing.

For this reason, **system leaders and staff** must constantly ask questions that get to the heart of the delivery chain and to ask what's happening on the ground. Using these tools, and your own time, to keep a finger on the pulse of the work in the field will mark you as a different kind of leader. This could mean incorporating more of these questions and evidence into formal discussions of progress (of which we discuss more in Part 4 of this book). It could mean asking your teams to prioritize getting you this information. Or, as one of our colleagues from the United Kingdom taught us, it could mean walking into a local campus bar, striking up a conversation with a group of students, and asking, "What do you feel that the university is doing to help you graduate?" Remember the principle of Genchi Genbutsu: when in doubt, go and see for yourself!

Delivery Unit leaders have a similar responsibility. In addition to facilitating the planning conversations and making sure that goal and strategy leaders have developed robust delivery chains for their work, you'll be the ones connecting the dots between strategies, seeing where delivery chains overlap, and facilitating conversations about the development of common delivery systems for your system's strategies. You'll also be encouraging a culture of getting feedback from the front line, helping system leaders and staff build the habits described above. The delivery chain is also helpful for building trust with others in your system. It's an accessible tool whose usefulness is easy to grasp quickly. For skeptical leaders and teams, it can be your foot in the door for collaboration.

⊙ CONCLUSION

As we said at the outset, the delivery chain is one of the most popular tools we use with education leaders. It's also one of the richest and the most challenging. Leaders who get it right, who insist that we map out how we will reach the field at scale for our major strategies, will reap a dividend both in the effectiveness of their planning and of their monitoring of implementation.

The delivery chain provides the last piece of definition for your reform strategy. With that, there's only one task left to complete your plan: to make the connection between your goals and strategies explicit by setting targets and establishing trajectories.

⊙ NOTES

1. University of Wisconsin System. (2014, November). *Fact book 13-14: A reference guide to University of Wisconsin system statistics and general information.* Retrieved from https://www.wisconsin.edu/publication-resources/download/factbook.pdf

2. Fullan, M. (2011). *The six secrets of change: What the best leaders do to help their organizations survive and thrive.* San Francisco, CA: Jossey-Bass.

3. Barber, M. (2008). *Instruction to deliver: Fighting to transform Britain's public services* (Rev. ed.). London, UK: Methuen.

4. Guskey, T. (2000). *Evaluating professional development.* Thousand Oaks, CA: Corwin.

Chapter 3C

Set Targets and Establish Trajectories

 Develop a foundation for delivery
 Understand the delivery challenge
 Plan for delivery
 Drive delivery

 Create an irreversible delivery culture

System Leader Summary

One of the distinctive parts of the delivery approach is its insistence on drawing a clear connection between outcomes (your goals) and inputs (your strategies). Targets and trajectories make this connection explicit. A **target** translates a goal into a numerical commitment that is SMART—specific, measurable, ambitious, realistic, and time-bound. A **trajectory** is a series of interim targets that plot the planned path of the metric between now and the target date. Targets and trajectories are rooted in evidence that strikes the balance between ambition and realism, including benchmarks of current and past performance and information about the future implementation and impact of each of your strategies.

As the tools in this chapter make clear, trajectory setting is an art, not a science. A trajectory is a hypothesis about what you think will happen—one that enables problem solving and course correction when the actual data come in. As system leader, you'll want to set the right tone around this work, creating a safe space for people to make their best guesses, to be wrong, and to continuously improve.

⊙ **6,900**

In the first chapter of this book, we emphasized the importance of having an aspiration that can be broken down into a handful of goals for student outcomes.

We also said that each of the goals in an aspiration must have a specific, measurable target. If a goal is a call to action, a target with a specific number has an even more powerful effect. When Paul Pastorek began his K–12 reforms in Louisiana, he began with a goal of improving high school graduation state-wide. The target was already fairly specific: the legislature and governor had asked him to increase 4-year graduation rates from 66.6% to 80% in 5 years. But the first step his team took was to make it even more specific: they translated it into the number of additional *students*—6,900, to be exact—who would need to graduate during that period for Louisiana to hit the target.[1]

The number 6,900 made the target real: it showed up posted in office cubicles throughout the state agency, made its way into leadership discussions of progress, and served as a guide for local superintendents, principals, and teachers who knew just how many additional students would need to cross the stage for them to make their contribution to the goal. Where would they find those students?

Most of us have, at some point, been asked to create SMART targets for our schools: targets that are specific, measurable, ambitious, realistic, and time-bound. But experience teaches us that not every target will necessarily have the impact that Louisiana's did. Consider a few examples of target-setting in recent history:

- President John F. Kennedy's call, in 1961, to put a man on the moon by decade's end;
- The national commitment, enshrined in the No Child Left Behind (NCLB) Act of 2001, that every child would be proficient in reading and math by 2014;
- President Barack Obama's promise, in 2009, that "by 2020, America will once again have the highest proportion of college graduates in the world."[2]

On the surface, all these targets seem similar—both in their specificity and their potential to inspire action. But they've achieved different results. On the one hand, Kennedy's promise did result in a man walking on the moon before 1970, and while the jury is still out on Obama's higher education challenge, the early results are a start: the latest report for the 2012 school year shows that the United States has increased its share of degree-attaining adults from 39% to 42%.[3] More important, this target has driven the conversation in state university systems across the country, which are aligning their planning and their work around achieving this goal.

On the other hand, it's past 2014 and we are nowhere near achieving NCLB's target of 100% proficiency for our students; in explicit recognition of this, the U.S. Department of Education has issued waivers to most states allowing them to set new targets.

What separates the success of some targets from the failure of others? While there are many different factors at work, our main argument is this: for a target to fulfill its intended purpose, it must be *grounded in evidence* and *used to check progress*.

Three parts of the SMART framework—specific, measurable, and time-bound—are fairly easy to include in a target. The difficult part of target setting is balancing the tension between ambition and realism. If a target is too ambitious without being realistic, it becomes easy to write off as a meaningless number, like the 100% target in NCLB. And if we cannot be realistic about how difficult a target will be to reach, it may cause us to adopt the wrong strategy.

At the same time, it's also possible for a target to be too realistic. A target of 25% proficiency would have been rightly criticized as well; it wouldn't have spurred the action necessary to confront the challenge at hand.

Consider, by contrast, the use of evidence with our three "successful" targets.

1. Kennedy's moon landing promise was more than mere rhetorical flourish; it was the result of a careful review of American capabilities conducted by then–Vice President Lyndon Johnson, at Kennedy's request. In a memo dated April 28, 1961, Johnson estimated that the country had the capability of landing a man on the moon, in the best-case scenario by 1966 or 1967. Kennedy's ultimate promise added some room for error.[4]

2. With President Obama's higher education challenge, the realism and ambition of the target came from a look at past and present performance. The United States had been number one in college attainment in the past. It had fallen in the rankings—to 3rd place among all adults and 13th place among young adults. But in 11 years, it was plausible to believe that the country could repeat its past history.

3. In Louisiana, leaders initially didn't believe that they could hit the target, but they vowed to try anyway, adopting a combination of strategies designed to achieve the necessary scale and impact. The target thus influenced the planning of the work rather than the other way around.

The range of examples shows that grounding in evidence need not happen at the same level of detail or rigor, or even in the same order, for every target. What's important is that leaders forge a clear and believable link between the work they plan to do and the outcome they hope to achieve.

The tools in this chapter are designed to help you make this connection so that the targets you set for student outcomes—and the trajectories that estimate interim progress along the way—motivate your system to make real and substantial progress toward achieving its goals for students. Much of the evidence you will be relying on is contained in the work you've done thus far: your analysis of past and present performance, the strategies in your delivery plan, and the delivery chains that demonstrate how those strategies will reach the field at scale.

Making these estimates is some of the hardest work we do. The process is more art than science, requiring a willingness to be flexible and to rely on assumptions to fill the gaps between facts. Leaders who set targets and trajectories will also need to balance the substance of their work with the optics of their public commitments.

Nonetheless, by the end of these few pages, we hope to demonstrate that this work is worth doing. Targets and trajectories are the most direct expression of the first principle of delivery: that the work we do must be connected to our goals for student outcomes. By holding us accountable to that principle, they complete our delivery plans and give them ultimate meaning.

⊙ CORE PRINCIPLES

Defining *target* and *trajectory* requires that we define a few other related terms. As we've noted before, we use these terms for the sake of having a common language; more important than the terms themselves is the shared meaning beneath them.

- As defined in Chapter 1A, a **goal** is a part or whole of your system's overall aspiration, one that provides the answer to the first delivery question, "What are you trying to do?" An example would be to "increase student success in postsecondary education."
- As defined in Chapter 2A, a **goal metric** is a specific type of data or measure that you use to measure progress against your goal. For student success, a common metric is the 6-year graduation rate.
- A **target** brings together the first two concepts. Specifically, a target translates a goal into a numerical commitment using the metric for that goal—a commitment that is specific, measurable, ambitious, realistic, and time-bound. For example, we might say that our target for improving student success is to achieve a 60% 6-year graduation rate by the 2016–2017 academic year.
- Finally, a **trajectory** is a series of *interim* targets, set on an annual or more frequent basis, that plot the planned path of the metric between now and the target date. In the case of our 60% target for student success, our primary task will be to estimate how we will progress toward that target from year to year.

Targets and trajectories are really two sides of the same coin: if a trajectory is a series of interim targets, then by the same token a target is the endpoint of a trajectory. To be useful, both must be rooted in evidence that strikes a balance between ambition and realism. And both must answer a fundamental question of delivery: What impact do we expect our strategies to have on the goal metrics over time? This is why the last part of the strategy profile that we began two chapters ago is an estimate of impact for each strategy (see Figure 3C.1).

At the most basic level, targets and trajectories are yardsticks against which we can measure our progress. They force us to clarify and articulate our assumptions about how the work we plan to do will help us achieve our goals so that we may check, when the data comes in, whether those assumptions turned out to be true or not.

Figure 3C.1   The Strategy Profile

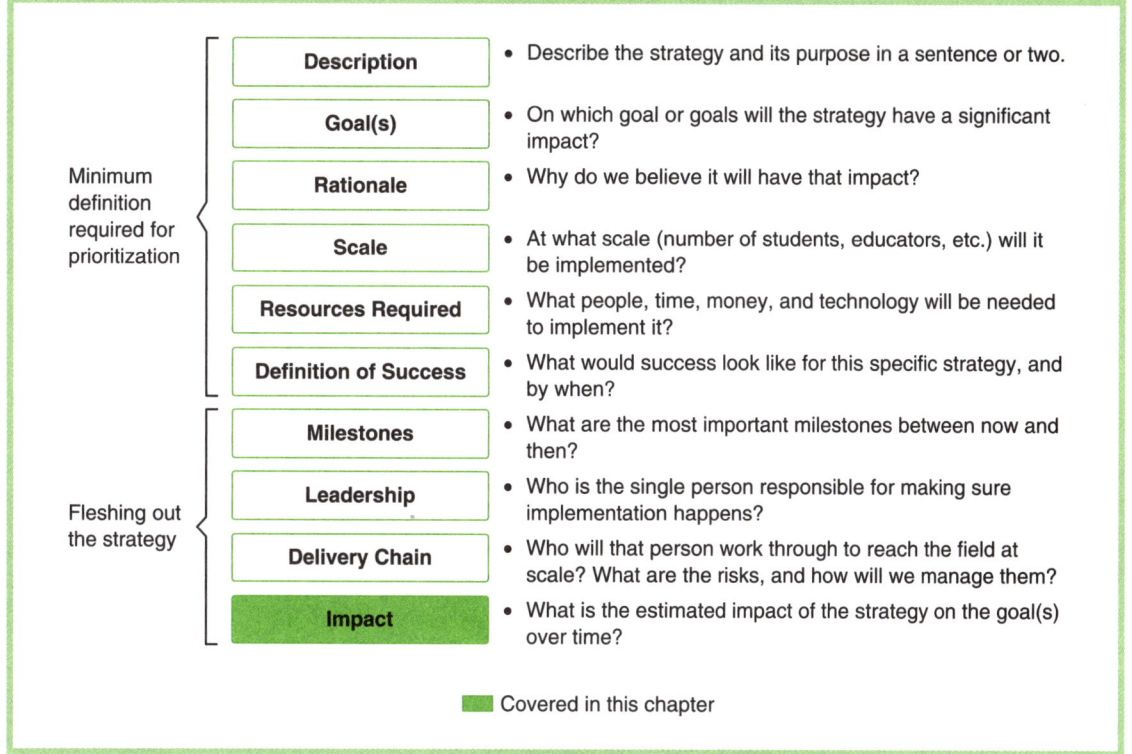

Minimum definition required for prioritization	Description	• Describe the strategy and its purpose in a sentence or two.
	Goal(s)	• On which goal or goals will the strategy have a significant impact?
	Rationale	• Why do we believe it will have that impact?
	Scale	• At what scale (number of students, educators, etc.) will it be implemented?
	Resources Required	• What people, time, money, and technology will be needed to implement it?
	Definition of Success	• What would success look like for this specific strategy, and by when?
Fleshing out the strategy	Milestones	• What are the most important milestones between now and then?
	Leadership	• Who is the single person responsible for making sure implementation happens?
	Delivery Chain	• Who will that person work through to reach the field at scale? What are the risks, and how will we manage them?
	Impact	• What is the estimated impact of the strategy on the goal(s) over time?

▇ Covered in this chapter

In short, targets and trajectories comprise our *hypotheses* about how our delivery plans will impact our goals. Just as we used hypotheses to understand past performance in Part 2 of this book, we can use hypotheses to project future performance as well. Implementation creates an ongoing test of those hypotheses—one that will enable us to see when we're off track to achieving our goals, to identify the underlying challenges and to address them before it's too late.

At the original PMDU, Tony O'Connor, the head of Michael's Operational Research team, distilled the practice of trajectory-setting down to eight questions, given in Figure 3C.2. The remainder of this section addresses how to use these questions to build trajectories for your student outcome goals.[5]

Put the Pieces in Place

The process of setting a target and trajectory begins with making sure the basic ingredients are there. A goal and a metric are the minimum requirements: every goal in your aspiration needs to have at least one metric to measure it. You'll also want to make sure that you know how your goals and metrics relate to the strategies in your delivery plans. This information will come from two places:

1. The work that you did to build an architecture for delivery planning at the beginning of this part of the book. What are your goals, what are your strategies, and how do they connect to each other?

Figure 3C.2 Eight Essential Questions to Consider When Constructing a Trajectory

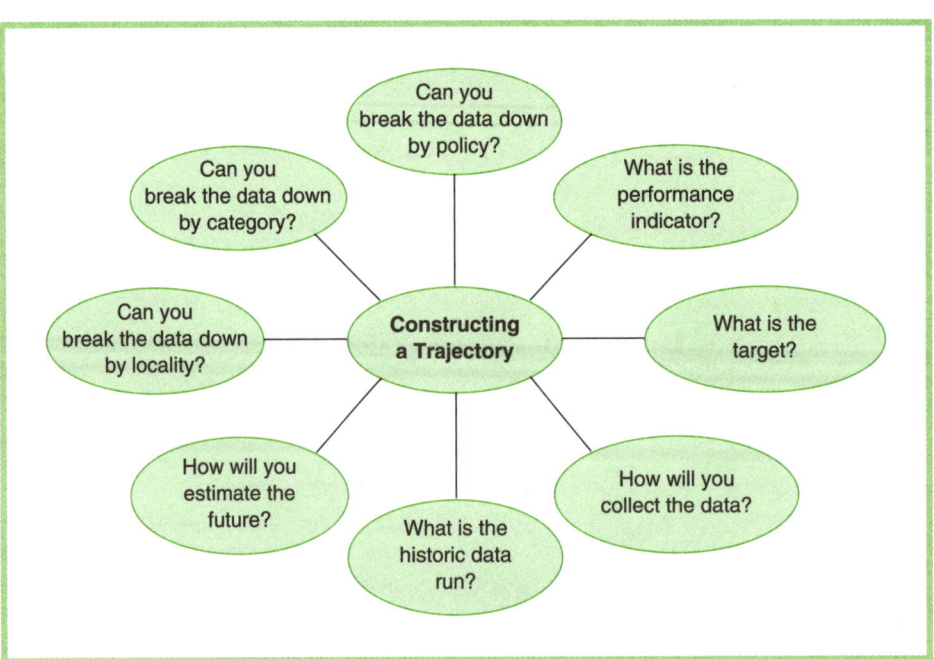

2. The profiles that you built for each high-priority strategy in Chapter 3A. What does each strategy profile say about which goal(s) it will impact?

It may be helpful to construct a simple map to visualize this information, like the one that the Massachusetts K–12 system created near the beginning of its delivery effort (Figure 3C.3).

The goals are coded by color—one in each corner of the diagram. Strategies are matched and connected to these goals by color, with a group of strategies in the middle that are connected to multiple goals.

This kind of overlap is quite common. In fact, you may need to resist the urge to throw up your hands and declare that "everything is connected to everything." In a large and cosmic sense, this is true, of course; it's just not very helpful. To narrow down the possible linkages, consider the question we posed in Chapter 3A: which goal or goals are *most directly* impacted by each strategy?

Please visit EDI's website at www.deliveryinstitute.org/3C for an exercise on establishing your connections between goals and strategies.

Build a Baseline

Once you know the metric for your goal and where it fits in to your delivery planning, you need to establish a **baseline** for that metric. What would happen to this metric if you did nothing between now and your target date? More specifically, what would happen if business continued as usual, without any of your strategies being implemented?

Figure 3C.3   Map of High-Priority Goals and Strategies in Massachusetts

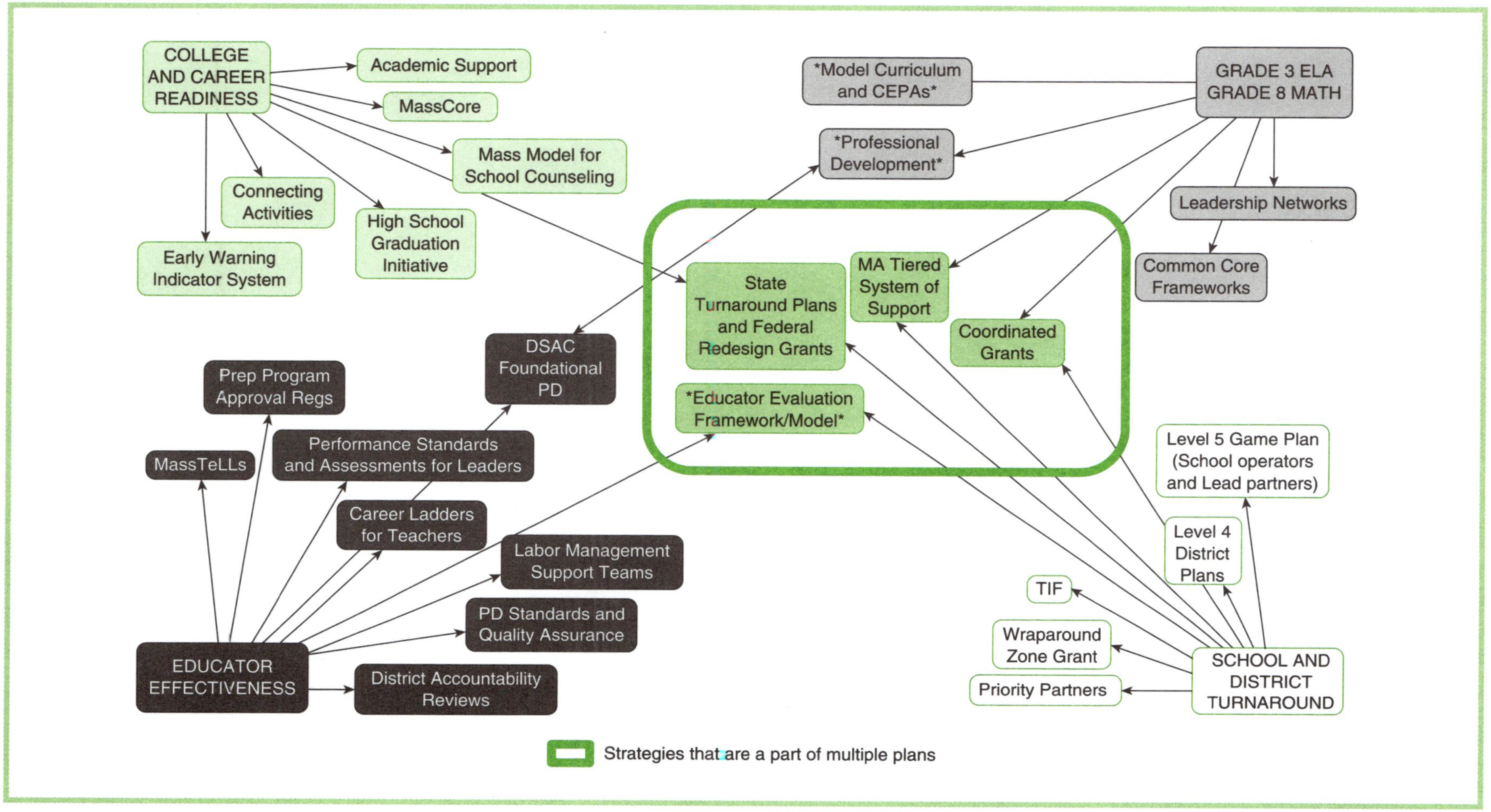

COLLEGE AND CAREER READINESS

- Academic Support
- MassCore
- Mass Model for School Counseling
- High School Graduation Initiative
- Connecting Activities
- Early Warning Indicator System

GRADE 3 ELA GRADE 8 MATH

- Leadership Networks
- Common Core Frameworks

Model Curriculum and CEPAs

Professional Development

Coordinated Grants

MA Tiered System of Support

State Turnaround Plans and Federal Redesign Grants

Educator Evaluation Framework/Model

SCHOOL AND DISTRICT TURNAROUND

- Level 5 Game Plan (School operators and Lead partners)
- Level 4 District Plans
- TIF
- Wraparound Zone Grant
- Priority Partners

DSAC Foundational PD

Labor Management Support Teams

Performance Standards and Assessments for Leaders

Career Ladders for Teachers

PD Standards and Quality Assurance

District Accountability Reviews

Prep Program Approval Regs

MassTeLLs

EDUCATOR EFFECTIVENESS

□ Strategies that are a part of multiple plans

169

A baseline is another one of those seemingly small things that have outsized importance. If we want to achieve a 60% graduation rate within 5 years from a starting point of 50%, setting a baseline forces us to ask: How much impact will we need to make to hit the target? Consider the scenario in Figure 3C.4.

Consider the scenario in Figure 3C.4. There has been a historical gain of 2 percentage points per year over the last 5 years, but the baseline projects that this will level off, so if we do nothing, there will be zero growth in the next 5 years. To maintain this trend and get to the 60% target by the 2016–2017 school year, we'll need to have an additional impact of 10 percentage points over that period. You can imagine why this might be the case: a system may have just experienced a wave of reforms that have brought great gains, but those reforms have run their course. New reforms (our strategies) will be needed to continue growth at this pace.

Now consider another scenario (see Figure 3C.5).

Here, the baseline actually projects continued growth if we do nothing, so we'll hit the target without changing anything. The story here is different but also plausible: perhaps more reforms are in place that have not yet run their course. Or maybe our students are changing, as more students enter college better prepared by the K–12 system to succeed in postsecondary work. Either way, a baseline gives us a reason to make the target more ambitious, like the one in Figure 3C.6.

Finally, consider a third scenario (see Figure 3C.7).

In this picture, graduation rates will actually *go down* if we do nothing, declining at a rate of about 2 percentage points per year. Even if our strategies "grow" graduation rates by 10 percentage points, the result would be a

Figure 3C.4   Zero-Baseline Trajectory

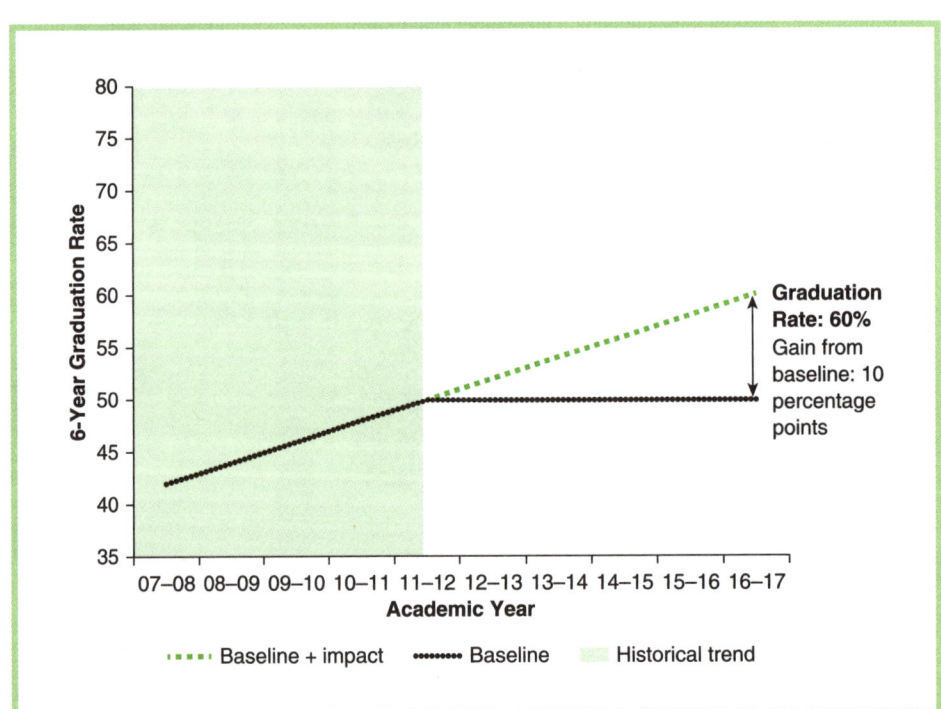

Figure 3C.5   Trend Baseline Trajectory

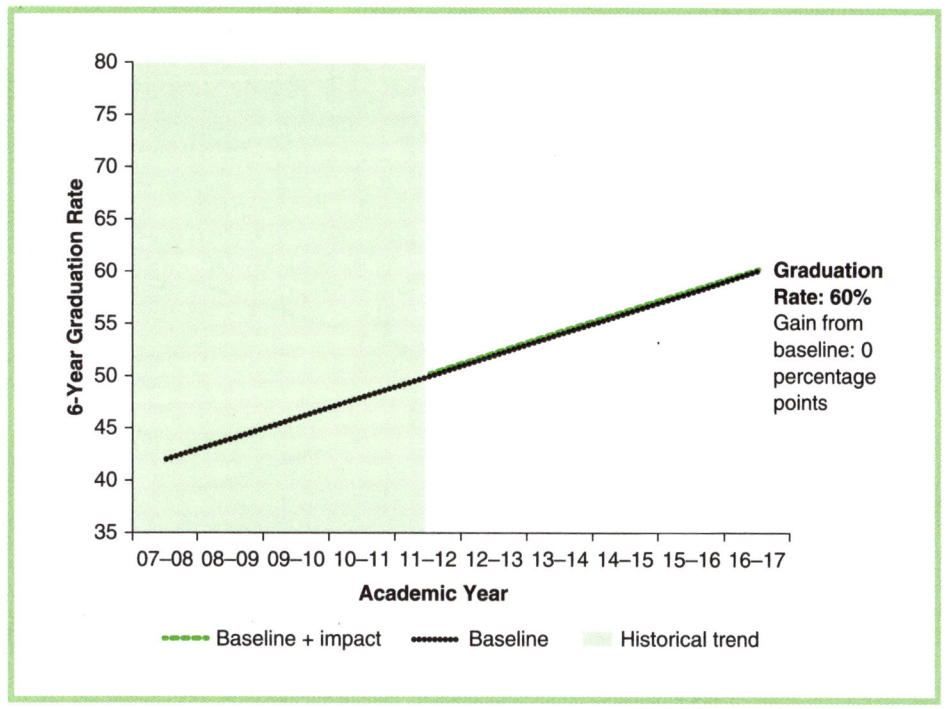

Figure 3C.6   Trend Baseline Trajectory: Adjusted

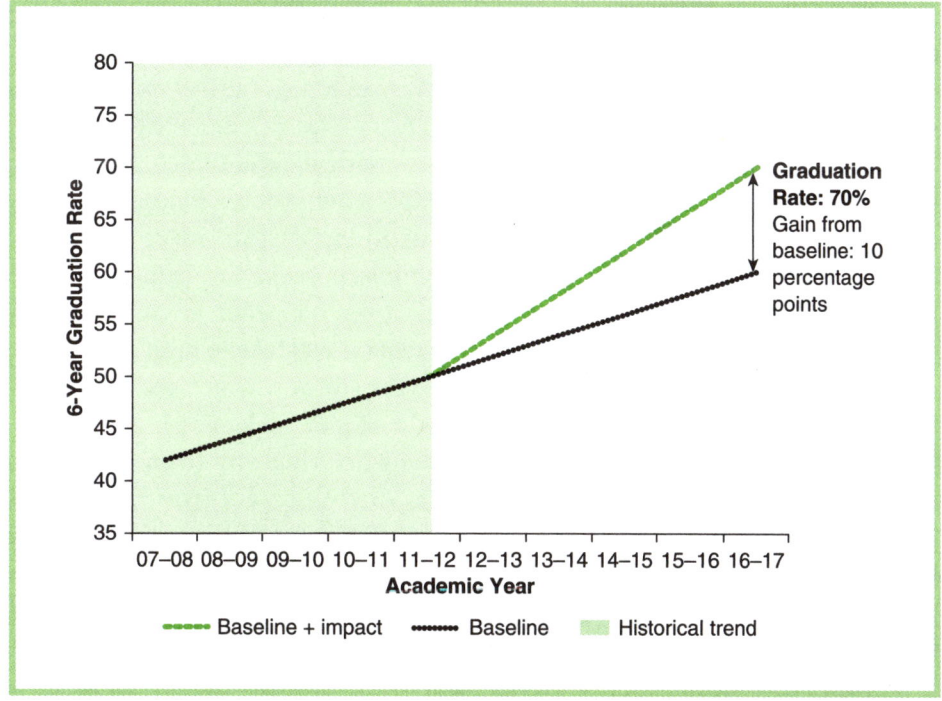

graduation rate that is the same in 2016–2017 as it is now. Again, it's not difficult to imagine why this might be the case: improved access to higher education might bring with it an increased share of students who are more

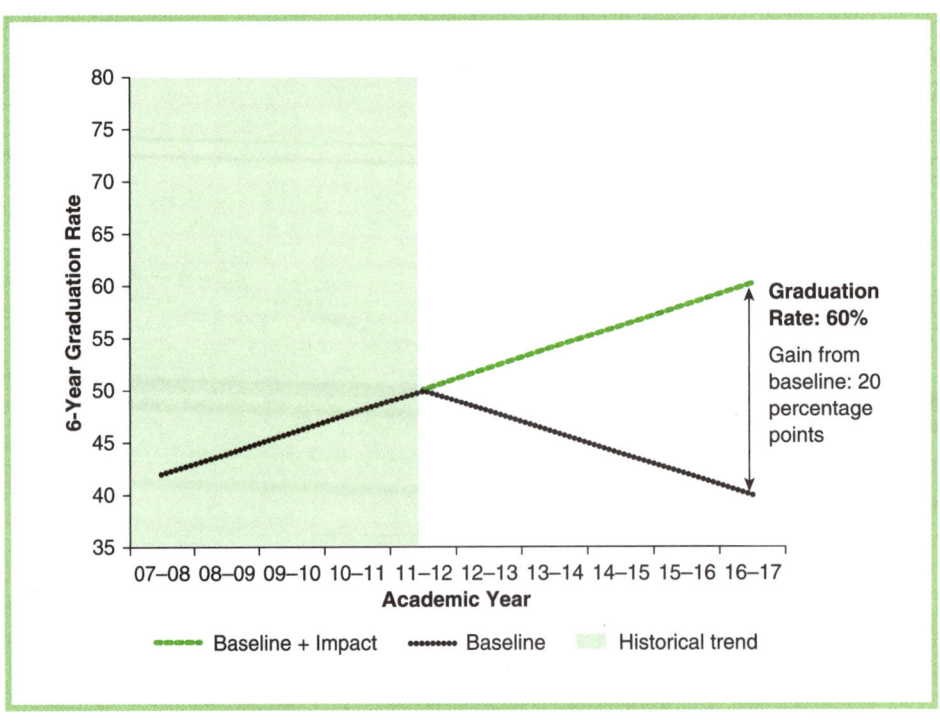

Figure 3C.7   Negative Baseline Trajectory

poorly prepared to succeed—students who will need additional help and attention to prevent a drop in overall graduation rates. In any case, a baseline like this is a signal that we have our work cut out for us to meet our target. It may even be a reason for revising the target downward.

Notice something about these scenarios: depending on the baseline, the same strategies will have very different results. That's why the baseline is such an important concept, not just in delivery but in many different disciplines. Social scientists call it a counterfactual; physicists call it a frame of reference. Measuring change (or, in our case, impact) requires us to know what we're measuring against. Without a baseline that accurately reflects reality, we run the risk of giving ourselves credit for things that would have happened anyway, or—the opposite problem—we risk underestimating what it will take to meet a goal.

Like a trajectory, a baseline is just an estimate. You won't get it perfectly right, and you may need to adjust it in light of new evidence in the future. Nonetheless, there are two key pieces of evidence that any team can use to determine the baseline for a goal. The first is the **historical trend**: What has happened to the metric in the past? What have been the root causes? Are they likely to persist in the future or to change? It's helpful to get historical data that goes back at least as far as your projection period; thus, if you have a 5-year target, you should have at least 5 years of past data to match it.

History may not predict future performance perfectly, but it's a good starting point from which to ask the question: does this make sense? Is there anything else we know that might cause us to revise this baseline? This brings us to our second type of evidence to consider: **external factors** that may have an impact in the future.

To give it a more specific definition: what factors *outside the scope of our strategies* are likely to have an impact on our metric between now and the target date? Some leaders refer to these as "forces outside of our control." That's a phrase we approach with caution: we never want these forces to become an excuse for inaction or lack of progress. For this reason, we must build them into the baseline and work from there. Some examples of factors to look for include:

- **Current or future reforms that will be taking effect:** Are there major expected changes in policy or practice that will occur regardless of your strategies?
- **Changes in demographics:** Will the student population that you are working with change in any significant way between now and the target date? What about teachers or faculty? This includes changes in the "pipeline" of students entering from other systems.
- **Changes occurring at the local level:** Are there individual regions, districts, schools, or campuses that are experiencing major changes (e.g., openings, closures, transformations, local reforms)?

You need not use every type of evidence detailed here. Your objective should be to establish a plausible baseline your leaders can agree on and to use whatever evidence is necessary to meet that standard.

Estimate Future Impact

Your baseline grounds your trajectory in one type of evidence, about the forces acting on your goal that are out of your control. The next step is to consider those things that are in your control: how much impact will you be able to make on the metric relative to its baseline?

As with the baseline, your objective here is not to use a specific type of evidence or analysis, but to use the evidence that is available to you to tell a realistic but ambitious story of future impact—one that passes muster with your system leader, staff, and key stakeholders. The tools in this section give you some options for doing this.

There are two types of tools. The first will help you estimate the impact of each of your **strategies**, while the second will help you use **benchmarks** to establish a range of impact that is both realistic and ambitious. You may take these in either order, using one set of tools to arrive at an initial estimate and the other to validate and (if necessary) revise that estimate. You can use these tools to help you decide what your ultimate target should be, or you can use them to plan your work toward a preestablished target.

Strategies

The first delivery trajectory predates the PMDU; it began when Michael led the Standards and Effectiveness Unit at the U.K. Department for Education and Skills in 1997. The new government had set a literacy target of 80% for England's primary school students, to be achieved 5 years later, by 2002. To achieve this target, they had adopted a national literacy strategy that revolved around a large-scale retraining of primary school teachers around best practices in teaching literacy.

As the team contemplated how the strategy would help them reach the target, they created a table that looked like Figure 3C.8.

The team made a simple assumption about the baseline: in the absence of a strategy, the current literacy rate of 63% wouldn't change in the next 5 years (the table depicts this by showing that the baseline has zero impact over this period). After that, the team's job was to fill in the blanks. How would each of these strategies contribute (or not) to overall literacy in each year—and would these contributions add up to make sufficient impact?

The team's estimates revealed more about how they expected things to unfold. For example, the team estimated some early gains from announcing the goal and asking practitioners to focus on it. This increased focus—known in management circles as the **Hawthorne Effect**—would generate early momentum. Another short-run strategy was assistance for teachers in preparing their students for the literacy tests that measured progress.

The remaining strategies had more lagged effects because they were more difficult or would take more time. Improved materials would bring two more points but would not be available for another year. School improvement strategies would also take at least a year to have an impact—and because of the challenges of transforming whole school culture, it would be 2 more years before they would bring about larger impact. Finally, the most difficult change to make was widespread improvement of teaching practice. This strategy promised high impact, but only in the second half of the 5-year period.

There's nothing overly scientific or precise about this story, but it has a believable logic that meets the test for a credible estimate. How accurate was it? Figure 3C.9 shows the projection against the actual results.

For the first few years, the projection was quite accurate, with an impressive 12-point gain in 3 years. Then a plateau came in 2000 that caused the system to ultimately miss its 2002 target. This divergence was a wake-up call to the

Figure 3C.8   The U.K. National Literacy Strategy: Trajectory

Year		1997	1998	1999	2000	2001	2002
Baseline		63	0	0	0	0	0
Impact of Strategies	Increased focus and priority	NA	+1	+2	+1	0	0
	Improved test preparation	NA	+1	+1	0	0	0
	Improved materials	NA	0	+1	+1	0	0
	School improvement strategy	NA	0	+1	+1	+2	+1
	Improved quality of teaching	NA	0	0	+2	+1	+1
Total		63	65	70	75	78	80

Figure 3C.9 Projection Versus Actual Results for U.K. National Literacy Strategy

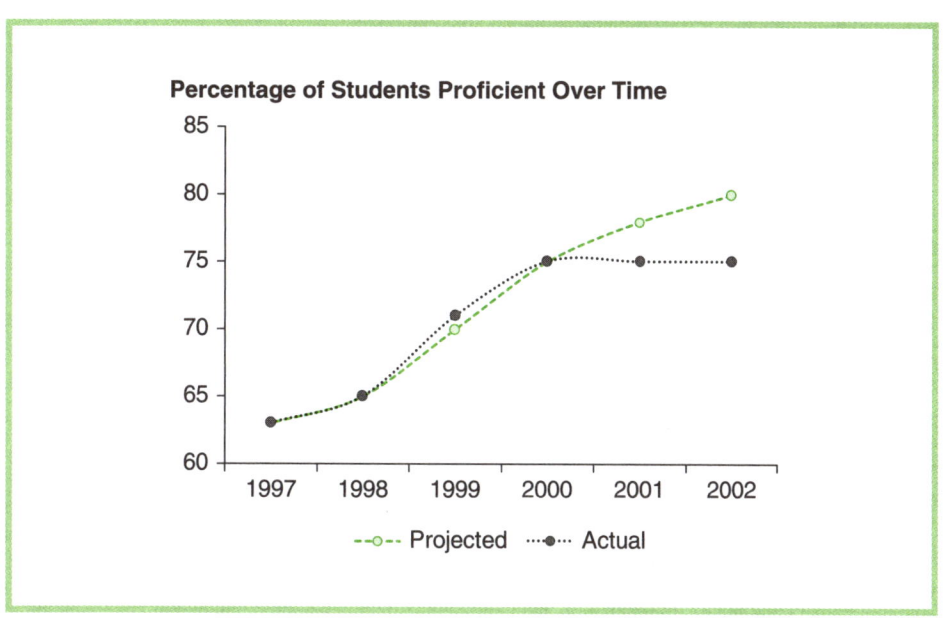

team at the Ministry of Education and to the PMDU, who made a renewed push for results in this area. It took several years to grind out those last few percentage points, but they finally managed to hit the target in 2007. Ironically, the trajectory had its biggest impact on the work in the year of its greatest *divergence* from the actual data. Even when they're not quite right (and they never will be completely right), this is the true value of a reasonably well-estimated trajectory.

The basic frame of that first trajectory is the same frame that we bring to our work with our K–12 and higher education partners: we fill in the current level of the metric, the baseline of changes we expect between now and the target year, and the target (if we have one). The remaining blank spaces are for our estimates of the impact of each strategy in each year.

How do we arrive at those estimates? Your primary evidence is in your strategy profiles from Chapter 3A, along with the delivery chains that you drew for them in Chapter 3B. These give you key information about how each strategy impacts the target metric, when, how deeply, and at what scale.

You can use this information in a few different ways to model your estimates. The simplest method is to use the information to fill in the blanks and tell a logical story, similar to the above example from the United Kingdom. To take it one step further, you can develop more calibrated estimates for each strategy based on a simple "High/Medium/Low" scale (see Figure 3C.10).

This team translated their overall High/Medium/Low estimates into numbers: .4 percentage points for low growth, .6 percentage points for medium growth, and a full percentage point for high growth. Adopting this approach will require that you scale your estimates similarly. One useful starting point is to consider the total distance between current performance and your target. In a single year, what would represent average progress (medium) toward that target? Above average

Figure 3C.10   "High-Medium-Low" Trajectory for Graduation Rates at a Higher Education Campus

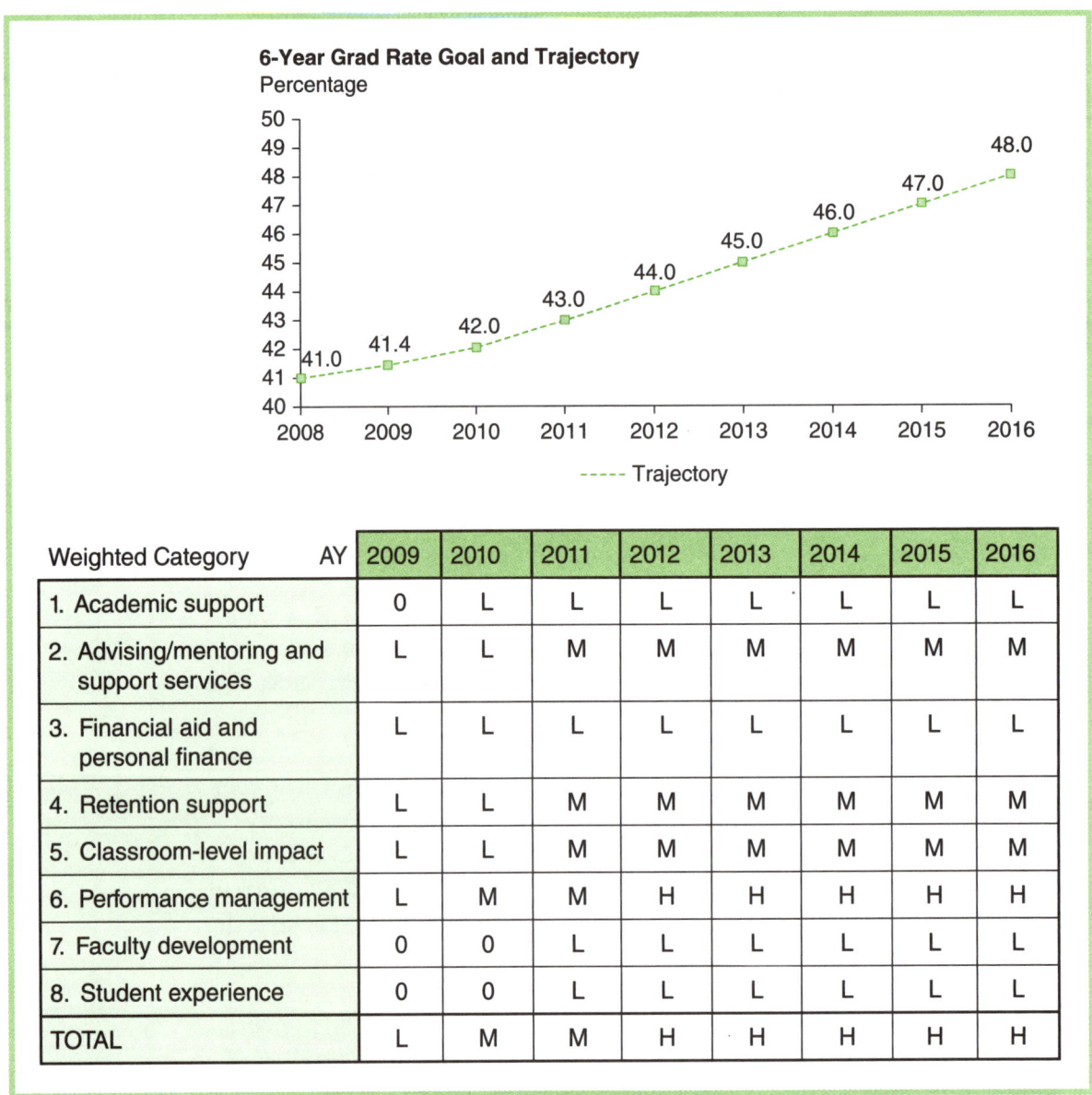

6-Year Grad Rate Goal and Trajectory
Percentage

Weighted Category AY	2009	2010	2011	2012	2013	2014	2015	2016
1. Academic support	0	L	L	L	L	L	L	L
2. Advising/mentoring and support services	L	L	M	M	M	M	M	M
3. Financial aid and personal finance	L	L	L	L	L	L	L	L
4. Retention support	L	L	M	M	M	M	M	M
5. Classroom-level impact	L	L	M	M	M	M	M	M
6. Performance management	L	M	M	H	H	H	H	H
7. Faculty development	0	0	L	L	L	L	L	L
8. Student experience	0	0	L	L	L	L	L	L
TOTAL	L	M	M	H	H	H	H	H

(high) and below average (low) progress? Your knowledge of your local context and your strategies will help you determine what's reasonable.

These are relatively informal methods for making estimates. At the other end of the spectrum is the analytical work that Louisiana's K–12 system did. Recall that they translated their graduation rate target into a specific number of additional graduates they would need: 6,900. To estimate the number of graduates each of their strategies would contribute, they used a simple formulation:

$$\text{Efficacy} \times \text{Scale} = \text{Impact}$$

Here, the efficacy of a strategy is the number of additional graduates produced per 100 students affected by the strategy. Scale is the number of students affected by the strategy. Multiply the two together (and divide by 100) and you get the impact: the total number of additional graduates produced by the strategy.

The team knew the scale of each strategy from its planning efforts. They estimated efficacy for each strategy using statistical analysis of that strategy's impact to date (or, when that wasn't available, a rougher estimate of future impact; see Figure 3C.11).

The result was a trajectory that combined these estimates for each strategy (see Figure 3C.12).

The efficacy x scale formula is an intuitive and powerful way to estimate the impact of a strategy. It relies on a known planning parameter—the scale at which you plan to implement—and an estimate of efficacy that can come from your assumptions about how the strategy will work. The statistical analyses that the Louisiana team did to estimate efficacy were right for their context, and they might be right for yours as well. But it's also all right to make an educated guess about efficacy based on your own thinking. Remember that your assumptions about efficacy are also testable hypotheses that you can validate or revise when the actual data come in.

Finally, a third option for estimating impact is to individually and flexibly model it for each strategy, varying your level of rigor as necessary. Leaders at the Kentucky Department of Education used this approach to estimate the impact of their turnaround school district, District 180, on graduation rates. To do this, the team started with an estimate of the number of *nongraduates* in the schools in this district (see Figure 3C.13).

Each cohort in these schools has approximately 3,900 students, and in the baseline year, their graduation rate is 50%. In that first year, the remaining

Figure 3C.11   Louisiana Graduation Rate Goal: Impact Estimates for Selected Strategies

Strategy Lever	Strategy Name	Strategy Summary	Efficacy	Scale	Impact
Support successful high school transitions for targeted incoming ninth graders	Connections	Targeted instructions and accelerated remediation for ninth graders who are overage and academically behind	1	52,000	520
	Diplomas Now	Inter-organizational collaborative case-management support for ninth graders in high-need schools	4	4,800	192
Support on-time promotion to tenth grade	Everybody Graduates! (ninth-grade academies)	Early warning data system and aligned interventions for at-risk ninth-grade students	4	14,500	580
Improve instructional quality	The system for Student and Teacher Advancement (TAP)	Develop communities of improving educational practice	2	107	2

Figure 3C.12   Louisiana Graduation Rate Goal: Trajectory

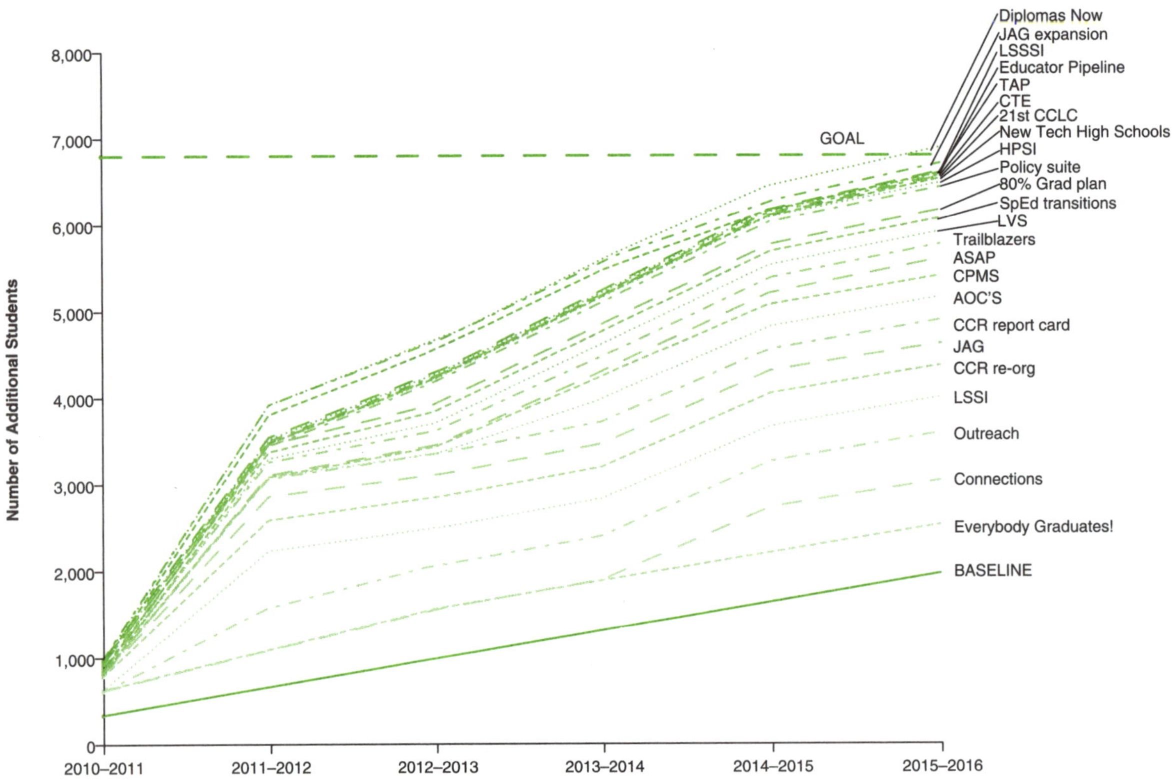

50% of students (1,950) are the at-risk population to which District 180's services are targeted.

The team assumed that in the first year, 5% of this at-risk population, or 98 students, would graduate who would not otherwise have done so. They then projected this percentage to increase over time, so that by the 5th year, District 180 services would "recover" 40% of this at-risk population (see Figure 3C.14).

Figure 3C.13   Trajectory Analysis: Baseline

Year	1	2	3	4	5
Number of Students	3,900	3,900	3,900	3,900	3,900
% of Students Noncomplete	50	45	37	25	20
# of Students Noncomplete	1,950	1,755	1,443	975	780

Figure 3C.14   Trajectory Analysis: Impact of District 180

Year	1	2	3	4	5
Number of Students	3,900	3,900	3,900	3,900	3,900
% of Students Noncomplete	50	45	37	25	20
# of Students Noncomplete	1,950	1,755	1,443	975	780
% Recovered	5	10	20	35	40
# of Additional Graduates	98	176	289	341	312

There's another dynamic at play here: as the strategy is successful, the percentage of noncompleters goes down, so the recovery services are targeted at a smaller and smaller pool of students. As a result, the strategy's impact peaks in the 4th year before declining, as many of the major gains have been realized.

This analysis isn't just an estimate; it's an operational blueprint for those administering District 180. The assumptions are like mini-targets for these leaders; if they buy in to this estimate, they will worry about how to increase their recovery rate from 5% to 40% over the course of the next 5 years. If this doesn't happen, it's cause for raising a red flag and discussing alternatives—because without this aggressive recovery rate, the strategy won't make its expected contribution. By making the assumptions explicit, trajectories further clarify the scale and impact of a strategy, and they create additional accountability for those who lead it.

> Please visit EDI's website at www.deliveryinstitute.org/3C for an exercise on estimating the impact of strategies on your trajectory.

Benchmarks

The other approach for estimating impact is to use data analyses to determine what realistic but ambitious progress should look like. How can we know what's in the range of possibility for our system, and what would be considered a stretch? The power of comparison is key to answering these questions: we examine our targets and trajectories relative to the progress made by different systems, campuses, districts, schools, or student groups in the past and present. These benchmarking comparisons were first introduced in Chapter 2A as part of your analysis of past and present performance. We can extend this analysis to include future performance as well.

Recall that there are three types of benchmarking comparisons you can make:

1. **Against history:** How has this metric moved in the past in our own system, campuses, districts, schools, and/or student groups? Would our target and trajectory represent a major departure from that trend? Is the difference plausible?

2. **Against peers:** How do our student groups, schools, districts, campuses, or system as a whole compare to similar entities in other states, or around the world?

3. **Against yourself:** What is the range of performance between our system's campuses, districts, schools, and/or student groups? How do they compare to the average? To others with similar characteristics? To the 80th percentile performer? The 99th?

You can do these comparisons at any geographic level of your system or between any set of student groups (e.g., the economically disadvantaged, underrepresented minorities). For any of these categories, you can further divide them into performance bands (e.g., performance quartiles of schools, campuses, students, etc.). It may be helpful for you to start with the analyses that were most relevant to you from Chapter 2A and reframe them as prospective, what-if statements. For example:

- What if our graduation rates grew by 50% more than the historic average for the last 5 years?
- What if our lowest-performing quartile of schools raised their reading proficiency levels to the current state average within the next 3 years?
- What if our statewide postsecondary enrollment rates for low-income students grew to match the national average in the next 4 years?

Underlying all these questions are the two essential ones: would that change be realistic? Would it be ambitious? This logic can flow in either direction. On one hand, you can use what-ifs like these to estimate targets and trajectories. In particular, if you use campuses, districts, or schools as your units of comparison, you may be building an evidence base for setting targets and trajectories at the local level as well (see the next section for more details on this). On the other hand, you could take a potential target or trajectory and translate it into a what-if: for example, "If we achieve this target, we would go from the 70th percentile of performance nationally to the 90th percentile in half a decade." Benchmarking comparisons can help you reassure yourself and your stakeholders that you've made sensible estimates.

Using Benchmarking to Set Targets and Trajectories in Hawai'i

In the early days of our partnership, leaders at the Hawai'i Department of Education (HIDOE) established targets and trajectories for their student outcome goals for the state as a whole and for each individual school, starting with reading proficiency. They needed these targets to be ambitious and realistic for each individual school; they also needed the targets to be fair to each school even as they differentiated between high and low performers.

The team examined reading proficiency rates in grades 3 through 8 from 2008 through 2012 and segmented individual schools in two ways. First, they established four quartiles of schools based on current reading performance (see Figure 3C.15).

Next, they established deciles of schools (ten groups) based on their average gains in reading proficiency over the last 5 years (see Figure 3C.16).

The logic of the next step was simple: the schools in the lowest performance quartiles would be asked to make future gains similar to those that the top gainers had made in the last 5 years. For the reading target, the lowest quartile was asked to make a 1-year gain of 6.4 percentage points—equivalent to the average for the 95th percentile of schools in the last 5

Figure 3C.15   Reading Proficiency, Grades 3–8

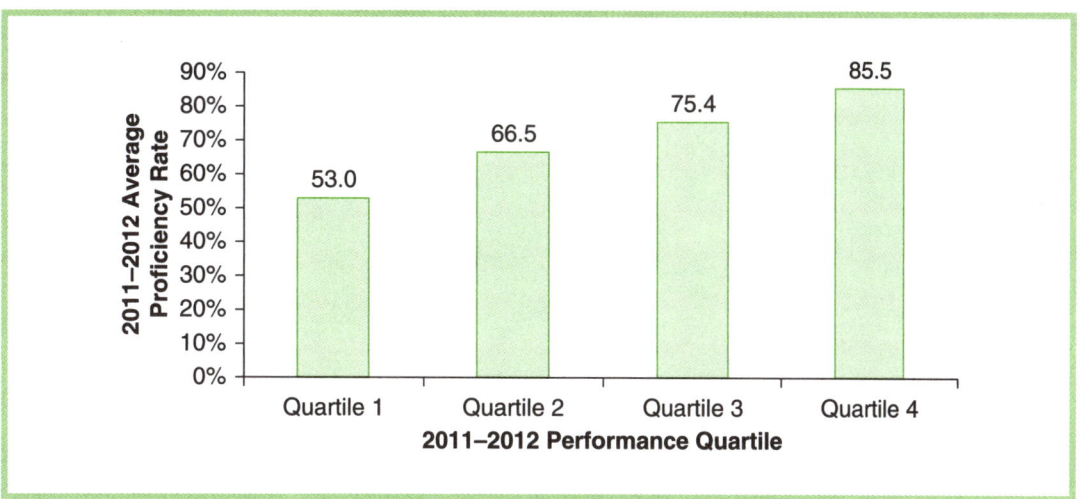

Figure 3C.16   Reading Proficiency Gain From 2007–2008 to 2011–2012, Grades 3–8

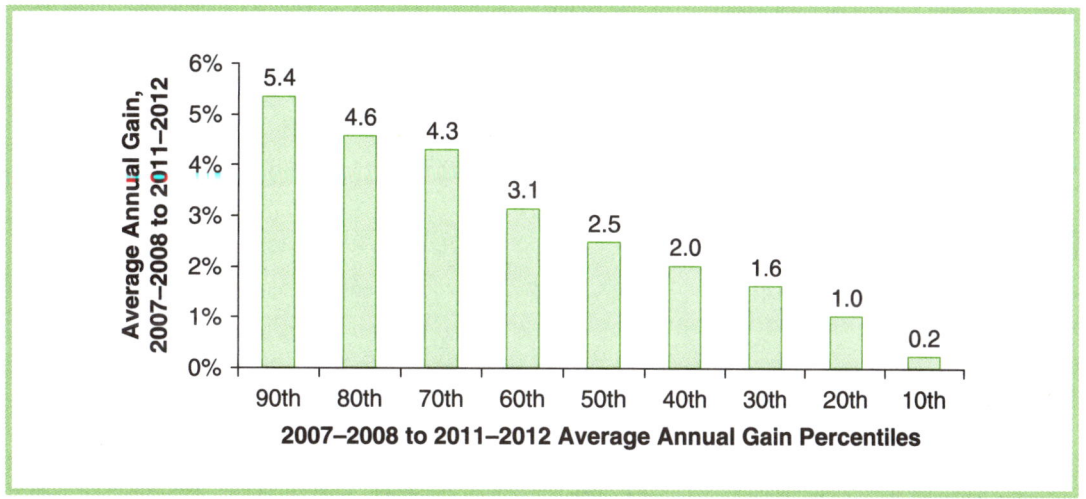

years. The highest quartile, by contrast, was asked to make a 1-year gain of 2.5 percentage points—equivalent to the 50th percentile.

These initial 1-year targets were extrapolated to the target year, 2017–2018, to create a complete trajectory (see Figure 3C.17).

There are two types of benchmarks that make this trajectory believable:

1. **Against history:** A comparison of historical performance and projected future performance shows that, while projected growth represents a steeper climb for some schools (particularly those in the bottom quartile), it does not represent a major break from those trends.

2. **Against yourself:** No school would be asked to make a gain in any year that had not been sustained by a similar school in Hawai'i over the course of the prior 5 years.

(Continued)

(Continued)

Figure 3C.17   Projected Reading Proficiency by School Performance Quartile, 2007–2008 to 2017–2018

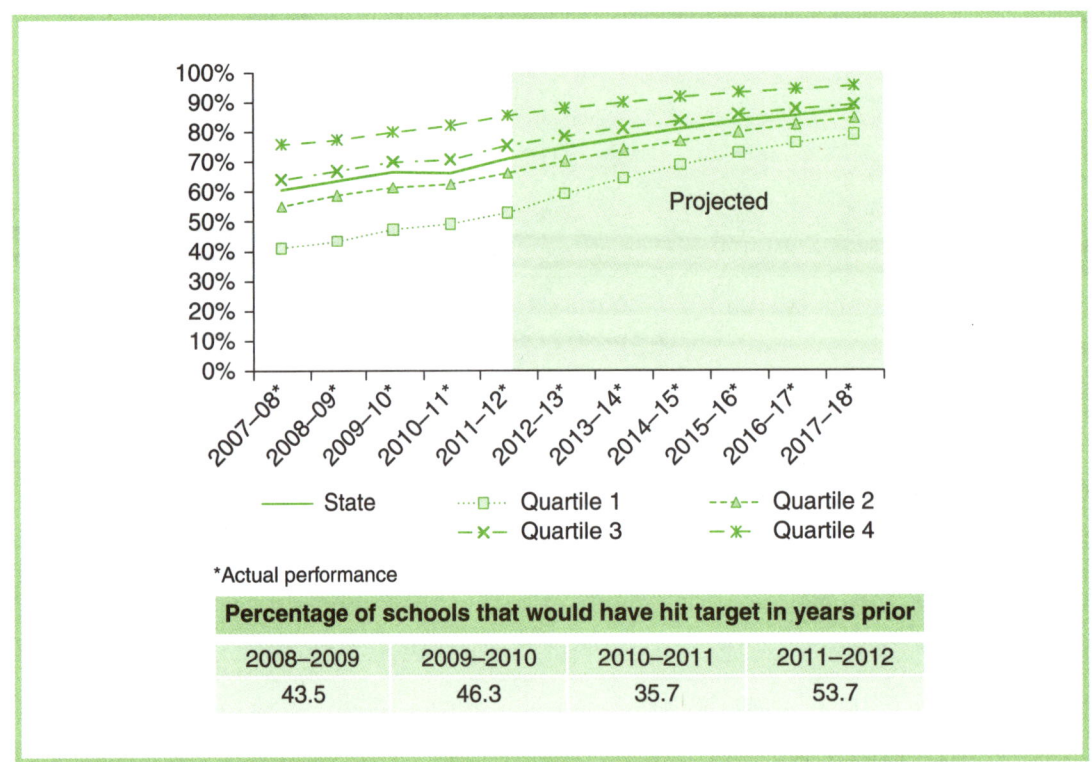

*Actual performance

Percentage of schools that would have hit target in years prior			
2008–2009	2009–2010	2010–2011	2011–2012
43.5	46.3	35.7	53.7

To test the ambition of these targets, the team did a what-if analysis using past data: if these rules had been used to set targets in 2007–2008, how many schools would have stayed on trajectory? Too few and the target may be too ambitious; too many and it may not be ambitious enough. Encouragingly, this number fell between 43% and 53%.

Finally, a look at the top-line number provides additional evidence of the target's ambition: if every school achieved its targets, the system as a whole would go from a 71.1% proficiency rate to an 87.7% proficiency rate—a 16-point gain in 6 years, greater than the 11-point gain it has seen over the previous 5.

In discussions that led to setting this target, leaders in the system raised a deeper question: "Are we giving up on 100%?" they asked, referring to the old proficiency goals under No Child Left Behind. This isn't an easy question: whatever the evidence tells us, how can we settle for anything less than success for all students?

After some discussion, the group came to a consensus: no, we won't settle for anything less than 100% and, philosophically, that remains our goal. But at the same time, when we're 30 points away from that goal, school leaders need to know what would represent substantial progress toward that ideal *next year*. If we're not willing to give them an annual target that is realistic, then the exercise is all optics and no substance. And so we must hold two things in mind at the same time: a long-term goal for all students, alongside significant steps that we plan to take toward that goal right now.

Rather than being a mere abstraction, a trajectory guides us through discussions like these and help us ensure that our targets are relevant to the work being done.

Communicate the Trajectory to Relevant Stakeholders

Once you've applied the right mix of analytical tools to build your targets and trajectories, you only have one step left: to put them into force by communicating them to the right people. This may be as simple as agreeing among your leadership team and some other stakeholders. Some systems make their trajectories part of the public discussion, like Kentucky's K–12 system, while others maintain them as internal estimates or only publish the end targets. In some cases, the logic and assumptions behind the trajectories become important tools for communication. Louisiana's K–12 system used its trajectory estimates to justify its funding priorities to the state legislature; they found it particularly effective to compare their requests for funding with the efficacy and impact that they had estimated for each of their strategies.

In some cases, target- and trajectory-setting will need to happen at a local level as well as system-wide. Sometimes this means, as in the Hawai'i example above, that the trajectory estimates themselves use internal benchmarks that connect system targets to local ones. While Hawai'i's system targets were driven by local-level analysis, the process itself occurred centrally; targets were effectively given to schools.

Other systems may choose to set local targets via a dialogue between the system and its campuses, districts, or schools. The California State University System did this for its Graduation Initiative; they knew they needed buy-in from their 23 campuses for new targets, so they convened a kickoff in October 2009 with campus leaders to discuss what targets would be ambitious but achievable. Through this dialogue, campus leaders eventually agreed to achieve graduation rates that would put them in the top quartile of peer institutions by 2015—a system-wide increase from 46% to 54%— while simultaneously narrowing their equity gaps for underrepresented minority students.

In dialogues like these, you may or may not use your own estimates as a starting point, but either way, it helps to have estimates in hand; they'll help you prevent your campuses, districts, and schools from adopting targets and trajectories that are too ambitious or not ambitious enough. With enough exposure, your analyses may even become contagious.

◉ LESSONS FROM THE FIELD

Respond to the Inevitable Pushback

Over the last several years, targets and trajectories have emerged as the most challenging exercise for our partners. This is understandable: as we learned in Chapter 2A, we tend to fear uncertainty, especially when it's bound up with a prediction about our own performance. The idea of a trajectory seems to compound this issue by asking us to make these predictions even more frequently and to make assumptions about how our work will impact our goals. Isn't there a false precision in doing this? Why invest time and energy in estimates that will almost certainly be wrong, no matter how strong the evidence?

The short answer is that these estimates are almost certainly better than what we're doing right now: adopting strategies, setting goals and targets, and hoping—maybe praying—that one will lead to the other. When we do this, we're effectively making a claim about the impact of our work, but without any supporting evidence. We've all felt the anxiety and uncertainty that comes with this approach. Imperfect as they are, the estimates in a trajectory at least offer us some assurance that our claims *could* be true.

But there's a larger point here: *nobody* can predict the future, and doing so is not the reason that we set targets and trajectories. We often take a very narrow, pressure-oriented view of the accountability that a target creates: positive consequences for "making your numbers," and negative ones for missing them. This view attaches such high stakes to our forecasts that we become reluctant to make them—or we try to marginalize their importance. More important, this view eclipses the real value that these tools provide as catalysts for managing and monitoring implementation. Remember: rather than being hard predictions, targets and trajectories are *hypotheses* about what will happen that can be tested against the facts as they come in. The comparison between hypothesis and actual data is what allows for continuous learning as we implement.

In other words, if we're to feel free to make these kinds of estimates, we'll need to shift our mindset. Targets aren't predictions that must be accurate *or else*; they are educated guesses that we must constantly check against and adjust. Being off track shouldn't be occasion for punishment and blame but for reflection and improvement of both our strategies and our estimates. We must be fearless about looking at our data. If this means lowering the stakes attached to our targets and trajectories, or making some of them internal (nonpublic) information, then it's worth it to do so. You should almost never hesitate to trade performance consequences for real performance dialogue; the most important accountability is the kind that truly engages the accountable.

Targets and Accountability at the Council of Chief State School Officers

When EDI partnered with the Council of Chief State School Officers (CCSSO) to support the organization's strategic planning, one of the toughest questions we faced concerned the Council's targets: should CCSSO, a member organization of K–12 state systems of education, set a student outcome target?

There were some natural hesitations. In particular, individual employees wondered about accountability: would *they* face consequences if student outcomes didn't improve sufficiently?

Eventually, we agreed that the Council would adopt student outcome targets against measures of high school graduation and college and career readiness. To make people comfortable with this decision, the leaders of the organization decided that the accountability for the targets would be "soft": the leaders and staff of the organization weren't going to be evaluated strictly on whether the targets were met. Rather, the performance against trajectory would become a catalyst for discussing the work of the organization, whether it was on track, and what the team could do collectively to improve progress.

CCSSO's willingness to put a stake in the ground, however imperfect, has contributed to their status as a leader amongst peer organizations and with the philanthropic community that supports them.

Be Flexible About the Tools You Use

This chapter presents a wide range of options for nearly every step of the process of setting targets and establishing trajectories. Some are more rigorous—and more time-consuming—than others. The more time-consuming the work, the more pushback you'll get. Is there any guidance for which tools a system should use?

As we've repeatedly noted in this chapter, there are no specific rules. There are merely two principles, which are in tension with one another. First, your targets and trajectories must allow you to tell a plausible story, using evidence, about how and why you believe that your delivery plan will help you meet your student outcome goals. This will depend on what your system leaders and staff need to feel confident, as well as what external stakeholders and the public are demanding.

Second, the work you do should be as simple as possible. Pick the easiest tool(s) you can get away with and still meet that first principle. For Hawai'i's leaders, internal benchmarking based on school performance was the most important evidence they needed to use. Many higher education systems work with the National Center for Higher Education Management Systems (NCHEMS) to estimate graduation rate goals; their analytic work is widely respected in the field and also carries weight with many higher education leaders. Meanwhile, many K–12 systems are feeling the pressure to connect more abstract student outcome goals with the tangible work that they are doing; for them, estimating the impact of strategies will be essential.

In the end, some tools will have more credibility in some systems than others. Experiment in your interactions with system leaders and staff until you find the mix that works best for you.

Use Imperfect Data If You Have To

Finally, some goals don't have good data, usually because the relevant metric doesn't exist yet. One common example of this is K–12 systems that have set goals for improving teacher and leader effectiveness. In most of these systems, a reliable metric won't be available for a few years. What should goal and strategy leaders do for these delivery plans?

There are a few steps that teams can take, most of which involve using imperfect data. They can use a proxy measure—usually, a different but related metric. They can also develop a baseline using data from individual campuses, districts, or schools (inside or outside the system) that already have the correct metric in place.

Whatever you choose, situations like this call for future refinements of the estimates once the data are available. The time line in your delivery plan should explicitly include a point where you look at the new data and revise your targets and trajectories accordingly. Again, the principles are clear: don't let the lack of data be an excuse for not doing what you can and use the planning process to hold yourself accountable for producing estimates as soon as possible.

◉ KEY CONSIDERATIONS FOR SYSTEM LEADERS AND STAFF

Because they're such a challenging part of delivery, targets and trajectories require substantial input and cooperation from leaders throughout your system. **System leaders**, in particular, have a special responsibility to fold public commitments into messaging about reform. You'll need to decide what can be shared and what must be kept internal. For those targets and trajectories that you do share, you'll want to take full advantage of the power that they have to make your aspiration real and tangible. Think back to Louisiana and the number 6,900, or consider the school systems that have used the what-if formulations of benchmarking to translate their targets all the way to the classroom level—for example, by showing that a graduation rate target asks every teacher to find just two new graduates in each of his or her classes of students. What's the specific number that you want in the hearts and minds of practitioners and the public?

As goal leaders and strategy leaders who "own" the trajectories, **system staff** will probably be the most uncomfortable with the tools in this chapter. Remember that your system is depending on you to establish the right culture of transparency and freedom to be wrong as you make your estimates. Show the members of your team that you're not afraid to embrace the discomfort and make an educated guess—or to revise it in light of new evidence in the future.

Because making these estimates can be tricky, **delivery leaders** may have to play an unusually strong role in teaching these tools and in facilitating the necessary discussions. We've seen some delivery teams hold "trajectory meetings" with each individual strategy leader to hash out the assumptions behind each estimate. You'll also be the ones called on most often to defend this practice. The arguments in this chapter represent our best responses to some of the most typical reactions you'll face; know them, use them, and let us know if we're missing anything. By playing this role, you will lend your system leaders and staff the courage to take this step.

⊙ CONCLUSION

We began this chapter by asserting that, while targets have great power to drive change, not all targets are created equal. The ones that are grounded in evidence—whether from benchmarks, impact estimates, a strong baseline, or other sources—are the ones which, if well communicated, will actually make a difference in your system. Hopefully, this chapter has persuaded you not only that this distinction is real, but also that we need not leave things to chance when it comes to the targets we have. There are things we can do—things well worth the cost in time and mental energy—that will help us build targets and trajectories that better articulate results for students.

Targets and trajectories take the elements of your delivery plan—the descriptions of strategies, the delivery chains, and the goals in your aspiration—and weave them together into a coherent whole. With their completion, your delivery plans are finished—or, at least, good enough to get started with. Now comes the opportunity for continuous learning, as you use your trajectories to judge whether you are making progress and answer that final delivery question: "If you're not on track, what are you going to do about it?" We turn to these tools in the next chapter.

⊙ NOTES

1. State of Louisiana B.E.S.E. (2010, May 20). Joint Meeting Board of Elementary and Secondary Education and Board of Regents [Meeting minutes]. Retrieved from http://www.louisianaschools.net/lde/uploads/12819.pdf

2. Obama, B. H. (2009, February 24). Address to Joint Session of Congress. Retrieved from http://www.whitehouse.gov/the_press_office/Remarks-of-President-Barack-Obama-Address-to-Joint-Session-of-Congress/

3. OECD. (n.d.). *Education at a glance 2014: OECD indicators*. Retrieved from http://www.keepeek.com/Digital-Asset-Management/oecd/education/education-at-a-glance-2014_eag-2014-en#page44

4. Papers of President Kennedy. Presidential Papers. President's Office Files. Series 2. Special Correspondence. Box 30, Folder: "Johnson, Lyndon B., 1961: January–May." John F. Kennedy Presidential Library and Museum. [See digitized folder here: JFKPOF-030-019]

5. Barber, M., & Moffit, A. (2011). *Deliverology 101: A field guide for educational leaders*. Thousand Oaks, CA: Corwin.

Part 4

Drive Delivery

Develop a foundation for delivery

Understand the delivery challenge

Plan for delivery

Drive delivery

Create an irreversible delivery culture

"However beautiful the strategy, you should occasionally look at the results." This statement, often attributed to Winston Churchill, tells us that a plan is only as good as the monitoring around it. You know what you're trying to do and how you're planning to do it, but don't forget the last two questions of delivery: At any given moment, how will you know whether you're on track to succeed? And if you're not on track, what are you going to do about it?

Your system's delivery plans—the aspiration, the goals, the strategies, the delivery chains, and the targets and trajectories—represent commitments made by your system, which, if honored, should lead to real results. As implementation gets under way, your Delivery Unit's role will be to track progress against these commitments, to identify challenges and change course where required, and above all to push your system to keep its promises.

In this part of the book, you'll be using the lessons you've learned and analyses and plans you've developed to drive delivery. The next three chapters take you through the tools that are at the heart of a Delivery Unit's ongoing work:

- Establish routines to drive and monitor performance
- Solve problems early and rigorously
- Sustain and continually build momentum

This is where your most important work happens—but at the same time, it's also the most difficult stage. Implementation is never easy, and sometimes, especially in the thick of things, it isn't even exciting. As the journalist Matthew D'Ancona described the PMDU's work, "There is no drama in delivery . . . only a long, grinding haul punctuated by public frustration with the pace of change."[1] But we dive into it anyway, because completing this long haul is the only way to get the results we've promised.

Chapter 4A

Establish Routines to Drive and Monitor Performance

 Develop a foundation for delivery

 Understand the delivery challenge

 Plan for delivery

 Drive delivery

 Create an irreversible delivery culture

System Leader Summary

Once you've done some planning, you will need to know—as frequently and meaningfully as possible—how well you're doing at implementing the plan and achieving the results it promises. This is the purpose of a **delivery routine**: a regularly scheduled and structured conversation between you and your accountable leaders to review progress against your goals, discuss and solve major challenges, and make decisions to drive delivery forward. These routines, brokered and managed by your delivery leader using the tools in this chapter, will create a consistent sense of urgency for your system to deliver results.

Your time, and the seriousness with which you take your delivery routines, are the single greatest investment you can make in ensuring your delivery effort's success. At the same time, a well-structured set of delivery routines is the greatest gift your delivery leader can give you: a consistent view of progress, with key decisions and questions teed up for you every time, no matter what other distractions are on your desk at the moment. Make sure you trust your delivery leader well enough to let them "manage" you through this process—and prepare to reap the rewards.

◉ TRUST, BUT VERIFY

On December 8, 1987, President Ronald Reagan met with his Soviet counterpart, President Mikhail Gorbachev, to sign the Intermediate-Range Nuclear Forces Treaty (INF). The treaty was a big step: it called for the disarmament and destruction of over 2,000 nuclear warheads that each side had pointed at the other. How had two old enemies overcome their mutual hostility to make this agreement? How did Reagan, a famous "hawk" on foreign policy issues, do it without appearing soft? The reasons were many, but one was the system of inspections that the treaty set up—allowing each side to credibly monitor the other's implementation of their commitments. At the signing, Reagan summarized this system with a Russian proverb that had become a signature phrase for him: "Trust, but verify."

What makes the difference between a treaty that has force and one that's meaningless? What makes the difference between a plan that drives your work and a plan that sits on the shelf? The answer is simple: the amount of attention you pay to verifying implementation. The more attention you pay, the more seriously the plan will be taken and the more likely it is that people will implement it.

Our plans come alive when we ask fundamental questions about progress: did we do what we said we were going to do? Did we do it well? Did it have an impact? And what are we going to do to improve implementation? These questions lie at the heart of continuous improvement, and good monitoring allows us to answer them in a consistent and actionable way.

The problem is that good monitoring is difficult to do. Even the word itself has a negative connotation; in our imagination, it usually keeps the company of bureaucratic contemporaries like "compliance" and "oversight." We react negatively to these words because they imply a loss of autonomy and professionalism: when monitoring turns to micromanagement, accountable leaders become disempowered and risk averse. On the other hand, the consequences of *not* monitoring can be just as bad. Monitoring creates the dialogue between system leaders and accountable leaders that allows them to set direction for the work. In the course of implementation, this direction must be constantly adjusted so that it's always relevant and always clear. Without direction, there's confusion—and when there's confusion, nothing happens.

So the challenge of good monitoring is well summarized by Reagan's words: we must trust people and empower them to do their work, but we must also verify that the work is being done and done well. We strike this balance by creating delivery routines: regularly scheduled and structured opportunities, brokered and managed by the delivery leader, for the system leader and accountable leaders to review progress, discuss and solve major challenges, and make decisions to drive delivery forward.

We emphasize the word **routine** because it's counterintuitive to manage an organization's highest priorities in this way. What is the opposite of a routine? An event. And by nature, we seem to be drawn to events: a special occasion rather than a normal one, an intervention rather than a prevention, an exception rather than the rule it breaks. We may allow routines to govern the mundane and peripheral things in our work—like how paychecks get sent out or how meetings get scheduled—but when it comes to things we really care about, we spend a disproportionate amount of our time managing events.

Yet it's through routine occurrences that most implementation happens: steady, persistent, sometimes even monotonous progress, achieved not through a blinding insight or an inspiring moment but ground out patiently over time. Our monitoring must capture and drive this progress, and so—like implementation itself—it must be routine.

Delivery routines are the engine of delivery for several reasons. First, they allow us to be proactive in our management of implementation. To borrow a phrase from the productivity guru David Allen, when we manage through events, we allow our work to be driven by whatever is latest and loudest—the proverbial squeaky wheel getting most of the oil. Routines ensure that, no matter what crisis is occurring or what fires are burning, the regular work of implementation always gets the attention it needs.

Second, delivery routines commit us to action ahead of the fact. The best routines follow the clock and the calendar, with no excuses for delay. Agreeing to put them on the schedule is tantamount to agreeing to have progress to show by the time they occur. Delivery routines create false deadlines for accountable leaders—and in so doing, they lend urgency to the work that would not otherwise have been there.

Finally, delivery routines amplify the authority of the system leader. As we noted in Chapter 1C, most leaders won't have time to stay on top of all their priorities; inevitably, they must be available to manage the public crises and challenges that arise in the course of leading a system. This puts them at a disadvantage when they engage in dialogues about performance and progress with accountable leaders: if they don't know what's going on or what questions to ask, they won't be able to use what authority they have to exert the right pressure for results. Inevitably, the vacuum of evidence will be filled by the accountable leader; this view will almost always be rosier than it ought to be, and the result will be a friendly conversation with little action or impetus to improve implementation.

Even Tony Blair faced this problem; it didn't matter how much power he had over his Cabinet ministers if he didn't know about the current state of their work. By creating a built-in mechanism for briefing the Prime Minister with the right facts and questions before each conversation, delivery routines created the illusion, in the view of each of those ministers, that their leader had been paying close attention to their work all along. His "hard" power was thus extended and strengthened by the "soft" influence of knowledge, evidence, and clarity brought by the Delivery Unit's constant focus on his priorities.

"Delivery never sleeps," Michael used to tell the Prime Minister. Delivery routines, and the work that a Delivery Unit does to prepare for them, are what make this claim a reality.

◉ CORE PRINCIPLES

In theory, most of us understand the value of delivery routines. Nonetheless, they're difficult to get right in practice. Even the emphasis on the word *routine*, useful as it is, can create confusion. We run the risk of confusing things that just happen to occur regularly—like a weekly meeting—for the sharp and focused conversations that take place during *delivery* routines. We've observed some common mistakes over the years. So before focusing on what a delivery routine is, it's helpful to point out what it is *not*:

- **A delivery routine is *not* a staff meeting:** A staff meeting—a time for teams to get together, to communicate about and coordinate their work, and to hear announcements—can be useful. But it's not a delivery routine because it's not focused on performance.

- **A delivery routine is *not* an update meeting:** Some leaders call team meetings and begin the agenda with an update from each member about the state of their work, the challenges they see, and (potentially) solutions and/or questions for group problem solving. This practice is of questionable value—updates usually take up more than half the agenda (if not all of it), and each update usually fails to engage more than a quarter of the room. But more important, such a format creates no clear consensus about the current state of progress. The narrative belongs mostly to accountable leaders, who have a natural bias toward reporting positive results. The dynamic that often results is one of leaders choosing not to challenge each other for fear of being challenged on their own work.

- **A delivery routine is *not* a data review meeting:** If participants in a meeting are reading data for the first time and trying to decide what it means together, it's useful and necessary *preparation* for a delivery routine, but it is not the routine itself. Participants have limited time: if they have to spend most of it interpreting the data, they'll have no time to prioritize and solve the most important challenges the data present.

What's the main difference between all these things and a true delivery routine? The answer, in a word, is *preparation*: preparation of the evidence and data, of the story it tells, of the roles and responsibilities of participants, and of the problems to solve and questions to answer. Careful, deliberate, even obsessive preparation is the thin line that separates a delivery routine from a waste of time. In the PMDU, it was not unusual for Michael and his team to spend several hours preparing for a single one-hour meeting.

For this reason, one of the most important responsibilities of a Delivery Unit is to take this preparation seriously and to coordinate it across all the major players. The rest of this section lays out the major steps for Delivery Units to follow as they do this.

First and foremost, you need to establish an **architecture** for your routines that mirrors the architecture for delivery planning that you created in Part 3. There are two steps here:

1. **Reflect on the characteristics of current routines:** Understand what you're already doing and how you can build on it.

2. **Organize routines:** Determine the topics you'll cover, the people who will be involved, the frequency, form, and schedule for each routine, and tools for assessing progress.

Once your architecture is set up, the remaining steps are ones that you take for each individual routine:

3. **Prepare for the routine:** Gather evidence, make initial judgments, set objectives, prepare materials, and brief the relevant leaders.

4. **Run the routine:** Bring all your preparation to bear on the event itself, generating follow-ups that will drive action and improvement.

Reflect on the Characteristics of Current Routines

Nobody begins this work in a vacuum. Most systems have some kind of routine for reviewing performance already, and many of these routines have some (and sometimes all) of the right characteristics. It helps to begin by reflecting on these current practices and seeing how they measure up to four essential elements of strong delivery routines:

- **Regularity:** Does the routine happen regularly enough to drive performance? Are the right people present and engaged, including the system leader and the relevant accountable leaders?
- **Strong execution:** Do participants buy in to the purpose of the routine and come prepared for a productive discussion? Are their roles and responsibilities clear? Are the supporting materials high quality? Is the meeting well facilitated? And are clear next steps defined?
- **Focus on performance:** Is the routine's *area of focus* clear—do we know what we're assessing progress on (goal, strategy, combination, etc.)? Does the routine allow participants to quickly form a *shared view of performance and progress*, based on strong, well-synthesized evidence about the area of focus? And does the agenda help participants focus on the most important issues impacting performance?
- **Action on performance:** Does the routine help participants identify and agree on the most critical barriers to progress? Are the tough questions asked? Does the routine result in creative problem solving that empowers participants to address these challenges and holds them accountable for doing so? And does the routine encourage continuous learning and improvement?

We've summarized these four elements in a brief rubric, similar to the rubric for assessing the current quality of plans we introduced in Part 3 of this book (see Figure 4A.1). Your first step is to identify existing interactions that could conceivably be delivery routines—staff or team meetings, review meetings, memos or reports on progress, and so on—and evaluate them against this rubric. What are you already doing well? How do you know? How could you improve one or more of these routines for the work you are trying to do? With so many meetings and other routines already taking place in most systems, it's good to begin with the assumption that you won't be starting from scratch, but repurposing existing work.

In several higher education systems we've worked with, for example, the system leaders already had regular meetings established with presidents and/or

Figure 4A.1 Characteristics of Strong Delivery Routines

Category	What Weak Performance (1) Looks Like	What Strong Performance (4) Looks Like	Rating/ Rationale

Regularity
 	
• Does the routine happen regularly enough to drive performance?
• Are the right people present? Including:
  – The "leader" holding the actors accountable?
  – The "actors" driving the work and reporting on progress?
  – The "broker" facilitating the discussion?
	• Takes place sporadically and is often canceled or rescheduled
	• So frequent that changes in performance are not observable, or so infrequent that performance "drifts" in between
	• Key players are rarely present
		• Provides a stable rhythm for the work; participants plan around the schedule of routines
		• Discussions are timely (not too early/ too late)
		• Key players—including the leader— attend; relevant actors are senior and/ or informed enough to account for performance and commit to necessary actions	

Strong execution • Do participants buy in to the purpose of the routine and come prepared for a productive discussion? • Are roles and responsibilities clear? • Are the supporting materials high-quality? • Is the meeting well facilitated? • Are clear next steps defined?	• Participants are confused about the routine's purpose/objectives or do not believe in them • Important participants are not sufficiently well prepared to contribute • Participants are unclear about their roles • Supporting materials are confusing, too detailed or missing important information • Starts late; runs out of time; departs from agenda • Next steps are not identified	• All participants can articulate the routine's objectives and want to play their role in achieving them • Key participants are well prepared (briefed in advance by the broker if necessary) • Agenda and supporting materials are clear, concise, relevant, and prepared in advance • Runs to time; changes to agenda are deliberate • Leader/broker ensure that objectives are met and clear next steps are identified	

Category	What Weak Performance (1) Looks Like	What Strong Performance (4) Looks Like	Rating/Rationale
Focus on performance • Is the area of focus for the routine clear—do we know what we are assessing progress on? • Does the routine allow participants to quickly form a shared view of performance and progress, based on strong, well-synthesized evidence? • Does the agenda/specific objectives of the routine allow for a focus on the most important issues impacting performance?	• Routine is merely a check-in during which participants give updates • Evidence is sporadic/inconsistent; discussion is mostly based in anecdote/opinion; data are disputed or not recognized by participants • Data are presented in raw format with little or no attempt to discern patterns or implications • All items get equal weight, with no attempt to make meaningful comparisons or focus on key issues	• Performance on specific goals, strategies, or entities is selected as the focus of the discussion • A wide range of evidence is presented in a way that is clear, sharp, and consistent, including outcome data, leading indicator data, and evidence on quality of implementation • Data is synthesized to identify key patterns and comparisons • Debate is vigorous but an overall picture of performance emerges quickly; the majority of discussion is on the biggest areas of challenge	
Action on performance • Does the routine help participants identify and agree on the most critical barriers to progress? • Are the tough questions asked? • Does the routine result in creative problem solving that empowers participants to address the challenges and holds them accountable for doing so? • Does the routine encourage participants to continuously learn and improve?	• Problems may be identified but are too vague to be actionable; their root causes are poorly understood, if at all • Data is discussed to no practical end; discussion tends to dwell on problems, with little attempt to seek solutions; key issues are left unresolved • Actions and next steps are superficial, with no real expectation that they will "move the needle" • There is no follow-up on actions between routines • Participants are reluctant to engage in open dialogue about their own/colleagues' performance; challenging conversations are either avoided or couched as a "gotcha" • Wider learning points are not identified	• Discussion allows participants to identify specific barriers to success, with a focus on root causes that are actionable • Leader/broker asks the tough questions, and presses for answers until adequate, realistic solutions have been identified • Between routines there is a shared expectation that actions will be followed up • Participants are open to supporting, challenging, and learning from each other • Cross-project comparisons create a spirit of friendly competition and professional learning across teams • Learning points are captured and shared	

Please visit EDI's website at www.deliveryinstitute.org/4A for the full rubric on routines.

provosts of their individual campuses. Some of these meetings were one-on-one, and others gathered the relevant leaders together as a group. These meetings created a natural framework for the delivery routines of many of these systems—and most of them didn't have to create any new interactions.

This initial evaluation of your existing routines has two benefits. First, it will help you deepen your own understanding of what makes a strong delivery routine. Second, it will help you identify any potential foundations to build on as you organize your delivery routines—the next step in the process.

Organize Routines

As with delivery planning, your delivery routines will need an organizational structure that makes them coherent. The PMDU, for example, had to create a system of routines to review 20 targets—and progress against the plans for each—in a way that would not overwhelm the Prime Minister but would ensure that he had comprehensive, up-to-date information about his priorities.

Their solution was rooted in the way that they organized delivery planning—what we called an architecture in Part 3—and the way that organization interacted with the structure of the relevant Cabinet agencies. Because the 20 targets were each attached to one or more of four Cabinet agencies (Transport, Education, Health, and Home), the Cabinet agency became the organizing unit for the routines (PMDU members would have a "Health" stocktake or an "Education" stocktake, or they would write monthly notes about "Transport"—and each of these included updates on multiple goals).

Similarly, you'll need to make some fundamental decisions about how your routines are organized before you start running them. The task at hand is to craft a combination of routines—and the topics they review—that maximizes the use of available data and holds the right combination of people to account often enough to continuously drive results. You can make these decisions by answering four questions:

1. What are you measuring progress for?

2. Who should be involved in your routines?

3. What types of routines will you have, and how often?

4. How will you assess progress?

What Are You Measuring Progress For?

This may sound basic—which is why many people skip over this question. Fundamentally, there are two types of **areas of focus** (mirroring the areas of focus in your architecture) for which you can measure progress:

- A **goal**: Is it being achieved? Are we likely to achieve it?
- A **strategy**: Is it being implemented well? Is it likely to make a significant contribution to the goal?

At this stage, you need to choose which goals and strategies will become areas of focus. You can also use schools, districts, campuses, departments, or other organizational entities as your areas of focus by bundling together all the goals and/or strategies for which they are responsible. This is similar to what the PMDU did with the four Cabinet agencies, each of which was responsible for multiple goals.

As we noted above, the way delivery planning is organized—your architecture—should have an influence on how you choose the areas of focus for your routines. The easiest solution is to have the same areas of focus for your routines as you do for your plans. For example:

- The Massachusetts Department of Elementary and Secondary Education has five goals, with a delivery plan for each; those are its areas of focus.
- The Tennessee Board of Regents has 10 strategies with a delivery plan for each; those are its areas of focus.
- The Delaware Department of Education uses its 19 districts as its areas of focus, running one routine with each district about progress toward overall goals.

Who Should Be Involved in Your Routines?

Clearly defined roles and responsibilities are crucial to a good routine. At its essence, a routine is a dialogue about performance between two leaders, one of whom is holding the other responsible for a specific area of focus. As such, it requires us to be very clear about which is which. Though not every routine is a face-to-face conversation, one useful image for this dynamic is conveyed by the idea of the two leaders sitting "across the table" from one another, with the Delivery Unit brokering and managing the conversation from the "side." Figure 4A.2 gives an example of these roles and responsibilities from one K–12 system's stocktake for one area of focus: their college- and career-readiness goal.

On one side of the table is the person playing the role of **system leader**. This is the person whose authority is being leveraged and amplified by the routine, in a manner similar to what the PMDU did for Tony Blair. The fact that the meeting will include this person lends the preparation a sense of urgency. With the help of the Delivery Unit, the system leader will hold the other leader(s) accountable for results by asking tough questions that provide challenge and support, focusing on certain priority areas identified by the data, and making decisions unique to his or her role that help drive progress.

On the other side of the table are the **accountable leaders** who are responsible for making progress on the area(s) of focus. There must be at least one accountable leader for each area of focus you've identified. In this example, a senior and a junior accountable leader are responsible for developing and implementing the agency's delivery plan for college- and career-readiness—and they are answering for its progress to the system leader.

In general, accountable leaders are goal leaders, strategy leaders, or leaders of entities (schools, divisions, departments, districts, campuses) that are responsible for multiple goals and strategies. Where possible, each area of focus should have a single leader, and there should be separate leaders for different areas of focus.

Figure 4A.2   Roles and Responsibilities: College- and Career-Readiness Stocktake

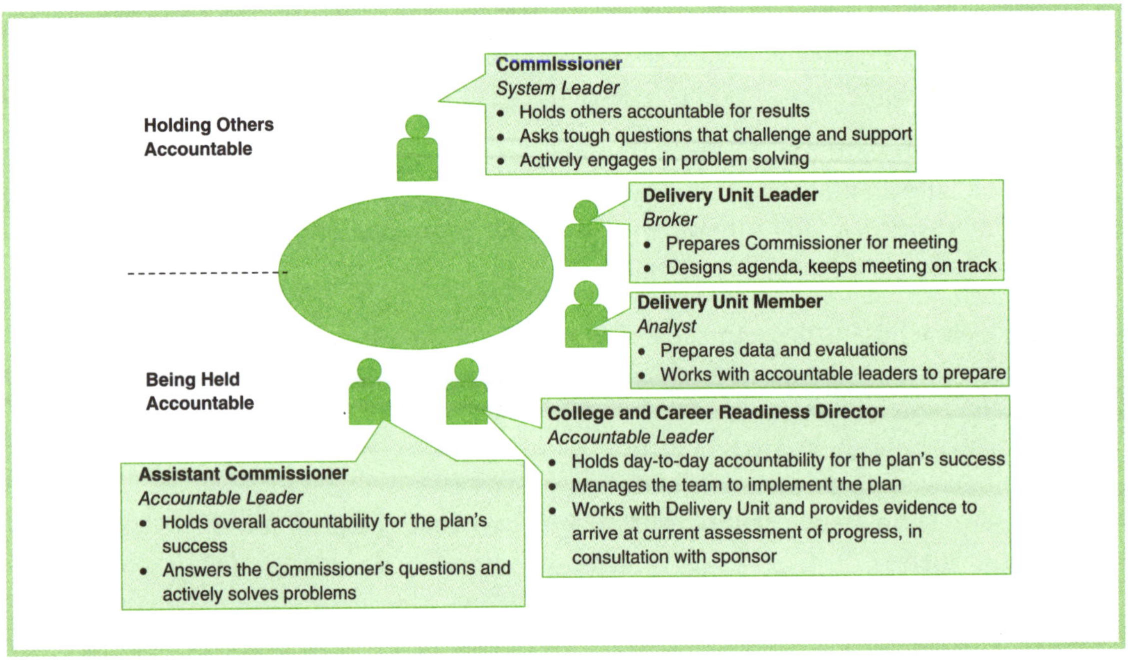

Holding Others Accountable

Commissioner
System Leader
• Holds others accountable for results
• Asks tough questions that challenge and support
• Actively engages in problem solving

Delivery Unit Leader
Broker
• Prepares Commissioner for meeting
• Designs agenda, keeps meeting on track

Delivery Unit Member
Analyst
• Prepares data and evaluations
• Works with accountable leaders to prepare

Being Held Accountable

College and Career Readiness Director
Accountable Leader
• Holds day-to-day accountability for the plan's success
• Manages the team to implement the plan
• Works with Delivery Unit and provides evidence to arrive at current assessment of progress, in consultation with sponsor

Assistant Commissioner
Accountable Leader
• Holds overall accountability for the plan's success
• Answers the Commissioner's questions and actively solves problems

The last roles listed here are played by the Delivery Unit: **broker** and **analyst**. The broker of a routine sets up the conversation between the system leader and accountable leader. He or she has final oversight over the routine's content and agenda and briefs the system leader ahead of time, preparing him or her to focus on the right issues and ask the right questions. If the routine is a meeting, he or she will facilitate it. If the routine takes place in written form, the broker will send the note to the system leader and coordinate the communication of the resulting decisions and actions.

The analyst is the person who prepares the information that is crucial to the broker's work. He or she will work with the relevant accountable leader(s)—and their teams if applicable—to get an initial view of progress on the relevant areas of focus. They will then incorporate additional evidence to arrive at an objective perspective, which they will work with the broker to package for both the system leader and accountable leader(s).

Take a moment to get clear about who's playing what role. Then you're ready to get into the substance of the routines themselves.

What Types of Routines Will You Have, and How Often?

There are two basic types of routines, and you will need to choose how many of each you will have over the course of a given year:

- A **stocktake** is a face-to-face meeting between the system leader and one or more accountable leaders. As the name implies, the purpose is to "take stock" of current progress against one or more areas of focus.
- A **note** or **report** is a written briefing of progress about one or more areas of focus, prepared by the Delivery Unit and sent to the system leader with input from the relevant accountable leader(s).

Both types of routines can be done for an individual area of focus or for multiple areas of focus together. Every system we work with uses stocktakes as a starting point; there's no substitute for the healthy tension created by a vigorous, face-to-face debate about progress. Some of those systems add notes and reports to the mix, particularly if their system leaders are willing to engage meaningfully with them.

How often should routines occur? There are two overall principles to balance against one another:

- **Comprehensiveness:** Set up your routines to allow for a consistent view of progress against all your identified areas of focus.
- **Minimal burden:** Set up your routines so that they achieve comprehensiveness with the least possible burden on the participants in all roles.

One structure that works well is to rotate through areas of focus on a regular, staggered schedule. The Massachusetts Department of Elementary and Secondary Education provides an example of this structure: for each of its five goals, the Delivery Unit held a stocktake once every 6 months, with notes to the Commissioner at 2-month intervals between stocktakes. Figure 4A.3 shows this schedule for the first year, with the staggered start times for each goal.

Notice how this calendar balances the principles of comprehensiveness and minimal burden. Viewed from the perspective of the Commissioner, he was getting an update about one of his top priorities an average of once every 2 weeks, and the cost of this information was about 2 hours a month of meetings (including briefings) and 1 to 2 short notes to read. Viewed from the perspective of an accountable leader, each of them had to work with the Delivery Unit to report on progress once every 2 months. And viewed from the perspective of the Delivery Unit, it was a large number of routines per year (about 30), but manageable for a team of three people.

Figure 4A.3   Calendar of Delivery Routines for Massachusetts Department of Elementary and Secondary Education, 2011

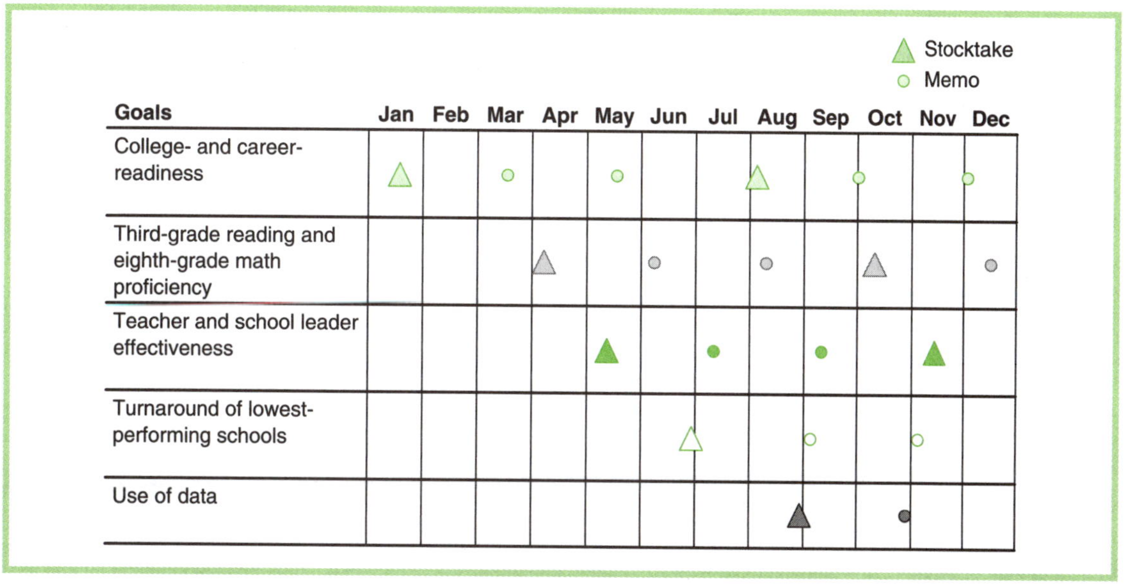

Goals	Jan	Feb	Mar	Apr	May	Jun	Jul	Aug	Sep	Oct	Nov	Dec
College- and career-readiness	△		○		○			△	○		○	
Third-grade reading and eighth-grade math proficiency				△		○		○		△		○
Teacher and school leader effectiveness					△		●		●		△	
Turnaround of lowest-performing schools						△		○		○		
Use of data								△		●		

Legend: △ Stocktake   ○ Memo

For some systems, it's helpful to add an occasional summative stocktake or report that compares progress across all areas of focus. The Tennessee Board of Regents, which has 10 strategies as part of its completion goal, rotates through those strategies in a series of stocktakes and progress notes each year. But once a year, in August, they hold a global stocktake to review all 10 strategies at once. Several other partners have adopted this approach, as has EDI; we hold two global stocktakes each year.

Once you've drafted a schedule of routines like the one above, check to see if they meet the tests of comprehensiveness and minimal burden:

- **Look at the schedule from the perspective of the system leader:**
  - Do the routines give her or him a comprehensive look at her or his priorities on a frequent-enough basis to be meaningful?
  - What is the longest amount of time that will pass before he or she gets an update on any given priority? Is this cycle short enough?
  - How many hours per month of her or his time will it require to participate in all the routines, including preparation? Is this reasonable?

- **Look at the schedule from the perspective of the accountable leaders:**
  - Do the routines give each leader frequent-enough access to the system leader for decision making?
  - Do the routines impose a reasonable burden on each leader—that is, are there not too many too frequently? How many hours per month will this require on average—including both preparation for and participation in routines?

- **Look at the schedule from the perspective of the Delivery Unit:**
  - Is it possible to sustain the total number of routines with the staff in the Delivery Unit?
  - Does each individual team member have a reasonable burden for the routines where they have primary responsibility?

By asking these questions, you can adjust your schedule to make the calendar more comprehensive or less burdensome, as needed.

In the end, it's better to have a few strong routines than to have a large number of poor-quality routines. In fact, if you don't have sufficient time to prepare properly for each of your routines, then it will be difficult to distinguish them from the many other, lower-quality interactions that take place in the day-to-day life of an organization, and the credibility of your delivery effort will be called into question. Create a calendar that allows you to focus on quality rather than quantity with the capacity that you have—or consider whether your current capacity is sufficient to get the job done.

How Will You Assess Progress?

A clear structure and schedule are prerequisites for successful routines: the areas of focus, the leaders responsible for them, and a calendar all make up an important infrastructure for this work. With these questions settled, you can move on to the question at the heart of any delivery routine: how will we assess progress? More specifically, how will we bring the various participants in a delivery routine to a shared view of progress?

Good assessments are based on good **criteria** for determining what constitutes progress, along with evidence that you can use to test those criteria. To arrive at a shared view of progress, participants in a delivery routine must agree on the criteria to use ahead of time—otherwise, they will spend their time arguing over these things rather than discussing progress itself.

What do good criteria look like? Outcomes are a good place to start: a particular metric provides the evidence, and our criteria for progress are the targets, trajectories, or other expectations that we've set for that metric. The same logic applies to metrics for leading indicators or feedback loops that we've discussed in prior chapters.

In education, however, this method runs into a problem that we're familiar with from Part 2: most outcome data—and even a great deal of leading indicator data—are available on an infrequent basis. Graduation rates, for example, are only available annually, and they usually lag beyond the end of the school year. Retention or proficiency data might be available more frequently, but that usually means once per semester or quarter. Some data, particularly the leading indicators and feedback loops we discussed in Parts 2 and 3, may be available more frequently than that. But in the end, the ideal—a real-time review of information that allows for daily or at least weekly decision making—may seem out of reach.

Moreover, the release of data often doesn't line up with your calendar for delivery routines. A key feature of an effective routine is *regularity*—once a month, once a quarter, twice a year, and so on—that builds a steady sense of progress and momentum. The staggered schedules that we saw previously allow for a regular and frequent review of every area of focus. However, data releases are unlikely to cooperate with a calendar like this: not only can the releases be irregular, but they also may not adequately cover every area of focus. You may have excellent outcome data about a target on daily attendance rates, for example, but only annual data on teacher effectiveness. You may have a survey that gives you leading indicator data on implementation of one kind of strategy, but nothing similar in place for the others.

Faced with this challenge, many leaders let the calendar of data releases dictate what they talk about and when. The result is a system-level version of the "what gets measured is what gets taught" problem: our focus is diverted mainly to those areas where we have data, while we may pay little or no attention to areas where we don't.

This gets it backward. Your priorities, expressed by the structure of your routines, should determine what information you collect and when you collect it rather than the other way around. You can adjust the schedule to account for some of the biggest data releases, but there will inevitably be gaps that you have to fill in. This means using qualitative information, which is tricky because it's more subjective. Your method for assessing progress will therefore need to harness qualitative information and bring it to a level of reliability that is similar to, if not exactly the same as, your hard data.

In its earliest days, the PMDU invented a tool called the **assessment framework** that has helped us meet this challenge. The assessment framework is a set of **common criteria** for measuring the progress of any area of focus—a goal or a strategy, at any level of your system. The criteria are centered around one crucial question: *What is the likelihood of delivery?* That is, what's the likelihood that we'll deliver on this goal? The likelihood that a particular strategy will make its promised contribution to the goal? Or the likelihood that a campus, district, or school will implement their strategies and meet their goals?

The assessment framework has been adapted for use by different Delivery Units in multiple contexts over the years, but its basic contours remain the same. The likelihood of delivery is determined by up to five criteria, as shown in Figure 4A.4:

- **Degree of challenge:** What do we know about the scale of the task and the obstacles to be overcome? How difficult is the goal to achieve or the strategy to execute? Does it represent a significant change from historical progress or something less ambitious?
- **Quality of planning:** Does the goal, strategy, or campus/district/school have a leader and team who will be responsible for delivery? Does it have a plan for implementation with clear measures of progress? Most important, does that plan actually drive the team's day-to-day work?
- **Capacity to drive progress:** Have leaders specified the roles that everyone will need to play, across the delivery chain, to deliver real results? How well are leaders engaging with these people to support them in playing these roles? How confident are leaders that these people have both the skill and the will to play these roles at sufficient scale?
- **Stage of delivery:** What is the current phase of implementation—policy and planning, early implementation, late implementation, or conclusion?
- **Evidence of progress:** Do leaders have and regularly review robust evidence of any type—outcomes, leading indicators, achievement of milestones, or other qualitative information—that shows whether progress is being made? Does this evidence suggest that the goal, strategy, or campus/district/school is on track to deliver its promised results?

Each of these criteria can be evaluated on a 4-point scale—as with the capacity review, the 4-point scale prevents a regression to the middle and forces a decision about whether something is more on track or off track.

These criteria are captured in a series of simple rubrics, similar to the delivery planning rubric from Part 3, that pose key questions for each criterion and give a clear description of both the high and low ends of the scale.

The original assessment framework was a very detailed instrument, which contained several subcriteria for each of the main criteria listed above. The ones that we use at EDI are condensed versions that focus on these main criteria and are about two pages long.[2] We've developed separate versions for assessing progress for different areas of focus—goals, strategies, campuses, districts, and schools—and our partner systems have experimented with several variations beyond these initial templates.

Figure 4A.4   The assessment framework helps teams assess likelihood of delivery.

Judgment	Rating	Rationale Summary
Degree of challenge	L/M/H/VH	
Quality of planning		
Capacity to drive progress		
Stage of delivery	1/2/3/4	

Evidence of progress

Likelihood of delivery

Red	Highly problematic—requires urgent and decisive action
Amber-Red	Problematic—requires substantial attention, some aspects need urgent attention
Amber-Green	Mixed—aspect(s) require substantial attention, some good
Green	Good—requires refinement and systematic implementation

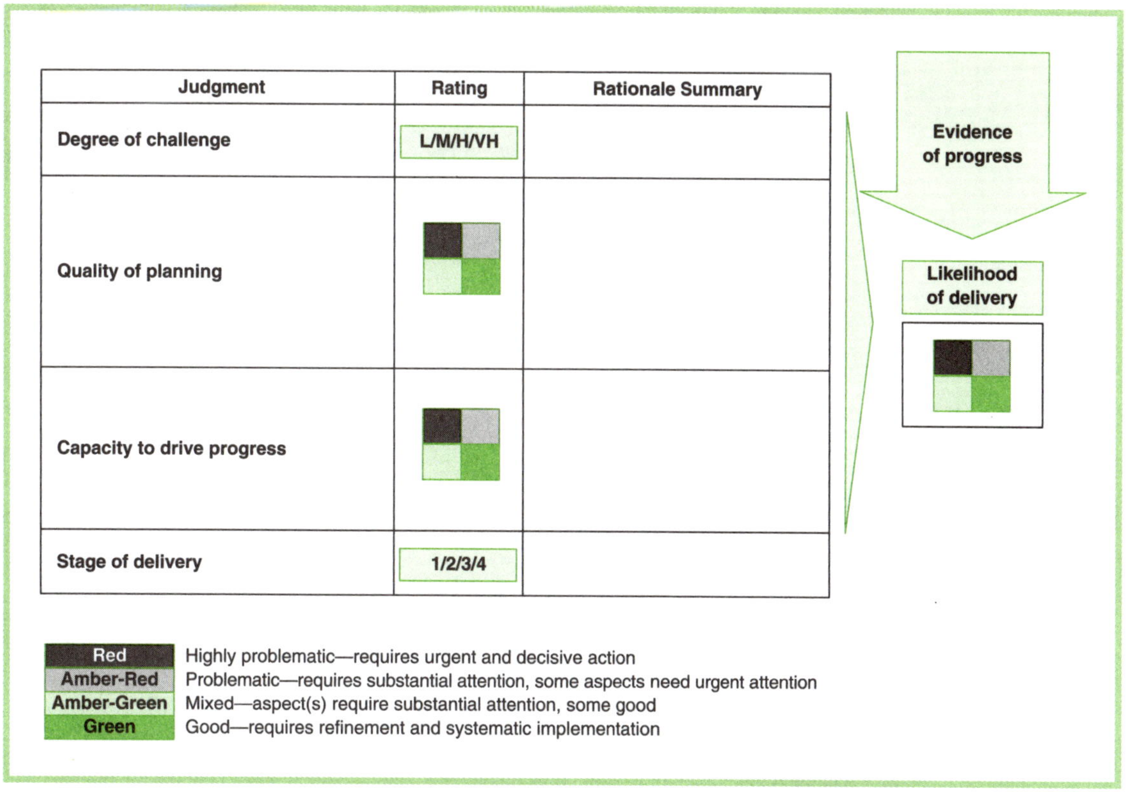

There is no single "right" assessment framework. But the concept of a single framework for assessing progress is powerful for two reasons.

First, the assessment framework helps address the challenge of infrequent or irregular data. Recall the third question of delivery: at any given moment, how will we know that we are on track? The assessment framework gives you a way to answer this question *at any given moment*, by taking the criteria and applying them to the area of focus in question. This is possible because the criteria in the framework include data and quantitative evidence, but go beyond them.

The criterion on "evidence of progress" is deliberately vague about *which* evidence to use. This allows leaders flexibility to look at whatever the most recent evidence is—be that progress against milestones, recently released outcome data, or leading indicators—and to draw a conclusion about whether things are on track. Again, this turns the usual way of doing things on its head: rather than waiting until data are available to make a judgment on progress, you commit to making judgments of progress on a sensible schedule that will support decision-making, and use those times to size up whatever data are most recently available. Moreover, translating the raw evidence into a rating is a critical and oft-overlooked step in interpreting this information; it's what distinguishes a delivery routine from a mere data meeting.

Whereas the criterion on evidence of progress is backward-looking, the other criteria are forward-looking. This provides a crucial complement to the evidence. A strategy may be on track right now, but a lack of capacity in the field may not bode well for its likelihood of staying on track at a later stage of implementation.

Conversely, we may be behind trajectory on a particular goal, but if we've significantly improved the plan to achieve the goal in the last month, this might presage a turnaround. The criteria combine to give a clear and balanced picture of the likelihood of delivery that is richer than what the data alone would provide.

Figure 4A.5 shows what a typical use of the assessment framework might look like: a rating or judgment for each of the criteria, with a few sentences describing the rationale for each. Notice that the evidence section is as specific

Figure 4A.5   Sample Assessment Framework Ratings for a Single Strategy

Strategy:		Common Core Implementation
	Rating	**Rationale**
Quality of Planning	AG	There is a plan for Common Core Implementation, but it is mostly new and has not yet begun to shape the work.
Capacity to Drive Progress	AR	School leaders know that his shift is coming, but it is less clear whether there is much traction for it amongst teachers. We have not yet communicated expectations clearly here.
Evidence of Progress	R	In general, our teachers do not yet believe that something different is required of them by the Common Core. This must change before they will ever change their teaching practices.
Data Points		Survey results suggest that nearly 50% of teachers in our Complex Area do not believe that Common Core will require them to do anything differently.
Overall Likelihood of Success	AR	Based on our low starting point, we will need an excellent plan that nearly shapes the work, along with a clear understanding of roles and expectations for every teacher, to have a good chance of being successful.
Potential Changes		Low teacher awareness is a major barrier, and it is also key to making the Common Core real in our schools.
Potential Next Steps		At next meeting of principals, share the plan with them and work with them to think through how they can carry out its expectations. Ask each of them to share basic introductory presentation or Common Core and its expectations with their teachers.
Potential Help Needed		Need additional resources from HIDOE that communicate about the Common Core, what it is, and what its expectations are, as well as resources and materials that can be used in our trainings with teachers.

■ Red   ▨ Amber-Red   ▨ Amber-Green   ■ Green

Source: Hawai'i Department of Education, 2013.

as possible about the data or information that support the rating, without showing all the underlying raw data. This is the practice of authentic cherry-picking we discussed in Part 2—a way to interpret the data and its implications that is accessible to others.

The second source of the assessment framework's power is the potential it provides for *comparative assessment of progress*. Thus far, we've only spoken of progress with respect to the objective criteria in the assessment framework. But one other way to sharpen an assessment of progress is by comparing judgments across your areas of focus.

Under normal circumstances, this is difficult. How do we compare our progress on achieving a postsecondary access target with our progress on achieving a success target? The metrics are different, and the targets may differ in their ambition and realism. Likewise, how do we compare progress on two different strategies? The definitions of success for any two strategies will vary widely, if they are well defined at all.

The assessment framework addresses this problem by reducing this complex array of information to a series of common color judgments based on balanced criteria. We may not be able to compare data on two different goals directly, but we *can* compare the judgments we've made on evidence of progress for each of them using the criteria in the assessment framework. In similar fashion, we can compare the quality of planning and capacity to drive progress for each goal, while taking into account the differences in degree of challenge and current stage of delivery. In short, the assessment framework allows us to valuably compare unlike things as if they were alike. Figure 4A.6 shows the "league table" that can result from this exercise—in this case, for a stocktake that EDI recently had on the various strategies in its own delivery plan.

These comparisons have an inherent usefulness: they help us prioritize our time and energy toward those areas of focus (in this case, strategies) that need the most attention. But just as important, the comparisons actually help us *improve* the accuracy of the individual ratings. To prepare the league table above, the EDI team engaged in a series of **calibration exercises**: Each strategy leader would share initial judgments on the work for which they were responsible. Then, other team members would question and challenge these judgments based on their own experiences and the judgments they had made, debating and discussing each goal until they had arrived at a set of judgments that were consistent across them all. Sometimes, this meant debating multiple strategies with similar evidence and different ratings. Sometimes it was the opposite: several goals would have the same ratings, but different evidence.

This is how comparative assessment adds its greatest value. Just as K–12 teachers benefit from similar debates about what kind of student work constitutes an A and what merits a B, education leaders can use this kind of dialogue to improve the objectivity of their ratings *and* their own understanding of what good looks like against all the criteria in the assessment framework. This dialogue is not only useful for delivery leaders as they bring participants in a delivery routine to a shared view of progress before the conversation begins; it's also useful as a tool for self-assessment and reflection. In our work with higher education systems in the Access to Success (A2S) initiative, we regularly used the assessment framework to frame *cross-system* dialogues about the likelihood

Figure 4A.6   League Table of Progress on Multiple Strategies

| Goal | Strategy | Ratings | | | Overall Likelihood of Success |
		Quality of Planning	Capacity	Evidence of Progress	
K–12	New engagements and partnerships (strategic partnerships and types)	AG	AR	G	G
Culture	Work/life balance	AG	AR	AR	G
Operations	Maintain expert and engaged board	G	G	G	G
Operations	Maintain strong internal controls	G	G	AG	G
Operations	Retain Gates Foundation as major funder	G	G	G	G
Operations	Obtain new sources of revenue to diversify base of support and reduce organizational risk	G	G	G	G
Higher Education	Special projects and partnerships	AG	AG	G	G
K–12	Deepen and sustain the delivery approach in K–12 education systems through intensive delivery engagements	AG	G	AG	AG
K–12	K–12 network	AR	AG	AG	AG
K–12	Delivery for nonprofits practice	AG	AG	G	AG
K–12	District and school practice	AG	AG	AG	AG
Expert Resource	Effective communications	AG	AG	AG	AG
Culture	Teamwork	AG	AR	AG	AG
Culture	Training	AR	G	AG	AG
Culture	Feedback	G	AG	AG	AG
Operations	Operate within budget	G	G	AG	AG
Higher Education	Support intensive engagements	AG	AG	AR	AG
Higher Education	Develop a campus strategy	AG	AG	R	AG
K–12	Turnaround practice	G	AG	AG	AG
Expert Resource	Curricular materials	AR	AR	AR	AR

Goal.	Strategy	Ratings			Overall Likelihood of Success
		Quality of Planning	Capacity	Evidence of Progress	
K–12	Capacity building and leadership development practice	AG	AR	AR	AR
Expert Resource	Network interactions	AR	G	AG	AR
Expert Resource	Library of resources	R	AG	AR	AR
Expert Resource	Data and data tools	AR	AR	AR	AR
Operations	Maintain healthy surplus of operating funds	AG	AG	AR	AR
Higher Education	Maintain a strong network	AR	AR	G	AR

■ Red   ▨ Amber-Red   ▢ Amber-Green   ▪ Green

that each participating system would deliver on their goals to cut achievement gaps in postsecondary access and success in half.

In summary, the assessment framework allows you to rigorously make use of all your evidence about implementation—both quantitative and qualitative—through the application of objective criteria and the power of comparison. As you set up your delivery routines, it will be important for you to adopt an assessment framework of some kind—the one in this book, an adaptation of it, or something else constructed with similar principles—to have a consistent way to measure progress across all your areas of focus.

Prepare for Routines

We said at the beginning of this chapter that preparation is what makes the difference between a true delivery routine and a waste of time. Thus far, most of this chapter has dealt with preparing for your routines by organizing them properly: defining areas of focus, leaders to be held accountable, a schedule of routines, and a method for consistently assessing progress. Suppose now that your routines are on the calendar, and the first one is coming up in a few weeks. What do you do now?

At EDI, we've developed a five-step protocol for preparing for each routine:

1. Gather evidence and arrive at an initial view of progress

2. Arrive at your own view of progress

3. Develop objectives for the routine

4. Develop supporting materials for the routine

5. Brief the relevant leaders

Routines work best when the agendas, structure, and even the format stay as consistent as possible; this helps everyone involved learn to play their roles well over time. The purpose of these steps is to produce this consistent experience for each routine.

Step 1: Gather Evidence and Arrive at an Initial View of Progress

You'll start by applying the criteria in your assessment framework to the area or areas of focus under review. This first step will often occur jointly with the relevant goal, strategy, campus, district, or school leaders, and it is usually a self-assessment facilitated by a delivery team member.

> Please visit EDI's website at www.deliveryinstitute.org/4A for a template that you can use to arrive at initial judgments of progress using the assessment framework.

In K–12 systems like Massachusetts and Kentucky, for example, the goals are the main areas of focus for each routine, and each goal is broken up into a handful of strategies that are evaluated individually. In preparing for a given routine, delivery team members meet with goal and strategy leaders to evaluate progress toward the overall goal (using whatever data are available) and the likelihood of delivery for each strategy—the likelihood, that is, that each strategy will make its projected contribution to the goal. In these meetings, the Delivery Unit's role is to facilitate, to push participants to link their judgments to evidence and to the criteria in the framework, and to ask challenging questions where necessary.

The result is a series of initial judgments on one or more areas of focus using a template like the one we saw above in Figure 4A.5. They can be combined into a league table of judgments, as we saw in Figure 4A.6.

Step 2: Arrive at Your Own View of Progress

Accountable leaders are good sources of information and evidence for making your judgments, but they should not be the only sources of evidence. Most will, for obvious reasons, have a bias for evidence that casts a more favorable light on their work. Delivery leaders and team members bring an objective perspective to this process, and over time, they will also bring the experience of having seen these judgments made in multiple contexts over longer periods of time. Once you have your initial judgments, test them internally with the Delivery Unit: are they consistent? Is each one backed up by sufficient evidence? Is there additional evidence you'll need to get in order to confirm or adjust a particular rating?

Remember the adage: Trust, but verify. The final judgment for any area of focus must belong to the delivery team; you'll need to be able to stand behind it under the scrutiny of the system leader and, possibly, the public. For this reason, every Delivery Unit must have the right to disagree with the self-assessment made by the accountable leaders. You should notify them if you do this and give them an opportunity to respond by accepting the new judgment or presenting compelling evidence that backs up their initial rating. Doing your homework is crucial here: the clearer your criteria and the better your evidence, the less likely there is to be any controversy. The final decision, however, is yours.

Step 3: Develop Objectives for the Routine

While he was Secretary of State, Henry Kissinger once opened a press conference by asking, "Does anyone have any questions for my answers?" Kissinger is a controversial figure, but nobody could ever accuse him of being unprepared.

A delivery routine has something in common with Kissinger's press conference: anticipating and answering the key questions ahead of time is crucial. Michael always used to say that when he attended a delivery routine, he had a fairly clear idea of about 80% of what he hoped would be said and decided. He knew what the evidence suggested should be the major topics of conversation, and he and his team constructed the routines to focus on these topics and reach a clear conclusion and next step for each.

To engage in this type of preparation for a routine, you'll need to develop an **agenda** for how participants' time will be used. This agenda must be driven by clear **objectives**: what do you want the participants to accomplish and walk away with?

At first glance, this kind of preparation seems only to apply to face-to-face routines, such as stocktakes. But whether the routine is a meeting or a note or report, you'll need to consider the objectives you want to achieve and how you want to use your participants' time to accomplish those objectives. The structure of an agenda can just as soon become the outline of a memo or report. Knowing that this kind of dual application is possible, we focus here on preparing an agenda for a meeting. For a more detailed discussion of the principles of meeting preparation and agenda building, please see Chapter 5A.

Every routine should be structured around three kinds of objectives. These objectives make the discussion "T-Shaped," as Figure 4A.7 shows, by striking the right balance between breadth and depth of discussion.

Figure 4A.7   Three Types of Objectives for a Routine

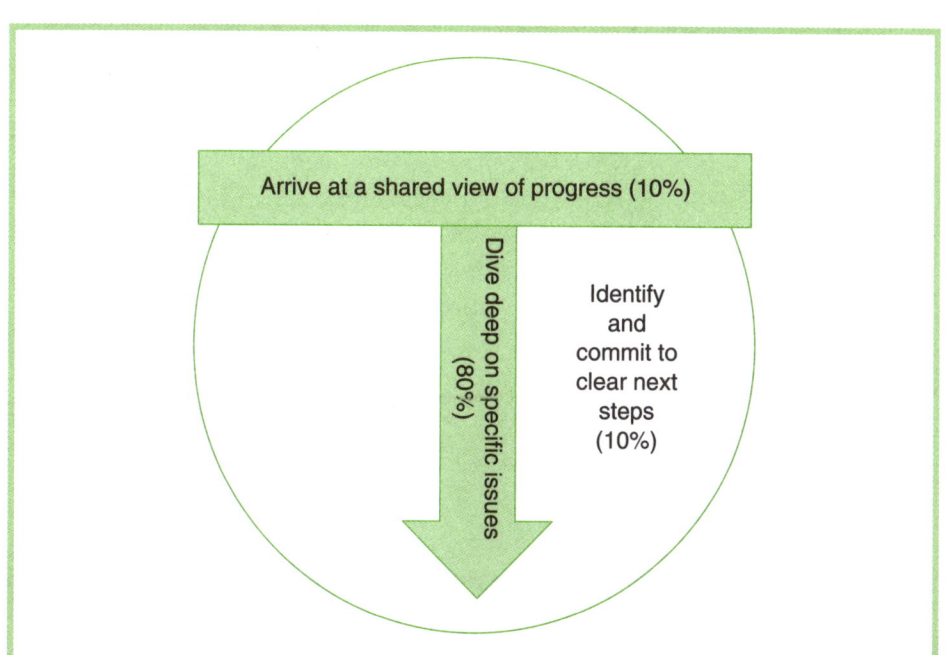

Arrive at a shared view of progress (10%)

Dive deep on specific issues (80%)

Identify and commit to clear next steps (10%)

The first objective for any routine is to **arrive at a shared view of progress**. To frame the conversation, participants need a broad overview and presentation of what the evidence says about progress and its implications for how you want to focus your time. Based on all the work you have done in Steps 1 and 2, you'll be able to summarize the current state of progress (often by copying the color judgments from those exercises) and note any patterns you see. What do the overall outcome data say? Are there strategies and/or goals that are most at risk? Are there areas of the assessment framework—like capacity or quality of planning—where there seems to be weakness, or strength, across the board? These patterns of strength and weakness will help you choose the highest priority **issues** to discuss during the rest of the meeting.

Because all the participants will have worked with you to define these judgments, this should be a short part of the routine—no more than 10% of the time that you've asked for. You will generally want to present a summary of this information, such as a league table and/or written description of the most important successes and challenges, and affirm its implications with participants: "These are the key facts about progress. And they have led to these issues for us to discuss during this meeting. Can we all agree that these are the right issues?" Getting the first objective right thus helps you frame the entire agenda for the routine.

The second type of objective—and the one that will take up the most time—is to **dive deep on specific issues** that you have identified in your review of progress. This portion is where the real work happens; it should take up about 80% of the time in the routine.

How do you come up with objectives for each issue? Colin Powell, the former Secretary of State and military leader, has four rules for analyzing intelligence that are useful to consider here:

- Tell me what you know;
- Tell me what you don't know;
- Then tell me what you think; and
- Always distinguish which is which.[3]

These rules will help us identify specific objectives for each issue:

- Tell me what you know: what are the "killer facts" to bring to bear? What makes this issue so important and so critical for us to spend time on? These facts, drawn from the evidence you have already gathered, should cause participants to pay attention.
- Tell me what you don't know: what are the key unanswered questions? Try to focus on questions that, if answered, would lead to a resolution of the issue and/or drive significant progress.
- Tell me what you think: what is your interpretation of the facts? And what do you think the way forward is? This is where you propose solutions and answers to those unanswered questions, either for debate or for further investigation.

Consider how this information could help you arrive at a clear objective for participants. Some examples are given in Figure 4A.8.

Figure 4A.8 From Issues to Objectives

Issue	Key Facts: What You Know	Key Questions: What You Don't Know	Potential Answers: What You Think	Objectives: Participants in the Routine Will . . .
Teacher effectiveness systems	• We have staked our success on this strategy • It is at risk of failing because fewer than 20% of teachers have confidence in it	• Why do teachers have such little faith in the system?	• Execution has been fairly strong, but communication has been weak • There is a natural skepticism toward change that we must overcome	• Understand the challenge posed by low teacher support for the new evaluation system • Identify additional questions to investigate about the root causes of the challenge • Identify specific ways to boost teacher confidence in the new teacher evaluation system
First-year retention rates	• Retention rates have been flat across the system in the last 3 years • However, three campuses are real "bright spots": they have higher than average URM [underrepresented minority] and Pell enrollments and have achieved substantial gains in retention during this period	• What has caused our "bright spots" to be so successful?	• These three campuses are leaders in using data to diagnose student needs and target services to them, with an emphasis on the first-year experience • We need to aggressively replicate this capacity on other campuses	• Understand and reflect on lessons learned from "bright spot" campuses • Agree to develop a new strategy to bring these lessons learned to all campuses
Low capacity across the system	• All our strategies score lowest in "capacity to drive progress" • This is despite a recent influx of resources—both money and people—to implement these strategies	• Where on the delivery chain is implementation breaking down? • Is it the same for each strategy or different?	• Most of the new people were hired into regional offices, but we have not yet hired a coordinator in the system office to support and communicate with them	• Understand and agree on the capacity challenge • Agree to expedite hiring of a coordinator for new hires in regional offices

By working through these questions for each issue, you'll develop a much better sense of what you want participants to walk away with. Sometimes, "tell me what you think" will be so well developed that you'll have a specific solution to propose; in this case, your objective would be to have participants debate, adjust, and agree on the solution. In other cases, the unanswered questions will dominate and your objective will be to have everyone think together about what the answers to those questions could be (or how to get them). In general, drive as far toward a solution as you can before bringing each issue to participants in a routine; this will ensure that the discussion is as clear and sharp as possible.

The last type of objective is to **identify and commit to clear next steps**. Much of this will have happened throughout the routine, but the last 10% of your time should be reserved for summarizing, clarifying, affirming, and committing participants to next steps. This means being very specific about what each step is, who is responsible for it, and by when; the next time this area of focus is reviewed, one important piece of evidence will be the participants' progress on completing these steps.

Notice the shift that these objectives imply. Without adequate preparation, most meetings never get past the broad discussion of progress in the first objective. By taking the time up front to curate the evidence, to get agreement on its meaning and implications, and to design the rest of the routine to focus on these implications, a Delivery Unit can set up these interactions to accomplish much more.

Developing Objectives for a Routine in Eagle County Schools

In Eagle County Schools (CO), the district established routines that allowed district staff to regularly report to the superintendent on the progress of implementation of their core strategies and tactics. Ahead of each routine, the delivery leader (called the Chief Strategy Officer, or CSO) would sit down with the relevant leaders for those tactics and strategies that would be in the "hot seat" for the upcoming routine. Because this process was new in Eagle County, the CSO also invited leaders of other strategies and tactics to join as they were available, both to give their feedback and also to learn from the process.

In these preroutine meetings, the CSO would walk through the assessment framework rubric with the accountable leads and help them reflect on progress. Based on the ratings, they would identify strengths and challenges to discuss in the routine, then identify key objectives for the routine.

One such example is outlined in Figure 4A.9. The assessment framework ratings showed a mixed picture in terms of progress on this particular tactic. Based on those ratings, the group identified key strengths and challenges (see Figure 4A.10).

From the preroutine conversation, the group realized that the biggest challenge they faced was getting agreement on really how to make pathways available at scale. Because agreement on this was so vital to planning and implementing the work, they decided to make that a large focus of the discussion at the upcoming routine with the superintendent, and generated the following objectives for that routine:

- Arrive at a shared view of progress;
- Understand the strengths and challenges of implementation so far;
- Understand options for structuring pathways goals/targets;
- Discuss options and agree on that which makes the most sense for Eagle County; and
- Identify and commit to clear next steps.

Figure 4A.9   Assessment Framework Ratings for a Single Tactic in Eagle County, CO

Tactic	Quality of Planning	Capacity	Evidence of Progress	Overall Likelihood of Success
Create clear and customized pathways to college or careers that include abundant opportunities for experiencing college-level work, earning college credits while in high school, and with local employers and experts engaging in experiential opportunities.	Amber-Red	Amber-Red	Amber-Green	Amber-Green

Figure 4A.10   Key Strengths and Challenges

Strengths	Challenges
<ul><li>There is a good foundation to build on; we have a system that has been successful in some cases that we want to improve.</li><li>Stakeholders are engaged and agree broadly with the goals of this work.</li><li>We have the basis of a strong plan and are moving into the implementation phase.</li></ul>	<ul><li>We see that engaging all key student subgroups and their parents may be a challenge, and we have not yet planned for that.</li><li>While we agree broadly on the goal of increasing pathways available to students, we haven't gotten agreement on the specifics of what that means—should the focus be on increasing AP participation or on increasing participation in internships? Or all the above? We need more discussion of and agreement on these questions.</li><li>Some structural barriers exist that limit our capacity to provide access to pathways at scale, but we have begun to address these already.</li></ul>

Step 4: Develop Supporting Materials for the Routine

Once you know your objectives, the rest of the preparation for the routine follows. How will you use the routine to achieve each objective? And what supporting materials and/or information will you need to do this? Whether your routine is a memo, a report, or a meeting, you will need to build an agenda that sets up the right decision points or discussions for each objective and provides the right supporting material (information, graphs, charts, and so on).

Figure 4A.11 is an example of a 90-minute stocktake agenda using a few objectives from the above examples and our agenda template from Chapter 5A.

You can see here how a clear understanding of your objectives leads to the "run of show" in the How column. This, in turn, helps you allocate time, assign responsibility for pieces of the agenda, and determine what evidence and materials you need. In fact, the Materials column serves as an initial outline of the content you will need to prepare for the stocktake (or, if it were a memo, the content to include in it).

> For more information on agenda building, please see Chapter 5A. For more information on how to build supporting materials, such as PowerPoint presentations with clear story lines, please see Chapter 5B. And for more information on supporting materials that involve data visualization, please refer to Chapter 2A.

A good agenda thus helps you customize each routine in a way that's driven by the evidence you have gathered, while maintaining an overall structure that participants can become familiar with from routine to routine. It also helps you pinpoint which evidence and data will be most important to bring for the participants to use. This is different from the data meeting approach, in which participants interpret large amounts of raw data together; instead, participants work from focused information that you've selected to answer specific questions and achieve specific objectives to move the work forward.

Step 5: Brief the Relevant Leaders

With your agenda and materials in hand, there's just one final step to take: briefing the participants to prepare them for the routine. There are two kinds of briefings to give: to the system leader and to the relevant accountable leader(s).

The system leader briefing is especially crucial. Recall what we said in the introduction to this chapter: a good delivery routine helps amplify a leader's formal authority by giving them access to the right facts, information, and questions to ask before each conversation about performance. This creates the useful illusion that she or he has been paying close attention all along. The briefing is where we create this reality: by taking all the hard work and preparation we have done and translating that into a particular role for the system leader.

What does this look like? The format is fairly straightforward: a 10- to 15-minute check-in between the delivery leader and the system leader within a day or two before the routine itself. In this time, your job is to help him or her benefit from all the preparation you've done. As with any other meeting, this one should have objectives as well. In general, every briefing should accomplish two things:

- **Affirm the objectives and agenda of the routine:** It will help you immensely if your system leader is on the same page with you and trying to accomplish the same things in the time you have together. This is the space for them to understand the agenda you have prepared, to give feedback on it if necessary, and to commit to it.

- **Affirm the role the system leader will be playing:** Depending on the way you structure the agenda, your system leader may have specific things you need them to do. There may be introductory remarks you want them to make, for example, or key things to emphasize during certain parts of the routine. There are at least three questions you want to answer firmly:

  - What messages do you want the system leader to send? You might want him or her to frame the importance of the issues at hand, for example.
  - What are the key facts that you want him or her to emphasize? Think back to the "killer facts" you came up with in your preparation.
  - What are the questions that you want him or her to press? Again, think back to your preparation and the "key questions" you came up with for each issue.

A useful device for selecting these key messages, key facts, and key questions is the "leaving the room" test: what's so essential that you wouldn't want to let participants in the routine leave the room before they address it? Phrase it to your system leader that way: "Don't let them leave the room without a satisfactory answer to this question," for example.

Once a system leader becomes accustomed to these briefings, she or he will come to appreciate the clarity they provide for the purpose of each routine. One Delivery Unit we worked with quips that the briefings have helped them "train" the system leader to say and do exactly the right things at the routine. This is not because the delivery team is in charge, but because they've mastered the art of giving their leader the very information and questions that he would have prepared himself, if he had the time.

The other kind of briefing you'll hold is for other participants in the routine. You will likely have already spent some time with these people during your preparation. The purpose of this final briefing is to give them a heads-up about what to expect during the routine. As one delivery leader who's been doing this work for a while told us, "If the goal team goes in and gets hammered by the Commissioner, we lose credibility with them if we haven't prepared them for that." If your judgments of progress disagreed with theirs, this is the time to let them know and to invite them to bring any additional evidence that might change your view. It's also the place to make sure that you're addressing all the topics that are important for them by inviting feedback on the agenda.

Remember that, in many cases, this will be some of the only times that these participants get with the system leader. This is an important opportunity for them to identify the biggest obstacles to their own success and to ask for help. You want to encourage this kind of openness; as that same delivery leader told us, "People now come to us and say 'My project is Amber-Red, here are the reasons why, and I want the Commissioner to know.' This is the point you want to get to."

Figure 4A.11 Sample Stocktake Agenda

What (Objectives)	How	Who	Time (Mins.)	Materials Needed

• Arrive at a shared view of progress	• Present data on goal and league table of "likelihood of delivery" of each strategy (7)
	• Discussion (3)
	  – Are these the right challenges to prioritize?
	  – Anything we should change about the agenda?
		• Delivery leader
		• Group
			• 10	• Latest data on goal
				• League table with supporting evidence
				• Flipchart
				• Markers

• Understand the challenge posed by low teacher support for the new evaluation system
• Identify additional questions to investigate about root causes
• Identify specific ways to boost teacher confidence in the new teacher evaluation system
	• Present evidence about implementation progress and teacher survey feedback (10)
	• Discussion (30):
	  – What are the root causes of low teacher support? What should we investigate?
	  – What can we do right now to improve teacher confidence?
		• Strategy leader
		• Group
			• 40	• Report of milestones met and missed on implementation of teacher evaluation system
				• Teacher survey data
				• Flipchart
				• Markers

• Understand and agree on the capacity challenge
• Agree to expedite hiring of a coordinator for new hires in regional offices
	• Present evidence (10):
	  – Capacity is where we are rated lowest
	  – Yet our spending and FTEs have increased dramatically in recent months
	  – We believe that the vacancy of the coordinator position is holding us back
	• Discussion (20):
	  – Do we agree with this hypothesis? If not, what would we have to see to be convinced one way or the other?
	  – If we agree, what would it take to expedite the hiring of the coordinator?
		• Goal leader
		
		• Group
			• 30	• League table with supporting evidence on capacity to drive progress
				• Data on trends in spending and FTEs for the major strategies over the last year
				• Evidence from interviews with field staff about what is holding them back
				• Flipchart
				• Markers

• Identify and commit to clear next steps	• Brainstorm next steps, responsibility, and dates (10)	• Group	• 10	• Flipchart • Markers

Dive Deep on Specific Issues

More generally, this briefing is important because, while there should be real accountability in a routine, it shouldn't be because people are kept in the dark about what will happen. Surprise is a cheap way to achieve accountability, and even then, it's a temporary accountability based more on fear than on empowerment and constructive dialogue. Participants should know what the key topics will be, where they're likely to be pushed by the system leader, and what questions they should be prepared to answer. They should know, too, that the questions will be tough. If you've prepared well, you won't need the element of surprise to have a constructive routine.

These five steps—gathering evidence, arriving at a view of progress, developing objectives, creating supporting materials, and briefing relevant leaders—will help you prepare thoroughly for each routine. Some systems, like the Hawai'i Department of Education, have even formalized these steps as part of their calendar of routines. For each stocktake with the superintendent, there are actually a number of preparation routines that are part of each quarterly cycle: a stocktake preparation meeting with the strategy team, an initial memo describing progress, a meeting with the deputy superintendent, and finally a revised memo to brief the superintendent before the main stocktake. Institutionalizing these practices can be a helpful way to ensure that the right preparation happens and that routines are of high quality.

Routines at the Massachusetts Department of Elementary and Secondary Education

The Massachusetts Department of Elementary and Secondary Education has been running routines for its core goals (and their constituent strategies) since early 2011, longer than most of our K–12 partner systems. Here is a sample of some of the slides of a stocktake presentation from February 2013, on their "Success After High School" (college- and career-readiness) goal. The team began by looking at the overall data on one of their key outcomes—the 5-year graduation rate—and noted that they were above trajectory (see Figure 4A.12).

They then turned to the individual strategies underlying the college- and career-readiness goal, noting that most were on track but that there were a few trouble spots (see Figure 4A.13).

Finally, in February 2013, the team was in the midst of a significant shift: they were expanding the college- and career-readiness goal to include Career/Vocational Technical Education and Adult and Community Learning Services. At the stocktake, they shared the results of their initial thinking on how to organize this work, which added several strategies to the delivery plan.

With this context in mind, the team identified two sets of issues to dominate the discussion in the stocktake:

- **Organizing the shift to the new delivery planning architecture:** The addition of Career/Vocational Technical Education to this plan was the result of a great deal of work and stakeholder engagement, with strong support from a member of the Massachusetts Board of Elementary and Secondary Education who led a task force on the subject (with the Delivery Unit's help). The Delivery Unit had a number of "asks" for the Commissioner in this area, including his continued engagement with the task force and support in thinking about the right high school equivalency assessments to use.

(Continued)

(Continued)

Figure 4A.12   Performance Against Trajectory for 5-Year Graduation Rate Target

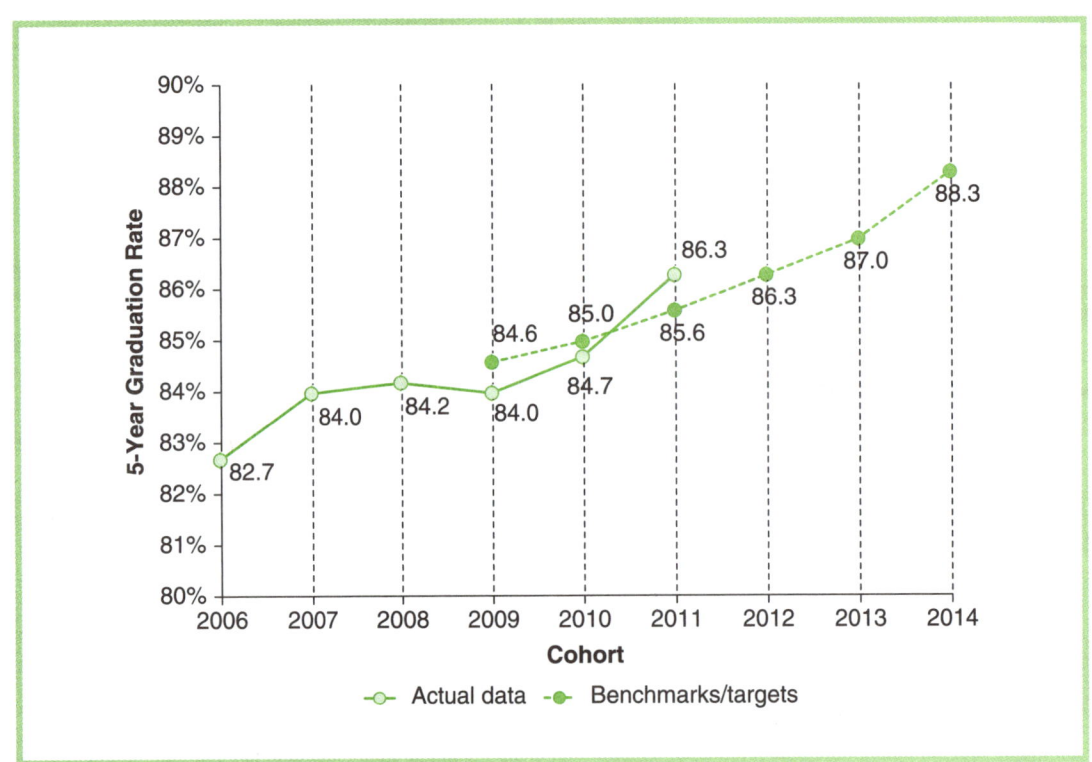

Figure 4A.13   Progress on Strategies Contributing to College- and Career-Readiness Goal

	Overall Likelihood of Success									
Original C and CR Priority Projects	Sept. 2011	Dec. 2011	Feb. 2012	April 2012	June 2012	Aug. 2012	Oct. 2012	Dec. 2012	Feb. 2013	Rationale
MassCore	AR	AR	AR	AR	AR	AR	AR	AR	R	Will not reach original trajectory/target
Academic Support	AG	AR	AR	AR	AR	AR	AR	AR	AR	Do not have the capacity to implement the initiative beyond grant giving
Mass School Counseling Model	AG	G	AG	AG	G	G	AG	G	AG	Project 4C Summit 2/13 to assist counselors in using Edwin Analytics reports
Early Warning Indicator System	AG	AG	AG	AG	AG	AG	G	G	G	Close to 1,000 listeners for the Edwin Analytics webinars featuring EWIS reports
Connecting Activities	AG	AG	AG	AG	AG	AG	AG	AG	G	New Connecting Activities Coordinator on board in March
MassGrad	AG	AG	G	G	G	G	G	G	G	Average increase of 1.6% in 5-year graduation rate for participating MassGrad schools (133 schools)

■ Red   ▢ Amber-Red   ▢ Amber-Green   ▮ Green

- **Improving the MassCore work:** The single "red" strategy was MassCore, an initiative designed to encourage districts to help all students graduate with a certain college preparatory course of study (the MassCore). The strategy was crucial because improving MassCore completion amongst high school graduates was the other key goal in this delivery plan. The strategy was at risk for a number of reasons—in particular, the postponement of a hoped-for policy change that would have required districts to make MassCore the default curriculum—so the Delivery Unit used part of the meeting to identify ways that the Commissioner and team could work together to get things back on track.

The same T-Shaped structure, with a broad overview followed by a deeper focus in a few areas, is evident in the bimonthly memos that come between the stocktakes. Figure 4A.14 is a snapshot of the first page of the memo for the same college- and career-readiness goal from four months later, in June 2013.

Notice the similarities: early on, there's a league table to provide a broad overview of progress, and we can see that while the MassCore initiative has improved, it's still at risk. The league table is followed by a deeper dive on each of the strategies, with the most at risk coming first. In the case of MassCore, the team had spent the last few months coming up with new activities to shore up this strategy and improve MassCore completion rates. The next steps here, as listed in Figure 4A.15, are much clearer than before: in the absence of a policy requiring

Figure 4A.14   First Page of June 2013 Memo on College- and Career-Readiness Goal

Massachusetts Department of Elementary and Secondary Education

75 Pleasant Street, Malden, Massachusetts 02148-4906

MEMORANDUM

To: Commissioner Mitchell Chester
From: Delivery Unit
Date: June 6, 2013
Subject: Bimonthly Memo for Success After High School Agency Goal

FOR YOUR IMMEDIATE ACTION/ATTENTION

For your attention: ESE recently released the **Integrating College and Career Readiness Demonstration Initiative Grant RFP** (Fund Code: 105). This is a new competitive grant program designed to provide start-up support to districts to create a comprehensive approach to college and career readiness through the creation and integration of activities that mutually support both academic and workplace readiness goals. The program offers two years of funding, with up to a year to create a plan, and then an implementation phase upon completion of the plan so that participating districts can launch their plans. The awardees will serve as demonstration sites. The funds were privately raised by Gerald Chertavian for a total of $250,000. Each of the five grant recipients will receive ~$50,000. Applications are due on Friday, June 28th.

(Continued)

(Continued)

OVERALL LIKELIHOOD OF DELIVERY

Last 4 ratings

	Rating	Project	Note
○ ● ○ ○	At Risk	MassCore Policy and Implementation	Need aggressive communication and marketing
○ ○	Likely	Academic Support	Changes to grant language and summer '13 increases
	Likely	MA School Counseling Model	Setting measurable goals
● ● ●	Highly Likely	Connecting Activities	Promoted ICCR agenda
● ● ● ●	Highly Likely	MassGrad	Sharing promising practices in Malden
● ● ● ●	Highly Likely	Early Warning Indicator System	Revising risk model and promoting use

STATUS OF 2014 PRIORITY PROJECTS

MassCore ○ At Risk: Need aggressive communication and marketing

In the previous iteration of the Success after High School delivery plan, the MassCore policy and implementation project relied heavily on changing the policy to a default course of study for high school students. The team revised the MassCore activities and time lines based on the decision to postpone changing the policy until a further date. The revisions categorize activities into two major buckets; providing more individual and group technical assistance and guidance to the current MassCore framework and expanded the framework to include more career development activities, per the Integration of College and Career Readiness recommendations. Although we documented new activities, we are still unsure of how much impact this will have on the MassCore completion rate. A strong agency communication and marketing campaign and a heightened sense of internal urgency for such a campaign (beyond the CCR unit) are needed in order to increase the MassCore completion rate.

■ Red   ▣ Amber-Red   Amber-Green   ■ Green

Figure 4A.15   Next Steps From June 2013 Memo on College- and Career-Readiness Goal

Proposed MassCore Framework Implementation Strategy	Inclusion of Career Development Activities
• Host webinars about implementation of MassCore • Host regional meetings about implementation of MassCore • Provide individual TA to districts and schools • Build a communication campaign both internally and externally about the importance of MassCore • Integrate MassCore into other ESE initiatives • Emphasize data collection and reporting through Edwin reports, DART, and SCS • Inventory district graduation requirements • Identify on-track indicators for MassCore completion (e.g., using SCS to track course-taking patterns)	• Present "expanded" MassCore framework to BESE • Develop definitions and examples of career awareness, exploration, and immersion activities • Develop guidance for incorporating career development activities into school curricula • Explore using SCS codes in tracking career development activity completion • Disseminate Career Development Activity survey to high school principals and guidance counselors • Share best practices/case studies of those schools that implement career development education

Next Steps: **Based on the revised activities, update the MassCore completion delivery target and present at next stocktake meeting.**

districts to take action, the target would need to be recalibrated and levers of softer influence (like communication and engagement) improved.

This is just a small snapshot of how delivery routines drive progress in Massachusetts for one goal. Please see EDI's website, **www.deliveryinstitute.org/4A,** for full versions of both the stocktake document and the memo.

Run Individual Routines

With preparation for a given routine complete, you're ready to implement it. In the case of a memo, this means writing it, delivering it, and getting feedback from the system leader receiving it. In the case of a meeting, it means conducting the event itself. For the most part, there's not too much to discuss here: if a routine is well prepared, much of the actual execution should follow easily from the agenda and materials you've created.

Nonetheless, there are a few key things to remember when you conduct a routine, particularly if it's a meeting. In particular, the delivery leader or a member of the Delivery Unit should facilitate the meeting whenever possible. This doesn't necessarily mean that this person dominates the discussion, but it does mean that she or he is in control of it, watching the time and moving things along to meet the objectives laid out in the agenda. The meeting facilitator can also occasionally raise key questions or make suggestions to help focus the discussion.

There's a simple division of labor here: the Delivery Unit manages the process toward the meeting's objectives and worries about achieving those objectives, freeing everyone else in the meeting to participate fully and engage with the content under discussion. The system leader should play their assigned role here, for example, but they shouldn't run the meeting, because it will impose a burden of preparation on them beyond that of the basic briefing discussed above. Likewise, the participants shouldn't run the meeting, because they may face an incentive to avoid topics that are less comfortable for them.

Once these roles have been established, running the routine is just a matter of following the agenda and exercising facilitative leadership and judgment during the meeting. In particular, whatever the specific objectives are, the person facilitating the meeting should take responsibility for making sure it meets the general characteristics of a good routine that we explored at the beginning of this chapter. After the routine, you can do a short debrief with the delivery leader and system leader to discuss how well the routine met these criteria (this is particularly helpful when the practice is new in your system). You can even use the rubric as a yardstick of success.

⦿ LESSONS FROM THE FIELD

Don't Wait

In the early days of our work, we took planning and routines in sequence: we would help teams create delivery plans (see Part 3) and then hold routines for the various areas of focus after the plans were completed. The first stocktake for each area of focus would be a review of the plan.

There were a few drawbacks to this approach. For one, it gave the false impression that there is such a thing as a "completion" date for a delivery plan, which should really be a living document that's never quite finished. This notion would cause teams to labor longer and harder on planning than they probably should have. Many of them would ask for a delay of the stocktake if they didn't feel like the plan was "done" by the scheduled date, which almost inevitably turned out to be the case.

The other challenge this created was the repurposing of routines for revising plans. While it's appropriate, in a first routine, to dedicate most of the time to testing the substance of the relevant delivery plan, it will be counterproductive if this happens repeatedly. If leaders spend all their time discussing (and effectively revising) the plan, they'll never get around to discussing whether any *progress* is being made in implementing it. The result is one of the great clichés of implementation: we spend all our time planning and none of our time doing. Routines should have the opposite effect, transforming plans into real drivers of the work.

The lesson we learned was simple: set the schedule of routines, stick to it, and let planning catch up. We realized that, as long as the areas of focus are well defined, you can hold a routine assessing progress even *before* a plan is written (after all, a part of the Assessment Framework is used to assess the quality of planning). When plans are nonexistent or inadequate, this regular routine puts additional and appropriate pressure on the relevant leaders to improve their plans as quickly as possible, but maintains the focus on progress. In this sense, plans are like the collection of data: you should let your routines drive them rather than the other way around.

Use Dashboards Carefully

Until this point, one concept has been missing from our discussion of delivery routines: the **data dashboard**. We've deliberately delayed our discussion of dashboards because, in most cases, they should *not* be your starting point in setting up routines.

A dashboard is a standard format for regularly analyzing and displaying important data and evidence on performance. Dashboards are common and popular in the performance management literature, both inside and outside the field of education. Their value to delivery routines is in their consistency: from routine to routine, participants grow so familiar with the format of the dashboard that they can immediately engage with the data and see what's changed since the last review.

One example of a dashboard, from the University of Hawai'i system, is given in Figure 4A.16. The delivery team at the system office generated these key reports on campus data to help guide regular conversations about performance between campus leaders and the system leader.

Dashboards are clearly useful tools, and Michael took care to apply the principle of standardization in data displays throughout his time at the PMDU. Why, then, do we advise you not to start with a dashboard?

Figure 4A.16   Hawai'i Graduation Initiative Campus Scorecard

University of Hawai'i Campus A

HAWAI'I GRADUATION INITIATIVE

STRATEGIC OUTCOMES	2012–13 Actual	2013–14 Actual	2013–14 Goal	Met/Exceeded Goal?
Total Degrees & Certificates Earned by Fiscal Year [1]				
Campus Total	4,737	4,949	5,456	No
Native Hawaiian [2]	664	687	500	Yes
Pell	1,482	1,518		
STEM [3]	1,111	1,256	1,069	Yes
Going Rates of Public and Private High Schools (Fall 12 and 13) (%) [4]	8.9	8.7	10.4	No
Disbursement of Pell Grants by Academic Year ($m)	19.1	18.5 [P]	11.1	Yes
Number of Pell Recipients by Academic Year	4,813	4,683 [P]	3,855	Yes

REDUCE TIME/CREDITS TO DEGREE [5]	2011-12	2012-13	2013-14	Positive Change?
4-yr Graduation Rate by First-time, Full-time Cohort (Fall 08, 09, and 10) [6]	19.8	21.2	24.7	Yes
6-yr Graduation Rate by Cohort (Fall 06, 07 and 08) [6]				
First-time, full-time (%)	55.7	56.6	56.2	No
Native Hawaiian (%) [2]	41.1	56.3	49.1	No
Pell (%) [7]	59.2	56.6	56.7	No Change
Transfer (%) [8]	61.3	60.4	62.0	Yes

	2011-12	2012-13	2013-14	Positive Change?
Average Credits to Degree for Undergraduates [9]				
Native Students (excludes 2nd BA) [10]	141.4	140.3	139.6	Yes
Native Hawaiian	139.5	134.7	136.4	No
Pell	142.6	140.8	142.0	No
Transfer - Internal transfers only (excludes Native Students and 2nd BA)	148.4	148.9	146.5	Yes
Transfer - external transfers only (excludes Native Students and 2nd BA) [12]	146.9	145.5	145.8	No

BACHELOR DEGREE SEEKING STUDENTS [5]	Fall 11 Cohort	Fall 12 Cohort	Fall 13 Cohort	Positive Change?
First-time, full-time freshmen with 6 or more credits at entry (%) [13]	19.1	21.3	21.1	No Change
Freshmen completing at least 30 credit hours within 1st academic year (%) [14]	41.3	48.8	53.2	Yes
Students completing college level English & math within 1st academic year (%) [14]	51.1	54.0	56.5	Yes
Freshmen with a declared major by start of second year [15]	76.4	77.0	74.6	No
Retention rate of freshmen to sophomore year [16]	78.7	77.4	78.6	Yes

RESTRUCTURE DELIVERY TO ACCELERATE SUCCESS [5]	Fall 12	Fall 13	Fall 14	Positive Change?
% of undergrads taking 15 credits or more	45.2	46.8	47.8	Yes
% of undergrads with 120-139 credits [17]	9.0	9.2	8.9	Yes
% of undergrads with 140+ credits [17]	6.1	5.7	6.6	No
% of DL credits taken by undergrad degree seeking students [18]	6.1	5.8	6.7	Yes
% of credits taken during summer by undergrad degree seeking students (AY 2011-12, 2012-13, and 2013-14)[19]	6.6	6.3	6.3	No Change

	Fall 08	Fall 09	Fall 10	Positive Change?
Campus share of Transfer-out to ANY 4yr from Other UH [20]				
UH 4yr to Campus A within 4 years	40.5	42.7	43.1	Yes
UH CC to Campus A within 4 years	55.8	49.7	36.2	No

PRODUCTIVITY MEASURES	2011-12	2012-13	2013-14	Positive Change?
Baccalaureate Degrees Awarded per 100 FTE Classified Undergraduates [21]	25.0	25.6	27.0	Yes

P = Preliminary

Source: The University of Hawai'i System.

A dashboard is only as useful as the data it holds. The more frequently updated the data, the more relevant the tool is for helping us make sense of the changing landscape. In fact, an actual dashboard (in a car, for example) is a quintessential example of this: most of the data it provides—your speed, the amount of fuel you have left, the miles you've driven, and so on—are literally updated in real time. But in education, as we've noted (or lamented!) repeatedly, frequent data such as these are difficult to find, particularly as you get farther away from individual classrooms, campuses, and schools. Consider the dashboard above: none of its information is updated more often than twice a year, and a great deal of it is only updated annually.

The challenge arises when education leaders ask for dashboards with this kind of data to be used for routines that happen much more frequently (say, once a week or once a month). The result is a mismatch: leaders expect dashboards to provide all the evidence they need for day-to-day decision making and are disappointed to see the same numbers turn up again and again when they are hungry for new information and insights. Moreover, even a dashboard with good information is still just a bunch of raw data; it doesn't relieve you of the burden of interpreting that data and creating an agenda to get at the most important issues.

To see what this is like, imagine a car dashboard that tells you how much fuel you had 6 months ago. Imagine further that we left it at that and never connected the dots to answer the really important question: do we need more fuel? That basically summarizes the most common approach to dashboards that we see in the field. When we lean on dashboards to do more than they're designed to do, the resulting frustration can discredit the idea of a dashboard and even the idea of a routine, which is a risk you don't want to bear.

The lesson: dashboards play an important role in delivery routines, but they don't play the only role. This is why we introduced the assessment framework and tools for agenda building above: to fill in the gaps in the evidence and to provide context for decision making. In fact, the assessment framework, and the league tables and other reports it produces, is a sort of qualitative dashboard that combines all our real-time evidence into actionable judgments about progress.

Dashboards can play a role in your work. But they shouldn't be the first or only tool you reach for.

Intervention in Inverse Proportion to Success

Whether you're talking about differentiating instruction in a classroom or "segmenting" campuses based on their student results, the principle of focusing increased attention on areas of challenge is time-honored and proven. In fact, it undergirds the delivery approach through and through—in capacity reviews (Chapter 1B), analysis of data (Part 2), and solving problems (Chapter 4B).

We saw this principle applied in delivery routines, with the concept of the T-Shaped agenda and the use of time in a routine to concentrate on those areas where the challenge is greatest. But the principle also applies to the schedule of routines themselves. Your calendar may start with an equal amount of time devoted to each area of focus, but as the results and evidence come in, you'll start to discover that some deserve more attention than others. When a particular goal is off track, for example, a system leader may ask the team to report back to him or her more frequently than the schedule of routines requires until the problem is resolved.

Routines are powerful tools for driving progress, but they're even more powerful when you adjust their architecture based on the evidence they surface. Each routine should provide your system leader with a level of information and opportunities for decision making that are commensurate to the urgency and importance of the challenge at hand. For more on this, please see the next chapter, where we more fully explore the "triage" model of addressing challenges as they arise.

"Theater" Matters

One of Michael's colleagues at the PMDU once described its routines as "great theater." At first glance, this doesn't seem like a desirable thing. Theater, at least in the context of public service, seems more like a tool for obfuscation than for bringing clarity. Moreover, we earlier ruled out the use of tricks, like surprise, as a way to make a routine effective. How could theater be useful in routines?

There's a difference between surprise—in which we catch people off guard—and *suspense*, in which we craft an event to sharpen everyone's focus on a matter at hand. Theater is about creating suspense in an honest and straightforward way. The management guru Patrick Lencioni notes that the most important element to make any meeting interesting is conflict: a tension of some sort that the team must resolve together. He even encourages teams to "mine for conflict" to make their meetings more productive.

Any good delivery routine relies on this principle. After all, what is all the preparation a Delivery Unit does for a routine—assessing progress, identifying the biggest problems to solve, and setting the agenda and materials accordingly—but a careful and deliberate conflict-mining expedition? In fact, one thing that sets delivery routines apart from other meetings is the fact that all the conflicts have been identified and teed up in advance on the agenda. All the preparation aims to bring these conflicts up in just the right order, with just the right information, so that the participants can maximize their productivity in addressing them. This will mean that delivery routines should be characterized by more concentrated conflict and suspense than any other interaction.

In many systems where we've worked, teams have struggled with this idea. We once showed up to a pre-stocktake briefing with a K–12 system leader and the Delivery Unit, only to find that the goal leader and the entire goal team were there at the delivery leader's invitation. In effect, we were having a stocktake before the stocktake—one where participants were trying to "pre-discuss" some of the topics to defuse the tension. Of course, this defeats the purpose of the briefings, which are to help each participant prepare to play their specific role, asking the right questions and bringing up the right facts. After all, what is a theater without the actors playing their parts?

It may seem strange to deliberately put this kind of distance between participants in a delivery routine, particularly in smaller, more collegial workplaces. Even the idea of setting up a goal or strategy leader to sit "across the table" from the system leader can be difficult. To see why it is necessary, though, consider the original PMDU. In British government, the Prime Minister was someone you saw so rarely that any interaction already had this sort of tension and suspense—a sense that every minute must be used wisely. This sense of urgency is something you want to recreate with your system leader's time, if only for an hour or two each month.

Routines should *feel* different. There should be an understanding that more is at stake. The amount of edge and "drama" in a stocktake will have a significant bearing on how seriously people take it and how accountable they feel. Ask participants to give you the benefit of the doubt and to embrace the "theater" inherent in your delivery routines.

Keep the Purpose of Routines Focused

One other mistake that leaders make is to try to make a routine do too many things. On the one hand, it's good to be efficient; as we noted above, repurposing a regular meeting to become a delivery routine is often the right idea. But there's always a danger when we do this, because we're usually displacing some other meeting that had a legitimate purpose. When we don't acknowledge that purpose and find an outlet for it, one of two things can happen.

First, the purpose of the original meeting can be dropped or ignored altogether. Imagine a system with a leadership team that meets twice a month. Now imagine replacing those meetings with delivery routines, but not giving the leadership team any other opportunity to meet. You can see the problem: while delivery routines are important interactions, they don't comprise the sum total of what the business leaders must do when they meet together. We said at the very beginning of this chapter that a delivery team wasn't a staff meeting, an update meeting, or a data meeting. But most of the time, with most teams, these kinds of meetings must happen *in addition* to the delivery routines for systems to function at a basic level. When they don't happen, the routine that replaced them is blamed and the process loses credibility.

Second (and sometimes, after trying the first solution with poor results), leaders will try to cram additional objectives into the time reserved for delivery routines. This leads to something that Patrick Lencioni calls "Meeting Stew":

> Imagine a clueless cook taking all of the ingredients out of the pantry and the refrigerator and throwing them into one big pot, and then wondering why his concoction doesn't taste very good. Leaders do the same thing when they put all of their issues into one big discussion, usually called a "staff meeting." All too often they combine administrative issues and tactical decisions and creative brainstorming and strategic analysis and personnel discussions into one exhausting meeting. And like that cook, somehow they are surprised when the result doesn't turn out so well.[5]

If delivery routines truly are to be a different experience, they need to be protected from this fate. A delivery routine requires a great deal of preparation. And it's precisely because this burden of preparation is so high that we shouldn't mix routines with other, more spontaneous interactions that serve other purposes. After all, if we took several hours to prepare for each hour of *every* meeting, we'd run out of time! For these reasons, a leader hoping to establish strong delivery routines must carve out the time and space for them, while at the same time creating or maintaining other opportunities for leaders to meet to deal with other day-to-day business.

> For more information on how to run strong meetings for day-to-day business, we highly recommend Patrick Lencioni's book *Death by Meeting*.

What if this leads to additional meetings on the schedule for the team? It might. But the problem in most organizations isn't the number of meetings we have; it's the number of *bad* meetings. Good meetings—like delivery routines—actually help you get your work done; they don't produce the same drain of time and energy (with nothing to show for it) as the bad ones do. Invest your team's time in thoughtful interactions at every level, so that leaders have as many meetings as they must, but as few as they can get away with. This will allow your delivery routines to fulfill their true purpose.

Routines Are Useful at Every Level

Finally, delivery routines aren't just for system leaders and leadership teams. The practice of reviewing evidence of progress and using it to make course corrections is useful both within and between every level of a system.

The delivery routines we've described are about organizations monitoring themselves, without any external influence. This is what education scholar Richard Elmore calls "internal accountability": "coherence and alignment among individuals' conceptions of what they are responsible for and how, collective expectations at the organizational level, and processes by which people within the organization account for what they do."[6] External accountability, by contrast, is the more formal publication of data, ranking of schools, and application of rewards and consequences that we usually think of when we hear the word *accountability*.

Much of Elmore's work demonstrates that the two are complementary and that internal accountability must come before external accountability. This is because an organization's internal accountability will determine its ability to respond to pressure brought to bear by external accountability. So when departments, schools, and districts adopt the tools and practices of delivery for themselves, they enhance the formal authority that the system exercises through external accountability. In other words, it's to your benefit not just to create delivery routines for yourself, but to encourage leaders at every level to do the same.

Sometimes this happens on its own. In the early days of the PMDU, Michael and his colleagues noticed that leaders in the Ministries of Health and Education had begun to run their own stocktakes, partly because they had learned from the example of the PMDU's routines, and partly because doing it made it easier for them to be prepared for those routines. Over time, they even established their own Delivery Units. They had discovered an enduring truth about accountability: that the most efficient self-monitoring you can do is the kind that both helps you improve your work and gives you what you need to report on progress externally. You need to do both, so why not use delivery tools to do it?

Elmore's insight into the two types of accountability brings to mind an adage of Niccolo Machiavelli, who famously wrote that the ideal ruler should be both feared and loved, but that if he had to choose between the two, he should choose fear. If you apply this to external and internal accountability, the logic is reversed: it's better to have both, but if you must just choose one, choose internal accountability. Internalization by campuses, departments, districts, and schools is the only thing that will lead your reforms to be self-sustaining at scale. Perhaps more to the point: unlike Machiavelli's prince, you are not a "ruler," and you will *never* have enough formal authority to force, let alone sustain, the change that you want. There's only so much you can accomplish through fear alone.

From External to Internal Accountability:
School Turnaround in Oregon

Like most state K–12 systems, Oregon has designated a list of about 92 focus and priority schools—schools that are performing in the bottom 15% in the state and need intensive support. To support them, the state divides the schools into six geographic regions. Each school is assigned a coach who's responsible for working with the school and its district to improve performance.

The very designation of these schools, and the structure of increasing supports and scrutiny for their work, is itself a feature of external accountability. What's interesting about Oregon's approach is how it handles the "scrutiny": by creating a set of delivery routines to regularly review progress of schools and the impact of coaching supports. Called the "How Are Schools Doing" (HASD) routines, these progress reviews are quarterly conversations between the coach, the regional coach supervisor, and the state school turnaround staff. They are focused on the likelihood that each school will meet its student performance goals by the end of the year. The reviews involve the usual elements: a review of performance data against the goals, an assessment of implementation quality for each school's top three priority strategies to achieve these goals (as perceived by the coach), and a drive toward identifying bright spots, key challenges, solutions, and next steps for the school and for the coach's support.

Though the routines are nominally a form of external accountability between multiple levels of a system (state, district, and school), they lend themselves to a true partnership and dialogue between each coach and school. They are as much about how the coach can improve his or her support as they are about how the school can improve its work. As such, they create a powerful sense of internal accountability. The result has been so powerful that the districts where these schools are located have expressed interest in replicating these conversations at the local level so that their staff can form similar partnerships.

⊙ KEY CONSIDERATIONS FOR SYSTEM LEADERS AND STAFF

If you're a **system leader**, your time, and the seriousness with which you take these delivery routines, is the single greatest investment you can make in ensuring your delivery effort's success. In fact, as Michael noted about his system leader, the time that Tony Blair spent in the stocktakes was the clearest indicator that they mattered and that the Delivery Unit had influence. Likewise, the time you invest here will reap immense returns in the capacity of your Delivery Unit to get results for you. Make sure it's a team you trust and let them direct and "train" you to play the role you need to play. There's no greater gift they can give you.

If you're a part of the **system staff**, you have a tough job; it's always a bit uncomfortable to be on the receiving end of any kind of accountability. But this kind of accountability really should be different: it should empower you to be successful and give you access to the resources and decision makers you need to move things forward. If everything's working well, the greatest pressure you feel might be the kind you put on yourself. If the delivery routines don't make you feel this way, it's worth having a conversation with the delivery leader to share your feelings and impressions. Sometimes you'll give him or her vital feedback to improve the routines, while at other times you may discover that aspects of your own view need to change as well.

If you're a **delivery leader**, delivery routines are the most critical milestone of your delivery effort. They're where a great deal of your work comes to fruition—or doesn't—in the problems they surface, the solutions they identify, and the action they drive. And because they're so visible, they can make or break the credibility of your effort. Don't let a bad routine strangle your delivery effort in its infancy; instead, obsess over every detail of preparation for these interactions until they are rock solid and your system leader depends on them.

⊙ CONCLUSION

That little phrase—"trust, but verify"—contains multitudes. Its two tenets are mutually reinforcing and yet in constant tension at the same time. Trust too much, and your routines will be ineffective at driving progress. Verify too much, and you'll join the long list of bureaucrats derided for "monitoring" that hinders the work and makes little sense.

The practices covered in this chapter are tools designed to help you strike the optimal balance between these extremes. But your judgment is an important factor as well. Depending on your context, you may need to emphasize trust more (or first) before verification, or the other way around. Keep asking yourself whether you are where you need to be on the spectrum between the two. An adjustment to a framework here or a schedule there can make all the difference in earning you the credibility you need.

A great deal is at stake here: if a delivery plan represents a commitment to change, the delivery routine is your most powerful means for honoring that commitment. It helps you understand the work, keep it on track, and identify and eliminate the most challenging barriers to implementation. But what happens when the biggest barriers are so large and so complex that they defy easy solutions? That's the subject of our next chapter, on problem solving.

◉ NOTES

1. Barber, M., Kihn, P., & Moffit, A. (2011). *Deliverology 101: A field guide for educational leaders.* Thousand Oaks, CA: Corwin.

2. Hawai'i Department of Education. (2013). *Academic review teams: A resource guide for complex area leaders.* Washington, DC: U.S. Education Delivery Institute.

3. Powell, C., & Koltz, T. (2014). *It worked for me: In life and leadership.* New York, NY: Harper.

4. University of Hawai'i System. (n.d.). *Campus scorecards: Hawai'i graduation initiative.* Retrieved from http://www.hawaii.edu/hawaiigradinitiative/campus-scorecards/

5. Lencioni, P. (2012). *The advantage: Why organizational health trumps everything else in business.* San Francisco, CA: Jossey-Bass.

6. Ontario Ministry of Education. (2010). Leading the instructional core: An interview with Richard Elmore. *In Conversations, 11,* 3.

Chapter 4B

Solve Problems Early and Rigorously

 **Develop a foundation for delivery**  **Understand the delivery challenge**  **Plan for delivery**  **Drive delivery**

 Create an irreversible delivery culture

System Leader Summary

Problems will inevitably arise during the course of implementation. The challenge is to know which ones are the most pressing and how to deal with them. Your delivery routines provide a framework for identifying these problems; the tools in this chapter will help your delivery leader prioritize and solve them.

Problem solving is more than a set of tools, however; it's a mindset. Your delivery leader will use what's in this chapter to set up the right conversations, but it's your job to engage in them meaningfully and to set the tone and example for everyone else. Let your delivery leader drive the agenda, lest you and your team become caught up in firefighting (the lowest common denominator of problem solving). Take care to be solution-oriented, resisting the urge to merely admire the problem. And encourage innovative, even risky thinking among your colleagues. This is how a problem-solving culture gets built.

Nobody would deny the value of being able to solve problems. Ask any leader in an organization what skills they look for in members of their team, and problem solving usually makes the list. In fact, the whole notion of delivery—and, in particular, the whole structure of routines that we described in the last chapter—exists to help you monitor progress on implementation and make course corrections as evidence comes in. This is just another way of saying that delivery helps you solve problems.

However, problem solving is difficult to define. To paraphrase Supreme Court Justice Potter Stewart, people know it when they see it. But that's of little help when you're trying to help people and organizations get better at it.

What makes the discipline of problem solving so hard to pin down? Part of the challenge is that there are too many problems to be solved. As one delivery leader we worked with has remarked to us, "Most people solve problems every single day—in their day-to-day lives, with their families, and at home. They wouldn't be able to survive without doing it. This isn't about people's ability to solve problems; it's about getting them to focus on the *right* problems." Problem solving without prioritization is essentially firefighting: letting the urgent trump the important, dashing from situation to situation, paying attention only to the things that are right in front of us. If an organization's main mode of problem solving is to fight fires, the most valued people will be those with the largest hoses. This reinforces all the wrong behavior: as one management expert puts it, when you reward firefighting, you create a culture of arsonists.[1]

And then there are the problems that actually do resist easy solution, even when we prioritize them—the ones that keep us up at night, or worse, the ones that we've long since given up on. For these big, complicated problems—an outcome measure that stubbornly refuses to improve, despite massive effort, or a situation where political constraints seem to leave no room for a good resolution—you've tried the standard stuff, and it hasn't worked. So what do you do?

Here's a working definition for the title of this chapter: to solve problems *early* is to have a system in place for identifying and prioritizing the right problems to solve, before they become too big to handle. To solve them *rigorously* is to take the toughest problems, break them down into manageable pieces that will yield to analysis, focus on the ones that matter most, and draw out the insights that lead to real solutions.

Like the problems themselves, the discipline of problem solving can be broken down into concrete pieces—a series of specific practices that any person or organization can use to take on the toughest challenges. We introduced some of these practices in Part 2, where we took steps to understand the biggest problem of all: the barriers to achieving our overall aspiration. That was problem solving in the service of delivery planning, a before-the-fact analysis of what it would take to make an impact. This chapter borrows some of those tools, but focuses on analyzing and solving problems during implementation. Unlike the big challenges in Part 2, these problems can be wide or narrow in scope: they not only involve barriers to achieving the overall aspiration, but they can also focus on implementation challenges with just a part of one particular strategy.

The presence of these tools in multiple parts of this book is a reminder to us that the delivery approach isn't linear. Just as problem solving is a skill that leaders value in all their people, it's also a useful practice throughout your delivery effort, not just at this stage. As you become familiar with these tools, be thinking about how they apply to every aspect of your work. In doing so, you'll strike a blow not just for delivery, but for the culture of your system, away from firefighting and toward something much better.

◉ CORE PRINCIPLES

Problem solving is a four-step process:

1. **Identify** and **prioritize** the right problems to solve;

2. Clearly **define** the problems that you have prioritized;

3. **Analyze** those problems; and

4. Develop **solutions**.

As we dive into these steps, it's worth noting that the actual tools for undertaking them don't always correspond one-to-one with each of them. Some of them, such as the priority review process, span three of the steps or more. In other cases, there are multiple tools for accomplishing a given step. Think of the different tools as ways to undertake the steps at different levels of rigor. Your prioritization in the first step will help inform how you apply them to the various challenges you identify.

For the tools in this chapter, we owe a particular debt to our colleagues at McKinsey & Company who are well known for their problem-solving tools. Because the organization helped incubate and launch EDI, McKinsey thinking has influenced some important aspects of our work, especially in this area.

Identify and Prioritize Problems

An ounce of prevention is worth a pound of intervention. Surfacing and understanding challenges quickly will help you prioritize them, which will help you solve them as efficiently as possible.

First things first: how do you know that something is a problem? Recall the different types of benchmarking that we reviewed in Chapter 2A. These were ways of comparing and contrasting data on performance to look for patterns. You can use many of these same types of comparisons to identify challenges in both quantitative data (on leading indicators and outcomes) and qualitative information (for example, the traffic-light judgments signifying the quality of implementation of your strategies):

- **Benchmarking against history:** Is there a plateau, or even a decline, in performance over time? Or is progress slower than in the recent past?
- **Benchmarking against peers:** Is there significantly less progress or lower performance for a particular area of focus (goal, strategy, campus, department, district, or school) compared to its peers?

- **Benchmarking against yourself:** Are there wide unexplained variations in performance between areas of focus inside your system?

In addition to benchmarking, you can consider at least two other possibilities:

- **Problems with the theory of action:** Is the link between your strategies and goals not supported by the evidence? Or is there evidence that causes you to question that link (and, thus, the wisdom of the strategy)?
- **Unintended consequences:** Are the data showing any?

If you've followed the advice of the previous chapter, the best source of evidence for doing these analyses will be your delivery routines. Through them, you will have done the hard work of sifting through the available information, curating it to create a clear picture of progress, and using comparative tools—particularly the league tables showing the likelihood of delivery across different areas of focus—that enable these types of comparisons and searches for patterns. A well-structured delivery routine won't just give you the evidence; as we've seen, it will identify the biggest challenges and tee up the right discussions to address them.

However, even if your routines aren't set up just yet, there's a great deal you can do by looking at the sources of evidence you're familiar with: outcome data on the aspiration, data on leading indicators, and whatever qualitative evidence you use to track the quality of implementation. At the very least, you can apply the assessment framework on your own and gather evidence on implementation through a few well-placed conversations with goal and strategy leaders, reviews of critical documents or artifacts of implementation, and spot checks through visits or phone calls to the front line. A little feedback can go a long way in finding out where the challenges are, especially if it's from an independent source of evidence.

Once you identify the problems, how do you prioritize them? This was one of the big innovations of the original PMDU: taking a culture of firefighting around the Prime Minister—what Michael called "government by spasm"—and replacing it with a more systematic approach. As Michael wrote, "I thought that if I could develop a system which not only categorized challenges, but also anticipated and managed them before they exploded, this would be a significant contribution to improving government."[2] Out of this thinking came the idea of classifying and responding to problems according to different levels of intensity—similar to the way that hospitals use triage processes to manage medical cases (see Figure 4B.1).

As you can see from the characteristics described for each level, they revolve around three questions:

- How severe is the problem in terms of impact? How big an adverse effect is it having on delivery—of a goal, a strategy, or both?
- How difficult to solve is the problem? How well understood are the root causes? How clear are the solutions, and how difficult would they be to implement?
- How politically salient is the problem? How much public attention is on it? How exposed or vulnerable will your system leader be if it's not solved soon?

Figure 4B.1   Levels of Intensity

Classification	Characteristics of Problem	Approach	Potential Delivery Unit Actions
Level 1	• Delivery is off track • Root cause and/or solution are relatively clear	"Timely nudge" from Delivery Unit	• Personally contact individual accountable for relevant aspect of delivery (e.g., phone call, e-mail) • Offer support, but ask individual to fix the problem • Follow-up to ensure problem has been resolved • Continue routines as usual
Level 2	• Problem is **significantly** affecting delivery • Cause and solution are not obvious	Standard problem solving	• Designate Delivery Unit staff responsible for "co-owning" problem with relevant delivery plan owner • Conduct collaborative problem-solving, potentially with challenge meetings, problem structuring, hypothesis-driven data analysis • Adapt normal routines to incorporate more frequent and/or deeper monitoring of problem area as needed
Level 3	• Problem is **severely** affecting delivery • Cause and solution are not clear, even after standard problem solving • There are politically salient factors in play	Intensive problem-solving drive	• Designate special problem-solving team (with Delivery Unit and front-line staff) to conduct "priority review" or similar method for deep problem solving • Loop-in and receive input from delivery leader • Develop temporary new routines for reporting progress on problem (e.g., weekly)
Level 4	• Problem is one of the top one to two challenges in the system • There is a great deal of complexity involved in the cause and solution • Problem is highly visible and urgent to solve	Crisis management	• Involve delivery leader full-time in problem solving • Request active and frequent participation of system leader • Utilize your system's crisis management techniques to keep attention of all relevant players on the problem • Develop new routines for monitoring problem (e.g., daily monitoring); incorporate problem insights into routines

Categorizing a problem involves assessing it against all three of these questions. The first level consists of the problems that are small enough and easy enough that they can be mostly or completely solved through the delivery routines themselves. In these cases, the delivery team would work with the goal team to propose solutions or tee up the right problem-solving questions for discussion with the system leader, and the objective would be to leave with the issue resolved. These cases almost always require some follow-up—hence the "timely nudge" from the Delivery Unit until things are on track again.

From there, the levels proceed from least to most challenging. In the second level, teams will find themselves employing more deliberate problem-solving tools. The big difference here is a recognition that a good conversation with the right people might not be enough, and the allocation of resources—particularly the time of the Delivery Unit and the relevant people on the goal team—to work together on the problem between routines. There also may be an ad hoc review scheduled with the system leader to check progress at some point between one routine and the next. This is a zone where a little bit of ad hoc feedback or extra evidence gathered can make a big difference to the effort.

The third level is distinguished by the presence of significant political factors that complicate the problem (and perhaps a failure of the tools in Level 2). As a result, the frequency of routines increased until the problem was solved. At this point, the PMDU used a process called a **priority review** (as in a deep review of a priority that is off track). The PMDU would establish a joint team consisting of PMDU staff, goal team staff, and front-line staff who were likely to understand the issue well, and task them with solving the problem together over a limited period of time (usually 6 weeks). The process is summarized in Figure 4B.2.[3]

Over the years, EDI has adapted the priority review process and applied it in partnership with several systems. The most important adaptation that we've made is to scale down the approach to fit with the capacity and personnel available. A priority review is a useful way to bring together many of the tools in this chapter in a concentrated effort to solve a particular problem. Whatever you call it, you should reserve capacity for this kind of work for a handful of the most severe cases.

The final level, called *crisis management*, was invented almost by accident, when a street crime epidemic was in full force in the United Kingdom. Tony Blair had been frustrated with the pace of change and numbers that had not improved for years. "Why is it that when we have a real crisis," he asked, "we get the job done? Perhaps we should call together COBRA [the Cabinet office emergency committee] and deal with robbery through that mechanism."[4] The goal leader agreed, knowing that this would be an opportunity for him to demonstrate leadership on this important issue, and regular meetings of COBRA—involving Blair himself and anyone who was even remotely connected to the street crime issue—kept the government focused on the problem for the next several months. The work itself was accompanied by a media blitz to keep the public informed of the magnitude of the problem and the government's evolving response to it.

What the PMDU leaders discovered here was a bit of ju-jitsu. As we said before, we advise avoiding the firefighting mentality. But in a few rare instances,

Figure 4B.2 Conducting a Priority Review

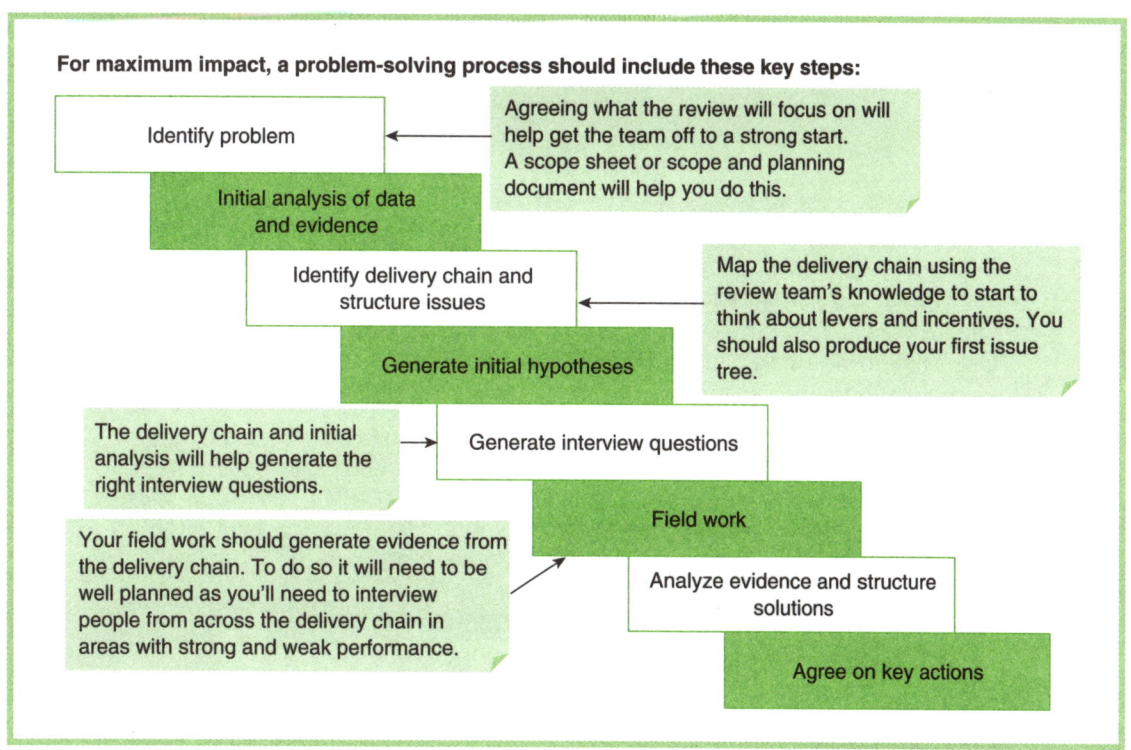

we can put firefighting energy to productive and focused use by using strong crisis mechanisms to deal with delivery challenges that are, in fact, full-blown crises.

What this looks like will vary from system to system. In the Massachusetts Department of Elementary and Secondary Education, for example, most of the delivery routines for a given area of focus occur every 2 months. Then, the results of a federal inquiry required the state to take significant action to improve its teachers' proficiency in working with English-language learners.

This work had been one strategy in one of Massachusetts' delivery goals—the one that focused on improving proficiency for all students. But it suddenly took on a prominence it had not had before. The state's leaders knew that, as a matter of both substance and optics, they needed to take decisive action and keep implementation on track.

The result was the Rethinking Equity and Teaching for English Language Learners (RETELL) initiative—a comprehensive effort to get every teacher in the state the training they needed for this work. Because this work was both highly visible and off track, the Commissioner asked the Delivery Unit to provide an update on progress every 2 *weeks* rather than every 2 months. Moreover, the notes dive into more detail than usual: they provide a color rating for every step of implementation for the plan, as the excerpt in Figure 4B.3 shows.

Like the PMDU's use of COBRA, this kind of focus ensures that leaders in Massachusetts are paying close and consistent attention to a priority with a high public profile.

Figure 4B.3   RETELL Note in Massachusetts

RETELL Update
June 13, 2013

SNAPSHOT

○ Overall Status of RETELL Initiative
  ○ Self-Registration System Development
    ● Registration system funding
    ● Onboard vendor to build and manage registration system
    ● Create statewide schedule of SEI Endorsement Course offerings
    ○ Launch registration system
    ○ Hire registrar to support registrants
  ○ RETELL Course Development and Launch
    ● Revise SEI Endorsement Course: flow, materials, workload
    ● Work with vendor to develop Bridge courses A and B
    ● Create MTEL test (offered in lieu of SEI Endorsement Course)
    ● Collect and analyze results from Data Collection Tool
    ● Work with vendor to develop Administrator Course
    ● Launch Bridge Courses
    ● Launch Administrator Course
    ● Acquire instructors
  ○ Governance
    ○ Funding
    ● Legislation
    ○ Communication

■ Red   ■ Amber-Red   ■ Amber-Green   ■ Green

Regardless of what crisis management looks like for you, there are a few elements that seem to be foundational to this approach: frequent routines involving the system leader are one, and a coordinated media campaign is the other (due to the public and politically salient nature of the challenge). You may or may not encounter a crisis like this during your tenure. But if you do, it's important to be prepared. After all, as the economist Paul Romer once said (and many have since echoed), a crisis is a terrible thing to waste.

Define Problems

Once you've prioritized the problems that you need to solve, the next step is to define them clearly. This, too, is an intuitive step, making it dangerously tempting to avoid. But make no mistake: assuming that you understand the problem to be solved—and, worse, neglecting to articulate it explicitly—is a recipe for disaster.

Why is this? A poorly defined problem is like the elephant in that famous Indian fable: a group of blind men each feel a different part of the elephant, and each draws very different conclusions about what an elephant is truly like ("A snake!" says the one holding its tail; "A spear!" says the one with a tusk in hand; "A fan!" says the one with its ear—you get the idea).

The moral of the story is that our perspectives are limited and limiting. Only by joining them with the views of others and coming to consensus can we hope to uncover a full picture. It may be true, to use a different metaphor, that you eat an elephant one piece at a time, but, first, you'd better know that it's an elephant you're eating!

We have found this to be true time and time again in our work with systems. We recall one workshop with the leadership teams of the Delaware and Massachusetts K–12 systems that brought this point home for us. The teams had been brought together by our colleagues at the Aspen Institute to work together on "problems of practice" that each team had brought. These were preidentified problems that the teams had already spent quite a bit of time defining. Nonetheless, the Aspen facilitator spent an hour with the Delaware team pushing on, probing, and sharpening their problem of practice. We were worried that this might be a bit much. But at the end of the day, the system leader in Delaware, in reflecting on and praising the day's work, actually said that that hour was the most helpful part of the entire process! We haven't questioned the value of defining a problem since.

The tool for defining a problem is fairly simple: a **scope sheet** (or, as our McKinsey colleagues call it, a problem statement). You can use it individually or with a team to answer some key questions that give shape to each problem you have prioritized (see Figure 4B.4).

Of all these prompts, the most important is the first: the basic question to be resolved. This is the question which, if you answered it, would solve the problem. It should be a thought-provoking and specific question—one that is both debatable

Figure 4B.4   Scope Sheet

Basic question to be resolved

1. Perspective/context	3. Decision makers

2. Criteria for success	4. Other key stakeholders

5. Key sources of insight

6. Out of scope

(not a statement of fact) and actionable. It should also be appropriately "sized"—you don't want to take on the whole universe of problems, but neither do you want to frame the problem too narrowly. A good basic question has embedded in it a sense of which options are likely to be on the table and which are not.

For example, suppose that you lead a higher education system and want to reverse a recent decline in the number of students who graduate within 6 years. There are many possible ways to frame the basic question, but not all will work:

- "The number of students graduating within 6 years has declined." This is a statement of fact rather than a provocative question.
- "Should we try to improve student graduation rates?" For most leaders, this will not be a debatable question.
- "Can we improve student graduation rates?" This gets closer to the mark but is still a bit too general and too wide a scope.
- "How can we reverse the recent decline in graduation rates through programs that target students in all stages of the pipeline?" This statement is specific and clear, and it points out something important: for this system, it is important to consider options for students in all years of study (not just those in the first one or two).

Once you have a basic question you feel good about, the rest of the scope sheet should come more easily. As with all things nonlinear, the answers to these questions may help you improve your basic question to be resolved as well.

- **Context:** What are the most important circumstances surrounding the problem? What do the key data say, and what is the history behind this?
- **Success criteria:** How will you know (and how will everyone agree) that you have solved the problem? Try to express in terms of both the quantitative and qualitative evidence that you would see.
- **Scope and constraints:** What is "in" and "out" of scope? What explicit constraints do you face as you come up with potential solutions? Some of this may be implied in the basic question, but here is where you make sure to state it explicitly.
- **Decision makers:** Who will need to agree to the solution? Who may have the power to block it? You may also note how you will keep them informed and help them make the right decisions.
- **Other key stakeholders:** Who else needs to be consulted or informed as you work through problem solving?
- **Key sources of insight:** What are the most important sources of evidence that you will turn to as you solve the problem? Make this list as specific as possible—it will help you in the next step.

One example of a completed version of the scope sheet, from a priority review we did with the Massachusetts Department of Elementary and Secondary Education, is shown in Figure 4B.5.

As you work through your scope sheet, keep three things in mind. First, remember to keep the focus on opportunities for improvement. It can be easy, especially given our language around problem solving, to dwell on the challenges

Figure 4B.5   Problem Statement and Scope: MA ESE

Basic question to be resolved: How can the ESE accelerate improvement in early literacy throughout the Commonwealth?

If we take a concerted and multifaceted approach that includes more intensive outreach, tools and resources that will serve as models for educators, higher standards, better coordination with other state education agencies (especially EEC), tight integration with the educator evaluation system, and a well-designed professional development available statewide, then we will develop a strong statewide system to support teachers and administrators and improve literacy in the early grades.

1. Perspective/Context
- MA has dedicated a substantial but decreasing amount of resources and staff time to its early grades literacy initiatives. Overall student performance has remained flat over the past decade.
- A few projects are under way that may contribute to improvement, most notably, the new Model Curriculum Units (MCUs), Curriculum Embedded Performance Assessments (CEPAs), and District Determined Measures (DDMs).
- ESE is leading field work to better understand the "bright spots" that exist and will share promising practices this year.

3. Decision Makers
- Mitchel Chester, Commissioner
- Alan Ingram, Deputy Commissioner
- Bob Bickerton, Senior Associate Commissioner
- Jonathan Landman, Associate Commissioner
- Julia Phelps, Associate Commissioner
- Sue Wheitle, Director of Literacy and Humanities

2. Criteria for Success
- Fewer funds available and no new funds expected—only existing or repurposed funds may be used.
- Solution(s) must include actions that can be taken in the short term (ideally, within the next few months) and are likely to generate improvements and gap closures within the next year (SY14–15 NAEP).

4. Other Key Stakeholders
- Department of Early Education and Care (not highly engaged with the ESE at this time)
- USED (RSN)

5. Out of Scope
- Organizational changes in ESE's structure

and barriers. Take the time to define and understand these, but try to move on as soon as possible. Otherwise, in the words of one delivery leader, we may fall into the trap of "admiring the problem" a little too closely!

Second, be sure to capture hypotheses as you go. In the natural course of defining a problem, hypotheses about the solution are bound to present themselves. Jot them down and carry them with you into the next step.

Please visit EDI's website at www.deliveryinstitute.org/4B for an exercise on using the scope sheet to define and sharpen a problem to solve.

Finally, remember that you can always revisit your problem statement. The analysis you're about to do not only will help you attack the problem with rigor, but it also may show you that the problem you need to solve is different from what you thought. In these cases, don't be afraid to come back to this step and revalidate or reframe your problem.

Analyze Problems

With one or more well-defined problems in hand, you're ready to take the most important step: breaking each problem down into manageable pieces and analyzing them to determine the solution.

Unfortunately, this is more difficult than it sounds—one reason why the skill of problem solving is so elusive and difficult to define. After all, we've all heard the stories of analysis paralysis: we risk drowning in our data, lamenting our lack of it, or getting stuck at multiple points in between.

To avoid these traps, we must begin by structuring a problem into questions we can answer—or, more precisely, into hypotheses we can test. At the heart of this process is the cycle of inquiry between hypotheses and data that we explored in Part 2 (see Figure 4B.6).

Recall that hypotheses and data form an iterative cycle of learning: you generate hypotheses, you look for the right data to test them, the data validate or disprove your hypotheses, and you generate new hypotheses to test based on what you've learned. Or you start with a few basic data analyses and use those to generate your first hypotheses, and so on. This allows us to make our data analysis and gathering of evidence efficient. Without a good hypothesis, we'll get stuck wanting to look at everything.

Hypotheses

For this reason, it's critical to take your problem—specifically, the basic question to be resolved—and structure it into a series of hypotheses that can be tested.

The key word to remember here is *structure*. The aim at this stage is to create a structure that divides the problem into discrete, mutually exclusive pieces that are small enough to work on and that, taken together, are collectively exhaustive—hence an acronym you may have heard of (and one that is almost a creed with our

Figure 4B.6 Problem solving is a process of rapid hypothesis generation and testing.

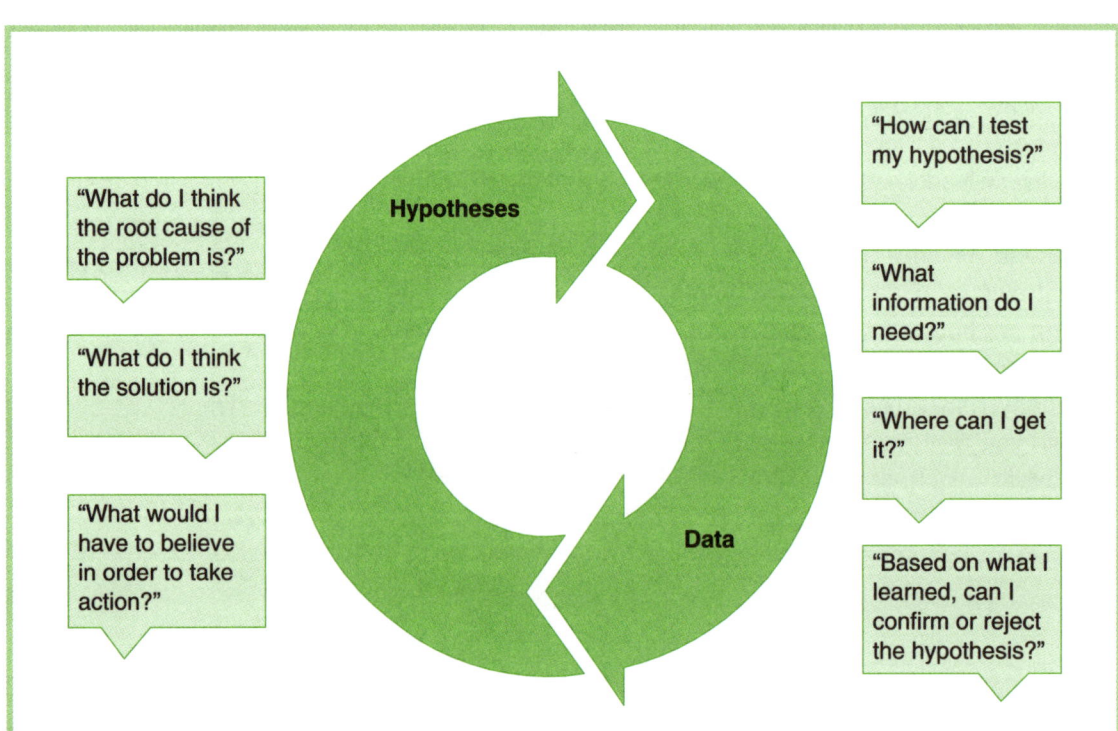

McKinsey colleagues): MECE, for "Mutually Exclusive, Collectively Exhaustive." The value of a MECE structure is again rooted in prioritization: it not only allows you to assure yourself that you're covering all the possible ground for a difficult problem, but it also covers that ground in small pieces that can be prioritized and worked on accordingly. To put it another way, a MECE structure allows you to consider the whole ocean without boiling it. When you ignore a part of a problem, you can be confident that you are choosing to do so deliberately rather than because you ran out of time to do every analysis.

Creating a MECE structure can be challenging, but there are a few tools you can use to do it. To illustrate how these tools work, let's walk through them using the higher education problem from above: "How can we reverse the recent decline in graduation rates through programs that target students in all stages of the pipeline?"

You can use any of these tools or none of them; your objective is to get to a series of hypotheses you can test, which may be as simple as sitting down and brainstorming a list. Use one of these tools only if it will help; in the end, there's no substitute for your common sense.

Reminder: What Makes a Good Hypothesis?

As we first defined it in Chapter 2A, a hypothesis is a *tentative* statement about the relationship between two variables (usually your proposed solution and the outcome you are trying to change) that is verified or rejected through further investigation. As you generate a hypothesis consider five questions to ensure that it is robust:

1. Is it **testable?** Can you prove or disprove it with available data and a reasonable amount of effort?

2. Is it **plausible?** Does it broadly comport with existing evidence and theory? This is just a sense check—you do not necessarily want to rule out more far-fetched hypotheses, but the bar to prove them will be higher.

3. Is it **debatable?** If it can't be wrong, it is simply a statement of fact and unlikely to produce very much insight.

4. Will it lead to **insight?** If you shared your hypothesis with the system leader, would it sound naïve or obvious?

5. Is it **actionable?** If you test it, will the result point directly to an action or actions that the system might take?

Hypothesis Trees. The first tool you can use is a **hypothesis tree**, which we introduced briefly in Chapter 2B and which also comes from our colleagues at McKinsey. Starting with the basic question to be resolved, create an overall hypothesis about what the answer is (see Figure 4B.7).

Figure 4B.7   Hypothesis Tree

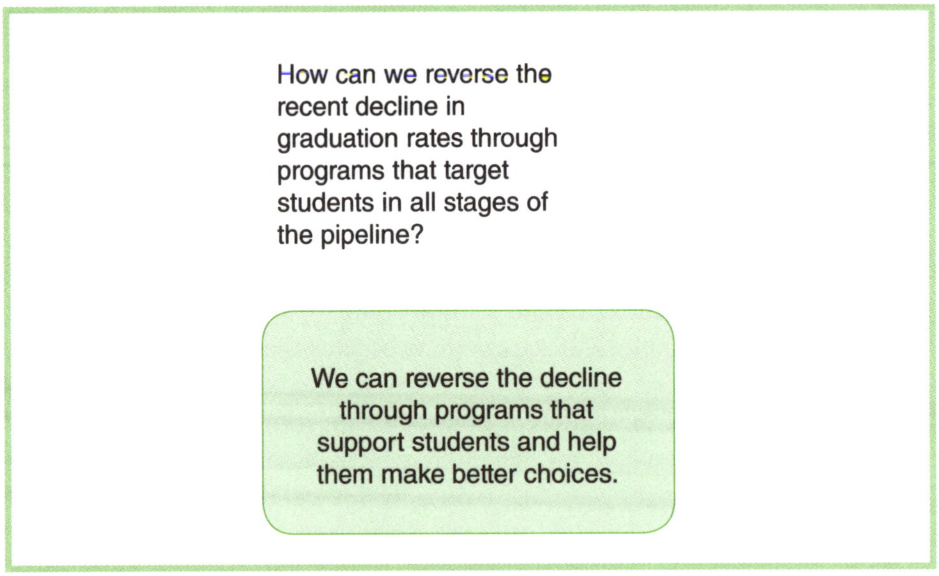

How can we reverse the recent decline in graduation rates through programs that target students in all stages of the pipeline?

We can reverse the decline through programs that support students and help them make better choices.

This hypothesis is fairly basic—and in truth, we need to get more specific before we have something testable. This will happen as we build the tree. This first hypothesis is the "trunk"; from there, create a set of MECE hypotheses as the first set of "branches" (see Figure 4B.8).

Notice that the split is fairly simple: new and existing programs. But though it's basic, it's a helpful and MECE way to break down the hypothesis. You can then build a set of MECE "branches" off of the ones you've created (see Figure 4B.9).

If you ensure that each set of branches is MECE, then the whole thing will be. In a few simple steps, you've generated five testable hypotheses about the potential solution to the problem.

Figure 4B.8   Hypothesis Tree

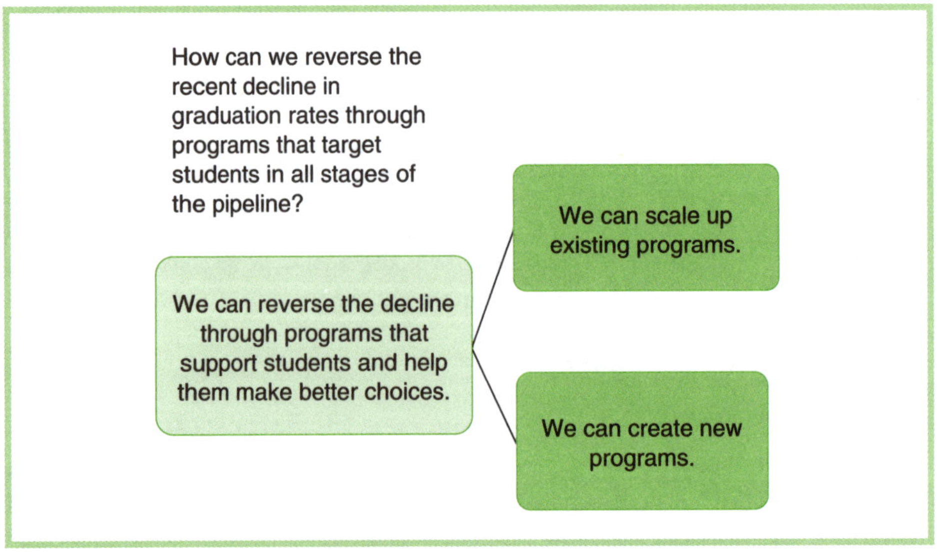

How can we reverse the recent decline in graduation rates through programs that target students in all stages of the pipeline?

We can reverse the decline through programs that support students and help them make better choices.

We can scale up existing programs.

We can create new programs.

Figure 4B.9 Hypothesis Tree

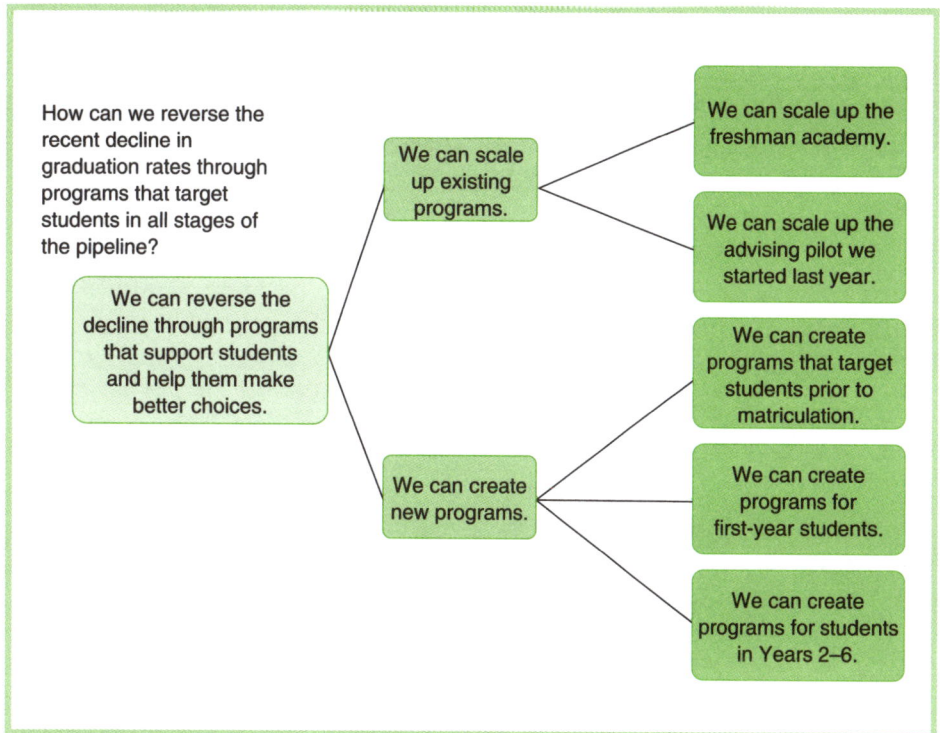

To understand how to test a hypothesis, a useful question to ask is, "What would you have to believe?" That is, what would you have to believe to confirm the hypothesis? For example, to accept the hypothesis about the freshman academy, you'd need to believe (1) that the freshman academy had significant room and resources to scale up and (2) that the freshman academy's work with existing students had made a significant difference in graduation rates—one which, if applied at scale, would make an even bigger impact. The analyses you will need to do follow easily from this.

A hypothesis tree is one of the most efficient tools you can use, because it brings you straight to generating hypotheses (the other tools are a bit more roundabout). It allows you to get to your insights efficiently and helps you start thinking about solutions as soon as possible.

Issue Trees. The second tool you can use is an **issue tree**. The idea of an issue tree is very similar to that of a hypothesis tree, but you don't come up with hypotheses right away. Instead, you literally break the basic question down into its logical parts. So here, the basic question to be resolved becomes the trunk of the tree, and the branches follow (see Figure 4B.10).

You can see that an issue tree is more expansive than a hypothesis tree. Because it doesn't start with a proposed answer, it breaks down the problem into all its possible pieces (and, as you can probably tell, this one can be broken down much further if necessary). You then form your hypotheses as answers to questions at any level of the issue tree. This approach is useful when it's more difficult to formulate an initial hypothesis.

Figure 4B.10   Issue Tree

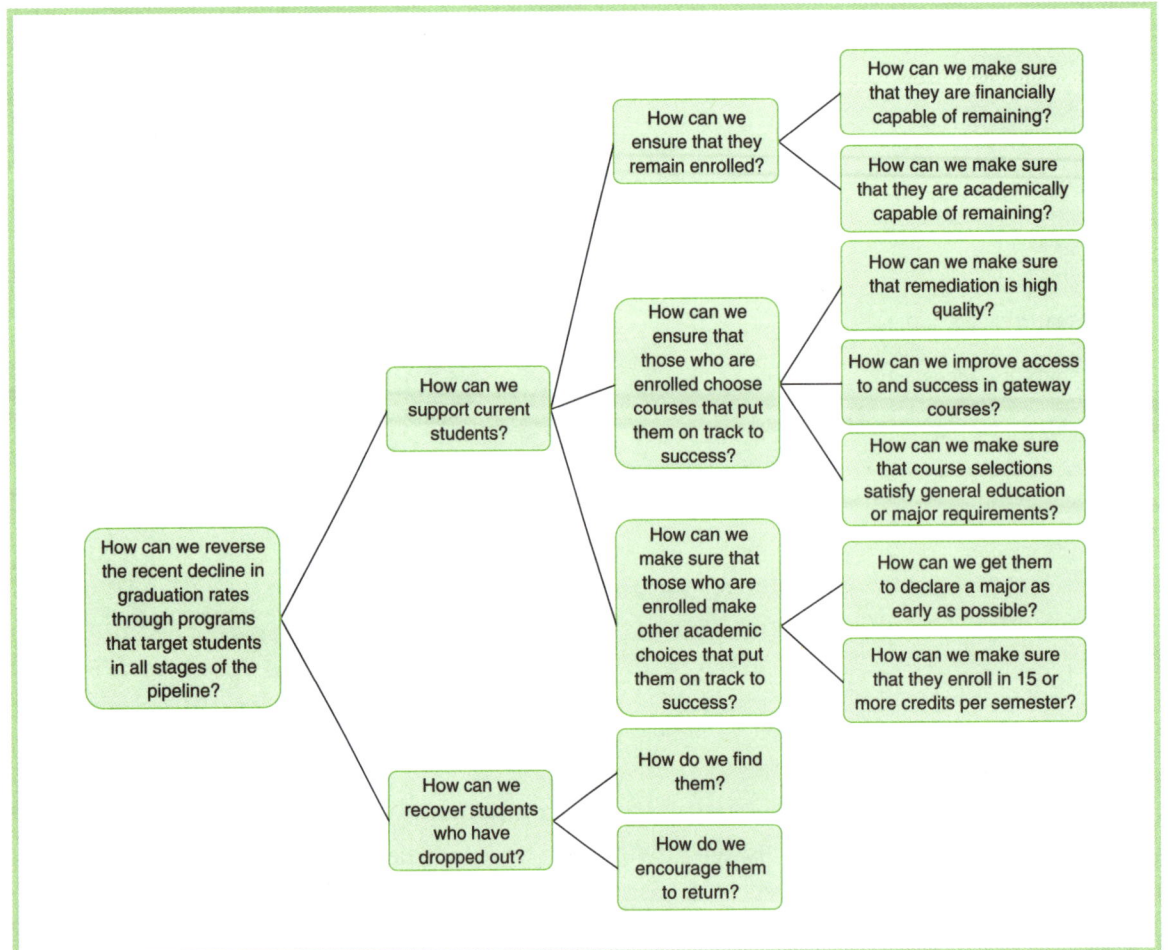

Toward a "Standard" Issue Tree

At one of our convenings of Delivery Units, we decided to focus on the theme of problem solving and field work. To prepare, we worked with each team ahead of time to select and define a specific delivery problem, complete with scope sheet. As we looked at all the problems, we realized that delivery challenges often follow similar patterns. They involve a particular goal that is off track, a set of strategies that are supposed to help achieve that goal, and a set of questions about which of the strategies to achieve that goal are falling short of making their planned contribution to the overall outcome. Using this insight, we generated a "standard" issue tree that may prove to be a useful shortcut for system leaders engaged in problem solving (see Figure 4B.11).

Notice that the issue tree assumes a goal and at least one strategy that you're trying to implement to achieve the goal. But the major issues identified are (mostly) MECE, and they're the most common issues that system leaders encounter. When the goal and strategy are known, it may make sense to start with this tree, adjust it as needed, and use it as a checklist to think through the possible challenges.

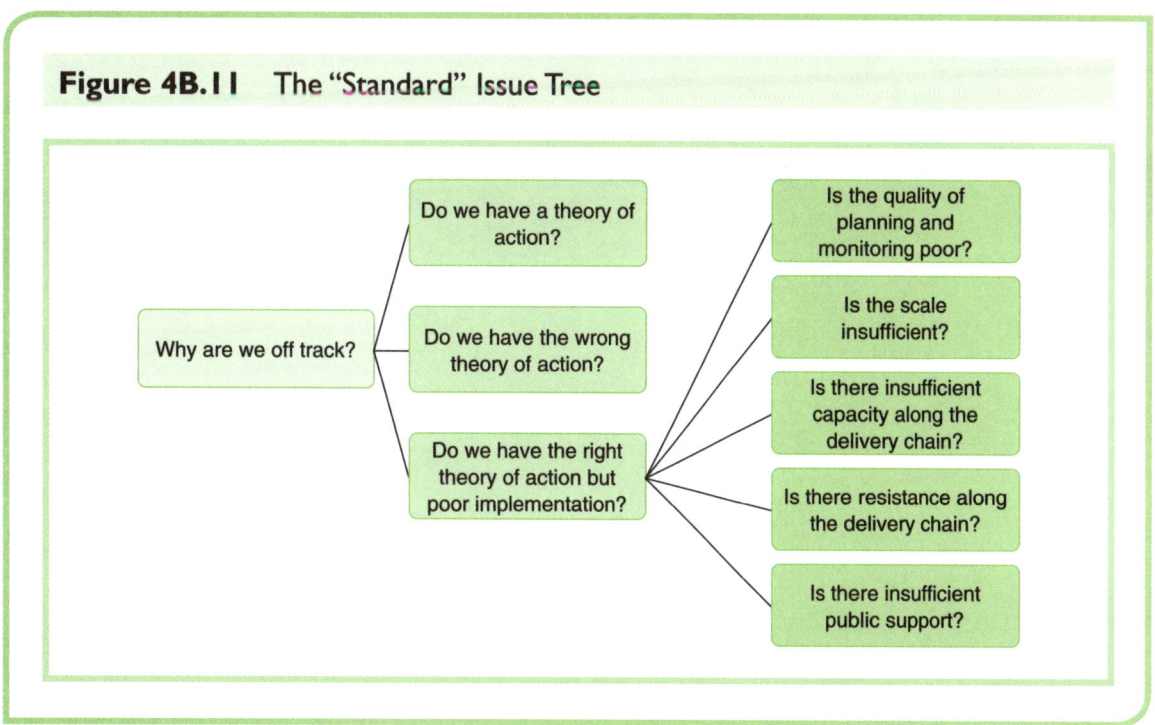

Figure 4B.11   The "Standard" Issue Tree

Delivery Chains. The third tool that you can use is the **delivery chain**, which we explored in detail in Chapter 3B. This is a clear structure that is almost MECE by design. The challenge that prevents delivery must reside at one or more points on the chain—and, in fact, the delivery chain was the most common structure that the PMDU used in its problem solving work (remember the way they described their priority reviews: "checking every link" in the delivery chain to see how strong it was).

This approach is particularly helpful when you already know the strategy or strategies that are going to be the focus of problem solving. In the case of our higher education example, we would need the problem to be more specific, i.e., "How can we improve the quality of implementation of the advising pilot to improve graduation rates?" The resulting analysis might look like Figure 4B.12.

We said in Chapter 3B that a delivery chain is essentially a hypothesis about how you expect a strategy to work. As we can see here, it's not just a hypothesis; it's a hypothesis with clear MECE parts, each of which can be tested. Was the working group able to produce good content? Was the training effective? Are the chancellors and vice chancellors reinforcing the message? And so on.

Story Lines. Finally, you can create a **story line** of the answer to the problem. This is a variant on the hypothesis tree, which we also explored in Part 2. Imagine yourself at the end of this problem-solving effort, presenting your final solution to the system leader. If you had to guess (or hypothesize), what do you think the outline of that presentation would be? This forces you to be even more specific about your solution and to present it as a series of linked hypotheses, each of which can be tested. Figure 4B.13 is an example of what that might look like for our higher education system.

Figure 4B.12   Delivery Chain: Advising

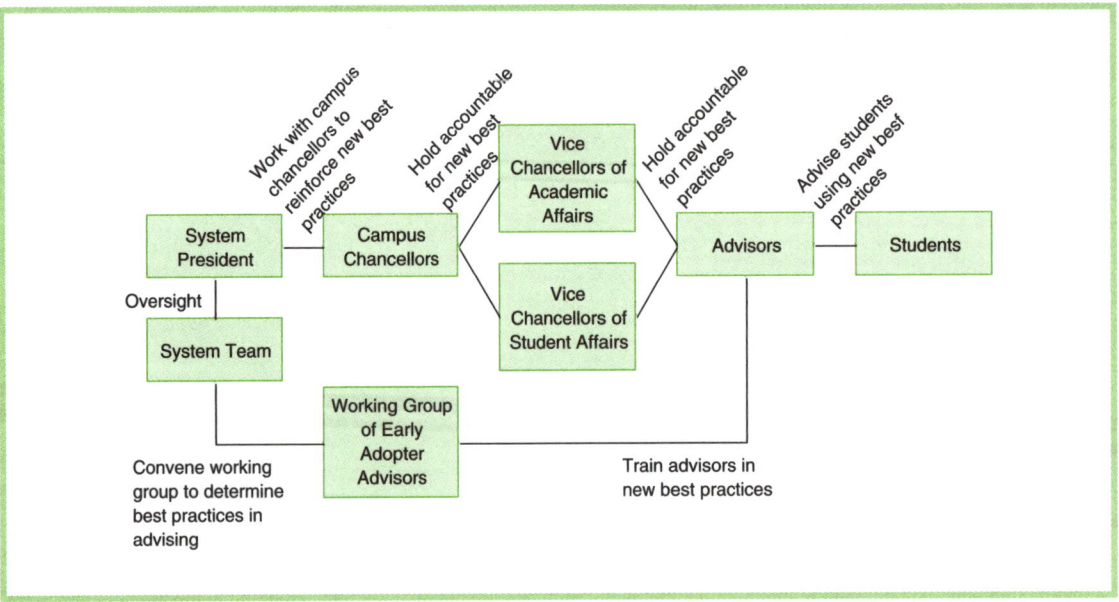

Figure 4B.13   Sample Story Line

Overall headline: We can reverse the decline in graduation rates through a combination of existing and new programs.

- First, we must expand the advising pilot to cover 100% of all students
  - In its first 2 years, the pilot has served 10% of students
  - Those students are on track to graduate at a rate **X%** above that of their peers
  - This difference suggests a strong **return on investment,** so we should find the resources to maximize it through a 100% expansion

- Second, we must create more programs for students who struggle in Years 2–6
  - Right now, these students represent **X%** of dropouts—a number that cannot be ignored if we are to achieve our targets
  - **All** our current programs target students in the first year
  - There are **proven models** for targeting students in these years that we can try
    - Model X is . . .
    - Model Y is . . .
    - Model Z is . . .
  - We should pilot Model X as a prelude to further work in this area

You can see the benefits of the approach from looking at the story line. It almost reads like a plan for data analysis, with an emphasis on the most debatable assertions (the ones we've marked in bold). A team with this story line would immediately know what they have to investigate: Is the pilot generating a significant difference in on-track results? Is it doing so at a reasonable cost per student? Do we really have no programs targeting students in their second years and beyond? And are there proven models that are worth trying for students in this category?

This approach generates clear hypotheses and has the benefit of forcing you to connect them so that you're forming a more robust solution from the beginning. It can also be the most difficult approach. "Inventing" a story will seem disingenuous or arrogant to some—and it would be, if we meant to leave the answer there. But a story line like this is a starting point at best—one that should evolve over time as the hypotheses are tested and confirmed or rejected.

> For more on principles and best practices of strong story lining, please see Chapter 5B.

Story Lining as a Tool for Problem Solving:
Grade 3 Reading in Massachusetts

One of our earliest priority reviews took place in partnership with the Massachusetts Department of Elementary and Secondary Education (ESE). As we've noted above, third-grade reading is a critical goal for ESE, and the scores had been flat for years. Despite new efforts and a new strategy, little was changing, so we worked with them to undertake a priority review and recommend solutions to this ongoing challenge.

Early on in the process, we drafted an initial story line to guide our work (Figure 4B.14).

You can see how rough it is by how many question marks and Xs we had to insert. But it guided our analysis and our work with ESE for several months, and it changed dramatically over that time so that by the time we gave our final report, the recommendations looked like Figure 4B.15.

The point was not that the story line in the beginning was 100% right; it could never have been. But it focused our actions and our work, while leaving us open to other possibilities

Figure 4B.14   Initial Story Line

- For existing strategies, we have good content, but we need to accelerate and spread our reach to equip all XX K–3 teachers to be working toward this goal
  - Major delivery chain changes: more aggressive use of web, partner more with professional associations
  - Limited ability to accelerate development of content given current resources but. . .

- Regarding new strategies, there are opportunities to collaborate with initiatives already in the works and learn from best practices in other states
  - Incorporate WIDA into work to reach ELL
  - Best practices?

- Perhaps, most important, this needs to be about equipping our "army" of XX third-grade teachers and XX K–2 teachers to prepare kids to reach this goal. To this end, we want to launch a communication strategy to make sure people are aware of the goal and are aware of resources available to them (Frameworks, CEPAs, PD). Moreover, we want this to be a two-way process, so people can indicate their interest and we can continue to reach out to interested teachers with more information and tools

(Continued)

(Continued)

Figure 4B.15   Executive Summary of Final Presentation

- We have identified third-grade reading as an area of challenge to focus on for Massachusetts
  - CPI in this area declined overall and for high-need students in 2011
  - Early grade reading results in NAEP suggest large achievement gaps relative to other states
- Massachusetts' strategies for addressing this issue are a good start, but challenges remain with:
  - Defining an integrated picture of what each K–3 teacher, principal, and district leader should know and be able to do for the strategies to improve practice
  - Scaling and implementing the strategies in enough time to make a significant impact on third-grade reading proficiency
- Addressing these challenges will require a comprehensive approach that includes building awareness, capacity, and continuous feedback loops
- With a strong and dedicated person to support the goal leader, we can begin implementing these strategies immediately, for quick wins in 2011–2012 and larger impact in 2012–2013

Whatever method you use to generate your set of testable hypotheses, you may find yourself with a long list of them by the time you're done. The next step is to prioritize the hypotheses and select which ones to analyze. If you used a story line, or even a hypothesis tree, this may not be too difficult to do, as those tools force you to narrow your views quickly. When dealing with an issue tree, by contrast, it's more likely that you'll need to do some pruning of the branches.

There are several criteria that you can use for prioritization. You may eliminate some hypotheses right away because they're impossible to test, they would lead to unworkable solutions if true, or acting on them does not comport with your values or mission. More positive criteria to use include potential impact (how much of the problem would this solution solve?), feasibility (would the solution be aligned with our current capabilities?), and fit with your current strategy. You might also borrow the prioritization exercise from Chapter 3A to help you narrow down your options.

Data Analysis

Hypotheses are useful tools, but they can't drive action until they're tested using real data and evidence. Doing this requires you to identify the specific analyses to do, gather (or create) the necessary data and evidence, run the analyses, and then read the results for insight and implications.

We should stress again here, as we did in Part 2, that data analysis is not necessarily the second step. The cycle is decidedly nonlinear, and depending on your situation, you may start with data or you may start with hypotheses. It's helpful to start with data, for example, when you already know a few standard analyses that will shed light on the problem and help you form even better hypotheses as a second step.

However, we present the two steps in this order because it's a common mistake to go straight to the data without a clear plan for how to analyze it. Some people are gifted at coming up with those plans intuitively and in real time—but what they're really doing is rapidly forming hypotheses and testing them in their own minds. This practice works for individuals but is much more difficult to translate to teams, which is why we recommend that groups begin by considering what their hypotheses are together.

The fruits of a prioritized set of hypotheses will be evident in the very first part of this step: constructing a work plan of analyses to do. In Chapter 2A, we introduced a work-planning template to help you make the leap from hypothesis to analysis. We can use that same template to plan analyses for the example we've been following (see Figure 4B.16).

- The starting point for the work plan is the issue and hypothesis. If you used an issue tree, you'll fill in both of these; if you just went straight to hypotheses, you can start in that column.
- From there, you define a specific analysis for each hypothesis you've identified. The "end product" column is meant for you to be as specific as possible about the output; as we noted in Chapter 2A, it helps to draw the data analysis charts that you want before you've even gathered the data for them.
- Then, define the source(s) you'll consult for each analysis, the owner of the work, and a deadline.

At this point, it's worth stepping back and noting what you've accomplished by the time you get to this stage. You started with a large, possibly ambiguous, and difficult problem to solve. By following these steps, you've broken it down into manageable pieces, prioritized the most important issues, defined analyses for them, and created a concrete action plan for doing them. That is the power of this process: taking a tough problem and breaking through to a specific set of next steps to solve it.

Once you've done this, you're in a great position to dive into the data analysis. However, creating the work plan can sometimes be easier said than done. One area where you may get hung up is on the sources of evidence, which are often few and far between. What do you do when the "killer analysis" that you know would solve the problem requires data that aren't readily available? Or what if the data simply don't exist?

We've run into this problem before. But as we learned in Part 2 and the last chapter, data and evidence are all around us if we are willing to be creative, and the bar for "validity" is far lower when you're putting data to use in internal problem solving. Recall the four types of data and evidence we learned about in Chapter 2B (page 100): statistics, new collections, artifacts, and field work. In the context of problem solving, the best area for exploration will likely be in your qualitative information: artifacts, which are an underestimated and (often) readily available resource, and field work, which allows you to generate new evidence to test your hypotheses.

Figure 4B.16 Work-Plan Template With Example

	Issue	Hypothesis	Analysis	End Product	Sources	Timing and Responsibility
Definition	What is the key unresolved question?	What do you think the answer might be?	What work must you do to prove or disprove the hypothesis and resolve the issue?	What will the output of the analysis be?	Where will your data and evidence come from?	Who will do the analysis and by when?
Example	How can we make sure that our students enroll in 15 or more credits per semester?	We can significantly increase the number of students who do this by making 15 credits per semester a requirement to be a full-time student	Compare average number of credits per semester at similar institutions with a requirement vs. those that do not have one	• Bar chart comparing average credits per semester across the two groups • Raw data listing institutions in both categories	Reach out to colleagues in IR departments at peer institutions	• Nick, by May 30

Field work is particularly important. As our PMDU colleagues would tell you, nothing beats a visit to the front line to understand what is really going on. The essence of this practice is well summarized by the Japanese phrase we learned in Chapter 2B: "Genchi Genbutsu," which means "go and see." Recall the four types of field work we learned about in that chapter: interviews, focus groups, experiencing the work, and site visits. For more detailed guidance on how to use these tools, please consult the section on field work in Chapter 2B.

Generate Solutions and Decide What to Do

At this point, you've successfully broken the problem into manageable pieces and analyzed the highest-priority ones. Solutions, however, are not simply the results of your analyses; they're actionable recommendations that synthesize the most important things you learned from the work.

The process of generating solutions actually starts long before you get to this stage. Many hypotheses are early stage solutions of a sort (e.g., "We can improve our graduation rate by scaling up the freshman academy"). Even when they're not, you can tease out your early solutions by asking a simple pair of questions:

- What would we do if the hypothesis were true?
- What would we do if it were false?

Sometimes, when we do this, the solution is obvious in the sense that it follows from the results of your analysis. If you're testing the hypothesis that scaling up the freshman academy would improve graduation rates, for example, and you prove that the freshman academy has made a huge difference in graduation rates for those who participated, then the headline recommendation is clear; what's left is to flesh out the details of implementing the solution.

At other times, however, the solution will not be immediately apparent. Perhaps the obvious solution is unfeasible due to resource or political constraints, or you're working with multiple hypotheses whose findings need to be combined to see the way forward. Perhaps your findings have raised additional questions, which require you to go back to earlier steps to design and conduct additional analyses. If this is the case, don't hesitate to do this; in a nonlinear process, it shouldn't be unusual for you to double back from time to time.

Tools for Testing Solutions: The WRAP Framework

In their book *Decisive*, brothers Dan and Chip Heath lay out a four-step process for improving the quality of decision making as you generate and consider solutions to your problem:[5]

1. Widen your options: Can you increase the number of choices available to you? Consider having multiple people come up with different

(Continued)

(Continued)

ideas, looking for and speaking to other leaders who have already solved your problem, and running the "vanishing options" test (if none of your current options were available, what would you do instead?).

2. Reality-test your assumptions: Look for ways to test whether your potential solution(s) would work. Look for disconfirming evidence and seek out others who have already tried this solution, and look for ways to test it in your own system before committing fully to it.

3. Attain distance before deciding: Overcome the emotional biases we all face by stepping outside your own shoes as decision maker. What are the core priorities you need to honor? What would you tell your successor, or your best friend, to do in this situation?

4. Prepare to be wrong: As we've said before, nobody can predict the future. Consider what the best possible outcome will be if you implement this solution. Now consider the worst-case scenario. Are you prepared for dealing with the consequences of either? Can you set a "tripwire"—a particular bit of evidence or feedback on implementation—that would signal to you when it's time to consider changing course?

For more resources on applying the WRAP process, visit the authors' website at www.heathbrothers.com.

Once you've chosen and defined your solution, you'll want to flesh it out a bit more for implementation. Here's where you go back to your delivery plan. Is your solution a minor or major adjustment to the existing plan, or something entirely new? If the solution represents a big enough change, you may want to use your planning tools from Part 3—particularly the strategy profile and the delivery chain—to further define it and make it a part of your overall delivery plan. This way, your solution will live in a place where it's likely to be implemented and its progress monitored.

◉ LESSONS FROM THE FIELD

Be Deliberate About Triage

As we reflect on the "levels of intensity" that are the starting point for our problem-solving approach, we admit that the idea of categorizing and prioritizing problems by severity is fairly natural, even obvious. In fact, everyone engages in triage like this every day; it's the only way to make choices about what to do in a world of limited time.

However, as we have often noted, a group of individuals engaging in a particular practice does not always translate into a team doing the same.

Without a shared mental model of what is most and least important, the individual decisions we each make will still amount to chaos when added together.

Moreover, our natural triage practices leave a blind spot: problems and issues that are important but not urgent. In a contest between the former and the latter, the urgent almost always wins when we're left to our own devices. But when a team commits deliberately to a collective process to identify, classify, and prioritize problems, they're more likely to leave room for problem solving beyond urgent firefighting.

This is one of the many delivery tools that benefits from making the intuitive explicit. By making the levels of intensity a shared agreement and practice within a team, you'll add a ton of value at a very low cost. You don't even need to reinvent the wheel; just lift the system described in this chapter and adjust it as you go.

Try the Methodology Step by Step (at First)

As it goes with levels of intensity, so it goes with problem solving on the whole. Because we're all natural problem solvers, thinking of problem solving as a deliberate, step-by-step process may seem like an unnecessary complication. As we noted at the beginning of this chapter, we solve problems every day; isn't that enough?

If this approach were sufficient, however, we wouldn't face some of the massive, unsolved challenges that we do in education. We will inevitably solve *some* problems in the course of our work, but we may gravitate toward the ones we know we can solve rather than the ones that need to be solved. And when we do encounter the biggest challenges in our field, the dialogue inevitably falls into a familiar rut. Consider whether you have ever been a part of one of these conversations:

- The kids who can't read are the ones from disadvantaged families. We can't do anything about that.
- We can't really change anything because the faculty doesn't want to change anything.
- We can't affect what happens in classrooms because of local control (also known as: local control means never having to say we're sorry).
- We don't have the budget to do what is necessary to make a difference.

These are the dead-ends that trap us when we rely only on our intuition to solve problems. They represent the limits of conventional thinking, and they're exactly what the problem-solving process laid out in this chapter is designed to address—by breaking down the problem, looking at it from multiple angles, and using hypotheses to sift through the evidence.

Even with the help of good tools, we don't want to pretend that these challenges are easy to address. But without these tools, we fall victim to a whole host of embedded assumptions that we never surface, let alone question. The real value of the problem-solving process is in getting us to think comprehensively but efficiently about the various issues and possibilities on the table, and to only accept a constraint or eliminate a potential solution after we've considered it deliberately.

By using these tools to open up your thinking in this way, you may surprise yourself. To take one simple example: when we worked with our partners at the Massachusetts Department of Elementary and Secondary Education to conduct a priority review on their Grade 3 reading goal, we found that one of their core strategies was to create model Common Core–aligned units for every grade level and subject area. The problem was that they were working to draft all these units simultaneously—104 units, covering four subjects across Grades P–12—so that none of them would be ready for another 2 to 3 years.

There was a logic of equality there—the idea that no grade level or subject should be left out. But this logic was at odds with the decision that leaders in Massachusetts had made to prioritize third-grade reading. After the team pointed this out, department leaders decided to change course and to accelerate the development of modules related to early grades literacy so that they were ready much earlier.

Here was an implementable solution—but it had been held up by an assumption that just needed some questioning. At its best, the problem-solving process in this chapter forces us to confront every one of those assumptions, maximizing the likelihood that we can find creative and innovative solutions we might not have thought of otherwise. The process need not be applied to every problem—but we would encourage you to try going through it for at least some of the challenges you face. Over time, if you use these tools as a team, they will come more naturally to you and will become part of your intuitive approach to problem solving.

Go and See

We cannot overstate the importance of being willing to engage in field work. Not only is it valuable, but it's also underutilized—which means that you will distinguish yourself from others by doing it.

However, in our experience working with system leaders and teams, we have found a relatively consistent aversion to field work. This is not because people don't want to do the work; rather, the cause is rooted in our fears about rigor. As we learned in Chapter 2B, qualitative information—whether in the form of existing artifacts or new information generated by field work—often does not get the attention it deserves in discussions of data and evidence. For many of us, the paradigm of rigorous information is set by what we know from working with validated quantitative data. Set against this backdrop, we underestimate what we can learn from spending even a little bit of time in the field, and fear that our efforts there can never be comprehensive enough to yield meaningful information.

Of course, this line of thinking is self-defeating; by refusing to act on information that isn't validated and quantitative, we let the perfect become the enemy of the good. As a result, we either delay our decisions until we have the "right" information, or we act from no information at all, which is worse than the imperfect alternative that field work offers. Moreover, field work really does tell us something that no amount of validated quantitative data can: the actual state of things on the ground.

Field work can take up quite a bit of time, and because you have to make choices about where to go, it may be daunting to think about where to start. Our advice: use the prioritization tools laid out in this chapter, and where all else fails, start *somewhere* and use that experience to build better hypotheses about where you should focus your time. In all our years working with system leaders and teams, nobody who's tried out field work has regretted it or wished that they'd done less of it.

◉ KEY CONSIDERATIONS FOR SYSTEM LEADERS AND STAFF

If you're a **system leader**, your main role is to insist on innovative thinking and do whatever you can to create the space for it. Your actions will send signals every day about what kind of thinking is "permissible" and what's frowned upon. Do you actively encourage dissenting voices? Are you transparent about the pros and cons of your own decisions? Are you persuaded to change your mind by the evidence your colleagues bring? These behaviors will give your team permission to become true problem solvers.

You know how people talk about building a "problem-solving culture" in their organizations? If you're one of the **system staff**, nobody is a more important building block of this culture than you. And as we learn in Part 5, culture is just the sum of actions taken repeatedly by people like you. Consider applying this methodology to your own work, whether it's a part of the overall delivery effort or not. Pick a problem that's vexing you and design your own mini problem-solving process to address it.

Beyond that, start using this process to suggest outside-the-box solutions or hypotheses to test. You may be surprised at how they're received: often, in systems governed by unseen assumptions, everyone's just waiting for someone to ask the right question to give them permission to talk about something differently. You can be the one who makes that difference, even if your leaders aren't yet role modeling it. If you're rebuffed, consider doing some preliminary analysis to test your hypothesis or solution, and using that evidence to make your case from a different angle.

Finally, if you're a **delivery leader**, your role as a facilitator here is paramount. A lot of these exercises and tools emphasize process, and the value from them will not always be immediately apparent. Motivated by good instincts, people will be impatient to just get on with it and do something.

We would never want to bias you toward inaction, but this is one of those cases where going slow(er) will help you go fast later. If raw analytical power were enough to solve the crisis in education, we'd have solved it by now, at least in some places. The evidence suggests that much more is needed. The tools in this chapter provide the structure to help people push beyond convention. They will see the value eventually!

⊙ CONCLUSION

At first glance, problem solving seems like an elusive art, or perhaps a talent that only some are born with. In this chapter, we've attempted to show the opposite: like delivery, problem solving is actually a *discipline* that can be broken down into concrete practices. As such, it can be learned; using these practices—consistently, repeatedly, until they become almost instinctual—will improve both the quality of your current work and your skill in solving future problems.

The stakes are high at this stage. A central premise of this book is that our reforms often fail not because we're short of good ideas, but because we don't think rigorously or creatively enough about how to implement them with excellence. One reason for this is that, once we've started implementing a reform, we don't know how to change course when circumstances warrant it—or even how to know *when* we should change course. These tools for identifying, prioritizing, and solving problems help you avoid this trap. They close the loop of continuous improvement by looking at the stream of evidence coming from your routines and translating it into positive action for tomorrow.

In this way, good problem solving ensures that you'll always be ready with an answer to that last question of delivery: If we're not on track, what are we going to do about it? If your delivery effort is to make a real difference for students, then these are tools you must master.

⊙ NOTES

1. Leppert, J. (2013, July 19). *Reward firefighting and you'll create a culture of arsonists.* *Forbes.* Retrieved from http://www.forbes.com/sites/johnkotter/2013/07/29/reward-firefighting-and-youll-create-a-culture-of-arsonists/

2. Barber, M. (2008). *Instruction to deliver: Fighting to transform Britain's public services* (Rev. ed.). London, UK: Methuen.

3. Ibid.

4. Barber, M., Kihn, P., & Moffit, A. (2011). *Deliverology 101: A field guide for educational leaders.* Thousand Oaks, CA: Corwin.

5. Heath, C., & Heath, D. (2013). *Decisive: How to make better choices in life and work.* New York, NY: Crown Business.

Chapter 4C

Sustain and Continually Build Momentum

 Develop a foundation for delivery    Understand the delivery challenge    Plan for delivery    Drive delivery

 Create an irreversible delivery culture

System Leader Summary

When the going gets tough in implementation, you'll face pressure to back down. When the opposite happens, and you see your first positive results, the excuse will be different: people will be tempted to declare victory and slow things down. And sometimes, when neither happens, the threat of boredom will open your team up to distraction.

Implementation follows a cycle of ups and downs, each with its own perils and challenges. Sustaining your delivery effort through the inevitable setbacks,

(Continued)

(Continued)

transitions, and events in the news will be a collective challenge for you, your delivery leader, and your team. This chapter articulates a series of principles for being sensitive to the cycle and managing through it. As system leader, you need to role model a drive for urgency, steel in the spine, and a refusal to be satisfied with partial results. And even when you have to handle the crisis of the moment, remember and support your delivery leader: it's their job to push forward even when you and your team are distracted.

⊚ VICTORY AND DEFEAT

These last several chapters have brought you through some of the core elements of delivery—the practices and processes that make it a distinctive approach to getting results. These practices will increase your system's focus and lead you to some early wins. What will you do with them?

On the one hand, you will (rightly) feel some euphoria in these moments—progress at last! On the other hand, these early results will also bring the challenges you face into sharper relief. Jean-Paul Sartre once said, "Once you hear the details of victory, it is hard to distinguish it from a defeat." Your early wins might feel this way: costly, tiring, ground out amidst more resistance than you ever imagined you would encounter.

Together, these two feelings will tempt you to declare victory and move on to something else. Over the years, we've helped many system leaders get their delivery efforts off to a strong start. But some of them have struggled to sustain that momentum. They've lost focus in the out years, shifting their attention to the next fire—or even the next new strategy. They've celebrated too early and allowed themselves to get discouraged when the results went flat. Or they've seen their delivery teams become victims of their own success, pulled in to assist with special projects that need immediate help, even as the "mundane" things that make delivery work—the focus on results, the plans, the routines—start to slip.

You can avoid this fate. The key is to understand that implementation follows a cycle of ups and downs and to be ready to manage your system through that cycle. There are five overall stages, summarized in Figure 4C.1.

What makes this a cycle is the fact that, at each stage, you must make choices that will either move you forward or backward. In particular:

- How do you handle the early wins and early challenges? Do you seize the momentum from the good news and use it as fuel to take things to the next level? Or do you squander that momentum in self-congratulation?
- Do you plan for the implementation dip? You may not always be able to acknowledge publicly that an implementation dip is coming—sometimes it's not politically feasible—but you should always plan for it internally.
- When you're in the implementation dip, do you push through the challenges or give up because things are too difficult?

Figure 4C.1   The Cycle of Implementation

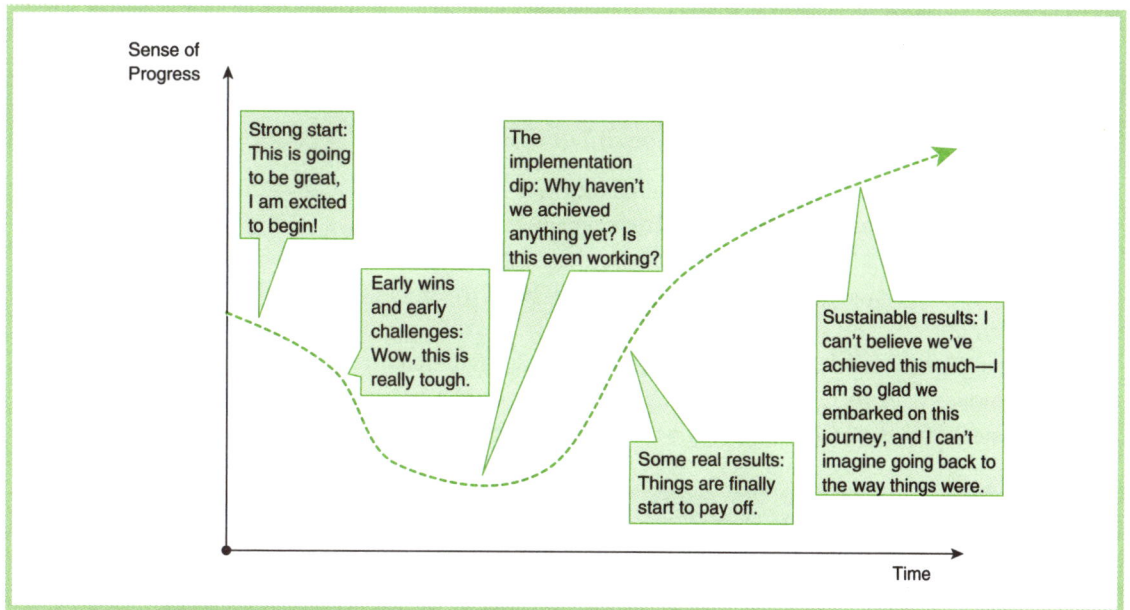

- And finally, when you start to see some real results, do you push for sustainability or do you give in to the (even stronger now!) temptation to take your foot off the gas pedal? Are you satisfied with good or do you insist on greatness?

One of the hallmarks of delivery is that it remains anchored on the aspiration, no matter what. Every victory—and every defeat—offers an opportunity to keep pointing at the aspiration and urging your system toward it.

The Delivery Unit will have a particularly important role to play here. Remember the image we introduced in Chapter 1C, of Ulysses and his Delivery Unit of rowers, driving toward the destination despite the distractions? The steps in this cycle of implementation will test your mettle, but these are the moments that matter most in keeping the work on track. As Michael put it in his final note to PMDU staff: "Someone has to be the unreasonable one."[1]

Sustaining Race to the Top Reforms

In 2012 and 2013, the U.S. Department of Education (ED) started to consider how the Race to the Top (RTT) states would sustain their reforms when their grants ended in 2014 and beyond. These states faced a funding cliff; more significantly, many of them faced renewed opposition to their work as implementation got more difficult. How could ED support the states to face these challenges?

In 2013, ED partnered with EDI and others in the Reform Support Network (RSN) to answer this question, forming a Sustainability Work Group of seven states that were keen to work through the problem together. The work group's approach was simple:

(Continued)

(Continued)

- Define *sustainability* rigorously;
- Help states use this definition to self-assess the sustainability of their reforms; and
- Support them to build on their strengths and shore up any areas of weakness they find through that self-assessment.

For the first step, we defined sustainability like this: "sustainable reforms are durable, adaptive, and persistently focused on priority goals for improved student growth in the face of changing conditions." From this definition, we created a **sustainability rubric** that lays out all the elements of a sustainable reform. There are 20 of these elements, as Figure 4C.2 shows.

Each element has a row in the rubric that includes key questions for self-assessment, descriptions of weak and strong practice, and sample evidence to look for. Like the capacity review framework from Chapter 1B (page 23), this tool can be used to help states assess the current state of their work. We designed a series of exercises to help states:

- Identify their most important student outcome goals;
- Prioritize the reforms that must be sustained to achieve them;

Figure 4C.2　Elements of Sustainability

System Capacity	
SEA Capacity	• Align human capital decisions to support reform goals • Build a culture of continuous improvement toward reform goals • Align organizational structure to reform goals
State Capacity	• Extend capacity through partnerships • Extend capacity in the field
Performance Management	
Clarity of Outcomes and Theory of Action	• Set student outcome targets to achieve priority goals • Establish a theory of action and strategies for implementing priority reforms • Develop plans that align strategies to priority goals
Alignment of Resources	• Direct resources to priority reforms • Establish clear leadership of priority reforms
Collection and Use of Data	• Ensure quality data on performance • Ensure quality data on implementation • Use data to review progress and make decisions
Accountability for Results	• Link internal accountability to results • Link external accountability to results • Engage stakeholders about results
Context for Sustaining Reform	
Alignment of the Statewide System	• Align the policy agenda to support priority reforms • Build a coalition to drive priority reforms
Public Value	• Build stakeholder support for priority reforms • Build broad public support for priority reforms

- Identify the elements of sustainability that are strongest and weakest for each of these reforms; and
- Develop and implement plans to improve sustainability in their areas of greatest challenge.

This work showed us how important it is to plan for sustainability early, especially in the context of a time-limited grant like RTT. But we also learned that the work had much broader application beyond RTT states. Whether funded by a grant or not, all reforms have a limited shelf life unless we put thought and energy into how they will be sustained through the challenges that come. The RTT end date gave some states an excuse to have these conversations, but sustainability is a vital topic for any reformer who's hoping to have a lasting impact on a system's work.

You can download the sustainability rubric and associated tools at this link: http://www2 .ed.gov/about/inits/ed/implementation-support-unit/tech-assist/resources.html#capacity-building.

Note: This project has been funded at least in part with federal funds from the U.S. Department of Education under contract number ED-ESE-10-O-0087. The content of this publication does not necessarily reflect the views or policies of the U.S. Department of Education nor does mention of trade names, commercial products, or organizations imply endorsement by the U.S. government.

⊙ CORE PRINCIPLES

We must be deliberate about how we build momentum and create sustainability for our delivery effort. But there's no concrete set of steps that will do this; what you need to do will vary widely by situation. Instead, we offer five principles for managing through the cycle of implementation:

1. Persist through distractions;

2. Persist through monotony;

3. Persist through resistance;

4. Challenge the status quo; and

5. Celebrate successes.

We'll illustrate each of these with lessons that we've learned from the field and with case examples of what those lessons looked like in practice.

Persist Through Distractions

Distractions will be with you throughout the cycle of implementation. As we learned in Chapter 4A, the routines you create as part of a delivery effort are the exception rather than the rule; left to our own devices, it is in our nature to be distracted by events as they come.

Some of these events are cyclical: legislative sessions, and their pull on staff time to provide data and testimony, are the most obvious. In some systems, elections exert a similar gravity. For these, we return to a question Michael once asked the British railway service, when they explained that the trains slowed down every autumn because the falling leaves blocked the lines: "Why does autumn take you by surprise every year?" In other words, why not have a plan for dealing with predictable distractions?

Of course, most distractions are not predictable. Even legislative sessions throw up plenty of surprises, and sometimes big events in the news intervene: natural disasters, scandals, gaffes of one kind of another, or dramatic failure in a campus or school district. And let's not forget unexpected leadership transitions: as of this writing, the average tenure for K–12 state chiefs and urban superintendents is about 3 years.[2] Campus presidents and provosts have average tenures of 7 and 4 years, respectively, and in our higher education network, we have observed a System Head transition in at least a third of our systems and turnover of the Chief Academic Officer in several more.

Distractions like these often demand engagement from system leaders and leadership teams; we shouldn't pretend otherwise. Like Ulysses, they must be free to listen to the sirens' call, responding to criticisms, handling the questions from the press, and being present at key moments to handle the crisis at hand directly. So we must rely on the division of labor that we agreed on when we created a Delivery Unit: the Unit persists in focusing on the goals and strategies, even though—especially because—the system leader is preoccupied.

Our most famous example of this comes from the PMDU. During Michael's time there, the war in Iraq began in 2003, with Tony Blair standing as America's closest ally. Michael stressed to his team that the Delivery Unit was created precisely for situations like this—to ensure that delivery never sleeps, even when the system leader is busy. Most of our system leaders won't be trying to fight a war—though we're sure that they feel that way on some days. Nonetheless, the challenges we've seen them face are real:

- In 2011, the Massachusetts Department of Elementary and Secondary Education (ESE) took over the Lawrence Public School District. This sensitive move required a great deal of the Commissioner's time. The Delivery Unit also had to be involved, since the takeover had a direct impact on one of the delivery goals: school and district turnaround. The Delivery Unit took the changes in stride, but continued with the routines for the broader turnaround goal without missing a beat, ensuring that the team would not be distracted from attending to the dozens of other turnaround schools and districts that also needed attention.
- In the middle of EDI's strategic planning partnership with E. L. Haynes Public Charter School in Washington, DC, the Head of School resigned to take a post as the mayor's chief education advisor. But the board, the leadership team, and the new delivery team stayed committed to the strategic planning process: now, more than ever, they said, it would be important to complete the plan and maintain the delivery routines to set the next Head of School up for success.
- In South Dakota's 2014 legislative session, several bills were proposed to roll back that state's adoption of the Common Core State Standards (CCSS). The Secretary of Education, Melody Schopp, spent a great deal of

time that year working to defeat the bills in question. Meanwhile, the Delivery Unit's routines allowed the South Dakota Department of Education to maintain its focus on implementation.

The division of labor is evident: system leaders get drawn in to events of the moment where necessary, but the Delivery Units remain free to focus on the core work. You can't ignore all distractions, but you can compartmentalize them.

For Delivery Units, there are two lessons. First, maintain delivery routines, even when there's pressure on you to let the schedule slip. They're the only way you can generate a sense of urgency to compete with the distractions at hand.

Second, Delivery Units will have to resist the tendency to become a rapid-response team. A good Delivery Unit is filled with talented people; in tough times, the pressure to repurpose them to handle the crisis of the moment will be strong. Sometimes you may make a calculated judgment that dealing with a specific issue is in the best interest of the overall delivery effort. But you should be wary of requests like this.

Persist Through Monotony

Let's face it: delivery can be monotonous, and monotony can be even more dangerous than a crisis. The excitement that comes from planning that first stocktake may lessen after months or even years, of reviewing the same old goals and strategies. Crises bring at least some excitement to a system office, which is one of the reasons why people fight fires: not because they have to, but because it's more interesting.

More broadly, you'll often find your focus threatened by the call of the latest reform, big idea, or other shiny object. In America, implementation has always fought a losing battle with policy for supremacy in the hearts and minds of leaders. Policy—the "what" of reform—is far sexier, far grander, and, frankly, far *easier* than its more homely cousin. Leaders, especially elected officials, will always itch to announce new things, especially during the implementation dip, when nervousness sets in as the numbers refuse to move. We are reminded of the politician's fallacy, first popularized (appropriately) in the popular British sitcom *Yes, Prime Minister*:

1. We must do something.

2. *This* is something.

3. Therefore, we must do *this*!

To be clear: we're not saying that you should *never* change your approach. Indeed, most of this part of the book has been about the kinds of continuous improvement practices that allow you to review progress and adjust your work based on the evidence. It's that last part that's key—*based on the evidence*. Delivery routines and problem-solving practices allow you to make appropriate mid-course corrections as you observe what happens.

What we're talking about here, though, is a kind of political magical thinking—one that would wish away the challenges of implementation by focusing on something else. Giving in to this impulse will lead to all sorts of difficulties. If we change the goals, we're effectively abdicating our aspiration. Victory becomes easy to declare under these circumstances—it's whatever we want it to be—and it becomes meaningless. If we flit from strategy to strategy without relying on the evidence, we'll never be able to evaluate whether anything we tried actually worked. Most important, these misplaced shifts in focus will dissipate what energy we've tried to husband for wrestling with the challenges of delivery. Implementation may be the plainer cousin, but in the long run, it's the only route to real results.

For these reasons, you must persist through the monotony. Keep the aspiration, goals, and strategies front and center, and keep reminding people of the moral purpose associated with them. Emphasize the importance of results as the ultimate yardstick of success; if people want to change the strategies, invite them to make the case for change based on evidence of progress. Better still, ask them to use the framework you've set up through delivery routines to do this. And, of course, insist that the routines go on, no matter what.

Some people—powerful people—may still not be able to take no for an answer. If they really want to repudiate the existing goals, use polite (but firm) logical questions to make sure that this is what they really want to do:

- Are we still committed to dramatically improving outcomes for students?
- So what are you saying that we should do with these student outcome goals that we committed to?
- Are you saying that we need to walk away from them? Adjust them downward? Emphasize them less? If so, what's the rationale for the change?
- Are there other goals that are more important than these? How are they more important?

In some cases, this kind of dialogue can be persuasive; the weakness of a poorly conceived idea is far more evident when it's spoken out loud. In other cases, it will turn out that there actually is a strong case for making changes—and these questions, asked honestly and authentically, will help uncover that. Sometimes, however, the other person knows exactly what they're doing; they're under pressure and need to announce something new to change the subject. In this case, it's important to put yourself in their shoes, to empathize with their situation, and to suggest other ways to relieve the pressure without changing course. Announcing quick wins or evidence of progress may be a viable alternative to starting something new.

In the end, persisting through monotony is about letting evidence rather than ego drive the decisions you make. Mark Murphy, the Secretary of Education in Delaware, is a good example of this. At EDI, we had the privilege of working with his predecessor, Lillian Lowery, and then continuing the relationship with Delaware after the transition. Rather than wiping the slate clean and starting over, the new Secretary took some time to understand and evaluate the existing work; his first month coincided with the agency's end-of-year delivery routines with districts, so he used the opportunity to listen to his superintendents and get feedback on what was working. After that, adjustments came incrementally. The goals stayed the same, as did many of the core reforms. The Secretary even increased his emphasis on the delivery work and heightened its focus, using routines and delivery planning to further flesh out his strategy for improving college and career readiness.

> For more on building capacity to persist through monotony, please see Chapter 5A.

Eventually, other changes came as well: a refocused human capital plan, a stronger professional learning program around the Common Core, and a revised approach to interactions with districts. But these decisions derived from the evidence the Secretary saw, and they were built on top of the existing work. These adjustments also came in the context of a heavy investment in improving the Department's capacity and aligning its people around the work.

And that's the last important lesson about persisting through monotony: it's a lot easier when you invest in your people. The implementation dip can sap morale. When people believe in you and know that you'll support them to persevere, they will be that much more likely to do it.

Persisting Through Monotony at the California State University System

In 2009, the California State University System kicked off its Graduation Initiative, with the purpose of raising graduation rates and halving gaps in success for underrepresented minorities. The delivery team engaged all 23 of the system's campuses to participate in this effort:

- The team provided statewide workshops in pertinent areas of strategy (transfer, closing gaps, engaging faculty).
- The Chief Academic Officer visited each of the campuses and spent time with their core implementation teams.
- The team provided system-level supports for campuses, such as leading indicator data. They also provided some supports directly to students, such as an Academic Calculator that encouraged students to make choices that were more likely to lead to graduation.

Over time, outcomes began to shift. The system achieved record high graduation rates for all students and its underrepresented minorities. In time, the achievement gap that had been growing stabilized and even began to narrow.

Ironically, the system office team was concerned that this early success might result not in further momentum, but a loss of interest. It often becomes increasingly difficult to engage leadership who want to move on to the next big strategy, even though the goal was far from achieved and the target date was several years out.

In response, the team stayed focused on the work and found ways to keep the feel of the initiative fresh. Support to the campuses has varied in

(Continued)

(Continued)

format over time—directly from the team, from outside experts, and even peer to peer. The initiative kicked off at the Chancellor's office, but has been led by campuses—an important break from past practice. And in 2013, the Chancellor's office added competitive grants to the mix, encouraging campuses to propose ways that they could use a pool of additional funding to close achievement gaps further, with specific interventions related to data readiness and action research, the revision of bottleneck and gateway courses, and support for high-impact educational practices.

Most important, the delivery team didn't waver from their original goals. Their continued focus gave other leaders room to pivot—or get distracted occasionally—even as the broader system stayed focused on the most important thing.

Persist Through Resistance

The implementation dip will often include resistance to your work—the pushback that comes when a strategy does not (yet!) seem to be producing results. This resistance can be internal: skepticism about the work, a feeling that "this too will pass," or a tendency to make excuses about why it won't be possible to implement the strategies or achieve the goals. Even some leaders may make this argument. Resistance can also be external, because stakeholders lose patience and opponents of the strategy will sense an opportunity to strike during a moment of weakness.

We explored some of these dynamics in Chapter 1D on building a guiding coalition, and we learned there that planning for this resistance will help you when it inevitably comes. A strong guiding coalition, selected to be influential with the right mix of internal and external stakeholders, will act on your behalf to reinforce your core belief in the work at hand.

For that to work, though, you must maintain that belief. Persisting in the face of opposition will require some steel in your spine: you'll need to maintain your own confidence in the work while simultaneously engaging with the resistance you do meet.

This begins with making sure that you are centered. Don't be spooked at the first sign of trouble (or the second, or the third!). Don't fall for shallow arguments or rush to compromise because some people are making things uncomfortable for you and the team. Remember why you committed to the aspiration, and make sure that comes through as you continue through routines and problem solving to push for more progress. Progress itself will ultimately be your best argument against the naysayers.

In the short term, however, you'll need to engage with those who oppose the work. Resistance is often rooted in fear of personal accountability and change. What can you do to understand and address these fears? Can you take them off the table? Can you address them with an adjustment to the strategy?

On the other hand, some objections will sound more like excuses (though you can't call them that out loud). In these cases, you'll need to make the argument for why the current course is the right one. The PMDU actually compiled a list of the most frequent excuses they heard, and the recommended responses to them, in Figure 4C.3.[3]

Notice that some of these responses simply amount to standing your ground. Others involve using evidence and analysis; skepticism often collapses in the face of fact. Present your case, and then offer an authentic challenge:

- Do we still agree on these student outcome goals?
- Do you have a better way to meet them?
- How do you know that it's a better way?

That's the bar a skeptic has to meet if they want to change the work.

Facts and analysis can make a difference, particularly when your skeptics are internal to your system and genuinely need to be convinced. But sometimes the facts will not be the relevant point of conflict. Exhibit A is the recent pushback to the Common Core State Standards, where the opposition has been making a mostly emotional argument warning against the "federalization" or "corporate takeover" of education. You may use facts to deny that this is what is happening, but that doesn't make the fear any less real.

In situations like these, you'll need to respond with an emotional argument of your own. Come back to the moral case for what you are doing. And remember that fear can cut both ways: people are arguing about the risks of action, but have

Figure 4C.3   Responding to Excuses

Six Common Explanations	Your Delivery Unit's Response
1. We're already doing these things.	1. Improving what our system is doing in a coordinated way can have a tremendous impact on performance.
2. The changes you're asking for will have unintended consequences.	2. Maintaining the status quo is just as risky as what we are trying to do, and we'll have mechanisms for ensuring potential consequences aren't realized (e.g., monitoring perverse indicators).
3. The changes are impossible to make.	3. The changes were chosen from fact-based analysis, and the Delivery Unit will help you make them—no matter how daunting they seem.
4. The target is wrong.	4. The target was chosen from evidence-based analysis and makes sense when viewed as part of the trajectory.
5. Delivery is just the flavor of the month.	5. Delivery is a long haul, and we will not stop until the targets are reached.
6. Delivery is just another layer of bureaucracy.	6. The Delivery Unit is here to make less work, not more, and will work with you to ensure change happens as efficiently as possible.

For more information on managing resistance to change, please see Part 5. For more on guiding coalitions, refer to Chapter 1D.

they considered the risks of *inaction?* The 2010 film *Waiting for Superman* focused on the current state of K–12 education and made the risks of doing nothing abundantly clear: hordes of undereducated students with dim job prospects, an economy in permanent malaise, and injustice for families from disadvantaged backgrounds. What will happen if your reforms are unsuccessful? Can you paint a compelling picture that overwhelms the fears stoked by the opposition?

Persisting Through Resistance in Hawai'i

As we've noted in previous chapters, leaders at the Hawai'i Department of Education (HIDOE) boiled down their Race to the Top (RTT) reforms to six strategies that they committed to see implemented well in every school and classroom throughout the district. These include the transition to the Common Core State Standards, a new Educator Evaluation system, and a comprehensive system of student supports.

The team encountered resistance in many forms. Some school leaders were reluctant to abandon past practices to embrace these new reforms; others worried that they were too much, too fast. Some of these tensions came to a head in 2014, when a group of current and former principals started a campaign to convince the State Board of Education to change direction. The board has stayed the course, however; they even renewed the superintendent's contract for 3 more years that summer.

How did the leadership team manage to persist through the resistance? The answer lies in the groundwork that leaders had laid for implementation over the prior 2 years. The team overcommunicated about the six priority strategies and responded to the initial objections they heard. Amid concerns about a lack of support for implementation, they freed up nearly 100 positions so that each of the state's local school districts would have a team of six support staff (one to coordinate each strategy). They looked for ways to reduce other unnecessary burdens on schools, partly by reducing compliance requirements and partly by improving the quality of services such as facilities and IT support so that school leaders would be free to focus on the priority strategies. But through all this, they didn't waver from the strategies themselves.

And in July 2014, at the department's annual Educational Leadership Institute (ELI) for school and system leaders, the superintendent and her team reinforced this work by bringing the argument back to the emotional plane, reminding the assembled participants that the six priority strategies were not just reforms for their own sake, but critical pillars for the success of Hawai'i's students and economy. The motto of the Institute was a Hawai'ian proverb: "He wa'a, he moku. He moku, he wa'a," which translates to "The canoe is our island, and the island is our canoe." The broader translation: we're all in this together, and our future depends on getting this work right.

A combination of messaging, real responsiveness, and resolve allowed the team to persist through resistance. As a result, the six priority strategies became a part of the vernacular of education reform throughout Hawai'i. By the time the opposition organized itself, the system the team had built was resilient enough to survive it.

Challenge the Status Quo

Even as you face challenges in implementation, your successes will sometimes trap you as well. Whether during a strong start, early wins, or your first real results, success will lead to praise and a sense of accomplishment. You'll have achieved more than most others who have tried. And the greater your achievement, the greater the temptation will be to hold the victory party too soon.

You have to remember that this isn't the time to take your foot off the gas. In fact, the momentum from your successes is precisely the fuel you need to accelerate your efforts and push toward the target with even greater fervor. This is the time to use your evidence of what worked to narrow your focus even further if you can, zeroing in on those things that will make the biggest difference and obsessing over them. It's also the time to think hard about the distinction between "good" and "great" and to make sure that you never confuse the two.

So when the data come in with the good news, take advantage of these key moments and use them to telegraph three messages:

1. We've come a long way and we should be proud.

2. However, we have a long way to go still.

3. Here's what we must do to get there.

This frame balances celebration with the urgency to do more. This is critical, because the further you get into your delivery effort, the less time you'll have to reach your target.

Michael understood this during his time at the PMDU; their work had begun during the start of a 5-year Parliament. After 2 years, several outcomes had improved and the disciplines of delivery were being established in government. Michael wanted to build on this success, so he used the opening of the third year to assess the PMDU's own work and recommend ways to improve it even further. The recommendations fell into three categories: ruthless prioritization, more vigorous challenge, and stronger problem solving with deeper collaboration.

Notice the ambitious tone of this language; it gives no quarter to the idea of slowing down at all. Michael and his colleagues took what could have been occasion for premature celebration and transformed it into a springboard to the next level.

Celebrate Successes

As we've repeated several times now, it's important not to celebrate success too early. But don't make the opposite mistake and *never* celebrate success. The key is to celebrate success in direct proportion to accomplishment; not all victories are equal. The biggest rewards and recognition should come from achieving real results for students; smaller congratulations are in order for hitting a key milestone or moving a leading indicator.

There are many ways to do this. The PMDU would single out "delivery heroes" in government departments—civil servants who had gone above and beyond to contribute to achieving the targets—for recognition. Several Delivery Units that we work with, such as the one in the Kentucky Department of

Making the Most of Transition: Massachusetts and Sustainability

The Massachusetts Department of Elementary and Secondary Education (ESE) faced two big changes in 2015: the end of their Race to the Top (RTT) grant and a gubernatorial transition. Knowing this, the leadership team at ESE took a few important steps in the years leading up to 2015:

- As we chronicled in Chapter 1D, they participated in the creation of "The New Opportunity to Lead," a report chronicling the state's successes and challenges with the last 20 years of reform and laying out a blueprint for the next 20 years. This report gave them a long-term perspective on what it would take to accelerate the system's progress.
- In the summer of 2014, they zoomed in and examined their progress over the last 4 years, since beginning the RTT grant and their delivery effort. They used the sustainability planning process to review their goals and strategies and to take stock of the major successes and challenges. Weaving in the findings from "The New Opportunity to Lead," they proposed a series of adjustments to both the core strategies and their implementation of the delivery approach. The frame was simple: "This is what we've accomplished in the last 4 years. What will it take to make the next 4 even better?"
- The proposals eventually set the stage for the Commissioner's communication with the new governor-elect and the State Board of Education that autumn. As the slides from his presentation show (see Figures 4C.4 and 4C.5), he has framed the work as being consistent

Figure 4C.4   Evolving Standards-Based Reform Framework

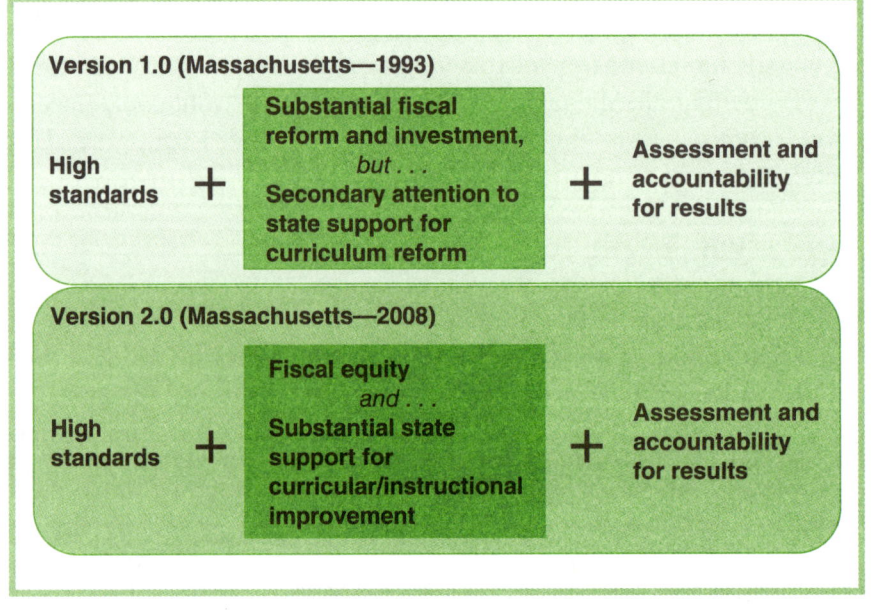

with a bipartisan tradition of support for education reform that goes back over 20 years, with an eye toward what will take things to the next level in the future.

The transitions in 2015 could easily have become an excuse for ESE leaders to pocket the progress they had made and give up on the rest of the agenda. Instead, they refused to be satisfied, and they used the transition as an opportunity to challenge the status quo and deepen their commitment to the work.

Figure 4C.5 Evolving SEA Role

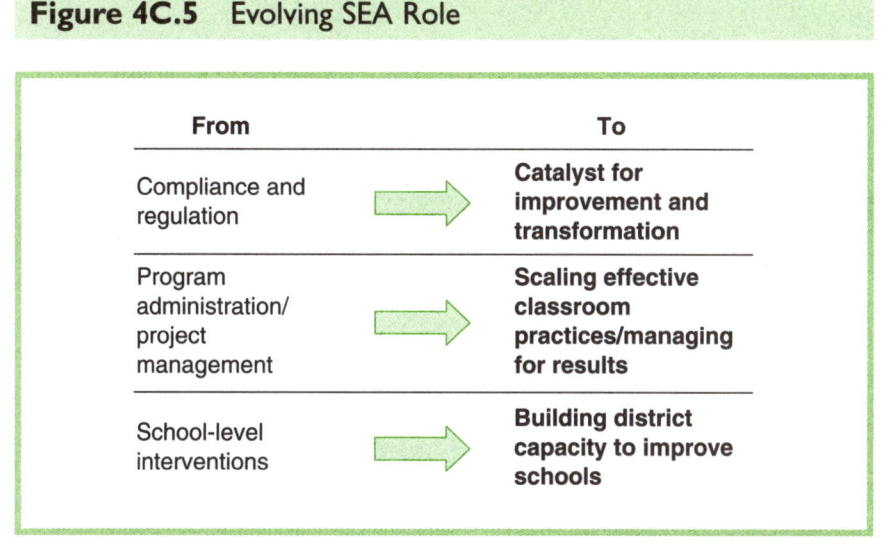

From		To
Compliance and regulation	→	**Catalyst for improvement and transformation**
Program administration/ project management	→	**Scaling effective classroom practices/managing for results**
School-level interventions	→	**Building district capacity to improve schools**

Education, have adopted a similar practice. Recognition can range from a public mention to financial compensation, depending on what tools are at your disposal.

In any case, pay close attention to the public message you send. Make every effort to frame your partial victories in a way that acknowledges the hard work of individuals, even as it lifts everyone's gaze to the horizon and the work ahead.

Celebrating Success at the University of Missouri–St. Louis

The delivery team at the University of Missouri–St. Louis began its work at the outset of the Access to Success (A2S) project, focusing on improving both access and completion rates for its nearly 14,000 undergraduate students.

The team decided to focus on improving advising in their first year. They developed a set of key strategies that every college within the university needed to undertake to ensure a positive experience for their students: mandatory orientation, first-year experiences, 4-year degree plans, and a series of measures to reduce drops, withdrawals, and incompletes in

(Continued)

(Continued)

student coursework. Each dean took on the responsibility of implementing or strengthening these actions within his or her college, and they tracked progress using a league table like the one we introduced in Chapter 4A (see Figure 4C.6).

As implementation improved over the course of the year, freshman and transfer graduation rates rose, retention increased for all students and for underrepresented minorities, and freshman scores on the National Survey of Student Engagement (NSSE) rose even more dramatically.

To celebrate these accomplishments, the team passed out awards at the end of the year. Trophies included Most Valuable, Most Potential, and even Most Likely to Improve Next Year (given to the college that had struggled the most). This recognition set just the right tone: congratulatory, but forward-looking. It gave the team a moment to pause and reenergize for the next leg of the journey.

Figure 4C.6   League Table of Traffic-Light Judgments for UMSL

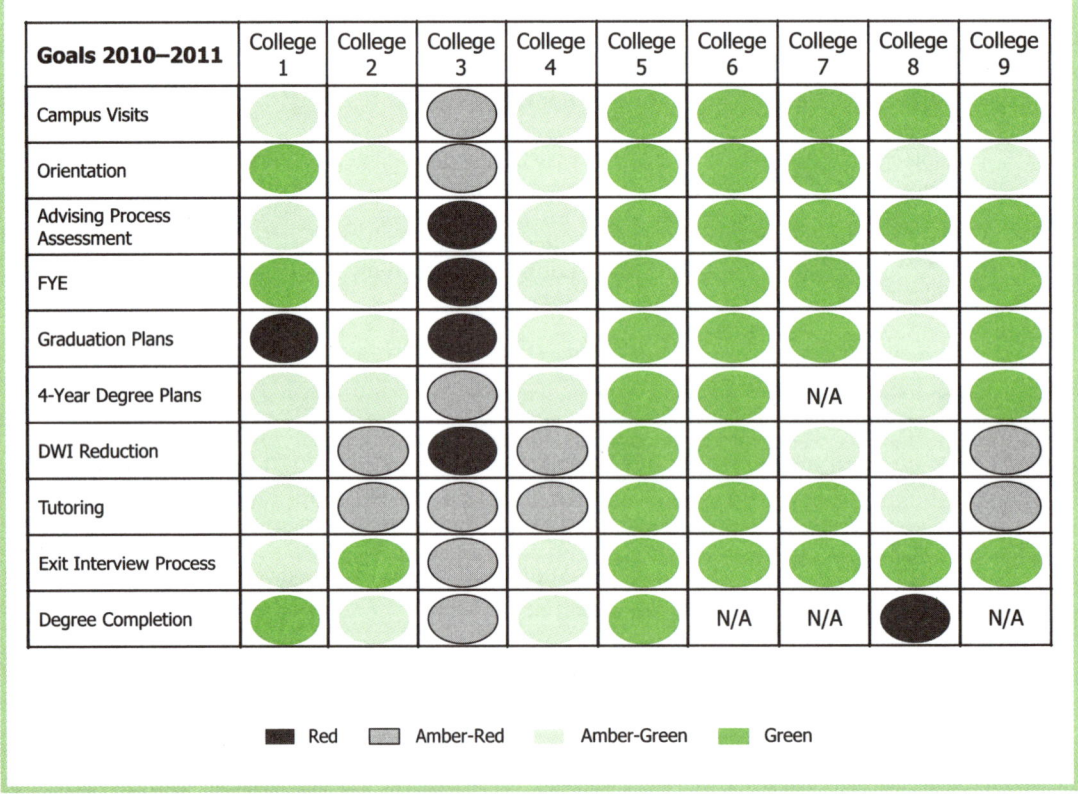

Goals 2010–2011	College 1	College 2	College 3	College 4	College 5	College 6	College 7	College 8	College 9
Campus Visits									
Orientation									
Advising Process Assessment									
FYE									
Graduation Plans									
4-Year Degree Plans							N/A		
DWI Reduction									
Tutoring									
Exit Interview Process									
Degree Completion						N/A	N/A		N/A

Red   Amber-Red   Amber-Green   Green

⦿ KEY CONSIDERATIONS FOR SYSTEM LEADERS AND STAFF

If you're a **system leader**, you will play a vital role as the cheerleader-in-chief. Your system needs to see the drive for urgency and for greatness come directly from you. Even as you handle the many day-to-day crises that arise, you will be the one who gives courage to other leaders to stay the course. You will be the one who reminds the Delivery Unit that it's their job to make this happen even while you are distracted. And, of course, you'll also host the victory party!

If you're a part of the **system staff**, recognize that the natural bias of your system—of almost every system—is to pull you away from a singular focus on the most important things. While you won't always be able to avoid that pull, it will make a huge difference if you're not contributing to it. Get excited about the core goals and strategies. Consider how you make a difference for students by contributing to this work as best you can. Learn to articulate this excitement as you advocate for spending more time on what matters most.

Finally, **delivery leaders**: remember that you're the rowers here. Ulysses won't get to his destination without you, however much he may protest. There will be times when you feel like a lone voice crying out in the wilderness about the importance of the goals and strategies. Expect this and take it in stride. Remember Michael's words to his PMDU: you were appointed to be the unreasonable one. Don't shy away from the task now; if you don't do it, nobody else will!

⊙ CONCLUSION

As one former PMDU staff member observed to us, a Delivery Unit is often the only organization that will press a system to "play to the final whistle." As much as possible, this is an attitude that everyone involved with your delivery effort should have. By applying these guiding principles, you will increase the likelihood of driving delivery all the way to an endgame where your goals are achieved and your aspiration becomes reality.

With this, we complete our treatment of the tools and techniques of the delivery approach. These last four parts of the book have laid out the steps that you should take to manage a delivery effort. By themselves, however, these tools don't guarantee a permanent change in the way your system does business. For that, a final component must undergird your entire delivery effort from start to finish: a culture of delivery. We turn to this subject in the next and final part of this book.

⊙ NOTES

1. Barber, M., Kihn, P., & Moffit, A. (2011). *Deliverology 101: A field guide for educational leaders.* Thousand Oaks, CA: Corwin.

2. Will. M. (2014, November 6). Average urban school superintendent tenure decreases, survey shows. [Web log post]. Retrieved from http://blogs.edweek.org/edweek/District_Dossier/2014/11/urban_school_superintendent_te.html

3. Barber, M., Kihn, P., & Moffit, A. (2011). *Deliverology 101: A field guide for educational leaders.* Thousand Oaks, CA: Corwin.

Part 5

Create an Irreversible Delivery Culture

 **Develop a foundation for delivery**

 **Understand the delivery challenge**

 **Plan for delivery**

 **Drive delivery**

 **Create an irreversible delivery culture**

⊙ WHY CULTURE MATTERS

In *Democracy in America*, his landmark study of the United States in the 19th century, Alexis de Tocqueville made a powerful observation about the challenge facing the young republic: "The central Government . . . must entrust the execution of its will to agents, over whom it frequently has no control, and whom it cannot perpetually direct."[1] De Tocqueville's point actually holds true for any type of government and for any type of large organization: we must work with and through many people to get anything done.

In Chapter 3B we explored the problem of scale—the fact that, for the strategies in your delivery plans to have real impact, they must work (almost) everywhere in your system. In truth, the problem is more universal: *anything in this book* that you try to do will depend on faithful implementation by "agents" you cannot directly control, from goal and strategy leaders in your building to educators and faculty in the field. Consider a few examples of the types of challenges we've seen up to this point:

- How will we design a program of training and support that helps tens of thousands of educators change their classroom practices (Part 3)?
- How will we help the person responsible for a strategy write an implementation plan that is meaningful to them and connected to our student success goal (Part 3)? How will we help them use data to shape this plan (Part 2)?
- How will we encourage a goal leader to make the shift from owning an "input" to owning an "outcome" that is a critical part of our aspiration (Chapter 1A)?
- How will we make sure that stakeholders and the public share our aspirations and goals for students (Chapter 1A)?
- As we start doing stocktakes and other delivery routines (Chapter 4A), how will we help participants understand the purpose of these interactions?
- How will our Delivery Unit (Chapter 1C) position itself as a trusted and helpful resource that can exercise influence without authority throughout our system?

Thus far, the various chapters in this book have offered tools, exercises, and examples for thinking through and addressing these types of questions. But there's a missing piece. While the challenges above are all different, the common thread that runs through them is the need for sustained changes in behavior by real people. Chip and Dan Heath put it simply: "For anything to change, someone has to start acting differently."[2]

There's a name for the discipline of getting people to do things differently: change management. Its challenges are best summarized by Nobel Prize–winning scientist Murray Gell-Mann: "Imagine how hard physics would be if particles could think."[3] People (including the writers of this book) are complicated and unpredictable. Put them in organizations and the complexity multiplies.

The "hard" tools of delivery can provide the structure and frame for our work; like theoretical physics, they can help us identify the changes we need and some models for getting there. But to succeed, these tools must be accompanied by "soft" skills and approaches—applied physics, if you will—that help us engage with the messy realities of people, their hearts, and their minds. Delivery succeeds or fails depending on whether you can make it an irreversible part of your system's culture.

That word—culture—needs to be unpacked as well. What exactly is it? Broadly speaking, an organization's culture is the values, beliefs, and norms that influence the actions and behaviors of people in that organization. Think of it as a set of unwritten rules that tell us what is and isn't acceptable to do. An organization with a strongly embedded culture is bigger than any one leader or person in an organization; like the fabled Ship of Theseus, you should be able to replace each part of it, bit by bit, and still emerge with a whole that's recognizably the same. The right culture is a valuable thing; it insulates an organization's actions from all sorts of transitions and changes that may blow it off course.

We tend to believe that the primary causal relationship with culture goes in one direction: the values and norms of a culture influence people's actions. So when we try to change culture, we try to change those values and norms directly, perhaps by telling people that we have new values and norms. This is a mistake. Culture may influence behavior, but culture change also works in reverse. As Michael Fullan likes to point out, people often act their way into believing—not the other way around.

John King, the former Commissioner of Education in New York, once made this point in a speech to education leaders in his state. He invoked the words of Nelson Mandela, who challenged his people, in the wake of apartheid, to ensure that their "daily deeds" produced a South African reality different from the one they had known before. "It's not enough for the leader to articulate a vision," said King. "The daily deeds have to match that vision."[4] He then issued his own challenge to the assembled leaders, asking them to identify and commit to the daily deeds that would bridge the gap between the state's vision for students and the current reality: Taking the time for thoughtful classroom observations. Role modeling the instructional shifts aligned with the Common Core. Having a courageous conversation with a teacher to give feedback and set new expectations. These daily deeds, he said, would be what created a different reality—a different culture—among New York educators.

Culture is nothing more than the the sum of the actions we take. Changing culture requires that enough people change what they do, and see the benefits of change, that they influence everyone else to do the same. Throughout this part of the book, we explore tools to change both behaviors and beliefs as a means of changing culture.

⊙ A ROAD MAP FOR PART 5

This part of the book focuses on change management and its application to delivery. Unlike the others, it is not chronological; it's not the "last step" of delivery, and it's certainly not an afterthought. Rather, the principles and practices explored here are for application alongside every other tool in this book, from setting your aspiration to establishing and running your delivery routines. If you're a **delivery leader**, the delivery tools will probably be the first place where change management comes into play. But these principles and practices can also be applied to the broader changes across your system that delivery is meant to support—changes identified in your high-priority strategies, like transforming educator preparation programs or improving counseling and guidance to students. Delivery leaders will need to think about these things as well—but, in particular, **system leaders** and **system staff** will want to consider how change management plays a role in this day-to-day work of theirs.

We use a simple frame for organizing these ideas that we introduced in Chapter 1D: Michael Fullan's "ever-widening circles of leadership"[5] (see Figure 5.1).

These circles represent the size of the change management challenge: you'll never be able to move this many people by sheer force of will. Rather, you must create leadership and ownership of your work at all levels of the system. The starting point is at the center: your system leader, leadership team, Delivery Unit, and members of the guiding coalition (see Chapter 1D). These people are the core of your effort and the first people to bring on board.

From there, each circle has a role to play in engaging the next: you'll need all the leaders in the center to bring along all the staff in your system office, you'll need the help of leaders and staff to energize the field, and everyone will need to be involved in reaching students and the public.

This engagement can't flow in just one direction. Just as you can't move this many people by force of will, you can't think for this many people as they literally make millions of decisions to implement your strategies. For this reason, as we explore below, change management must be about empowerment, about delegating authority alongside responsibility. It must also involve a willingness

Figure 5.1   Delivery Unit Relationships With Goal Leaders in a K–12 System

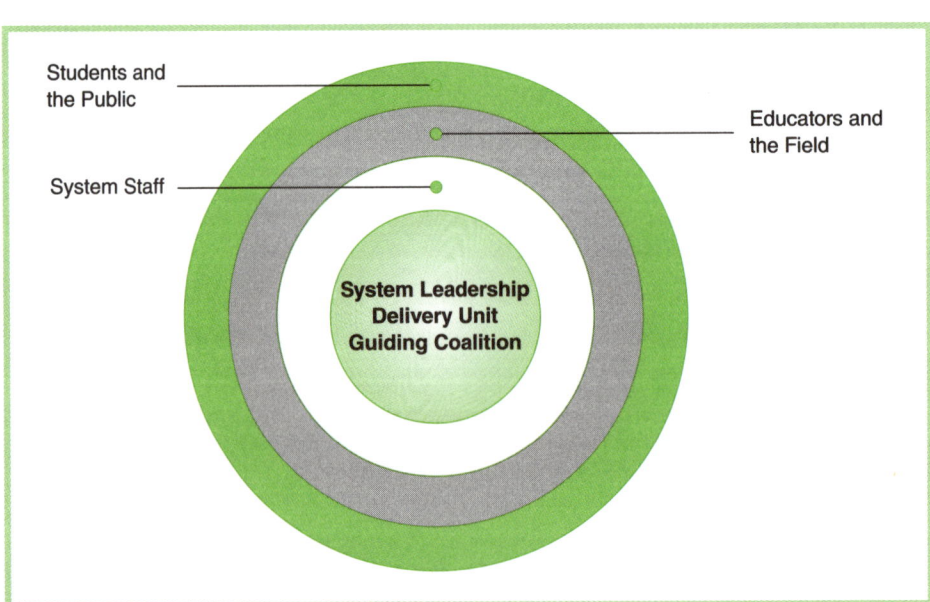

to continually listen to and learn from those who are experiencing implementation, especially the front line, students, and the public.

There are common and necessary practices for engaging each of these circles of leadership, which we cover in the following chapters:

- Chapter 5A is about building capacity. This term has a slippery definition, but it ultimately comes down to giving people the necessary **skill** and **will** to change their behavior. Capacity building is particularly important in the inner circles, where people will be most directly responsible for leading change. Delivery Units will often focus their efforts directly on capacity building for system leaders and system staff, while system leaders and system staff will need to build capacity in the field to implement their strategies.
- Chapter 5B is about communication and stakeholder engagement. This set of practices has a broader reach to every circle of leadership, including students and the public. Communication is about more than media management: it's about the messages you send, the audiences you identify for them, and the levers at your disposal for engaging in a differentiated dialogue with key stakeholders about implementation.
- Finally, Chapter 5C is about building relationships—the "glue" that holds the circles of leadership together. Whether you're a Delivery Unit trying to gain credibility within a system office or a district superintendent reaching out to principals, the quality of the relationships you build is your main currency for developing influence without authority. This chapter explores practices for building good relationships—and what to do when they break down.

None of these practices are new or revolutionary; they're a normal part of managing K–12 and higher education systems. What is new is how the principles of change management, rightly applied, can transform these practices.

Influence Without Authority: The Purpose of Change Management

Why is influence without authority such a critical ingredient in change management? We've talked about the problem of scale and the fact that formal authority will only get you so far. But there is another reason, rooted in the attitudes people have toward the work you are asking them to do. Our colleague Richard Eyre taught us to ask two questions about them:

1. Do they *have* to do it?

2. And do they *want* to do it?

This will tell you most of what you can expect in their reaction, as Figure 5.2 shows.

(Continued)

(Continued)

Figure 5.2   Attitudes Toward Your Work: Why Influencing Without Authority Matters

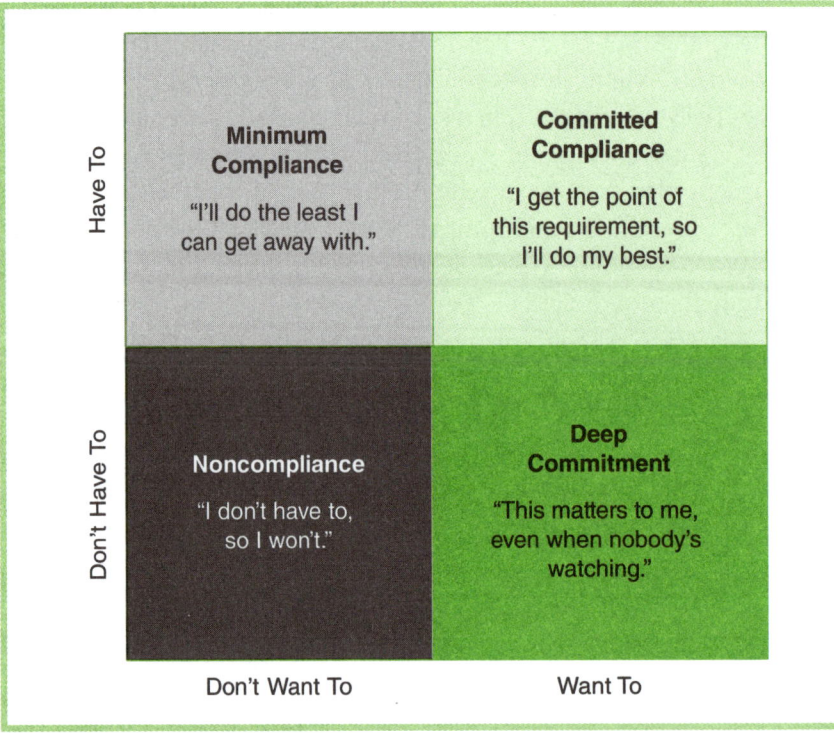

Source: Eyre, R. (2006). Unpublished.

Leaders who over-rely on requirements and incentives—even well-designed ones—will find themselves running into a compliance mindset at best. Moreover, they will resign themselves to active resistance when they do not have this tool to reach for. This creates a false choice between power and impotence that bedevils many education leaders.

Joel Klein, who led New York City's school reforms for a decade, once said that "you can mandate awful to adequate but you cannot mandate greatness; it has to be unleashed."[6] Only when people *want* to do the work you're asking them to do will you get the commitment that you need. For work that's required, you'll get compliance beyond the minimum and a powerful combination of formal and informal pressure. But the most important work is in the lower right quadrant—the thousands and even millions of decisions that people make every day, so numerous that you couldn't hope to mandate them even if you had the authority. People who care deeply about doing the work, even when nothing requires them to do it, are your greatest asset in change management.

As you read this part of the book, consider how you can combine what formal authority you have with the tools of informal influence described in these chapters—capacity building, communication, and relationship building—to engender deep commitment to change in a critical mass of people, particularly those at the front line.

⊙ NOTES

1. Quoted in Barber, M., Kihn, P., & Moffit, A. (2011). *Deliverology 101: A field guide for educational leaders.* Thousand Oaks, CA: Corwin.

2. Heath, C., & Heath, D. (2010). *Switch: How to change things when change is hard.* New York, NY: Broadway Books.

3. Baran, S., & Davis, D. (2010), *Mass communication theory: Foundations, ferment, and future.* Boston, MA: Cengage Learning.

4. King, J. (2013, July 10). Remarks at the Network Team Institute. Retrieved from https://www.engageny.org/resource/on-mandela-colonel-king-and-the-distance-between-our-values-and-our-reality

5. Hargreaves, A., & Lieberman, A. (2010). *Second international handbook of educational change.* New York, NY: Springer.

6. Mourshed, M., Chijioke, C., & Barber, M. (2010). *How the world's most improved school systems keep getting better.* McKinsey & Company. Retrieved from http://www.mckinsey.com/Client_Service/Social_Sector/Latest_thinking/Worlds_most_improved_schools

Chapter 5A

Build System Capacity All the Time

 Develop a foundation for delivery

 Understand the delivery challenge

 Plan for delivery

 Drive delivery

 Create an irreversible delivery culture

System Leader Summary

Capacity is the combination of the **skill** and **will** of individuals throughout your system to make the change you need them to make—whether it's adopting the disciplines of delivery or executing on your strategies. This chapter lays out a practical framework for capacity building that has three elements at its core: formal learning, deliberate practice, and reflection through feedback and coaching. The corresponding tools will help you design a capacity-building effort that is sensitive and responsive to how adults learn.

Capacity is necessary for everything that we do—but, in most organizations, capacity building is last on the list of priorities. It's often done so poorly that the entire approach has been discredited in many systems. As system leader, you will need to reverse these trends, by both protecting resources for high-quality capacity building and asking people to trust that this time will be different. Your delivery leader is the tip of the spear here; they will use these tools in the day-to-day work of delivery. In the long run, however, you want this to be everyone's job: everyone should have capacity to build capacity.

⦿ PROFESSIONAL DEVELOPMENT?

The word *capacity* can join the growing list of terms in this book that are often used but poorly understood. What most of us do know is that capacity is essential to delivering results of any kind and that the lack of capacity is an oft-cited reason for why change efforts fail.

But everyone has something different in mind when they think about capacity. Is it the number of people in your organization or division or school or campus? The skill levels of those people? The way they work together? The financial resources at their disposal? The flexibility and autonomy they have?

All these are arguably elements of capacity, but we use a simple and common definition: capacity is a combination of the skill and will of individuals or teams to make the change you need them to make.

Capacity can be individual or collective. It's specific to the task at hand, so that a person or organization might have capacity to do one thing but not the capacity to do another. And it depends on two crucial variables. Skill is the ability to do something; will is the motivation and drive to do it.

The need for capacity is evident throughout a delivery effort. Nearly every strategy we choose to implement will require us to build capacity to make some kind of critical change in behavior. In fact, the delivery chain (Chapter 3B) is a map of capacity-building needs: for every actor you've assigned a role, from teachers to district superintendents to a team at the state department of education, there's the possibility that they don't yet have the capacity to fulfill that role. Leaders attempting to use the tools in this book will need to build their own capacity—and that of their colleagues—to set clear goals, to build coalitions, to analyze data, to create delivery plans, to set the right tone in delivery routines, to solve problems, and much more. In Fullan's model of widening circles of leadership, capacity building is a crucial tool for reaching the field and the front line.

So how do we build capacity? One great irony in K–12 and higher education is that, despite a consistent focus on improving pedagogy for young people, we pay relatively little attention to how *adults* (including the adults who do the teaching) learn to change and improve their practices. As a result, many capacity-building efforts feel incomplete, disconnected, uninteresting, or just plain impractical. This sentiment is captured well in the title of a paper by Peter Cole: "Professional Development: A Great Way to Avoid Change."[1]

The solution to this problem is to insist that what's good enough for our students must also be good enough for our teachers, professors, principals, deans, campus presidents, superintendents, and bureaucrats. How can we help them engage in real learning and improve their practice? How do you do it at scale? And how do you set up an infrastructure in your organization that can do this consistently in response to the changing needs that you face?

This chapter lays out a framework for building organizational capacity at scale. The adults throughout your system are the "students" whose behavior you need to change; to avoid confusion with actual students, we refer to them as **adult learners** or **learners**. The principles in this chapter can be used by Delivery Units as they work with goal leaders and a system's leadership team.

More generally, they can be used by anybody who needs to train and motivate large numbers of people to do something differently as part of the core work of reform. In fact, these practices are very much at the heart of how we work with our partner systems to build their capacity as well.

◉ CORE PRINCIPLES

The major elements of capacity building are summarized in Figure 5A.1.

Your starting point is **defining the change** you desire. What is the change in behavior or practice that you are trying to make? With that in mind, there are then three core elements at the heart of capacity building:

1. **Formal learning:** Any planned interaction between you and your adult learners. It is the "lesson" in which you make expectations clear.

2. **Practicing:** An opportunity for adult learners to try changing their behavior, for you (or someone you work with) to observe, and for feedback and coaching to take place.

3. **Reflecting:** A space to discuss and debrief the experiences from formal learning and practicing.

The most effective capacity building is a continuous process that includes all three of these elements. By themselves, each element is inadequate: a training program with no follow-up feels disjointed; practice can't occur without some idea of what one is supposed to be practicing; and reflective conversations only add value if there is some experience to reflect on.

Figure 5A.1　Capacity-Building Elements

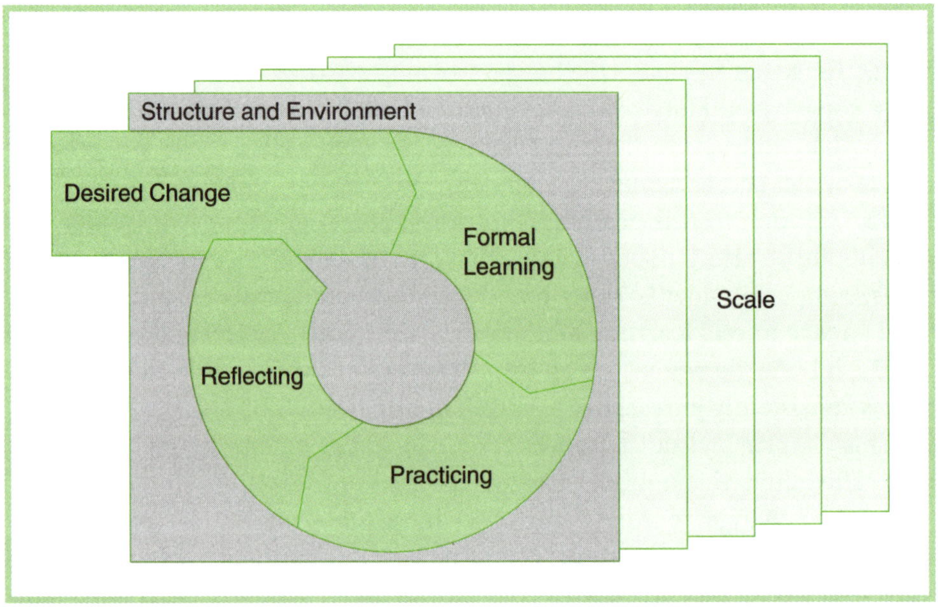

Structure and environment is the context in which this all takes place. It includes not only sources of formal authority such as incentives and reorganization, but informal influence as well.

Finally, you'll want to think about how to **scale** the change by setting up systems in your organization to multiply and replicate it.

Desired Change

In essence, this is the first question of delivery—"What are you trying to do?"— applied to individuals. There are three questions to consider.

First, who are your adult learners? Whose behavior do you want to change? Go through your system's organization chart, a list of goal and strategy leaders, and any relevant delivery chains (Chapter 3B) to see who needs additional capacity to get the work done.

Second, what's the change that you need your adult learners to make? It helps to be specific. In their management best-seller *Switch*, Dan and Chip Heath make a compelling case for "scripting the critical moves" that capture the desired change, or at least the most important part of it.[2] "You've got to think about the specific behavior that you'd want to see in a tough moment," they write.[3] Imagine you lead a higher education system that wants to implement a strategy to improve student advising for freshmen. As you contemplate the desired change for the advisors who will need to change their behavior, what are you going to tell them to do? "Help these students graduate" or "advise them better" would not be clear enough. Simple and clear guidelines, like "don't let a student leave your office without 15 units of coursework on their schedule," work much better.

The "instructional shifts" for the Common Core State Standards are another example of critical moves at work. In English language arts, there are three shifts that capture the most important first steps to implement nearly 30 pages of standards:

1. Make sure that at least half the texts you use are informational (vs. fiction);

2. Use questions that require students to read and interpret the text; and

3. Emphasize key academic vocabulary words for each grade level.

Critical moves make the change clear, and they also make it manageable. This follows another principle that the Heath brothers advocate: where you can, shrink the change that you ask for.

Finally, the third question is a sort of mini-diagnosis of the situation: What's holding your adult learners back from making the desired change? Is it a skill problem? Is it a will problem? Is it a problem with the structure and environment they face? We often confuse one type of problem for another, which leads to a mismatched solution. Answering these questions will help you shape a capacity-building effort that fits the challenge you face.

> Please visit EDI's website at www.deliveryinstitute.org/5A for an exercise on how to define your desired change.

Formal Learning

When we think of formal learning, we usually think of a classroom or a lecture hall—and indeed, a formal training or workshop is definitely a part of what we mean here. But our definition is more expansive: formal learning is any planned or deliberate interaction that we have with our adult learners. This can be something as small as an e-mail announcement or as large as a conference. It can include the distribution of materials and guidance, the delivery of training, or a working meeting. The keywords here are *planned* and *deliberate*—in every case, these are instances in which we explicitly ask for adult learners' time and attention so that we can help them understand something, equip them to do something, or motivate them in some way.

Formal learning is often the most visible aspect of capacity building. It's also where the weaknesses of many capacity-building efforts are most evident (if you have ever been to a mandatory training and would rather have been anywhere else, you'll know exactly what we mean). For this reason, it's also an opportunity to make a big difference quickly, by devoting time and attention to careful planning of your "teaching" moments. Just as teachers and professors invest hours in lesson and lecture planning, we'll be well served by treating our interactions with adults with the same care. In fact, the best formal learning opportunities contain all three elements of the cycle: we should strive to give our adult learners opportunities to practice and reflect *in the context of the lessons we plan* in addition to connecting those lessons to opportunities for practicing and reflecting outside the classroom.

How do we plan our lessons to accomplish this? We use a simple lesson planning template for every meeting we participate in, from a one-on-one dialogue to a large group workshop. Figure 5A.2 gives a worked example of the elements in this template.

As with any good lesson plan, it helps to begin with objectives for your adult learners who are participating in the meeting: when this lesson is over, what will they walk away with? What do you hope for them to accomplish in the time you've asked of them? Your objectives should follow directly from the "desired change" that you identified for your adult learners. Good objectives break this change down into manageable, measurable pieces that are appropriate to the context of your lesson with them. There are four types of objectives: new knowledge, skill-building, decisions made, and changes in attitudes. Some formal learning opportunities include all four; others just concentrate on one type.

Once you have your objectives, how will you achieve them? In the context of a lesson plan, this is where we develop *activities* that will help us deliver each objective. An activity can be nearly anything you need to do to fulfill one or more objectives.

There are at least three types of activities that we tend to rely on in designing our lessons:

1. A **presentation** is (mostly) one-way communication that's meant to convey some kind of information to participating adult learners. It can

Figure 5A.2   Adult Lesson Planning Template

Example: Partial agenda for workshop on planning and facilitating meetings

Time	Learning Objective	Activities	Person(s) responsible	Materials
9:00–9:10	• Understand the context for today's workshop and roles as liaisons	• Present	• Fac • Fac, Grp	• Slides with expectations for program, overview of LEA support program, definition of delivery • Flipchart • Markers
9:10–9:15	• Create shared expectations and agreements	• Welcome, introductions, review outcomes • Brainstorm expectations • Brainstorm agreements	• Fac • Fac, Grp • Fac, Grp	• Slides • Flipchart • Markers

9:15–9:40	• Understand the basics of meeting facilitation	• Brainstorm characteristics of good and bad meetings
		• Present Interaction Method
			• Fac, Grp
			• Fac
				• Slides:
				  – Introduction
				  – Key meeting roles
				  – Tools for reaching agreement

be a few casually delivered comments, a PowerPoint presentation, a review of data, or an update. The best lessons with adult learners use this tool sparingly. By contrast, the worst lessons lean on it almost exclusively; many of us dramatically over-estimate the effectiveness of presentation as a way to change skills or behaviors. As a general rule, you should have no more than 15 minutes of presentation for every hour you spend with your adult learners—and even less than that if possible.

2. In an **exercise**, the adult learners play the leading role. Your job is usually to supply a prompt or a set of instructions and give learners the space to work through them. An exercise could be as simple as a set of discussion prompts; it can be as complicated as asking adult learners to draw a delivery chain for a key initiative (see Chapter 3B). Exercises are perhaps the most critical tool at your disposal for building skills. After a brief presentation on feedback and coaching,

for example, a well-designed exercise with some role-play scenarios will help participants practice these skills and reflect on them. Exercises are also an important tool for changing attitudes. You may not be able to convince your adult learners that they need to improve their delivery plan, for example. But if you place some objective criteria on "what makes a good plan" in front of them and ask them to self-assess against those criteria, you help them reach that conclusion through self-discovery. This is the entire logic behind rubric-based processes for self-assessment, such as EDI's capacity review (see Chapter 1B).

3. A **facilitated discussion** is similar to an exercise but with a stronger role for you as "teacher." Of course, you can facilitate any exercise directly, but your role as facilitator becomes particularly important when meeting participants are discussing or deliberating challenging questions. In our work with systems, we've often facilitated discussions about what a system's goals should be, how to organize their Delivery Units, or developing strategies for engaging stakeholders. Facilitated discussion is also a good format for encouraging adult learners to reflect on their work and to learn from each other. In particular, there will be situations when the most qualified trainer isn't you, but an adult learner with unique experience engaging in the work. The best facilitated discussions don't just happen; like presentations and exercises, they're the result of careful planning and preparation, from the questions you use to the facilitative style you employ.

Once you've defined the objectives and activities in your lesson plan, the remaining details follow. How much time will each activity take? Who will play what role in making it happen? And what materials will you need (handouts, slides, flipchart paper, markers, etc.) to support the planned activities? A good lesson plan becomes a checklist for what you'll need to do to prepare for the event itself.

Practicing

We understand the value of practice from the old saying: practice makes perfect. But, as learning experts Doug Lemov, Erica Woolway, and Katie Yezzi make clear in their book of (nearly) the same name, practice is not the same thing as repeatedly doing something. Good practice is much more than that: it consists of "iterative rehearsal of activities done with intentional focus on improved performance."[4]

In his book *Talent Is Overrated*, Geoff Colvin extends the argument further: in any field, he claims, great performance is mostly (perhaps entirely) explained by something he calls **deliberate practice**.[5] It has four characteristics:

1. It's an activity designed specifically to improve performance, often with a coach's help.

2. It can be repeated a lot. Repetition isn't sufficient to improve performance, but it's certainly necessary.

3. Feedback on results is continuously available. To quote one expert that Colvin cites: "practicing without feedback is like bowling through a curtain that hangs down to knee level. You can work on technique all you like, but if you can't see the effects, two things will happen: You won't get any better, and you'll stop caring."

4. It's highly demanding mentally—and, as a corollary, it isn't much fun. Research shows that people who simply repeat a task for years often end up getting *worse* at it rather than better. That's because repetition is actually the path of least resistance; by contrast, if practice doesn't hurt, you're not doing it right.

The conclusion Colvin comes to—that great performers are made, not born—should be good news for anyone trying to change a large organization: no matter the team you inherit in the talent lottery, weak performers can become strong with deliberate practice. But there's bad news as well: life in most organizations, including education organizations, seems precisely intended to work against every principle of deliberate practice: few day-to-day activities are designed with performance improvement in mind, and repetition of work without feedback is the norm. This extends the irony we described earlier: everyone knows that *students* need deliberate practice to learn, but we don't extend the same respect to the adults who serve them. How can we change this?

As we've seen, the first opportunity for deliberate practice is during formal learning. Exercises during training sessions are a great way to design practice to isolate specific skills and to make immediate feedback available to adult learners. If you're training strategy leaders to improve their verbal communication skills, have them take turns practicing in front of the group. If you're training senior leaders on how to become better coaches, set up role-play sessions that test specific aspects of coaching skill. And, in all cases, invite feedback from peers (more on this in a moment).

Practice in the "classroom," however, must be accompanied by practice in the "real" world. A second way to help adult learners practice is to ask them to do so between formal learning opportunities, with tasks that are easily repeatable. If you need your adult learners to begin analyzing and using data better, you might deliver a training on it, with opportunities to practice using the data. But you might also give homework, asking them to continue what they've practiced in their day-to-day work after the training is over. This homework is often implicit. If your adult learners are responsible for producing delivery plans 2 months from now, and you organize a series of trainings during that period to help them learn how to produce a high-quality plan, you may not need to do much more to get them to practice in between. More generally, if the desired change has to do with a core skill that adult learners must apply in their day-to-day work—an educator's instruction, a trainer's presentation skills, a leader's ability to run a good meeting—then the opportunities to practice should come naturally.

However, you must make sure that a significant amount of practice includes opportunities to receive feedback. Sometimes the practice will automatically generate feedback, as a formative assessment tool might do for a teacher's instruction. But often you will need to create the feedback mechanism. One of the most common tools is observation; consider setting up regular opportunities to observe and give feedback to your adult learners as they engage in practice. (K–12 leaders: if it's good enough for principals in their observation of teachers, it's good enough for those who manage the systems they depend on.) Another option is to survey those who observe practice as a matter of course, such as the students who experience faculty instruction every day. Feedback like this is invaluable, and if the surveys are short enough, it can be a relatively light burden for those involved. This feedback sets us up for the third element of our capacity-building model: reflection.

Reflecting

"In times of change, learners inherit the earth, while the learned find themselves beautifully equipped to deal with a world that no longer exists."[6] These words, by the philosopher Eric Hoffer, capture a lesson we've learned over the last several years: the most important quality you can look for in a colleague or a teammate is their willingness and ability to learn. Without it, little else is possible. Though the other stages in the cycle are prerequisites, **reflection** is where learning truly occurs.

Reflection closes the loop of capacity building by creating a space for your adult learners to consider the work they have practiced and to think with you about how they can improve it. Sometimes it will take place in the context of a formal learning opportunity after practice has occurred; you might teach your adult learners to do something, observe them applying it, and then reconvene them to reflect on what they did. In other cases, it will take place in real time, because your adult learners engage in practice or immediately afterward. In either of these cases, good reflection depends on two things: the adoption of a **growth mindset** and robust **feedback and coaching**.

The concept of a growth mindset comes from the work of psychologist Carol Dweck. She defines the growth mindset in relation to its opposite, the fixed mindset:

People with fixed mindsets think that intelligence and ability are set in stone and can't be changed. They must repeatedly affirm that they are superior. Any setback is labeled as a failure. They avoid risks because failure is seen as a weakness, and they "get their thrill from what's easy, what they have already" . . . The growth mindset is the opposite. People with this orientation believe that they can get better through effort. By trying hard and figuring things out they think they could get smarter: "Not only were they not discouraged by failure, they didn't even think they were failing. They thought they were learning."[7]

Fixed mindsets are a hindrance to any capacity-building effort. And they're more common than they should be in education, a discipline that overvalues "natural talent" and "expertise" in its adults while underemphasizing learning (ironic once again). As a result, our field is overcrowded with experts who believe that what they already know is all they'll ever need to do the work. And it's often led by a host of cynics, who believe that the only way to improve talent in an organization is to recruit it from outside.

Whatever the change you seek, it will be important to start with the premise that it is possible *because people can change*. The culture of a growth mindset takes many forms in the literature: a culture of failing forward, of learning from mistakes, of being entrepreneurial, and so on. Whatever you choose to call it, this is a belief you must reinforce.

Of course, beliefs don't change overnight. Remember: people act their way into believing rather than the other way around. Creating a growth mindset will require the constant application of a critical practice: feedback and coaching.

Many of the leaders who understand this best are former coaches. When we first met him, Rob Saxton, the system leader at the Oregon Department of Education and a former district superintendent, summarized his approach to management with a story from his days as a football coach:

> We were at practice, and running play after play after play on the field. After a while, the head coach called us in, obviously frustrated. "How are these kids supposed to learn anything," he asked, "if you don't tell them what to do differently?"

Feedback and coaching are indispensable to individual and organizational improvement. Unfortunately, we must all overcome a natural aversion to giving and receiving feedback. Even when it's done well, it can induce anxiety and discomfort; done poorly, it can lock people out of the growth mindset by giving them a terrible experience.

The only remedy for this is a little courage and a willingness to try to get the practice right. We must not be afraid to be vulnerable in front of our colleagues, even when we fall short of expectations. Some of the best wisdom on this came to us recently in, of all places, a fortune cookie: "Failure is feedback, and feedback is the breakfast of champions."

Feedback can take two forms: *positive* (what we did well) and *constructive* (what we can improve). These two types of feedback have many synonyms: among the most common are *successes/challenges* and *pluses/deltas* (delta, being the mathematical symbol for "change," denotes what should change in the future). Figure 5A.3 gives an example of what this feedback can look like. This content is the (hypothetical) feedback that a delivery leader might give to a system leader on how they led a delivery routine (see Chapter 4A for more details on this).

The plus/delta structure implies two simple rules about the content of your feedback, both of which will help you encourage a growth mindset. First, **balance the constructive with the positive**. In the United States, at

Figure 5A.3   Feedback to a System Leader for a Delivery Routine That They Led

Pluses	Deltas
• Strong opening, reminding participants of the objectives at the beginning of the meeting. • Pressed the goal leader to be specific in his answers to your questions, probing where necessary. • Relied on the question framework that we gave you in our premeeting briefing, but deepened the inquiry beyond our questions where necessary. • Kept on drawing our focus to the data on performance we had prepared beforehand.	• When you state expectations for the goal leader, eliminate qualifiers like "if you don't mind." • Make sure that every next step is clear and well recorded (not sure the goal leader left with a clear understanding that he needed to revise his plan). • Push back more when the goal leader or a member of his team says "we can't do that"—ask why, ask what it would take to change that, how you can help, and so on.

least, we tend to associate feedback only with constructive suggestions. We forget to give positive feedback, or we make it an afterthought whose only purpose is to cushion the impact of the "real" feedback we're giving. This approach ignores half the potential benefits of feedback. Constructive feedback gives us concrete suggestions about what to do differently next time, but positive feedback helps us know—with equal specificity—*what we did right* that we should repeat in the future.

Second, **be positive but candid**. Notice that we call it constructive feedback rather than negative feedback; instead of pluses and minuses, we have pluses and deltas. We don't do this to spare the ego of the person receiving feedback (though it can make them more receptive). Rather, we avoid negativity because it's not useful to the person receiving the feedback. Telling a person that they did something wrong isn't feedback unless you can also tell the person what they should do differently in the future. In the list above, there's very little difference between the phrasing of the left column and the phrasing of the right column. The only difference is that the things on the left did happen, while the things on the right haven't happened yet. Today's deltas should be tomorrow's pluses.

How should we deliver feedback? At EDI, we use a six-part model:

1. **Self-reflection:** Ask the person to reflect on their own work. What do they think they did well, and where would they like to improve? This will get the person thinking about their own practice, and it may give you a starting point for the feedback you deliver.

2. **Observation:** The next step is to describe the specific behavior you'll be giving feedback about. Observations should be as specific and as objective as possible.

3. **Impact:** After establishing what happened, the next question to answer is: what impact did it have on you, or (from what you saw) on other

people who were present? This is where you go from the objective to the subjective. This is a critical stage in the feedback process—one in which you bring the other person face to face with the consequences (good or bad) of their actions.

4. **Pause:** It's a good idea to stop at this point and give the other person a moment to let your feedback sink in.

5. **Listen:** Give the other person an opportunity to respond and to give their own impressions. Do they agree with your feedback? Do they have questions about it? Is there anything you said that they need clarified?

6. **Suggestion:** This is the final "plus" or "delta" that you give to the other person. Based on the observation and the impact, what would you suggest they do in the future? What should they keep doing or do differently?

An important factor in encouraging deliberate practice is to create an expectation that this kind of feedback and coaching is normal, both in the classroom and in the real world. For people you supervise, you can set the standard by setting the example for them, by giving them feedback regularly, and by asking that they do the same for you. Be willing to ask permission to give and receive feedback with other people and to role model these practices in doing so.

Remember, too, that feedback isn't always an individual process. Feedback and reflection must also take place at the team level to debrief work that a group has done together. For these kinds of conversations, facilitating a simple list of pluses and deltas is the most straightforward approach. Sometimes, a more complex experience will benefit from a more detailed protocol, like the experiential learning cycle depicted in Figure 5A.4.

Bringing It All Together

Formal learning, practicing, and reflecting: this cycle of capacity building has a wide range of applications. For example:

- At the Kentucky Council on Postsecondary Education (CPE), capacity building became a primary strategy for engaging campuses. With little formal authority, leaders at CPE knew that delivery couldn't be a mandate or a requirement. So they invested in building a campus network that would learn—mostly from each other—how to use the tools of delivery themselves. The network convened campus teams every 3 months for formal learning, practice, and reflection on the work they were doing. Between meetings, EDI and CPE offered support and coaching to campuses as they applied lessons learned in their day-to-day work. This resulted in more and better collaboration between CPE leaders and their campus counterparts in pursuit of the system's delivery goals.

Figure 5A.4   The Experiential Learning Cycle

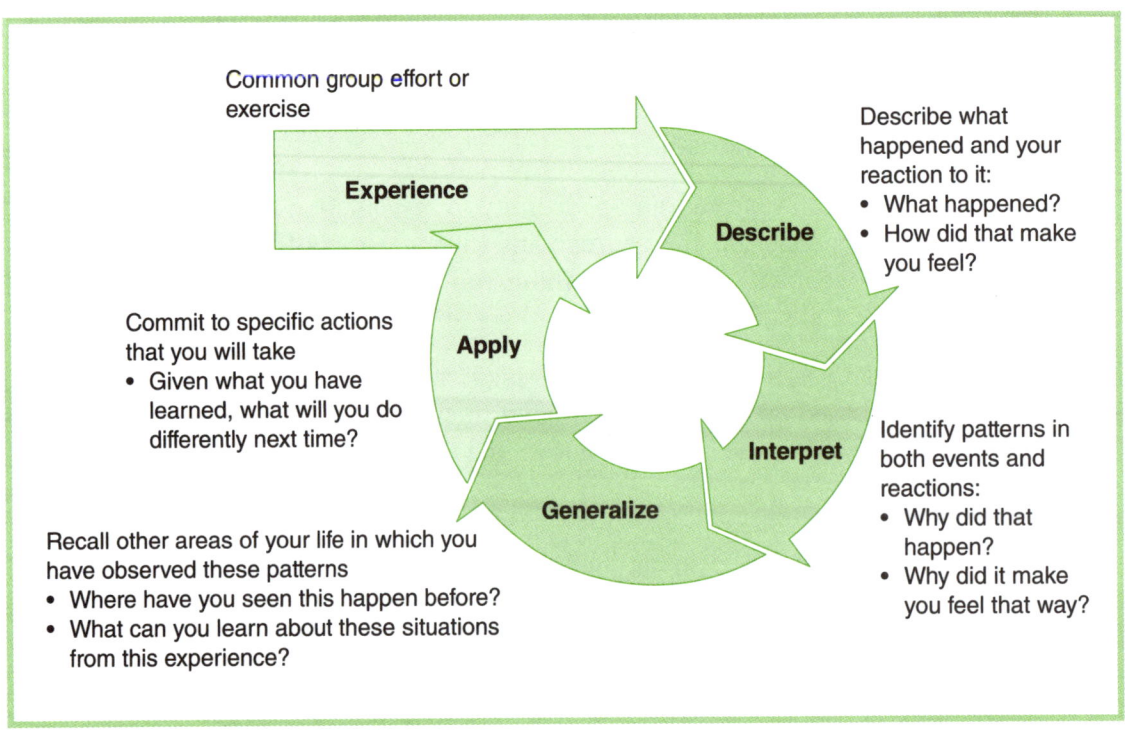

Source: Kolb, D. (1984). *Experiential learning: Experience as the source of learning and development.* Englewood Cliffs, NJ: Prentice-Hall.

- Leaders at the Maryland State Department of Education (MSDE) wanted to build the capacity of their top 20 leaders to analyze and interpret data (think of all the tools and practices we covered in Part 2 of this book). EDI facilitated a 6-month talent development program for this team that anchored on a series of capacity-building workshops (the formal learning opportunities). In between the workshops, each participant set job-embedded objectives for applying what they were learning to their day-to-day work, with individualized coaching and feedback to aid deliberate practice and reflection. David Volrath, who heads the Maryland State Department of Education's efforts to strengthen educator effectiveness, reflected on the process. "Training has to have an immediate connection to the work we're currently doing in order to be helpful in building our skills," he said. "Because we were able to tailor our work with you to a specific delivery project for us, the training was really valuable. I've applied the principles learned with everyone on the team."[8]

In both these cases, all three elements are present, along with a clear definition of the change desired. The application of this framework can be big or small; you can use it to run a large change program or to build the skill of a single individual (including yourself). We need not restrict these principles to one category of activity called *professional development*; rather, they should come into play whenever and wherever we need to help people grow into new behaviors, roles, or responsibilities.

A Competency Framework
for Education Leaders

In many workplaces, there's a discouraging pattern of valuing expertise over skill in evaluating employees. This makes feedback more difficult, since a great deal of feedback relies on observation of practice rather than knowledge.

To help with this problem, we've developed a competency framework for education leaders as a tool for aiding feedback. It defines seven competencies—displayed in Figure 5A.5—and includes a rubric describing indicators of progress for each one.

A competency framework is a useful anchor for any capacity-building effort. At EDI, we use our competency framework (similar to this one) to categorize and sharpen our thinking about day-to-day performance improvement and to do formal evaluations. It's also the basis for professional development, as we use the feedback from the framework to determine desired outcomes for capacity building in our adult learners.

Figure 5A.5 Competencies for Education Leaders

Competencies

Leads Change

Thinks strategically
- Sets strategic direction
- Brings logical and analytical rigor to decision making
- Synthesizes information to solve problems

Understands the work
- Understands the details of priority reforms
- Understands the national reform context
- Builds the necessary technical skills

Communicates effectively
- Structures clear communication
- Produces clear communication
- Engages stakeholders

Leads Others

Influences others
- Builds a strong network
- Collaborates effectively
- Facilitates clear decision making

Develops others
- Has a growth mindset
- Coaches and develops talent
- Inspires others to excellence

Leads Self

Delivers results
- Commits to priority goals and reforms
- Takes ownership of the work
- Manages and produces to deadlines

Learns continuously
- Pursues standards of excellence
- Demonstrates humility
- Receives and acts on feedback

Structure and Environment

The last element of capacity building in an organization is the structure and environment that people face. As Dan and Chip Heath note, "What looks like a people problem is often a situation problem."[9] What are the formal and informal systems and structures in your organization, and what kinds of incentives do they create for people? These norms and incentives create a path of least resistance that governs much behavior. What can you do to shape that path and ensure that these incentives nudge people toward your desired change in behavior?

There are at least five areas of consideration to keep in mind:

- **Organizational structure and "formal" authority:** Put simply, who reports to whom, and who has authority over whom? The way that lines of authority are drawn in your organization will obviously influence the behavior of people in it.
- **People management:** How is talent recruited into the organization? How are people evaluated and held accountable for their work? And how easy or difficult is it to remove poor performers? A team reforming an organization may want to consider ways to improve its people management processes, from recruiting and hiring to formal evaluations and associated rewards and incentives.
- **Incentives:** In general, do rewards, recognition, and resources follow the behavior you're looking for? Or do they work against it?
- **Norms and values:** Are there informal incentives that people in your organization face? What is considered "prestigious" work? Are there particular norms of behavior that are practiced by large majorities in your organization? It's important to name and surface your norms and values, if only so that you can know whether your desired change runs with or against the grain of accepted behavior.
- **Systems for capacity building:** To what extent do you have systems in place to promote the regular cycle of formal learning, deliberate practice, and reflection for all people in the organization? For example, are these principles embedded in the way the human resources department operates? Are they reinforced in internal professional learning? Systems like these give you an "infrastructure" for building capacity in your organization as your needs dictate.

Whole literatures exist on making changes to organizational structure and people management processes; a detailed treatment of them is beyond the scope of this book. In both cases, however, it's important to let your goals drive changes in formal structures rather than the other way around.

Building Capacity at Scale

This leaves us with one unanswered question: what do we do when the scale of change we need is so large that we don't have enough people qualified to train, observe, and coach our adult learners? Imagine that you need over 1,000 faculty members in a university system to start actively counseling their students to make wiser course selections. Or imagine that you're responsible for making sure that 1,500 teachers in your school district change the way they do lesson planning. Once again, you're up against the problem of scale: how can a small, central team apply these principles faithfully so that there's high-quality impact throughout the system?

The short answer: you need to train additional trainers.

The idea of "training the trainer" has a mixed reputation. For many systems, particularly those in K–12, it's the preferred theory of action for system-wide professional development: state leaders train regional and/or district leaders, who train school leaders, who train teachers. But in many of these systems, the results have been unsatisfactory, or at least unreliable and inconsistent. This is because *most of the approaches adopted by these systems are not true train-the-trainer models.*

How are the current approaches insufficient? The answer is in the description above: state leaders train regional and/or district leaders, who train school leaders, who train teachers. *There's only one touchpoint at each link in the delivery chain.* Moreover, it is only formal learning—the lesson—without any practice or reflection. This is the equivalent of a teacher teaching a lesson to a class of 30 students—say, on how to multiply and divide fractions—and then expecting each of those students to reteach the same lesson to a class of 30 new students the next day. You get to scale quickly—from 30 to 900!—but you have little to no control over quality and fidelity of implementation, because you haven't taken time to coach your students to the *mastery* they require to train others in the same material.

So what would a true train-the-trainer approach look like? Using the example above, a would-be trainer would need to develop two kinds of mastery:

- **Mastery as a student:** Before adult learners can even think about training others, they must master the source material to begin with. This would take place using the familiar cycle:

    - **Formal learning:** The teacher teaches the lesson on multiplying and dividing fractions to the class of 30 adult learners.
    - **Practicing:** The teacher builds student skills and assesses student understanding of the lesson by having learners solve multiplication and division problems with fractions.
    - **Reflecting:** One-on-one or as a group, learners discuss their strengths and weaknesses with the teacher based on the assessment results. The teacher selects the five best learners as candidates to be trainers.
    - **Continue the cycle:** The teacher or professor could theoretically reteach the lesson and assess again, surfacing additional learners who are potential trainers.

- **Mastery as a trainer:** It's not enough to demonstrate mastery of fractions; the knowledge and skills required to reteach are different and deeper. But the same cycle applies:

  ○ **Formal learning:** The teacher teaches the five trainer candidates a different lesson, one that involves reviewing the original lesson plan on multiplying and dividing fractions and sharing various techniques for helping new students understand the key concepts. In the context of this lesson, the trainer candidates might practice teaching all or part of the lesson to each other, with group feedback and feedback from the teacher. Based on this work, the teacher might clear some or all of them to try it in front of real students.

  ○ **Practicing:** Each of the five trainer candidates teaches the lesson to 30 new learners, *under the supervision of the teacher*, who observes the work and generates feedback.

  ○ **Reflecting:** One-on-one or as a group, trainer candidates discuss their strengths and weaknesses as trainers, and the teacher shares his or her feedback based on observation. The teacher selects trainer candidates who are ready to teach the lesson to other learners without supervision.

  ○ **Continue the cycle:** Again, this process could continue until, eventually, most of or all the trainer candidates are able to teach the lesson without supervision.

You could continue this process at one more level: training additional *trainers of trainers*. It would look similar to the process above: for trainers who have demonstrated mastery, an additional formal learning opportunity to learn how to train additional trainers, followed by opportunities to practice and reflect.

This model requires more patience than the traditional approach being undertaken in many systems. It takes longer to scale up for two reasons. First, trainers must undergo two additional stages—demonstrating mastery and then being trained as trainers—before they can even provisionally train new students. Second, because not every single learner will become a trainer, a given pool of learners will yield fewer trainers than in the traditional approach (which just assumes that everyone can do it). You also need to invest the time of trainers and trainers of trainers in observing and coaching their students, which can be difficult.

But by spending the time and resources to truly grow your trainers, you're making an investment to ensure quality and fidelity of implementation up front—and saving yourself a great deal of trouble on the back end. Moreover, the model is slow to start but can eventually grow exponentially. Figure 5A.6 shows how this can happen under some reasonable assumptions.

Figure 5A.6 Growth With Train-the-Trainer Model

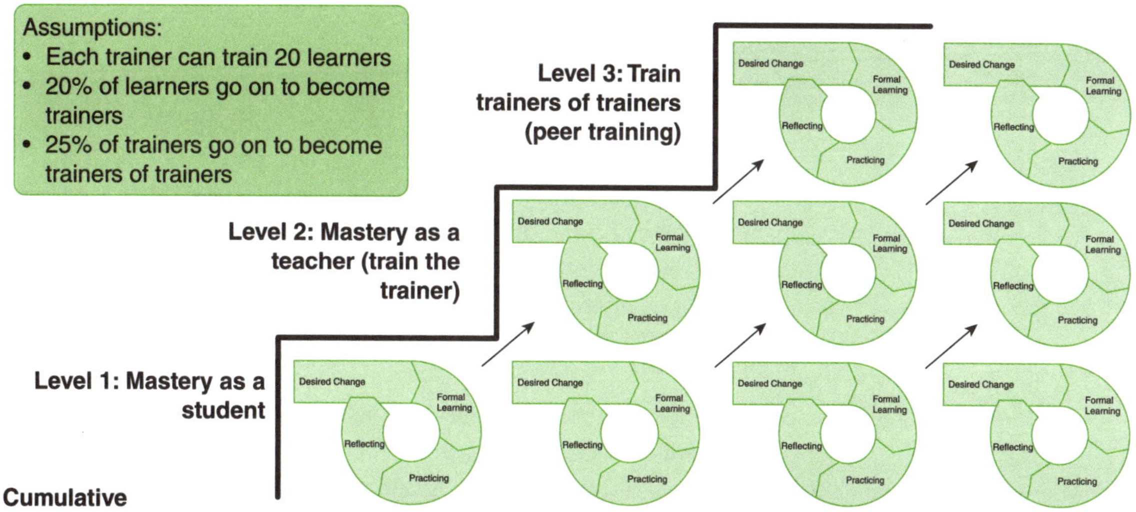

Assumptions:
- Each trainer can train 20 learners
- 20% of learners go on to become trainers
- 25% of trainers go on to become trainers of trainers

Level 3: Train trainers of trainers (peer training)

Level 2: Mastery as a teacher (train the trainer)

Level 1: Mastery as a student

Cumulative capacity built	Cohort 1	Cohort 2	Cohort 3	Cohort 4
Trainers of trainers	1	1	2	7
Trainers	0	4	20	80
Learners	20	100	500	2,100

A Checklist for Change

As we've seen throughout this chapter, the application of capacity-building principles can be wide and varied, ranging from a supervisor's relationship with one direct report to the transformation of an entire system. Because it encompasses so much, it's easy for the topic to become overwhelming. We offer here a simple checklist of questions to use as you think through and identify the type of capacity-building effort you need. Use these questions as a starting point to design a change program that works best for you.

- Define the **desired change:**
  - Who are your adult learners—that is, whose behavior would you like to change? How many of them are there? Are they inside your organization or dispersed across the field?
  - What's the change you'd like them to make? How will it help you achieve one or more of your student outcome goals? Try to identify one specific behavior.
  - What's holding them back from making it? What will be the most important barriers to overcome? How much do they have to do with skill versus will?

(Continued)

(Continued)

- Identify opportunities for **formal learning**:

  o What kind of formal learning will your adult learners need to make the change? Is it simply communication and knowledge of new expectations? Skill-building? A shift in attitude?
  o What formal learning opportunities will you make available to them, and how will you ensure that they participate? Is a note or an e-mail sufficient, or will meetings and/or trainings be necessary?
  o Are there current vehicles for interaction you can use for these learning opportunities? If not, what will it take to create new ones?

- Identify spaces for **practicing**:

  o How much practice will your adult learners need to make the change?
  o How will you ensure that this deliberate practice occurs and that it is observed by someone qualified to give feedback?
    o How much of it can you build into formal learning opportunities?
    o What will it take for you to observe it in the field?

- Create opportunities for **reflecting**:

  o How will you ensure that every instance of observed practice is followed by timely and actionable feedback?
  o When and how will your adult learners have an opportunity to reflect on their own practice, both with you and with each other? Can this be built into the agenda of one or more formal learning opportunities?

- Reform the **structure and environment:**

  o With all the above in place, are there still structural or environmental barriers that are likely to prevent the change from happening? What are they?
    o Organizational structure and formal authority?
    o Incentives?
    o People management processes?
    o Norms and values?
  o What can you do to overcome these barriers?
  o How can you use the structure and environment to set up systems that reinforce capacity building so that these practices don't end with your initiative?

- Strategize to **scale up**:

  o How many trainers/observers will your adult learners need? (Ideal ratio is no more than 10 adult learners for 1 trainer who is doing observations.)
  o Where will these trainers come from? How will you ensure that they have mastery both as students and as teachers of the desired change?

⊙ LESSONS FROM THE FIELD

Avoid the Temptation to Start With Structure and Environment

We've deliberately put structure and environment near the end of our list of elements of capacity building for four reasons. First, structural and environmental factors are the most difficult to change. Changing people management processes or rearranging the org chart can often require changes in policy, if not law. For many systems, these policies and laws pertain to all of state or local government, so changing them requires more than a simple lobbying campaign. Moreover, these types of changes impose substantial costs on an organization. They're disruptive. They create uncertainty and, for some people, fear of what's to come. It's no wonder that most of the organizational literature on "transformation" concludes that organizations that transform tend to underperform those that do not. The bottom line: don't invest a lot of energy in these kinds of efforts unless you have good reason to believe that the benefits will outweigh these costs.

Second, a focus on structure and environment crowds out other, more important factors. We noted in Chapter 3B that, in a large-enough system, the use of formal authority, even to the point of dictatorial power, will be insufficient to drive transformational change. To the extent that the soft levers of building capacity—the cycle of defining the desired change, learning, practice, and reflecting—are ignored or de-emphasized, the most sweeping of structural change efforts will amount to little.

Third, a focus on structure and environment can sometimes be disconnected from the fundamental question of what we are trying to accomplish for students. We may very well need to reorganize. But to what end? Too many structural shifts occur for their own sake rather than as the result of a deliberative process that uses the organization's goals as the starting point.

Fourth, the relative difficulty of changing the structure and environment can lead to fatalism about any prospects for change. When leaders turn to these kinds of solutions and don't get what they want, it can become an excuse for not pushing harder in other areas. Yet the consistent claim of this book—demonstrated by the vast majority of the examples we cite—is that, in most systems, real change is possible without a single change in law, policy, or resources available. It's nice when we can align these things to our goals. But it's hardly necessary—and when we fall for the notion that it is, we hold manageable reforms hostage to an ideal that may be unattainable in the short term. This is a variation on the problem of local control we explored in Chapter 3B, where leaders saw a lack of formal authority over campuses and districts and concluded that there was little they could do. To use a phrase the leaders of the original PMDU encountered from leaders in Britain's bureaucracy, they worry that they "only have rubber levers."[10]

The dirty little secret of reform, however, is this: those rubber levers, the soft capacity-building elements covered in this chapter, are the ones that matter most. They trump the hard ones every time. So by all means, we should labor to make sensible structural and environmental changes to our organizations. But we should pursue these changes in the medium to long term, and only after we've made a good start on the things that we can do right now.

What are the practical implications of this?

- Make your starting point your goals and the delivery plans to achieve them. These elements should be firmly in place before contemplating major structural changes. If you don't know what you're trying to do, you're likely to make costly investments without a clear purpose.
- Pull the "rubber levers" first. This means taking the aspiration and delivery plans and breaking them down into desired changes in behavior. Based on this, can you design a program of formal learning, practicing, and reflecting that encourages people to make the necessary changes within the current structure and environment?
- When you do make structural reforms, start with an infrastructure that supports capacity building. What changes will institutionalize formal learning, practicing, and reflection as a part of the daily life of your organization?
- Be incremental. This may seem counterintuitive. We've explicitly rejected incrementalism in our thinking about goals and strategies; why would we embrace it here? There's a difference here between ends and means; we should be radical in the former, but incremental in the latter. Remember what we said above: structural and environmental changes are costly and disruptive. If there's an arena where introducing change in bits and pieces is helpful, this is it. Once you've gotten all the mileage you can out of your rubber levers, it will be easier to identify the most important structural and environmental barriers that continue to hinder change. This will allow you to target your efforts more carefully. As one school leader we've worked with once reminded us, "Successful incremental change is better than ambitious failure."

The Limits of Structural Change:
Solving the "Silo" Problem

"Silo" is a dirty word in the organizational management literature. Its definition is simple enough: separate organizational units that don't communicate or collaborate with each other. "These departments are operating in siloes," complain would-be reformers. And the first solution they reach for is structural: a reorganization that breaks those siloes down.

Take one example of a K–12 state education agency that chose to reorganize for reform a few years ago. Per the advice in Chapter 1A of this book, they had just adopted a small number of student outcome goals—things like kindergarten readiness, third-grade reading proficiency, high school graduation, and so on. However, the various strategies to help reach a single goal were led by people who sat in different parts of the agency. The siloes between those different parts of the agency were hindering reform, reasoned the leaders at the time. So they reorganized the agency into "goal offices," each of which had responsibility for one or more of the student outcome goals.

A few years later, the leadership of the agency changed. Upon a close look at the organization they inherited, the new leaders discovered—surprise!—siloes in the goal offices. The solution for the new leadership team? You may have guessed it: another reorganization.

The point here is not to endorse one organizational structure or another. We've worked with organizations with few siloes and organizations with many. But the lines on their org charts rarely had anything to do with how collaborative they were. This is because *there is no organizational structure that is impervious to siloing.* An organizational structure, almost by definition, divides people into units—and this division always carries the risk of closing off cooperation. Yet we divide people into units anyway, because we recognize the usefulness of breaking larger problems into smaller pieces (recall our review of problem solving in Chapter 4B). To see why this is necessary, imagine the other logical extreme: one large team that is responsible for everything. An organization like that may not have siloes, but there will be plenty of other problems to deal with.

Siloing is a *learned behavior*; it will depend less on formal structures than on the capabilities, hearts, and minds of people working in those structures. The reformer who reorganizes without building the capacity of people to play their new roles and responsibilities—including the ways in which they work together—will inevitably be disappointed by the results of their work.

Take the Time to Do This

Most of the principles in this chapter are matters of common sense. Why are they practiced in so few organizations?

Time is a challenge. Higher education and K–12 system offices are beset by constant and urgent demands from the field, from the public, and from the elected leaders who oversee their work. But good capacity building requires a substantial investment of time, both on the part of those leading the change and those experiencing it. People will be justifiably suspicious when you ask them to devote time to a capacity-building effort, especially if they've been exposed to unsuccessful efforts to do this in the past.

More generally, capacity building suffers from the same challenge as delivery: we tend to think it's too obvious to be worth our time. Patrick Lencioni, the organizational health expert, once asked one of his most successful clients, the CEO of a major corporation, why more of his competitors didn't copy some of the practices that had helped him build the capacity of his organization. "You know, I honestly believe they think it's beneath them," he replied.[11] Many of us feel the same way, often without even realizing it.

What can you do to address this challenge? First, you need to believe in the value of this work and fight to create the space for it. Others may follow eventually, but you'll need to be out front.

Second, consider limiting the size of your initial effort just to prove the concept. Is there one particular behavior change that, if achieved, would be a quick and visible win? Can it be achieved by reallocating time from existing meetings or trainings? Use this opportunity to buy the right to deepen your capacity-building effort further.

Third, be obsessive about how you plan your formal learning opportunities and use each one to show people that "this time is different." In the words of one of our delivery leaders, "The greatest sin an educator can commit is wasting the future of a student. But the second greatest sin they can commit is to waste the time of a fellow educator." When you ask for the time of your colleagues for a formal learning opportunity, you're drawing on one of their most precious resources—one that's constantly taxed and often used poorly by others. Do what it takes to perfect your approach to these sessions. Your excellent use of the time you ask for will work wonders for establishing a brand for your work and give you the opportunity to expand it.

Finally, remember the old adage about going slow to go fast. The results of good capacity-building efforts often don't manifest quickly enough for many leaders. This is how we end up with train-the-trainer programs that don't attempt to build mastery or reinforce skills: impatient leaders take shortcuts, and the resulting work is sometimes worse than doing nothing at all. The good news, as we saw in Figure 5A.6 above, is that the progression of a good train-the-trainer program is exponential: it starts off slowly, but once you've built a small cohort of trainers with mastery, your organization's capability to deliver high-quality learning experiences grows large very fast. Keep this long view in mind as you begin your work.

⊙ KEY CONSIDERATIONS FOR SYSTEM LEADERS AND STAFF

Capacity building has perhaps the widest range of applicability of any concept in this book. Anybody at any level would do well to apply these principles to their daily work, whether their sphere of influence is large or small.

System leaders will be the ones most often worried about the problem of scale. As you look down the delivery chain, you'll want to try to isolate the desired changes that are most important to you and to create the time and space to build capacity for those changes. More than anyone else, you can at least make the demand that people spend time prioritizing this kind of work. The framework of capacity building in this chapter can help you get a handle on how to transform your system, perhaps with the help of a dedicated senior leader who takes responsibility for the work. Remember that your starting point should always be your organization's aspirations and delivery plans. If you don't have those yet, start there. If necessary, build the capacity for goal-setting and planning first!

System staff will face more variation in applying these principles. If you're a goal leader, your starting point should be your delivery plan. What capacity will your team need to carry it out? How can you build it? And how can you encourage them to apply these principles in the management of specific strategies? If you're a strategy leader, the question is different: as you look within your organization and down the delivery chain, what capacity will you need to build to make sure your strategy is implemented as intended? How will you build it? Can you work through current professional development channels, or is something else necessary? Where scale is a major issue, how will you train trainers?

Finally, in addition to constantly posing the above questions to system leaders and staff, **delivery leaders** will need to role model these practices relentlessly. In the course of your work, you're constantly building the capacity of others in the system to set goals, to analyze data, to plan, to review progress, and to participate in delivery routines. Be sure to apply this framework as you think about how to help system leaders, goal leaders, and strategy leaders to play their roles in implementing the delivery approach. And consider training them to use the checklist in this chapter as they think about capacity building in their own work. Your ability to build capacity will have a major influence on others' perceptions of your work; use these tools to build your credibility quickly.

◉ CONCLUSION

Capacity building is a double-edged sword. Poor work in this area can undermine the credibility of a reform effort, sometimes irreparably. But when it's done well, it can lead to systemic and lasting change for the better. Our experience suggests that there are so few examples of good capacity building out there that you can easily make yourself a hero by establishing yourself as one of them. It's a versatile framework, fit for campus and school leaders, system leaders, and everyone in between. It should run through your work with every delivery tool in this book, and you must maintain a continuous drive for it throughout your delivery effort. In short, it's the foundation for establishing a real culture of delivery in your system.

◉ NOTES

1. Cole, P. (2004, December). *Professional development: A great way to avoid change.* Melbourne, AU: IARTV. Retrieved from http://ptrconsulting.com.au/sites/default/files/Peter_Cole-PD_A_great_way_to_avoid_change.pdf

2. Heath, C., & Heath, D. (2010). *Switch: How to change things when change is hard.* New York, NY: Broadway Books.

3. Ibid.

4. Lemov, D., Woolway, E., & Yezzi, K. (2012). *Practice perfect: 42 rules for getting better at getting better*. San Francisco, CA: Jossey-Bass.

5. Colvin, G. (2010). *Talent is overrated: What really separates world-class performers from everybody else* (Pbk. ed.). New York, NY: Portfolio.

6. Hoffer, E. (2006). *Reflections on the human condition*. Titusville, NJ: Hopewell.

7. Dweck, C. (2012). *Mindset: How you can fulfil your potential*. London, UK: Robinson.

8. Rosenberg, M. (2003). *Nonviolent communication: A language of life*. Encinitas, CA: PuddleDancer Press.

9. Heath, C., & Heath, D. (2010). *Switch: How to change things when change is hard*. New York, NY: Broadway Books.

10. Barber, M., Kihn, P., & Moffit, A. (2011). *Deliverology 101: A field guide for educational leaders*. Thousand Oaks, CA: Corwin.

11. Lencioni, P. (2012). *The advantage: Why organizational health trumps everything else in business*. San Francisco, CA: Jossey-Bass.

Chapter 5B

Communicate the Delivery Message

 Develop a foundation for delivery  Understand the delivery challenge  Plan for delivery  Drive delivery

 Create an irreversible delivery culture

System Leader Summary

Communication is the Achilles' heel of many leaders, who find that no matter how hard they try, their message just doesn't seem to get through. Good communication is difficult: it's a two-way conversation between you and your stakeholders, and its aim is to motivate those stakeholders to support your goals and strategies. Most important, good communication is *anchored* in those goals and strategies—it's planned alongside them, and it's monitored just as rigorously.

The tools for communication in this chapter mirror the steps of the delivery approach, and your delivery leader will play a role in helping you use them. However, as the public face of your system, you have a special responsibility in this area. Some of the most important acts of communication can't happen

(Continued)

> (Continued)
>
> without your support and active participation, and you will need to be heavily involved to ensure that you believe in the messages you're sending. For these reasons, we recommend that you identify a communications leader who can focus on assisting you and your team to apply the tools in this chapter to their work. This dedicated and deliberate focus will turn a traditional weakness into an enormous strength.

⊙ IS IT POSSIBLE TO COMMUNICATE TOO MUCH?

The challenge of this chapter is best summed up in the words of George Bernard Shaw: "The single biggest problem in communication," he said, "is the illusion that it has taken place."

We've all experienced this before. Indeed, one of management theorist John Kotter's "top 8 reasons change programs fail" is "under communicating the vision by a factor of 10 (or even 100 or 1,000)."[1] Communication is critical to success for the same reason that capacity building is: it's a key lever to get people to believe and act differently than they did before. If nothing else, communication is a *prerequisite* for change: you can do a great deal of work to implement a strategy, but if people don't have basic information about the parts they are to play, nothing will happen.

We know and understand this intuitively. And yet, in most of the systems we've worked with, leaders have consistently ranked communication as one of their areas of greatest weakness. It seems as if we can never communicate too much. Is this true, and if so, why?

To answer this question, consider the stakeholders we need to reach. They will vary depending on the purpose of our work, but it's safe to assume that they'll include key people in the delivery chain—professors and teachers, school and campus leaders, and the like—as well as students, parents, and the public at large. In effect, communication widens the circle of leadership to include everyone who will influence or be influenced by your work.

Therein lies the first challenge: the problem of scale asserts itself once again. For some high-profile issues, you'll need to consider nearly the entire population of the district, city, county, or state your system serves. Getting that many people to hear you, let alone listen, will be difficult.

So do we simply need to follow Kotter's advice and multiply our communication efforts by 10, or 100, or 1,000? There's more to it than that. Consider what would happen if you multiplied the number of meetings you held with campus presidents, or e-mail that you sent to teachers, or press releases you put out, by 10 or 100 or 1,000. You might succeed in annoying some key stakeholders, but you would hardly be engaging them.

Consider the world from their point of view. The challenge isn't just that they're not hearing enough from you (though that may be true); it's that they're hearing far more from everyone than they could ever take in. This was probably true before the advent of digital technology, but it's even more true now: one study estimated that, in 2007, the total amount of information released through broadcast technology worldwide totaled 1.9 *zettabytes*—equivalent to every person in the world reading 174 newspapers per day. And that doesn't count information received in conversations, meetings, e-mail, and the like.

Quantity alone won't cut through all that noise. So what will? Before it can be voluminous and relentless, communication must first be sharp, focused, and targeted. Messaging must be compelling and consistent; if you're uninteresting or contradict yourself (which is surprisingly easy to do), you only add to the din and confusion. Some stakeholders will be more important than others; mapping and prioritizing some of them for deeper engagement will help cut down on the problem of scale. And the timing and tactics that you use to reach your stakeholders should be coherent and efficient, lest you waste anybody's time. In short, good communication has a lot in common with good delivery: it requires a clear vision of what you want to accomplish, a good understanding of whom you need to reach and why, and a good plan to reach them.

With this in mind, how do we define good communication in the context of a delivery effort? The above evidence should help us understand what it is *not*: good communication is not simply public relations or media management. It's not just one-way data transfer. It's not something that gets added in after the real work of planning your goals and strategies is done. Rather, good communication can be described by three characteristics:

1. It is both proactive outreach to, and feedback from, a range of stakeholders;

2. Its purpose is to motivate those stakeholders to understanding and action in support of your goals and strategies; and

3. It is anchored in those goals and strategies: it's planned alongside them, and it's monitored just as rigorously.

Good communication is inseparable from implementation itself. As Michael Fullan puts it, "Communication in the abstract, in the absence of action, means almost nothing."[2] We must keep this in mind as we walk through the tools and exercises for communication in this chapter.

⊙ CORE PRINCIPLES

There's a large literature on communications and a number of approaches and frameworks. The following six steps borrow from some of the best of these, with an emphasis on the relationship between communication and the delivery approach itself:

1. Develop a foundation;

2. Prioritize stakeholders;

3. Set objectives;

4. Develop messages;

5. Plan for communication; and

6. Drive communication.

Many leaders tend to focus only on the last three steps: they're the most tangible, and they give us a sense that something is being done. This is putting the cart before the horse: without a clear sense of your audience and goals, how can you know whether the message is right? Or your vehicle for communicating it? If you don't start with the simple but important work of the first three steps—understanding what you're communicating about, who you're communicating with, and what you're trying to accomplish with them—then doing the last three will amount to so much spinning of your wheels.

As you can see, the steps echo the steps of the delivery approach. This is why it makes so much sense to develop your communications efforts alongside your delivery work: otherwise, you'll run the risk of sidelining communications as an afterthought. More important, by doing this you'll find that thinking about how to communicate about your work will force you to clarify what the work is.

Anchoring Communications in the Work: Kentucky's K–12 Reform Effort

In 2009, Senate Bill 1 required the Kentucky Department of Education (KDE) to establish new standards and work closely with the higher education system to ensure that more students were ready for college and careers. To communicate about this work, KDE used the brand "Unbridled Learning"—a play on the state of Kentucky's slogan, "Unbridled Spirit"[3] (see Figure 5B.1). This connection to a familiar, statewide concept helped them connect with people and highlight the importance of college and career readiness to the future prosperity of the state.

KDE kicked off the work with an "Unbridled Learning Summit." This brought together leaders from all across the state: the Education Commissioner, the President of the Kentucky Council on Postsecondary Education, the Executive Director of the Professional Standards Board, the Governor, and representatives from every district and higher education institution in the state. The summit set the stage for the work moving forward, communicated KDE's vision and focus on college and career readiness, and sent a clear message that all the stakeholders were in this together and working toward the same goals.

The next step was to take the message out into districts and schools. KDE created leadership networks in eight regions across the state and held monthly workshops with school and district leaders from every region. The focus was on building the knowledge, capacity, and leadership skills of these district teams to train others in their districts, but also to serve as messengers and spread the word.

Figure 5B.1 Kentucky Department of Education's Unbridled Learning Program Logo

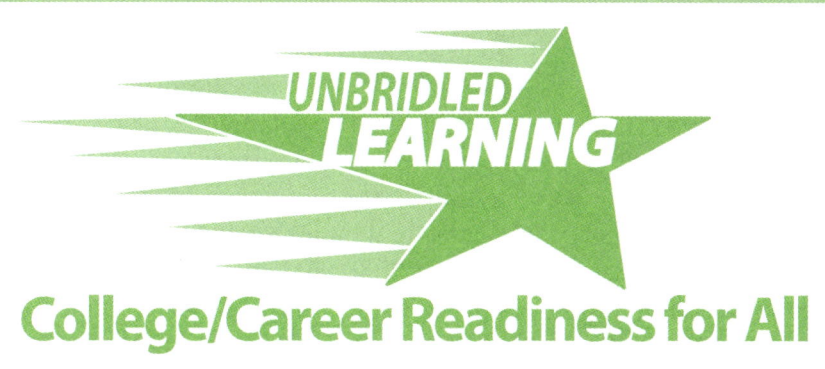

From their experience, KDE identified some clear lessons for communication efforts:

- Get key leaders in the system to set the stage
- Let the content lead the message and communications; work with communication experts, but make sure that those who are doing the work drive message creation and sharing
- Establish a clear vision and message early on, never waver from it, and repeat it over and over and over again
- Engage key stakeholders up front and ensure that they're echoing the same message
- Take advantage of social media to reach individual educators directly

Develop a Foundation

First things first: *what* are you communicating about? It may be that you're communicating about your whole delivery effort—the goals, the strategies, the plans, and the difference it will all make. But you may be choosing a narrower scope, and if that's the case, then you should be deliberate and clear about it with your leadership team. Perhaps there's a particular strategy that needs special attention and communications support, or perhaps you need people to understand and support the goals of your delivery effort without necessarily engaging on the rest of the detail. Whatever your situation, this is a critical step: it will set the context for the rest of your work on communications.

It will also help to appoint a communications leader for this work. Like a goal leader (see Chapter 1A), a communications leader should serve as the "single responsible official" for your system's work in this area. This can be challenging: because communications is inseparable from implementation, all the steps laid out here require the communications leader to work through and with *all* the people responsible for your system's goals and key strategies.

Many of the systems we've worked with stumble over this issue of leadership. Some have made the mistake of keeping their communications leader's scope too small. Communications leaders in these systems focus on narrower topics, like media relations, and they don't have the writ to think more comprehensively about an integrated communications effort. Other leaders in the system are likely to think of them as a service provider within the agency: when they have something to communicate, they tell the media person, who then issues a press release that may or may not reach the right people. Or, worse still, these leaders ignore the communications leader and handle their own messaging, without coordinating with anyone else in the system.

The ideal communications leader is senior and well respected enough to have a real influence, but collaborative in their leadership and development of the system's communications effort. They are experts in the topics covered in this chapter, but they know enough (or are willing to learn) about the core goals and strategies being pursued by the system to be a thought partner to the leaders who manage implementation. In this sense, their leadership is facilitative: they spend a great deal of their time convening the right conversations between these leaders, so that communication really does mirror delivery in the system.

Prioritize Stakeholders

Once you know what you're communicating about, *who* will you communicate with? Who are the most important stakeholders to engage in order to ensure that your delivery effort has the support it needs? There will inevitably be many more than you can handle, so once you've brainstormed an initial list, you should prioritize the stakeholders you will focus on during your delivery effort.

Two key questions will help you prioritize:

- How *influential* are they? Specifically, how great is their ability to influence whether your delivery effort succeeds?
- How *supportive* are they? Are they already on board, on the fence, or fiercely resistant to what you are doing?

The answers to these questions are difficult to pin down in an absolute sense. This is why it helps to identify and map your stakeholders based on where they stand along these two dimensions in Figure 5B.2.

Notice the typology that emerges:

- Those with the lowest support for your effort are the ones whose hearts and minds will not change, no matter what you do. Those who are influential are your **opponents**: you should watch them closely, but don't hold your breath about converting too many of them. Those who are not influential are **not a priority** for your work. Overall, these two groups tend to take up a great deal of leaders' energy and time, usually because they are the loudest. But spending time on them is rarely worth it: an hour invested here will translate to very little additional support, if any.

Figure 5B.2 Stakeholder Mapping Template

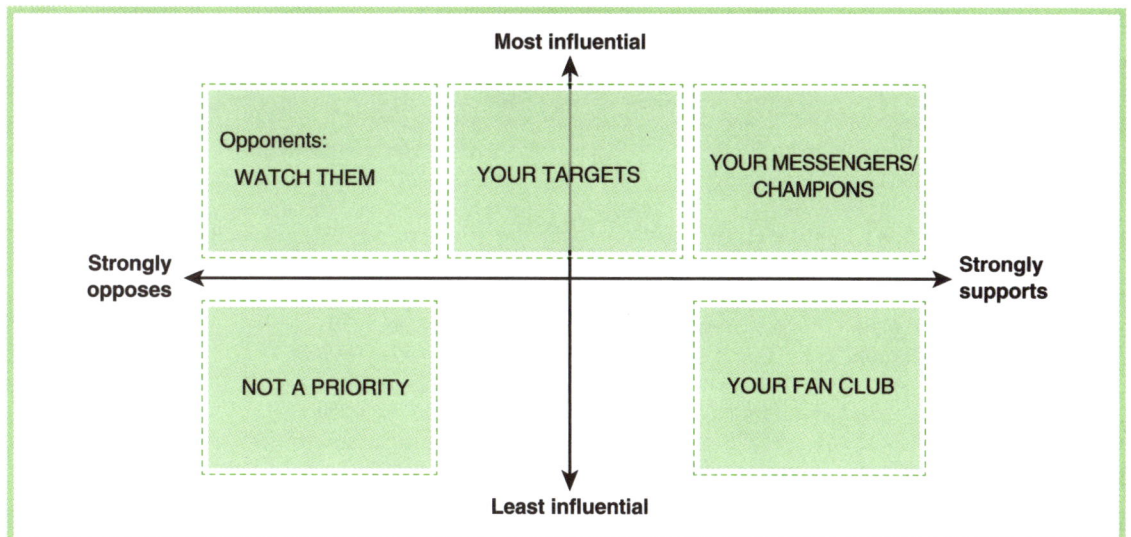

Therefore, you need to discipline yourself to give far less attention than you initially think to stakeholders in this category.

- Stakeholders who are both influential and supportive of your effort are your **messengers and champions**. The aim with this group is to activate them to multiply your message and make them an integral part of your communications plan. They will need little persuasion, but you will be working with them closely.
- Stakeholders who are supportive but not too influential are your **fan club**. You'll want to keep them informed, but devote as few resources as possible to doing so. Leaders are often too content to preach to the choir; if most of the people you engage with are in this group, an adjustment is in order.
- Finally, you will find **your targets** in the "moveable middle"—people whose support you will need and who can still be persuaded one way or the other. These groups are your priority stakeholders, and they should command the vast majority of your time and attention.

Over the years, we've found that people who are asked to brainstorm and map stakeholders onto this template tend only to think of stakeholders who are influential. As a result, only some of the template is filled out and the power of the exercise—its ability to differentiate—is diluted. The exercise is important not just because of who you prioritize, but also because of who you deliberately choose to deprioritize. Acknowledging that a group is not a priority for communication, or that they will need a little attention but not too much, is just as valuable as your decision to focus on a few key constituencies. For this reason, it often helps to start the exercise with a list of typical stakeholders in your system (such as the one in Figure 5B.3) and place them on the map, even if they turn out to be unimportant.

You may choose to be more specific than this list implies—for example, by naming a particular professional association or distinguishing supportive

Figure 5B.3   Typical Stakeholders to Consider

K–12	Higher Education
• System leader • Agency leadership team • Mid-level leaders in the agency • State Board of Education • Governor and Executive Office • Legislators (may split into members of relevant committees, supporters, opposition, etc.) • Regional leaders • District superintendents (may split by large/small, good vs. bad relationship, etc.) • School leaders • Teachers • Professional association leadership for superintendents, school leaders, and/or teachers • Parents • Parent advocacy groups • Third-party advocacy groups • Students	• System leader • System leadership team • Mid-level leaders in the system • Governing or coordinating board • Governor and Executive Office • Legislators (may split into members of relevant committees, supporters, opposition, etc.) • System chancellors • Campus presidents • Campus provosts • Deans (academic affairs, student affairs, etc.) • Faculty leadership • Faculty members • Parents • Third-party advocacy groups • Students

legislators from those who are opposed. You may discover, in the process of doing the mapping, that a group needs to be split more finely to define where certain members of it fall (teachers or faculty, for example, may have diverse viewpoints that aren't necessarily confined to one quadrant). The point is to develop a working list that creates useful differentiation for you across the two dimensions in the mapping template.

Mapping Stakeholders at the University of Texas System

In the summer of 2014, the University of Texas System brought together leaders from across its campuses for a workshop on how to lead change and drive student success. As part of this workshop, each campus team used a variation of the stakeholder mapping template above to plan how they would build buy-in and momentum for their most important initiatives.

The workshop started by introducing the campus leaders to an example in which a campus had mapped the stakeholders for a new advising strategy along two dimensions: influence over their work and interest in it (see Figure 5B.4).

This campus discovered that their engagement effort was lopsided; a lot of attention was focused on servicing a monthly working group for the deans (who had a high level of interest but relatively low influence over the success of the strategy), but nobody had really engaged with the campus advisors about what the strategy meant for them (see Figure 5B.5).

With this example in mind, campus leaders from UT mapped the stakeholders for their own initiatives, identified the key shifts in engagement that needed to take place, and identified the actions they would take to bring about those shifts.

Figure 5B.4 Example: One campus mapped the internal stakeholders for its new advising strategy . . .

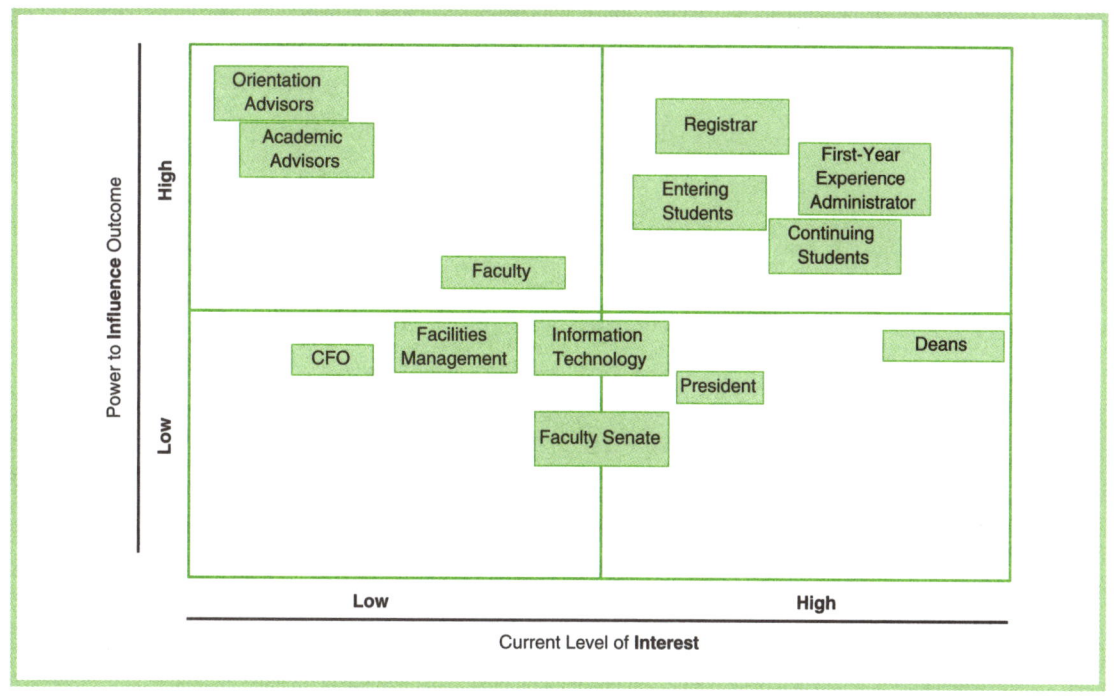

Figure 5B.5 . . . and realized they need to retarget their stakeholder engagement work.

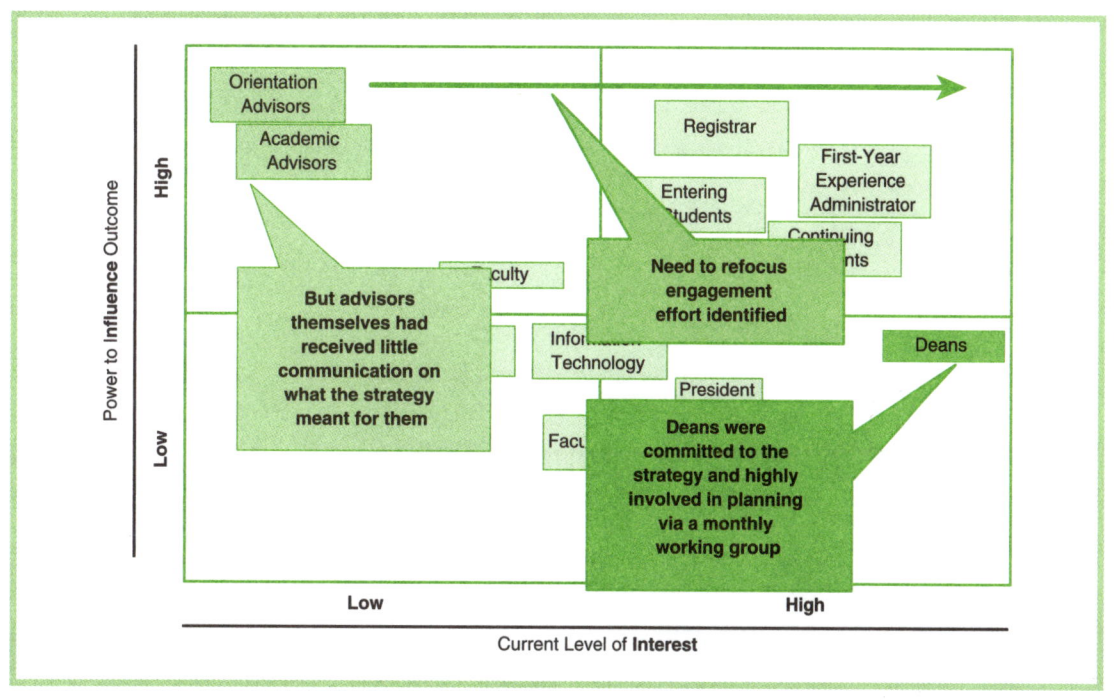

Set Objectives

As with many things in delivery, it will be important to set an objective for each stakeholder you've prioritized. This is particularly important in communications work: too often, we rush to communicate without thinking through the purpose first, and the result is more confusing than clarifying. Setting objectives helps you answer that crucial delivery question: what are you trying to do?

Please visit EDI's website at www.deliveryinstitute.org/5B for an exercise on identifying, mapping, and prioritizing stakeholders to engage.

More specifically, an objective answers one or more of three questions for a stakeholder group:

- If your effort to engage them is successful, what will they *think*?
- What will they *feel*?
- And what will they *do*?

The information from stakeholder mapping will help you come up with objectives for each prioritized group. Figure 5B.6 gives an example of what this should look like, for a K–12 system that's trying to engage stakeholders about an effort to get digital instructional tools into its classrooms.

Notice the specificity of each objective, even though thoughts and feelings can be harder to pin down. Knowing what you hope to accomplish with each priority stakeholder will both guide your efforts to engage them and give you a realistic sense of progress when the inevitable bumps and challenges arise.

Figure 5B.6   Stakeholder Objectives

Priority Stakeholder	Think	Feel	Do
Champion: Business Leaders	• Affirmation of support: "These digital tools are necessary for students to succeed in this century."	• Urgency: "We must make sure that the tools find their way into our classrooms."	• Influence: "We will support state legislators who are willing to continue to fund this effort."
Moveable Middle: Teachers	• Support: "These digital tools are among the best to help my students learn these new standards."	• Satisfaction: "If I use these tools, my students will have learned and I will have done my job well."	• Adoption: "I will make every effort to figure out how these tools work and work them into my lesson planning as soon as possible."

Goals for Communication: The 4 I's Framework

Figure 5B.7   The 4 I's

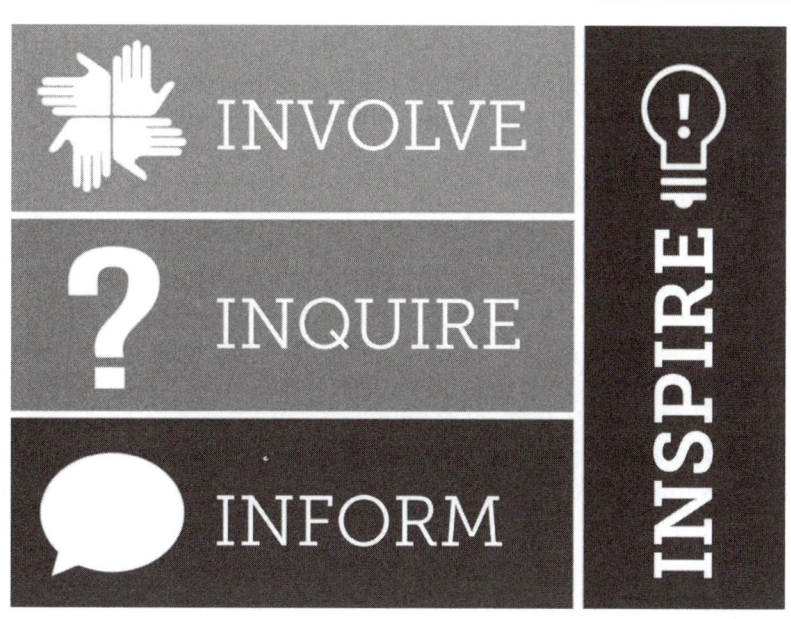

One tool for thinking about your objectives for each priority stakeholder is the "4 I's" framework developed by the federal government's Reform Support Network. In this framework, you can have one or more of the following goals for each stakeholder group:[4]

- You can seek to **inform** them. This is a necessary beginning and the foundation of all good practice: keeping your stakeholders abreast of changes in expectations, policy, and practice.
- You can seek to engage them in **inquiry**. This means that the stakeholder group responds to your communication by providing feedback and having their questions answered.
- You can **involve** them in your work. This could include codeveloping your goals, plans, and strategies; it could also include deploying them as spokespeople for these things.
- You can **inspire** them by appealing to them to act and to lead, based on what they have learned and on the work that they have codeveloped with you.

Often, we don't move past the "inform" stage. We tend to overemphasize it because we naturally start from what we want to say rather than what we want stakeholders to think, feel, and do. Use this framework to ensure that you go beyond the first stage and engage your stakeholders in a real dialogue.

Note: This project has been funded at least in part with federal funds from the U.S. Department of Education under contract number ED-ESE-10-O-0087. The content of this publication does not necessarily reflect the views or policies of the U.S. Department of Education nor does mention of trade names, commercial products, or organizations imply endorsement by the U.S. government.

Develop Messages

Finally, we are ready to develop that quintessential component of communications: the **message**. Whole other books have been written on this subject—including one that we reference below—so we'll endeavor to cover only the basics here. For each stakeholder group you've prioritized, you'll want to develop a core message that (1) will help achieve your objectives for that stakeholder and (2) can inform all the specific communication tactics that you undertake with them (more on this in a moment). This might mean that you have only one core message for multiple groups or that your messages are variations on a common theme. However, your starting point should be to consider each priority stakeholder and the objectives you've set for them.

Consider the example of a P-20 system that is trying to increase the number of postsecondary graduates in STEM fields. For the K–12 system, the main strategy is to adopt the Next Generation Science Standards, develop an aligned assessment system, and make sure that every science teacher is prepared to help their students meet the new expectations. For the higher education system, the main strategy is to encourage a more scientifically literate population of high school graduates to major in STEM fields, then to counsel and support them through to successful graduation. The priority stakeholder group you're starting with is the legislature, which will need to sign off on these strategies and fund them. What would the core message be?

It helps to start by thinking through what *questions* the core message should answer. Here are three common possibilities:

1. **The What:** Sometimes a message must be designed to inform the stakeholder and give them basic information. What is the goal? What will it mean for our state? What are the Next Generation Science Standards, and where did they come from? Are they better than the standards we have now? And what are you asking me to do about it?

2. **The Why:** Anything in the "what" category might need a rationale in the minds of your stakeholders. Why is this goal important to the future of our state? Why do we believe that the Next Generation Science Standards will actually help us achieve the goal? Why should I support this effort?

3. **The How:** Sometimes your stakeholders need additional detail about your plans or about the things you have asked them to do. What will the next few years look like as the new standards come online? What changes can I expect to experience? What do I need to do to support the effort?

The what, why, and how framework provides a starting point to make sure you're covering most of the likely concerns and questions in the minds of your stakeholders. Once you have a good list of your key questions, you can work with the relevant goal and strategy leaders to agree on answers to them.

Key Questions About
New Science Standards

In 2013, EDI partnered with Achieve and the authors of the Next Generation Science Standards (NGSS) to create a workbook with implementation guidance for states.[5] We defined several questions for states to consider answering as they developed their core messages for NGSS adoption and implementation. Note that they are all "what," "why," or "how" questions:

- What are we trying to accomplish for our students and the United States in science education?
- Why are we trying to do this?
- How will we know that we have done it? What are our specific goals and targets?
- What is holding us back from reaching our goals and targets?
- Why and how are the NGSS essential to our success?
- How are the NGSS different from what we already do?
- How will the NGSS help us overcome the challenges we face?
- What are the benefits to students, our economy, and the workforce by having college- and career-ready graduates in not only English-language arts/literacy and math but also science?
- What strategies are we undertaking to implement the NGSS?
- What are the biggest changes these strategies will require in our districts, schools, and classrooms?

These questions usually require clear knowledge of implementation to answer well. You'll need to know about time lines, milestones, and dates. You'll even need to understand the theory of action and rationale behind your strategies and how they connect to the aspiration. Again, communications can't be separated from delivery: a clear understanding of your system's goals and plans is essential to the development of a strong core message.

The answers to these questions are the raw material of your core message. You'll need to shape this material and put it together so that it's clear, consistent, and logical. You can do this at greater or lesser levels of rigor as the situation demands. For some groups, it will be a matter of reworking the language until it flows properly. For others, there are additional frameworks and tools that can be used to think about improving the clarity and structure of a core message, one of which we explore below.

Once you have a message that's clear and well structured, the last step is to bring it to life. Remember that the challenge of communication is not just how much you communicate; it's also how you make your communication stand out from everything else stakeholders are hearing. What will make your message memorable?

Structuring Communication: The Minto Pyramid Principle

One of the most useful frameworks for structuring messages is Barbara Minto's Pyramid Principle. Used by experts around the world for over four decades, the principle will allow any communications leader to create a compelling message for any situation.

Minto's claim is that we naturally order our thinking into "pyramids." Specifically, "The easiest order for a reader [to process information] is to receive the major, more abstract ideas before he is required to take in minor, supporting ones. And since the major ideas are always derived from the minor ones, the ideal structure of the ideas will always be a pyramid of groups of ideas tied together by a single overall thought."[6] Figure 5B.8 is an example of a message structured as a series of pyramids.

We've seen this idea of grouping and ordering before; it's why we do outlines of documents we write or presentations we give with major and minor points. The Pyramid Principle sharpens this approach by insisting on some simple but important rules for how the major and minor points relate to each other:

- Ideas at any level in the pyramid must always be summaries of the ideas grouped below them.
- Ideas in each pyramid grouping must always be the same kind of idea. Each idea triggers a question (Why? How?) and each idea underneath it provides an answer to that question.

Figure 5B.8   Pyramid Message

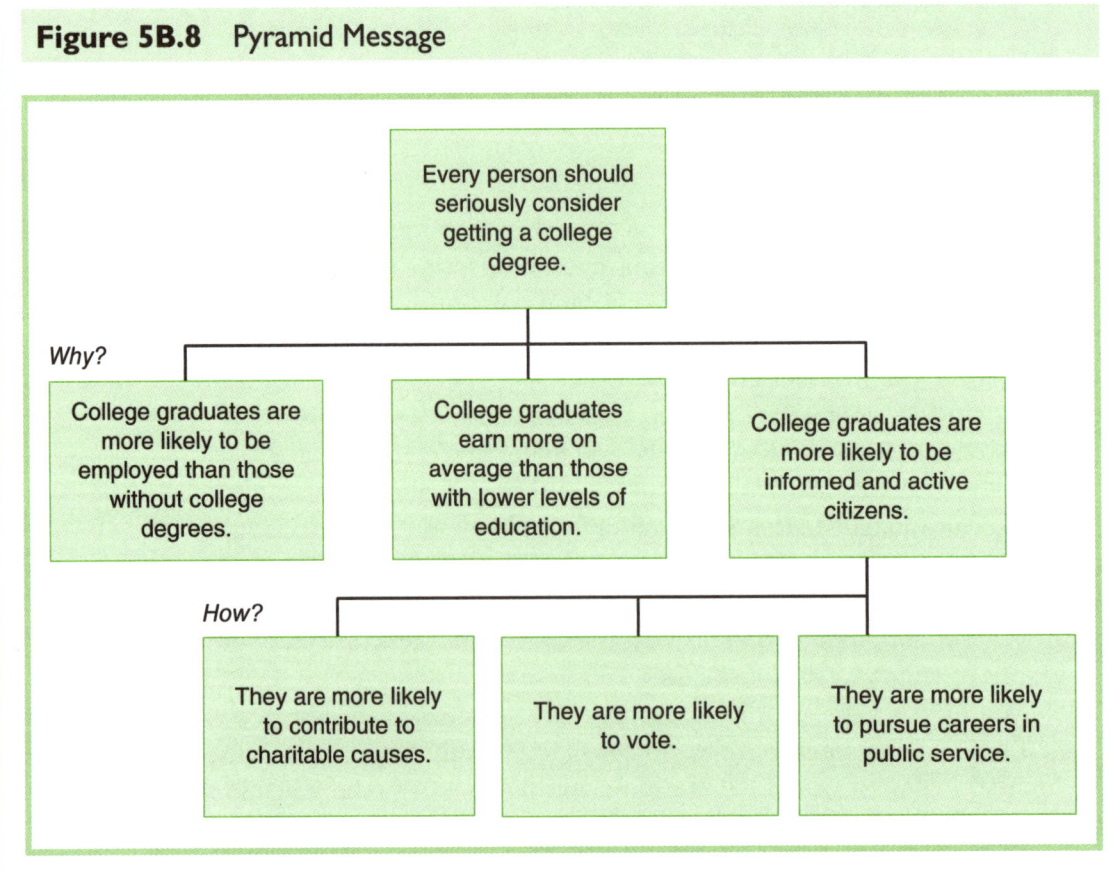

Figure 5B.9 Message Map: Implementing South Dakota Common Core Standards in English–Language Arts and Math

KEY MESSAGE #1 The new standards in English and math are challenging.	KEY MESSAGE #2 The new standards are necessary to prepare students for college and careers in the 21st century.	KEY MESSAGE #3 The new standards allow for flexibility and local control.
SUPPORT POINT #1	SUPPORT POINT #1	SUPPORT POINT #1
• They provide a clear and more rigorous set of expectations for what students should know and be able to do in English and math. • They raise the bar so students are ready for college and careers in the 21st century.	• Today's economy places high value on postsecondary education and training. • These standards are aligned to expectations for college and careers in the 21st century.	• Standards are not curriculum. Local school districts choose their own curriculum.
SUPPORT POINT #2	SUPPORT POINT #2	SUPPORT POINT #2
• They shift students from a focus on memorization and test taking to understanding key concepts and applying knowledge.*	• Today's employers need workers who can think critically, apply knowledge to real-world situations, read and analyze tests construct viable arguments, solve problems, and communicate effectively. • These are exactly the types of skills the new standards promote.	• Teachers choose how to teach the standards, using their own sound instructional practices and materials.
SUPPORT POINT #3	SUPPORT POINT #3	SUPPORT POINT #3
• They lead to richer, more authentic types of assessment.	• South Dakota must be able to compete in a global economy. • These standards are informed by the best models in the U.S. and benchmarked to top performing nations, which means our students will be better prepared to compete for jobs with students around the world.	• States led development of common standards and chose whether or not to adopt. (Currently, there are 45 participating states.) • Federal government did not play a role.

(Continued)

(Continued)

- The ideas in each grouping must be logically ordered—that is, there must be a reason why one comes after the other and not the other way around. Minto notes that there are four ways to order ideas:

  1. Deductively (a major premise, a minor premise, and the conclusion you can draw from the two);

  2. Chronologically (first, then second, then third);

  3. Structurally (breaking down the whole into parts); and

  4. Comparatively (starting with the most important according to some criterion, then the next, then the next, etc.).

One example of the Pyramid Principle at work comes from the South Dakota Department of Education, which developed a set of three key messages to support its implementation of the Common Core State Standards in 2013 (see Figure 5B.9).

By constructing a pyramid that starts with the most important idea, then works its way down through a question and answer dialogue to provide additional detail through logical and logically ordered groupings, the Pyramid Principle ensures a clear and consistent flow of information that mirrors the way that we think.

For more information, we highly recommend Barbara Minto's book, *The Minto Pyramid Principle*.

As you can imagine, there's no set formula for doing this, but there are a few practical tools to keep in mind:

- **Invoke your aspiration and your moral purpose:** Don't be afraid of making an authentic appeal to the most important reason we all do this work: to improve the lives and life chances of students.

- **Tell a story:** As the journalist Jeremy Hsu once wrote in a definitive article on the subject, "Storytelling is one of the few human traits that are truly universal across culture and through all of known history."[7] Be on the lookout for stories that will help illustrate your message and bring it to life.

- **Use metaphors:** If a picture is worth a thousand words, a metaphor comes close; it's a "word-picture" that gives stakeholders an image they can hold on to. Remember the metaphor we used to describe the Delivery Unit in Chapter 1C: the picture of Ulysses' rowers, rowing their leader toward his destination even as he was distracted by the sirens' song. Years after we first began to use that metaphor in our public presentations, we continue to hear delivery leaders and others in systems make reference to it as a way of understanding their own work.

- **Give real-world examples:** People, even senior leaders, relate to the experience of individual students, teachers, faculty, and administrators much more readily than to abstract ideas.

- **Quote your supporters (the messengers, champions, and fan club on the stakeholder map):** Use their support to emphasize that a broader coalition is behind your delivery effort.

- **Above all, surprise and entertain your audience:** People pay more attention to things they don't expect to hear.

Storytelling: Making the Case for NGSS

Stephen Pruitt, Senior Vice President at Achieve and a leader of the Next Generation Science Standards (NGSS) movement, tells a story from his time at the Georgia Department of Education to illustrate the need to give the audience context when communicating. He also teaches us something about the shifts that we need to make in order to understand the true purpose of science education:

> In 2006, Pluto was reclassified to no longer be a planet. I spent over an hour on the phone with a reporter from the local newspaper. In this interview, I gave some great insight (or so I thought) to what a great time this was for science in general and science education specifically. It did not matter. The reporter was mortified that I was not sending a personal message to each Georgia teacher regarding the assessment of Pluto. He could not believe that we did not focus on naming the planets in order (especially since Pluto and Neptune actually switch places for a while). For him, he had no context. He did not see that science is a way of knowing and that it changes based on new evidence. For him, it was about facts to be memorized.
>
> At the conclusion of the interview, the reporter asked me, "So, do you think students will still do science fair projects with the solar system?" I said, "Yes, but now they only need 8 balls instead of 9." That was the only quote that made it into the article. The following day, this cartoon was in the paper . . .

Source: Bob Gorrell by Bob Gorrell, Via @GoComics. (2006, August 25). Retrieved from http://www.gocomics.com/bobgorrell/2006/08/25

Though he was communicating about *miscommunication*, Stephen's story brings the main point home: Many people—even talented and capable people—misunderstand the true purpose and nature of science education. He uses this story to help audiences around the country understand just what makes the new standards so different and so much better than their predecessors.

A good core message makes a powerful case to its audience: it attempts to instill new beliefs (or reinforces old ones), then appeals to those beliefs to change behaviors. In this sense, it's different from capacity building, which tends to help people act their way into changing their beliefs. Communication and capacity building are thus two mutually reinforcing halves of the same coin.

Plan for Communication

With a compelling core message and prioritized stakeholders, you can now turn your attention to amplifying and repeating your communication. This is where your work in communications becomes operational and tactical. The next tool you'll need is a communication plan. Like a delivery plan, it builds on the foundation you've established—your aspiration/core message and your stakeholder analysis—to lay out how you will implement at scale. And like a delivery plan, it includes measures and milestones for implementation that can serve as a basis for monitoring and accountability. In fact, because communication needs to be integrated with implementation, much of the communication plan will depend on what's in your delivery plan or plans. You may even choose to integrate communication planning into your delivery plans.

You already have three elements for your communication plan:

- A list of priority stakeholders to engage;
- One or more specific objectives to achieve with each priority stakeholder; and
- A message for each priority stakeholder.

Because communications is an integrated exercise, this is the point where it makes sense to think about this work all together rather than stakeholder by stakeholder.

Your first step in bringing a plan together is to identify **key milestones**. In the next year, what are the make-or-break moments that will let you know that you're on track to achieve your objectives with stakeholders? Some of them will be obvious events for communication and decision making, like a positive board vote, a successful conference with stakeholders, the passage of a critical law, or the launch of a newsletter. Others will be more subtle—they may be accomplishments that you know you have to make with your stakeholders within a certain timeframe (e.g., "six months from now, mentions of our work in the local press will have doubled"). As with delivery planning, it's helpful to limit the number of milestones so that the detail does not become too unwieldy. What are the five (or fewer) most important ones, and when will they occur?

Next, you can start to think about the actions you'll take to achieve each milestone. For the time leading up to and during each of your milestones, consider a few key questions:

- Who are the **priority stakeholder groups** you'll engage to achieve this milestone?
- What **communication vehicles** will you use to engage them? You'll often find that one communication vehicle can be used to reach multiple

groups. Consider the list in Figure 5B.10, and think about the following questions to select the appropriate ones for each stakeholder group:

- ○ What are their regular information and dialogue sources?
- ○ Who are the people and institutions they trust most?
- ○ Where do they gather, socially and virtually? What existing interactions or communications vehicles can you take advantage of that already exist?
- ○ What unique communication vehicles can your champions or messengers bring to the table?
- ○ What is free, and what requires you to spend money?
- ○ How does the reach of each communication vehicle compare? (Get specific about scale here, just like in delivery planning.)

- • With what **frequency** will you engage? Is there one specific date or several contact points leading up to the milestone?
- • Who will be **responsible** for achieving this milestone?

For each milestone, then, you can create an action plan using Figure 5B.11 to guide your communication efforts.

Like all good planning tools, this one helps you go from the general to the specific—from questions about what you're trying to accomplish to tactical actions that your team can take to achieve your objectives for stakeholders.

Figure 5B.10   Potential Communications Vehicles

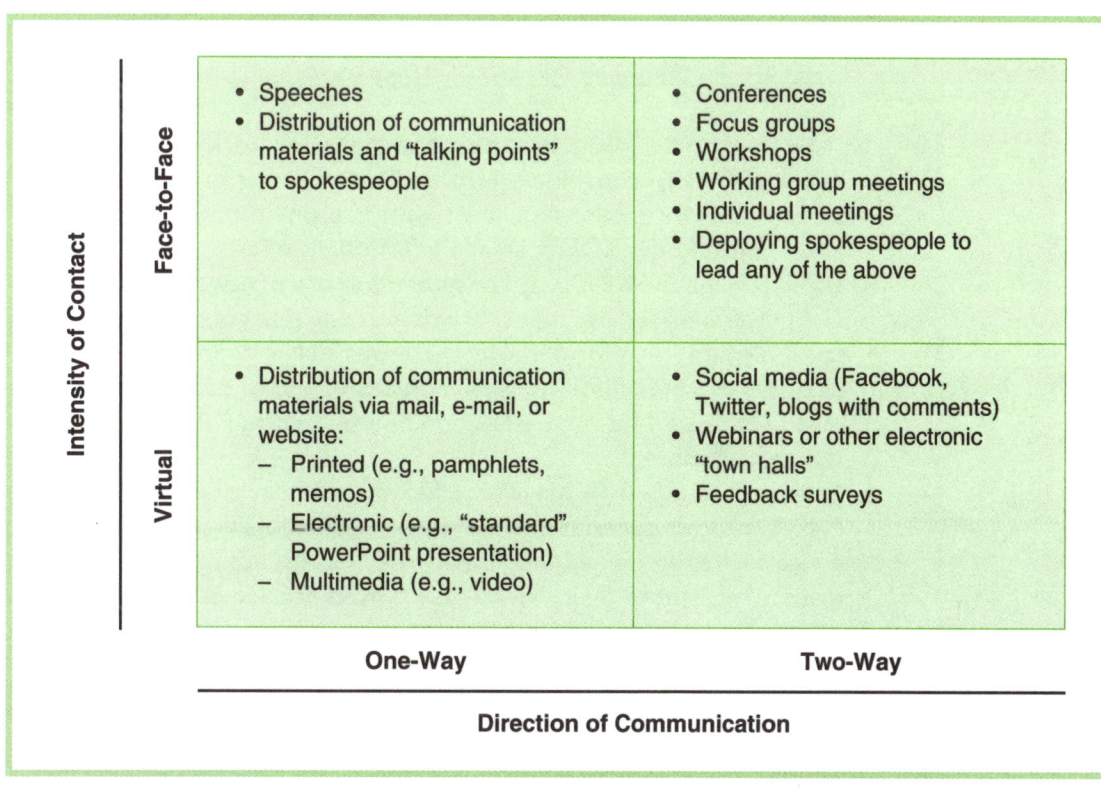

Figure 5B.11   Stakeholder Communication Planning Template

Milestone:			
Who (priority stakeholder)	**How (communication vehicles)**	**When (frequency with specific dates)**	**Responsibility**

Using Multiple Communications Vehicles in Kentucky

The delivery effort at the Kentucky Department of Education has been complemented by a robust communications operation. Commissioner Terry Holliday and his team use a variety of communication tools to help key stakeholders understand the system's priorities and future direction:

- **Webpage:** Commissioner Holliday has a dedicated webpage that serves as a one-stop-shop for his recent and archived communications with key stakeholders, including superintendents, principals, and teachers. The webpage also includes a catalog of presentations the Commissioner has made throughout the state and recordings of the webcasts he frequently hosts for superintendents, principals, and teachers.
- **Advisory groups:** In order to receive timely feedback on education issues from key constituencies, the Commissioner has developed several advisory groups that meet with him on an ongoing basis to advise him and the KDE team and inform their efforts.
- **Blog:** To keep the KDE's key constituents aware of news and updates, Commissioner Holliday regularly writes a blog that gives his personal take on education reform, and its challenges and its opportunities. The blog sets a standard for transparency: at the end of 2014, the Commissioner shared his own evaluation by the Kentucky Board of Education on the blog.
- **Friday Fast Five:** To maintain effective communication with Kentucky's district superintendents, the Commissioner sends out an e-mail each Friday called the "Friday Fast Five," to highlight hot topics that are relevant to their work. These e-mails provide brief overviews of new Department initiatives, resources available, or new laws or regulations pertinent to school leaders, with links to more information about the topics.

> • **Twitter Town Halls and #TeachKCAS:** To promote the introduction of college- and career-ready standards, KDE holds Twitter Town Halls where stakeholders can ask questions about this key change. Each month, KDE also "crowdsources" good practice in implementing the new standards by encouraging educators around the state to share resources using the hashtag #TeachKCAS.
>
> Thanks to these and other efforts, KDE has avoided or addressed much of the pushback on reform that has overwhelmed other states.

There's one last piece remaining in your communication plan: **measures of success**. Think about the feedback loops we defined in Chapter 3B. How would you use those techniques to gauge your progress toward your milestones and objectives for stakeholders? Start with the questions that you are trying to answer with your feedback loops. Remember: don't limit yourself to inputs. There may be a lot of communication going on, but are stakeholders getting the message? Do they understand it? Are they convinced by it? And are they acting on it?

Dan Cohen and John Kotter[8] identify a few key questions that help us get at these deeper levels of inquiry:

- Can stakeholders concisely repeat the message in their own words?
- Can they articulate the implications for themselves and/or their groups?
- Are they discussing these implications in their routine management meetings?
- Are they asking you an increasing number of questions about this work?
- Is the language you use becoming part of the language they use?

Some ideas for measurement are given in Figure 5B.12; as always, it makes sense to start by identifying and using the ones that already exist before creating new ones.

This is a good place to get creative. One partner of ours collected data on a teacher evaluation system by manning a booth at the state fair; this simple effort allowed him to speak to over 4,000 teachers.

With that, you have the components of your communication plan. Bring everything together in one document, or integrate it into existing delivery plans, and you'll be ready for the last step: monitoring progress.

Drive Communications

A communications leader can work to facilitate the right groups of people—with the right knowledge of your system's delivery goals and strategies—to work through each of the exercises we've defined up to this point. Ideally, these converstions would take place in parallel to or as part of actual delivery planning, which would set up communications as an additional item to monitor through delivery routines.

Figure 5B.12   Potential Ways to Monitor Stakeholder Engagement

Surveys and Polls	• Questionnaires that can be (semi-) regularly administered to the whole group of a significant sample
Check-Ins With Key Individuals	• Regular touchpoints with those who have a finger on the pulse of the group's opinion • Some of these may be members of your guiding coalition
Focus Groups	• Qualitative feedback from a cross section of members of the group • May be a regular advisory group or ad hoc
Attending Events	• Show up at events where large number of priority stakeholders will be present • Be prepared with a list of questions that can be used in short, casual conversations
Tracking Public Information	• Regular searches of publicly available commentary from group members (e.g., Google Alerts, LexisNexis, or informal internal sources) • Measures of digital engagement: website visits, number of downloads, e-mail opens, Facebook (or other social media) likes and mentions

Like a delivery plan, a strong communications plan should lend itself to this kind of monitoring. The goals, milestones, and measures of success are all evidence that you can use to determine the likelihood of delivery using the tools from Chapter 4A. The principles here are identical to those for monitoring delivery plans.

You'll need to decide how to integrate your routines for monitoring communications with the routines you set up for your delivery goals and plans. You might include "communications" as part of the rotation in the schedule; alternatively, you might add a communications component to each of the individual routines.

Go through these steps, and you will establish a communications effort every bit as formidable as the delivery work itself. This reflects a truth that should become obvious as you go through these exercises: good communication should be integrated with planning because good communication will help you achieve the goals and objectives in your plans. This is why stakeholder engagement deserves so much weight in the work you do.

⊙ LESSONS FROM THE FIELD

Be Proactive

Some of the most common mistakes that systems make in communication have to do with how they define it. We saw this already when we described the risk that a communications leader is only thought of as the media person. One other pitfall that we see is the conception of communications as crisis management, or at the very least a rapid-response operation for fielding inquiries. To put it in specific terms, the temptation is to take the list of questions that stakeholders are likely to ask (see above) and turn it into an FAQ rather than a proactive message.

To be clear: of course communications has a reactive component and must be responsive to crisis situations, as must nearly every other area of implementation management. But just as we worry when implementation management devolves into a series of fires to fight, we should have the same concern in communications. The core principles in this chapter lay out a set of proactive tools for identifying and analyzing stakeholders, setting objectives for them, and planning to engage them appropriately. You'll need to fight to create the space to use these tools and to have the right conversations. Naming a communications leader, and giving them the writ to work with other key leaders in your system, will itself be a sign of your willingness to invest in proactive communications.

This proactivity will pay off when crises do arise. In fact, continued proactive messaging is essential *during* a crisis, in addition to the reactive work you'll inevitably do. To take one example: as we've noted before, many K–12 systems are getting pushback on their implementation of the Common Core State Standards (CCSS). The backlash is coming from multiple directions, and it's fiercer than anything that's come before in the life of this reform effort.

> "In the absence of clear, concise, and purposeful communication about the Common Core, seeds of misinformation can start to take root. States that have won these communications battles have communicated thoughtfully and tirelessly in this time of great uncertainty."
>
> —Paul Ferrari, Program Director for College and Career Readiness Engagement, Council of Chief State School Officers

The leaders we work with are, naturally, trying to respond to the questions they're getting from the press, from other state leaders, and from the field and the general public. The problem with this approach—by itself, that is—is that it answers questions that have been framed entirely by those opposing the reform. Rather than talking about the benefits of college and career readiness, rigor, or next-generation assessments, for example, leaders are spending a disproportionate amount of their time explaining that the CCSS don't represent federal intrusion into local affairs or left-wing indoctrination for their students.

You should answer questions when people raise them. But they're hardly the only questions. Proactive communication allows you to set the terms of debate so that you can spend at least as much time (or more) explaining why a reform is good as you do explaining why it isn't bad. Even if your strongest opponents won't budge, they might at least move in your direction. More important, the strongest opponents of your work will almost by definition be a minority. Your proactive messaging may not reach them—but if you focus only on them, you ignore the opportunity to reach others who are more persuadable.

Do the Hard Work of Integration

Several times throughout this chapter, we've made reference to the importance of integrating communications with your broader delivery effort. While we've tried to give guidance on what this would look like throughout, this integration is usually more difficult—and messier—than it may first appear.

The most difficult tension you'll encounter is between centralized and decentralized communications. We've worked in systems where there's a single communications leader who is responsible for everything. So far, so good—it's what we recommended above. But what happens if communications planning takes a long time—and your system leader needs talking points for a speech on a specific goal or strategy now? What happens if a particular team, implementing a particular strategy, needs to start communicating about it now—but the other teams don't yet know what their messages are? How does that one team articulate its own "core message," knowing that a broader communications planning effort might change it down the road?

Likewise, we've been in systems with the opposite problem: a separate communications effort in every division. These divisions are more nimble and can more readily integrate communications with implementation at their own pace. But the quality of the resulting communication is variable, and there will be a huge risk that stakeholders receive more (and more redundant) communication than they need to, which will dilute the overall message. Or, worse, they get conflicting messages depending on who they're talking to.

Because of the need for a unified and coherent approach, we recommend a single, senior-level communications leader. If individual divisions have communications experts of their own, this leader could make a point of working through them to work with their teams. But we can't emphasize enough that this leader must be willing to do the hard work of integration. This doesn't necessarily mean that the leader is a gatekeeper (though this might make sense in some cases, like communications to the field). Instead, he or she must work across every division and every leader, understand how they work, and serve as a thought partner who is neither too aggressive or passive in planning communications with them. Your communications leader also has to strike the right balance between consistency and speed—letting some teams who need to move faster do so, and keeping track of how their work will affect the overall effort, even as they devote time and attention to the important but less urgent work of comprehensive communication planning.

Like we said before, your communications leader has to be a skilled facilitative leader. Consider carefully who will be the right fit for the job.

⊙ KEY CONSIDERATIONS FOR SYSTEM LEADERS AND STAFF

The tools of communication are flexible and applicable to a number of different contexts. Most of this chapter has been about communications with respect to your core goals and strategies—the ones that you worked through in Parts 1 to 4 of this book. If you're a **system leader**, this kind of communication won't happen without your active participation and support. One reason for this is that you yourself will often be a "communications vehicle": your communications leader will give you talking points for your speeches, ask you to mention specific things in your meetings with stakeholders, and the like. You may need to allow your name to be attached to blog posts, newsletters, and other missives that the communications leader coordinates on your behalf. The most powerful and symbolic communication comes from the top. You'll need to be comfortable enough with the work going on that you can give your assent to these things—all the more reason why choosing a communications leader you trust is so important.

If you're on the **system staff**, there are several applications for these tools. Some of the above may apply to you, to the extent that you lead specific large pieces of a delivery effort (in particular, if you're a goal leader). But these tools are applicable no matter how large or small your sphere of influence is. Imagine leading a particular strategy. You'll need to master the tools in this chapter so that you can solve the communications challenge for that strategy—then work with the communications leader to connect it to the work of the system as a whole.

Finally, if you're a **delivery leader**, it goes without saying that you may play a key role in facilitating some of the most critical communication decisions. Moreover, as the primary facilitator for system-wide goal setting, delivery planning, and routines, you have a responsibility to work with the communications leader to make sure that this work really does integrate with delivery.

But there's another, potentially separate application of these tools for delivery leaders: communicating about delivery itself. As we've noted, the introduction of delivery work brings its own changes that might arouse skepticism among those who are affected by them. As such, delivery may require a communications effort all its own. The tools in this chapter can be pressed into service for this purpose: working with your system leader (who will be a key communications vehicle), you can develop a core message around why the system is adopting this approach, identify and analyze the stakeholders likely to be affected, and develop a smaller-scale communications plan for making sure that your delivery effort has the internal support it needs.

Branding the Delivery Effort:
Communicating About the Goals in Massachusetts

Several years into their delivery effort, the Delivery Unit at the Massachusetts Department of Elementary and Secondary Education (ESE) started to turn its attention toward communicating externally about the work they were doing. This began with an effort to brand ESE's four main strategies for improving college and career readiness for students (see Figure 5B.13).

The logos may seem like a small touch, but they've created a visual marker and reinforced a common language around the state's priorities. They show up on every delivery plan, bimonthly note, and stocktake document. They are also used with external stakeholders, as ESE's most recent strategic plan summary (http://www.doe.mass.edu/research/StrategicPlan.docx) shows.

(Continued)

(Continued)

Figure 5B.13   Branding for Strategies in Massachusetts

 Massachusetts will **strengthen its curriculum, instruction, and assessments** by creating tools and resources to support the implementation of the Massachusetts Curriculum Frameworks, providing a support system for improving classroom practice and instruction, and offering high-quality professional development.

 Massachusetts will **improve the effectiveness of all its educators** by improving educator preparation programs, recruiting and hiring a more diverse workforce, and promoting a system of continuous improvement through the educator evaluation model system.

 Massachusetts will **turn around the lowest-performing schools and districts** by supporting schools in their implementation of improvement strategies, appointing receivers for chronically underperforming districts, and partnering with providers who have expertise and demonstrated effectiveness.

 Massachusetts will **use data and technology to support student performance** by providing data in an effective and efficient manner, producing relevant data and information, and promoting a culture of effective data-informed decision making.

As of this writing, this document is at the top of the Commissioner's page on the ESE website. It restates many of the goals and strategies that ESE leaders have been familiar with for years—but it uses them to help stakeholders understand the work of the agency.

⊙ CONCLUSION

Communication and engagement are integral parts of your delivery effort, influencing and being influenced by each step you take in goal setting, planning, and monitoring. And, like delivery, it's most likely to accomplish its purpose when there's a clear and competent leader in charge.

This chapter has given tools and examples to help you put all these things into place. In doing so, you will not just solve Kotter's problem of undercommunicating by a factor of 10, or 100, or 1,000. You'll also ensure that the most high-priority stakeholders are continuously engaged with the right messages that will motivate them to the right beliefs and actions. You'll widen your circle of leadership to include whomever you need to support your work. And you'll be ready to take on the last element of building a delivery culture: building the relationships that hold it all together.

⊙ NOTES

1. Kotter, J. (2012). *Leading change*. Boston, MA: Harvard Business Review Press.

2. Fullan, M. (2011). *The six secrets of change: What the best leaders do to help their organizations survive and thrive*. San Francisco, CA: Jossey-Bass.

3. Kentucky Department of Education. (2012). *Unbridled learning accountability model (with focus on the next-generation learners component)*. Retrieved from http://education.ky.gov/comm/ul/documents/white%20paper%20062612%20final.pdf

4. Reform Support Network. (2014, March 10). *Educator evaluation: Reaching and engaging the most critical stakeholders*. Retrieved from https://www2.ed.gov/about/inits/ed/implementation-support-unit/tech-assist/reaching-engaging-stakeholders.pdf

5. Achieve, Inc. (2012). NGSS adoption and implementation workbook. Washington, DC: U.S. Education Delivery Institute. Retrieved from http://www.deliveryinstitute.org/publication/next-generation-science-standards-adoption-and-implementation-workbook

6. Minto, B. (2008). *The pyramid principle: Logic in writing and thinking* (Rev. ed.). Harlow, UK: Financial Times Prentice Hall.

7. Hsu, J. (2008). *The secrets of storytelling: Why we love a good yarn*. Scientific American Global RSS. Retrieved from http://www.scientificamerican.com/article/the-secrets-of-storytelling/

8. Kotter, J., & Cohen, D. (2002). *The heart of change: Real-life stories of how people change their organizations*. Boston, MA: Harvard Business School Press.

Chapter 5C

Unleash the "Alchemy of Relationships"

 Create an irreversible delivery culture

System Leader Summary

We must never forget that a *system* is just a large collection of people—a diverse array of perspectives, interests, hopes, and fears that may or may not be aligned with what you're trying to do. You can't hope to understand them all, but understanding a vital few will almost always be crucial for making progress. No matter how strong the plans, routines, and process you set up to manage change, **relationships** are the glue that will hold your delivery effort together.

Most of the tools in this book are about influencing the behavior of groups of people. The tools in this chapter are about influencing people one by one: creating space for relationship building, building a strong "brand" through deliberate attention to each interaction, and using principled negotiation to work with those who oppose you. Though these tools are applicable to everyone in your system (including you), make sure your delivery leader internalizes them. Even with your backing, your delivery leader's effectiveness will depend on their ability to wield influence without authority. And more than anything else, that influence is the product of the alchemy of relationships.

⊙ STOP SEEING LIKE A STATE

The job of a system leader is often to simplify reality. It's an inevitable consequence of the problem of scale. The thousands of students, faculty, and school and campus leaders in a system—as well as all the organizations and people between us and them—aren't just numerous; they're also a diverse and chaotic bunch. This fact helps us appreciate the meaning of the word *system*: these people exist in a complex and ever-changing web of interactions, interests, hopes, fears, and emotions. Any one leader couldn't hope to comprehend them all.

This is why so much of the delivery approach provides you with tools for simplification. We set goals, write plans, and draw delivery chains as a way of reducing this complexity to its most essential elements. Likewise, in this part of the book, we've focused thus far on tools for analyzing and impacting large groups of people—building capacity throughout the delivery chain and engaging stakeholder groups to widen the circle of leadership to the public at large. This requires us to make assumptions and generalizations about these groups, about how they'll react to our work, and about what we can do to change their beliefs and behaviors.

This makes sense: as James C. Scott puts it, when we live at 30,000 feet in a system, we inevitably become experts in "seeing like a state." But we always run a risk when we do this. When we simplify, our generalizations are like averages: what will help us change the behaviors of the average teacher, faculty member, principal, or provost? This even includes our collection and use of data, which reduces complex reality to stylized facts.

These facts can obscure relevant information; as Scott points out, "The farmer rarely experiences an average crop, an average rainfall, or an average price for his crops."[1] And sometimes the individual data points are more important to understand than the averages. We once saw this principle in action in a session we facilitated with a team in a state education agency. We had drawn the delivery chain for their key initiatives and were collecting feedback on the quality of implementation via a survey. One of us gave the team a reality check question: "Who are you most concerned that you are *not* reaching?" One leader answered without hesitation: "We are not reaching teachers in the school districts in our largest cities." This was more than a minor challenge: over 40% of the students in the state are in that small handful of districts. But because relationships between state leaders and the leaders of these districts were historically challenging, a plan that worked for the rest of the state would not work for them.

This is a familiar story. A higher education system might not be able to get a new initiative off the ground without the assent of a few key campus leaders. A state K–12 system might be powerless to move a project forward without the help of a specific person in HR. Hidden among "average" people are outliers that can make or break a reform effort.

And this is the risk that Scott points out (in fact, the subtitle of his book—"How Certain Schemes to Improve the Human Condition Have Failed"—suggests that he is more pessimistic on this point than we are). When we view the people in our system as little more than objects to be moved around by our plans, we ignore the fact that they are people first—each with a unique background and set of motivations. And when the support of one or a small handful of them becomes pivotal to your prospects for success, simplifying tools no longer work. Instead, you must engage each critical individual in all their complexity. Hence this final chapter on the "alchemy of relationships."

The dictionary definition of *alchemy* is "a power or process of transforming something common into something special." When people work together, the quality of the relationships between them can make the whole into something greater than the sum of the parts. High-quality relationships, like alchemy, transform the common—a group of people—into something special—a system that delivers real results for students. Of course, the opposite is also true: poor relationships create dysfunction and terrible consequences for those same students.

For this reason, the relationships you build during implementation will determine your success. If capacity building and communication help you widen the circles of leadership for your delivery effort, then relationships help you hold these circles together. They reduce the inevitable friction that occurs between colleagues as they pursue the work of reform. Attention to them must run in and through and all around everything else you do. This is a chapter about how to make sure that happens.

The Importance of Relationships:
Educator Effectiveness in Hawai'i

The Hawai'i Department of Education (HIDOE) began implementing their Educator Effectiveness System (EES) in 2010, but things didn't quite go according to plan. Implementation fell behind schedule in 2011 and 2012, resulting in increased scrutiny from the U.S. Department of Education.

The delay was due to one critical factor: as a single district responsible for contract negotiations, HIDOE couldn't reach an agreement with the state's teachers' union. Without a contract for EES implementation, they wouldn't be able to link evaluation to compensation. It didn't matter how well designed their system was, how strong the communication about it was, or even how many teachers supported it. This crucial element depended on the relationship between HIDOE leaders and just a handful of union leaders.

In 2013, after a long impasse, HIDOE and the union reached an agreement to allow implementation of the EES. Seventy percent of all teachers voted, and of those, 95% agreed to approve the new contract—the largest margin for such a vote in the union's 40-year history. "By this vote, it clearly shows that teachers are ready to go on to the next level, and headed to education transformation,"[2] said Will Okabe, the union president.

We ignore critical relationships at our peril—but when we get them right, they can be a big advantage.

⊙ CORE PRINCIPLES

We know that relationships matter, but it can be difficult to define what makes them work or not. We believe that relationship building breaks down into three practices:

1. Create spaces for relationships

2. Build a strong brand

3. Help resisters get to yes

Because prevention always trumps intervention, the best relationships are cultivated *before* conflict or resistance arises. For this reason, our first two practices are about proactive relationship building. When challenges with specific people do arise, the best tools for dealing with them come from an unlikely source: the principles of good *negotiation.* For this, the seminal work of negotiation experts William Ury and Roger Fisher provides the insights and tactics that we've found most effective over the last several years. Our third practice is taken from the title of their best-known work: help resisters get to yes.

Create Spaces for Relationships

You want to build strong relationships before you need them. Of course, to have a good relationship, you must first have a relationship at all—which is, in its most basic sense, a series of interactions. So that's the first practice: we must create the spaces—the interactions—where we will invest in building these relationships.

To do this, it helps to know your highest priority targets for relationship building. If you're a delivery leader, one of your most critical relationships is with the system leader and with his or her leadership team. If you're a system leader, the members of your guiding coalition are a good starting point, as are the local leaders you work with. System staff could benefit from relationships with any of these and with other colleagues inside their organizations. A few questions that may help you identify your highest priorities:

- Are they key decision makers on one or more aspects of your work?
- Do they have access to a resource that you need? This could be money. But it could also have to do with systems or processes in your organization (again, think of the head of HR or IT). And don't forget another critical resource: the time of one or more busy leaders. Executive assistants often make the list.
- Are they an important link in the delivery chain? If you manage a strategy or a goal, you might have a clear idea of who the potential choke points are.
- Do they lead a high-priority group of stakeholders? In the last chapter, we focused on identifying groups of stakeholders to engage. One of the primary strategies for engagement may be to win over a group's leader.
- Do they have influence on others who have these characteristics? Sometimes, if access is the issue, a more indirect route may be the best option.

Often, it's not immediately obvious where power and influence sit. Don't be distracted by formal titles; ask who can really help you move the work forward. Finding and building relationships with "hidden" influencers can be very powerful—and often relatively easy.

Once you've identified your highest priority "targets," assess the current opportunities you have to interact with them. When—and in what context—do you see each person? If, for example, you have a weekly one-on-one working session with a person and also catch up over lunch once every month or two, you probably have all the relationship-building space you need. On the other hand, if the only time you see a person is once a month at a 50-person staff meeting, you may need to think about building in additional opportunities to interact.

You should also consider where each relationship currently stands. What impression does the other person have of you and your work, and how positive (or negative) is it? How much work will you have to do to build this relationship?

After this initial assessment, consider what you can do to create additional space where it's needed. In the context of your work, you might look for opportunities to work more closely with the person in question—whether that means side-by-side problem solving (a working group, a task force) or just additional exposure (supporting a project that they lead).

Sometimes these opportunities arise naturally out of the delivery work. In Kentucky's K–12 system, the Delivery Unit often found itself facilitating delivery planning for a goal team—only to find that they had no good way of continuing to interact with the team after the plan was completed. The Delivery Unit saw that if they were to get the information they needed—and build the right relationships—they would need to establish and attend regular meetings of these teams. By convincing the goal leaders and teams to do this, they created all the space they needed for relationship building and solved an important problem for the organization.

Sometimes, opportunities for interaction are more difficult to find, particularly for more senior leaders. In many of these cases, proximity and the chance meeting can be a good, nonintrusive solution. Michael perfected this practice during his time at the PMDU. The Prime Minister and his staff were busy people with limited time, but Michael still found a way to see them by spending time at their principal place of work, No. 10 Downing Street:

> Though my staff were on the other side of Whitehall in those early days, I always spent some time each day in my little No. 10 office. Throughout my time as head of the Delivery Unit, I spent much of my day tramping around Whitehall and, even if it was sometimes a slightly longer way round, I used to pass through No. 10 on the off-chance of running into one of these characters. And since they were inevitably in a hurry, I would try to have one piece of positive news about the Delivery Unit impact on the tip of my tongue so I could say it in a moment and then we'd both go about our business.[3]

Moments like these can add up. How can you be in the right place at the right time for busy people?

In addition to working meetings, consider social interactions—lunch, a drink after work, and so on. These are more appropriate for some than for others, but they're valuable because they allow you to focus purely on the relationship (indeed, our friends in Hawai'i have an idiom for this—"pau hana"—which literally means "finished work"). As any politician will tell you, when you need something from someone, some of the most important meetings you have with them will be the ones where you ask for nothing at all—except, perhaps, for advice, which nearly everyone is willing (and flattered) to give. One informal social interaction is probably worth 10 formal meetings in terms of relationship building; not making time for them (because we're busy, or it's awkward) is one of the biggest mistakes we can make.

> Please visit EDI's website at www.deliveryinstitute.org/5C for an exercise on identifying key relationships, evaluating them, and creating the space to strengthen them.

Build a Strong Brand

Creating the space for a relationship is the necessary first step. How will you fill that space? The stakes are high: a good relationship is transformative, but a bad one is worse than none at all. One way or another, you've asked for the time and attention of another person, and your challenge is to make every minute of it worth their while—to not be, as our CEO recalls some interactions from her days in state government, a "time suck."

How will you do this? Go back to the first question of delivery: what are you trying to do with this relationship? More specifically, what impression do you want them to consistently have about you, your work, and its implications for them?

This is where the idea of a **brand** comes in. Though the term originated in the private sector, its definition is useful here: a brand is a consistent idea or experience associated with an entity—in this case, you. Your desired brand is your aspiration for all your relationships with others, including and especially the ones you've prioritized. To build it, you must first define it.

The first component of your brand is your **values**. Values are your own deeply held beliefs about what is good or bad, desirable or undesirable, in the way you do your work. They are principles to live and work by. If you're creating a brand for a team, they are an anchor of that team's culture. In the context of a relationship, you'll know that you're living by your values when others use the language of those values to describe you.

As you think through what your values should be, consider the ideal rather than the reality. How do you want others to describe you and/or your team? And feel free to look to the examples of others—corporations, nonprofits, or other public sector agencies—for inspiration.

Values help you define your brand, but like relationships, they can feel intangible. How do we bring them to life?

There's a common saying among public speaking experts (and, we imagine, some educators): "It's the little things that make the big things count." The little things are the details of a speech—making eye contact, standing up straight, and so on. The impressions left by these small behaviors are instrumental to a

Values in the PMDU and EDI

Much of the PMDU's success can be attributed to the brand it established for itself throughout the government and the various Cabinet ministries. The Delivery Unit was consistently self-conscious about this brand, which came to be based on the five values we first introduced in Chapter 1C: ambition, focus, clarity, urgency, and irreversibility.

Years later, as EDI was founded to carry on the PMDU's work in the United States, our team followed suit. These are the current values of EDI:

- We are committed to EDI's mission and willing to **do what it takes** to achieve it.
- We are **team players**: responsive to others and our relationships with them, to the organization as a whole, and to EDI's partners.
- We are **reflective**, always seeking feedback on our work and continuously improving it.
- We are **flexible** and **adaptive**: we would rather ask "Why not?" than "Why?"
- We are **positive** and **forward looking**, always seeking solutions from the starting point we are given, whether it is in our own work, with a team, or with a partner.

We attempt to hold ourselves accountable to living by these values, and invite all those who interact with us to do the same.

speaker's credibility. If they're good, they reinforce the substance of the speech. If they aren't, they might prevent the audience from even hearing it.

In the same way, our daily practices demonstrate our values by framing the substance of our interactions with others. What practices are most important for relationship building?

First, consider **the way you prepare**. The word we use at EDI is *obsessive*. Many of the people we work with have enormous demands on their time, and it's not uncommon for some to spend most of or all their time in meetings. As we've already documented, most meetings are so poorly planned that you'll stand out simply by preparing well and thoroughly for the ones where you are involved. We learned about the importance of good preparation in the context of delivery routines (Chapter 4A). We can apply a version of those principles to other interactions. For example, if you're responsible for running a part of a meeting or presenting in it, it's not uncommon to spend 5 minutes or more preparing for every 1 minute of air time you have. The higher the stakes, the higher this ratio goes. For meetings you run, consider regularly using the meeting planning tools we laid out in Chapter 5A. And if you're just a participant, consider in advance (and write down) the three or so points you think will be important to make in advance. These are easier to predict than you might think.

Also, think about the information you gather before a meeting: If you're going to discuss financial aid policy, for example, have you read the latest research? Do you know your system's own financial aid policies? Do you know the data? It's a sign of respect and seriousness to know as much or more about the topic in question as the other people in the room.

Second, consider **the way you use others' time**. Besides preparing for meetings, here are a few practices that we've learned over the years:

- **Arrive early and end meetings early:** People rarely leave a meeting saying, "I wish that had gone on longer." For such a small gesture, ending early is a disproportionately symbolic and powerful way to serve the other person. Because time is such a precious resource, there's no better way to make someone's day than to give some of it back to them. Remember that most meetings are about accomplishing things rather than spending a certain amount of time together: if a meeting is scheduled for 60 minutes, but after 10 you've reached agreement on all the issues, have the courage to adjourn.

- **Consider and monitor your "airtime":** You want to contribute to these interactions without dominating them. What percentage of the participants at the meeting do you represent? Can you make sure you're not talking for more than that percentage of the total time allocated? If there are five people in the meeting, that means taking up 20% or less of the time. If it's a one-on-one, you should take up 50% or less. Your preparation will help you emphasize quality over quantity.

- **Think about your norms for using electronic devices:** We are constantly tempted to check our smartphones. Being the person who *never* does this in a meeting is a rare sign of respect that will differentiate you from others. A simple rule of thumb: think of checking your device as being equivalent to taking a phone call. You'd at least have to leave the room or wait for a break to do it.

Third, consider **the language you use**. As we learned in the last chapter, the repetition of a few focused ideas can leave a lasting impression. Are there words you can use regularly that provide consistent cues about your values? One delivery leader in Massachusetts, Matt Deninger, does this in his e-mail signature. Rather than sign all his notes with standard greetings like "Sincerely" or "Thanks"—or, our personal favorite, "Best" (Best what?)—he ends every e-mail with "Yours in Continuous Improvement, Matt." If the reader wonders what values Matt aspires to in his work with them, the note leaves little doubt.

This isn't an invitation to use jargon—quite the opposite, in fact. As we've pointed out, you're usually better off adopting language that already resonates with others rather than introducing new words—as long as this language describes the right underlying idea. We've worked in several systems where one of the most important things we did was to discover the anchor point for the system's aspiration—say, a strategic plan agreed to by their governing board—and to consistently refer to "goals in the board's strategic plan" rather than "delivery goals."

In the same vein, we should become experts at appropriately connecting each conversation to the impact that it will have on students. We must do this without letting the message become trite, cynical, or—perhaps worst of all—self-righteous. In particular, whenever the word "why" or "purpose" is mentioned, is there a way to connect it to impact on students? Is there a way to do it that's clear but nonthreatening? You really have two audiences here. For those who keep student impact top of mind, you want to signal that you share their values. And for those who don't, you want to help change their thinking without insulting them with the suggestion—implicit or explicit—that they're *not* putting students first already. One technique for this is to assume the best of intentions: "OK, I *know* that the most important thing to each and every one of us is to make a difference for the students in our system. Perhaps we should evaluate each of these potential strategies to see how well they do that?"

Sometimes, the language cues we give can be more subtle. Is your language positive or constructive? At EDI, we avoid words like *minus* or *weakness* in favor of words like *challenge*, *opportunity*, or *area to improve*. This isn't because we never deliver bad news; it's because we want to position ourselves with others as problem-solving partners.

Another key language cue is how you see yourself relative to others. Do you use the words "I" and "you" a lot? How often do you refer to "we" instead? One leader we know spends a great deal of time speaking to audiences of educators. Though she's never been an educator herself, most of her speeches feature only one protagonist: the "we" in the room. The underlying message is clear: *I'm not here to attack you. We're on the same team. Let's discuss the challenge and work through it together.* "We" is a powerful uniter—which is one of the reasons why it's a protagonist in this book as well.

Fourth, consider the **assertions you make** and the **questions you ask**. What's the balance between them? Relying on both, in roughly equal measure, will demonstrate that you're as committed to listening to what others have to say as you are to getting your opinion across. When you do make assertions, are they grounded in evidence? How can you show that as clearly as possible, without showing off? Do you use questions to push the thinking of others and challenge them? (As Michael likes to remind us, "Experts answer a question; leaders ask it.") And are your questions open-ended—do they invite discussion and new ideas?

Finally, consider **the way you give credit (or assign blame)**. Humility can be a powerful value in your brand. Demonstrating it requires that you be generous with the praise and credit that you give for others for successes, even as you take an increased share (or all) of the responsibility when things go wrong. Jim Collins, in his seminal work *Good to Great*, illustrates the point with the pattern of the window and the mirror:

> [The greatest leaders] look out the window to apportion credit to factors outside themselves when things go well (and if they cannot find a specific person or event to give credit to, they credit good luck). At the same time, they look in the mirror to apportion responsibility, never blaming bad luck when things go poorly.[4]

If you can become known as the person or team who has no ego, and who is willing to take responsibility to solve problems, you'll create a magnetic draw for people to cooperate with you. As the common saying goes, "A man may do an immense deal of good if he does not care who gets the credit for it."

The specific practices you adopt will vary depending on your context. At EDI, for example, we spend a lot of time traveling to and working directly with our partners in education systems. As a result, we have a whole set of practices—literally, rules of the road—for how we prepare for, conduct, and debrief one of these visits. Your team should define, adopt, and commit to practices that will demonstrate your values in every context where you interact with others and build relationships.

Influencing Ethically: Tools and Tactics

There's a great deal of literature on how to exercise influence in the context of critical relationships. From this, we've summarized a list that helps guide our work at EDI (see Figure 5C.1).

We've repeatedly pointed out the outsized importance of influencing without authority—and for that reason, informal influencing tactics dominate this list. Consider developing a shared language with your team about what types of influencing tactics work best for you and being collectively deliberate about where and how you use them.

Figure 5C.1   Influencing Tactics

Tactic	Description	Strengths/Limits
Legitimate Authority	Legal/position power	Only secures compliance
Rational Persuasion	Facts, data logic (expertise). You should do this because . . .	Important basis—but only goes so far
Inspirational/ Emotional Appeal	Appeal to values, emotions, beliefs	Can inspire commitment, but can be used unethically (emotional blackmail)
Consultation	Seek input/assistance	Builds shared ownership, but must be ready to compromise
Coalition	Getting advice, support, or advocacy from allies	There's strength in numbers, but may limit your independence
Ingratiation	Make them feel good—includes flattery	Effective ingratiation is honest, infrequent, and well intended—but overdoing it can backfire
Personal Appeal	Build rapport/friendship	Strong foundation for other tactics—but don't overuse
Exchange	Explicit or implicit quid pro quo (also, leading by example)	Shows reciprocal commitment/ authenticity—but could end up out of pocket
Pressure	Threats, ultimatums	Works in short term/crisis, but often unethical/counterproductive

Once you've defined the values and practices of your brand, we recommend that you set up a basic routine for monitoring your progress. This can be as simple as taking your list of values and practices, reviewing it once every 3 to 6 months, assessing how well you're living up to each one, and deciding on next steps to make further improvements. This lightweight feedback loop follows the "learn, practice, reflect" cycle that we introduced in Chapter 5A.

Of all the areas where you can spend time and energy, your brand is a high-return investment. Your reputation is the foundation on which all your relational capital is built; it will make things possible that you could not accomplish by any other means.

Building the Brand: Kentucky's Delivery Unit

In the Commissioner's Delivery Unit at the Kentucky Department of Education (KDE), leaders adapted the values and practices in the original PMDU "brand" and made them their own. They constantly seek feedback from others at KDE on whether they are living up to these values, both through surveys and informal conversations with the Commissioner and other leaders (see Figure 5C.2).

Figure 5C.2   Values and Practices of the Commissioner's Delivery Unit

Ambition	Focus	Clarity	Urgency	Irreversibility

The Unit will:	The Unit will not:
• Keep the system leader well informed • Consistently pursue key priorities • Use data and evidence • Be plain speaking • Identify problems early • Use imaginative problem solving • Learn from and spread best practice • Recognize differences and similarities between departments • Build capacity • Simplify things • Focus on action and urgency • Ask the important questions • Make heroes of people who deliver • Champion the belief that it can be done	• Be just another committee or task force • Be burdensome and bureaucratic • Distract people from their key tasks • Take the credit for delivery that belongs to others • Get in the way of delivery • Micromanage • Offer opinion without evidence • Have a short-term outlook • Change the goalposts

Help Resisters Get to Yes

The proactive principles we've presented thus far will help you address most of the relational challenges you will face. But no matter how well-targeted your relationships or how strong your brand, you'll inevitably encounter real resistance to your work from specific individuals. Sometimes they're the "outliers" we discussed at the beginning of the chapter—exceptions who need to be understood differently and who often have disproportionate power. Sometimes they will be people you proactively identified at the outset, but whose natural opposition is strong. Whatever the reason, you're now in the territory of dealing with a specific and difficult individual relationship—one that you must get right in order to succeed.

As we noted above, the principles of *negotiation* are the most useful tools for situations like this. Why? William Ury and Roger Fisher, two of the world's leading experts on negotiation, give the answer: we're all negotiators. "Like Molière's Monsieur Jourdain, who was delighted to learn that he had been speaking prose all his life," they write, "people negotiate even when they don't think of themselves as doing so."[5]

You are in a situation where you and another person want different things—their position is different from yours. You might need a reluctant goal leader to take charge of a team, while they clearly seem to prefer to do anything but that. Or you might be asking a leader in your organization for a larger budget for the program you are running—something they might resist as a matter of principle. In this situation, you can enter into a dialogue to try to resolve the conflict and agree on a course of action together. Or you can each go your own way and try for a different solution. These are the parameters of a negotiation, and so the wisdom of experts like Ury and Fisher is informative.

An Introduction to Negotiation

In their seminal work on negotiation, *Getting to Yes*, Ury and Fisher establish and define a method called *principled negotiation*. It's their way of resolving the false choice that confronts most of us when we approach negotiation:

> People find themselves in a dilemma. They see two ways to negotiate: soft or hard. The soft negotiator wants to avoid personal conflict and so makes concessions readily in order to reach agreement. He wants an amicable resolution; yet he often ends up exploited and feeling bitter. The hard negotiator sees any situation as a contest of wills in which the side that takes the more extreme positions and holds out longer fares better. He wants to win; yet he often ends up producing an equally hard response which exhausts him and his resources and harms his relationship with the other side.[6]

We need not make this choice. There's a third way, the method of principled negotiation, that is both hard and soft: "hard on the merits, soft on the people." They lay out four tenets of this approach:

- **People: Separate the people from the problem.** Conflict has both a substantive and an emotional dimension. Before working on the

(Continued)

(Continued)

former, you'll need to deal with the latter: "Figuratively if not literally, the participants should come to see themselves as working side by side, attacking the problem, not each other." This means understanding the perceptions and emotions of the other person, acknowledging them as legitimate, and doing what you can to deal with them directly.

- **Interests: Focus on interests, not positions.** Positions are specific things that you and the other person want. If the only space for negotiation is to compromise between these positions, it may be tempting to devolve into "hard" negotiating. But underneath opposing positions, you can often find shared and compatible interests. You need to identify your own interests, understand those of the other person, and see where there's potential for agreement.
- **Options: Invent options for mutual gain.** Negotiation can be tense, but problem solving requires creativity and innovation. How do you create the right environment for this under pressure? The key is to work with the other person to create the space and flexibility to think of a range of possible solutions to satisfy the interests of both parties. This means jettisoning some common assumptions that we bring into negotiations, such as the idea that they are zero-sum games.
- **Criteria: Insist that the result be based on some objective standard.** Sometimes you have to negotiate about the negotiation itself. In particular, what principle(s) will guide final agreement on a solution? Good criteria will protect both people from an unfair outcome—but to get to those criteria, they must be a part of the negotiation itself.

Principled negotiation is not about "winning" or getting everything you want; it's about making it possible for both people to win. We will apply these tenets in the discussion below, but for more detailed guidance, see *Getting to Yes* and Ury's follow-up book, *Getting Past No*.

What steps should we take to apply this wisdom? Suppose that you're the Chief Academic Officer of a university system and you've identified a difficult relationship with one individual: a campus president who refuses to participate in your initiative to increase degree production throughout the system. It helps to start by taking stock of the situation on your own. A few key questions apply here:

- What is your position? This may seem simple enough, but it's worth writing down: you want the campus president to participate in the initiative.
- What is your underlying interest? Why do you want what you want? In this case, your underlying interest probably has something to do with wanting to see the system achieve its goals for degree production.
- What is her position? Again, it's worth noting the obvious: the campus president does not seem to want to do what you're asking.
- What is her underlying interest? This is where the answers become more speculative. The campus president may be resisting because she has an

interest in focusing her institution's resources on something else. She may be concerned about the perception that her institution is just a "degree factory." This is the space to make your best guess about what's motivating her resistance. We will validate this hypothesis later on.

- What is her emotional objection, if any? Does the campus president have a bad relationship with you or with someone on your team? Is she naturally suspicious of the system office for historical reasons? Again, make an informed guess.
- Finally, what is her power relative to yours? Your wealth, strength, or authority is not the source of your power; rather, it's how attractive you find the option of not reaching an agreement at all. This is your BATNA—your Best Alternative to a Negotiated Agreement. In the case of our campus president, she might strictly prefer her BATNA—which would mean doing nothing—to a negotiated agreement. You, by contrast, start with a fairly weak BATNA: not getting any of what you're asking for.

Answering these questions will help you understand what your first objective should be in engaging with the other person. Can you jump right into problem solving? Or is their emotional objection so strong that your first few encounters will likely be entirely about building trust? Do you need to lay the groundwork for a better negotiating position by strengthening your BATNA? These are questions of negotiating strategy, which you can break down into two pieces: the emotional and the substantive.

The Emotional Strategy

What can you do to better understand the perceptions and emotions of the other person? There are three things: listening, acknowledging, and agreeing (where you can).

This requires some courage because it requires you to name the conflict. It means saying to the campus president, "It seems like you have some concerns about this initiative. I'd love to hear about them." It means listening to what they have to tell you and demonstrating that you really understand. As one colleague told us about his K–12 system's efforts to engage local leaders, "When you have a long history of distrust, you pretty much have to be wiling to take a bunch of criticism from them for about six months." And that's *before* the problem solving can begin.

This is what Michael Fullan calls *impressive empathy*—impressive because you're putting yourself in the shoes of a person who fundamentally disagrees with you. In the most contentious situations, it means something even more difficult: "you have to give other people respect before they have earned it."[7]

Another important element of emotional strategy is *disarming* the other person. If the other person is hostile toward you, how can you neutralize that hostility and step to their side? We've found a simple thought experiment to be the most powerful: Given the other person's perception of you, what will they expect you to do? Now: *how can you do the opposite?* How can you do it in the most visible and obvious way possible? For example, your campus president may view the system office solely as a bureaucratic compliance agency. What can you do that will give her the opposite impression? You might help her cut through some red tape she's dealing with. Or you might ban certain words from your vocabulary, like "monitoring," "performance management," or "compliance."

Think through what your emotional strategy will be. How will you demonstrate impressive empathy by listening, acknowledging, and agreeing? And how will you disarm any hostility they feel toward you and your team?

The Substantive Strategy

Once you've separated the people from the problem, it's time to think about the problem itself. The starting point for this is your interests and theirs. What are the areas of difference, and what are the areas of overlap? Where there's uncertainty about what their interests are, how can you learn more? Sometimes, you'll discover mutual interests: you may find that the campus president shares your interest in helping more students graduate but is worried that she won't have the autonomy to try the strategies most important to her. In other cases, you'll find diverging interests—as when, for example, the campus president worries that a focus on degree production detracts from the broader purpose of a university. In these cases, agreement is often based on disagreement. To reconcile the president's interest with yours, she might agree to focus on improving graduation rates as a means of increasing the number of graduates. You might, in turn, agree to let her keep all the resulting cost savings and invest them in her programmatic priorities for her institution.

Second, consider the criteria that you'll use. This isn't about searching for a standard that will give you the answer you want; it's about identifying criteria that both you and the other person will find fair. For example, you and the campus president might pursue a solution that is "in the best interests of students," if you can agree on what that means. Precedent is another powerful standard of fairness. Is there a decision or statement the other person has made that's consistent with your interests? If the campus president has set her own goals for improving graduation rates in the past, you may try to base your agreement on them. Using precedent allows you to take advantage of the human desire for self-consistency. Of course, the best criteria are the ones that the other person comes up with. Even if you think you know what their criteria will be, ask them for their ideas and let them be the first to propose them.

Third, consider the range of options you can invent with the other person for mutual gain. Are there options you can test with the other person, and if so, how can you test them? The important thing is to be specific without locking yourself in to one position. Think in terms of multiple options that meet criteria and meet both people's interests, and formulate them as potential ideas that preserve your flexibility. As with criteria, you might keep most of the options in your back pocket, create the space for brainstorming, and hope that the other person names some of them first.

Another barrier may assert itself here: the ego of the other person. If they've promised themselves or others that they won't cooperate with you, reaching agreement will feel like a betrayal of that promise. In these cases, having the right solution isn't enough: you must help them see a retreat from their position as an advance toward something better. There's another phrase for this: helping the other person save face. People often view the idea of saving face negatively, but in fact, it is at the heart of good negotiation; it's what allows people to preserve their sense of principle and consistency even as they change their positions.

One important way to help the other person save face is to help them write their "victory speech." Lyndon Johnson was famous for this in his negotiations with Congress. Often, when he had convinced a representative or senator to take a difficult vote for him, he'd encourage that person to tell the press and their supporters on how they had gotten the best of the president. Here was face-saving to the point of being self-sacrificial.

Finally, think about how to use the negotiating power you do have, as represented by your BATNA. Ury suggests that you use this power to educate the other person rather than to fight. Even when you can "win," you should negotiate, because no agreement is sustainable (especially in delivery) without buy-in from both sides. Throughout this book, we've documented the many ways in which people who don't want to support your work can undermine it, no matter how powerful you are. Forced agreements are nearly worthless when quality implementation is the main objective. We have another word for them: compliance.

Consider our campus president once again. What's the strongest possible BATNA you could imagine in your negotiation with her? In theory, you could secure a promise from the system leader to remove her from her position if she doesn't work with you. Higher education leaders reading this book will know how unrealistic this is, even if the system leader does have that authority. Why? Because firing someone is a nuclear option. You can only hang it over their heads so much before the relationship is poisoned beyond repair and cooperation is impossible.

Because power is such a blunt instrument, the most effective leaders wield it with responsibility, with humility, and as little as they possibly can. What does this look like? Rather than threatening the other person, help them understand what the potential consequences will be if you can't reach agreement. There are several "reality-testing" questions that will help you do this:

- What do you think will happen if we don't agree? What will be the costs of that?
- What do you think I will do? How will I satisfy my interests? What impact will that have on you?
- What will you do? How well will that satisfy your interests?

If these questions don't work, you may need to demonstrate your BATNA, while making it clear that you are not walking away (yet). Sometimes this means making preparations to exercise your alternatives that you know the other person will see. Suppose you have a more modest BATNA with the campus president: if she doesn't cooperate, you'll go around her and reach out directly to students on her campus. If she saw you making visible preparations to do that, it might change her tune.

Even when and if you do end up exercising your BATNA, it should be more in sorrow than in anger, and with the door left open as much as possible to resume the negotiation. Your BATNA is a real alternative. But you wouldn't be negotiating if you didn't think that an agreement would be even better.

⊙ LESSONS FROM THE FIELD

Most of the lessons that we've learned over the last several years are captured by the principles and examples above. One thing should be clear: like the people they represent, relationships resist simplification or easy answers.

For this reason, the one final lesson we've learned is this: to unleash the alchemy of relationships, we must reflect continuously and rigorously on this aspect of our work. In the context of our work at EDI, we put these principles to work just as much as our partners in state systems do. Like them, we need to create spaces for interaction (usually with them). Like them, we strive to develop and live by a specific brand, as we saw above. And like them, we must be ready to build relationships with outliers one by one, usually to persuade system leaders and others that the tools of the delivery approach are worth using.

Our best work in this area has always occurred when we've had the chance to learn, practice, and reflect on it (see Chapter 5A). This includes reflecting on our values and how well we're living them out. It also includes regular conversation about the quality of our relationships with others, and how we can strengthen them.

These kinds of situations are the most difficult to prepare for—which is why you should put extra effort into designing deliberate practice for yourself in this area. When one of us expects to go into a difficult conversation with another person, we don't allow the event itself to be our first take. We'll usually grab one or more of our colleagues, explain the situation, and ask them to role play it with us. Afterward, we debrief to see what we could do better.

How should you design a program of deliberate practice for relationship building? Use the exercises in this chapter as your opportunity for formal learning. Then create the spaces for reflection and practice—in particular, before and after your interactions with the key players in question. Involve someone you trust to coach you in this area. They can provide thought partnership as you reflect on your progress.

Doing this can be awkward, just like some of the difficult relationships you're trying to improve. But because so many people shy away from focusing on this area of their work, the rewards are great for those who choose to take it on.

⊙ KEY CONSIDERATIONS FOR SYSTEM LEADERS AND STAFF

If you're a **system leader**, you should think about what brand you want for the organization you lead. By insisting on defining values and practices and regularly assessing progress against them, you can take a big step toward transforming your organization. When you negotiate, you're more likely than others to engage in the type of "traditional" negotiation that Ury and Fisher wrote about: over who gets what, what price to pay, the terms of a contract, and so on. Those sitting across the table will be more "formidable" negotiating partners: governors, legislators, union leaders, and the like. But you do have an advantage here: the public profile of these people means it will be easier for you to learn more about their interests and values as you plan your negotiation. Even when you find yourself negotiating with those over whom you have considerable power, remember the importance of using your power to educate rather than to fight, to negotiate even when you can win. It's not a sign of weakness, but a gesture that will add to the authority you already enjoy.

If you're a part of the **system staff**, you will find yourself using these tools primarily as a way to engage the field or others inside your organization. Because influence without authority is so important in these systems, particularly those with substantial local-level control and autonomy, these tools will be important for you even if you're high up in the organizational hierarchy.

This goes double for **delivery leaders**, who have perhaps the least formal authority of anyone in the system. Not only will you need to build your own relationships, but you may also be called on to facilitate the improvement of relationships between others. The relationships that you build and facilitate will be the lifeblood of your delivery effort. Pay attention to them from day one.

⊙ CONCLUSION

We began this chapter by arguing that good relationships, like alchemy, transform the common—groups of people—into something special—a system that can deliver real results.

One reason that good relationships are so transformative is because poor relationships are the default. A great deal of an organization's dysfunction can be traced back to the low quality of the relationships in it, mostly because so few people focus on them. For this reason, relationship building represents a real opportunity for immediate improvement—the "low-hanging fruit" of organizational change—for those who are willing to work on it.

But, as we've demonstrated, good relationships aren't just a nice-to-have; they're at the heart of building a delivery culture in your system. Delivery relies almost exclusively on exercising informal influence, and relationships are the major source (often the only source) of this influence. Nearly every tool in this book will require this kind of relationship building. Study it, master it, and everything else will be possible.

⊙ NOTES

1. Scott, J. (1998). *Seeing like a state: How certain schemes to improve the human condition have failed*. New Haven, CT: Yale University Press.

2. Hawai'i State Teachers Association. (2013, April 17). *Teachers ratify new four-year contract*. Retrieved from http://www.hsta.org/news/teachers-ratify-new-four-year-contract

3. Barber, M. (2008). *Instruction to deliver: Fighting to transform Britain's public services* (Rev. ed.). London, UK: Methuen.

4. Collins, J. (2002). *Good to great: Why some companies make the leap—and others don't*. Concordville, PA: Soundview Executive Book Summaries.

5. Fisher, R., & Ury, W. (1991). *Getting to yes: Negotiating agreement without giving in* (2nd ed.). New York, NY: Penguin.

6. Ibid.

7. Fullan, M. (2011). *Change leader: Learning to do what matters most*. San Francisco, CA: Jossey-Bass.

Conclusion

Over to You

Let's try to imagine where you find yourself now. You've come to the end of this book. You've read through the best of the knowledge and lessons we've learned in the course of doing the work of delivery in the last 5 years. You've got some ideas for what to do—you've probably already started to try some of them out. But inevitably, there are gaps in your knowledge of what to do—gaps that this book hasn't answered.

Maybe you face a specific situation that's unlike any the protagonists in this book have encountered. Maybe the reform you're trying to implement is so different from the ones we describe that some entirely new thinking is needed. Or maybe nobody quite like you, in your specific context, has ever tried to use these tools before. Whatever the case, how do you fill those gaps?

The answer shouldn't surprise you by now: this is the part where you become the innovator and we become the students.

So many of the solutions and recommendations in this book came not from our own thinking, but from joint problem solving between us and the education leaders applying these tools on the ground. The story was always the same: there was a gap in knowledge or practice, much like the one you're probably experiencing. We jumped headlong into the breach with our partners to figure out what to do. We thought carefully about the right course of action but tried not to get stuck in or overwhelmed by that thinking—and instead to just "go." We applied the principles as best we could, understanding the facts on the ground and what made them unique, trying a solution, and being humble about changing direction when the evidence warranted it. And the result made its way into this book.

In most cases, of course, our partners did this by themselves. Our job was to write it down to see what we could do to help other leaders benefit from this learning.

And that's the point: the movement to solve America's implementation problem depends on practitioners like you who want to take this kind of work seriously. So consider this our invitation to innovate.

To start with, don't treat this book as an orthodox set of instructions; treat it as a guideline and a starting point. We often like to say that, 20 years from now, the big principles of delivery—the four questions—won't change, but the tools will almost certainly be different. Delivery is still an emerging science, and we know that there's a lot more learning to do about excellence in implementation. So hold fast to the principles. The four questions are a useful North Star: keep asking whether what you're doing is helping you ask and answer at least one of them. But always be willing to experiment with the tools.

Second, don't worry about undertaking the entire delivery approach all at once; start somewhere and let that build momentum for your work. Thinking about getting all the tools right at once can be overwhelming, and in any case, it's unnecessary. The capacity review (Chapter 1B) is a useful way to figure out where to start. But at a more basic level, remember that all these tools—the data visualizations, the planning rubrics, the protocols for routines—start from simple, open questions and then narrow down to specific solutions. So when in doubt, start simple: ask yourself the four questions, use those to figure out where you need to go, and draw in other delivery tools when you think you need them. Or just find a tool that resonates with you and start there (like we said before, the delivery chain is often a popular choice). Over time, as you build the habits of delivery, you'll figure out what's most important for you and for your context.

Finally, share your feedback with us. As you do this work, you're going to learn things about the delivery approach that are far beyond what we know now. We'd love for you to get in touch with us and share your stories (you can find the most updated way to contact us at our website, www.deliveryinstitute .org). Let us know what's working and how you've improved results in your system. Let us know what was challenging or what didn't work. Tell us if you tried something different and would recommend it to others. And let us know if you'd like to be put in touch with other practitioners who are doing this kind of work.

As we said at the beginning, our aim is to make delivery into a true discipline and an essential skillset for every education leader—to build a movement for excellence in implementation that's bigger than any one organization. We hope you'll join that movement with us. But more important, we wish you great success in changing the lives of the students you serve.

Index

CORWIN

A SAGE Company

Helping educators make the greatest impact

CORWIN HAS ONE MISSION: to enhance education through intentional professional learning.

We build long-term relationships with our authors, educators, clients, and associations who partner with us to develop and continuously improve the best evidence-based practices that establish and support lifelong learning.

Solutions you want. Experts you trust. Results you need.

AUTHOR CONSULTING

Author Consulting

On-site professional learning with sustainable results! Let us help you design a professional learning plan to meet the unique needs of your school or district. www.corwin.com/pd

INSTITUTES

Institutes

Corwin Institutes provide collaborative learning experiences that equip your team with tools and action plans ready for immediate implementation. www.corwin.com/institutes

ECOURSES

eCourses

Practical, flexible online professional learning designed to let you go at your own pace. www.corwin.com/ecourses

ELIBRARIES

eLibraries

Your online professional resources library. Create a custom collection with more than 1200 eBooks and videos to choose from. www.corwin.com/elibraries

READ2EARN

Read2Earn

Did you know you can earn graduate credit for reading this book? Find out how: www.corwin.com/read2earn

Contact an account manager at (800) 831-6640 or visit
www.corwin.com for more information